THE NEW FIELD BOOK OF
American Wild Flowers

THE NEW FIELD BOOK

HAROLD WILLIAM RICKETT

THE NEW YORK BOTANICAL GARDEN

# of American Wild Flowers

*With 96 illustrations in full color
and over 700 drawings by the author*

G. P. Putnam's Sons   New York

TO MY FATHER

Copyright © 1963 by Harold William Rickett

Library of Congress Catalog
Card Number: 63-14464

Manufactured in the United States of America

PREFACE

IN the preparation of this book I have had the assistance of many of my colleagues, most of whom were unaware of playing any part in it. To all of them, too numerous to list here, I tender my grateful appreciation.

The professional, the specialist, will find much here with which he may not agree. I ask only that he remember that the book was not written for him, but for the amateur naturalist.

Most of the drawings were made from living plants or from photographs of living plants. Details were verified or added in the herbarium, and a few species were illustrated from preserved material, with some inspiration from the published illustrations of others. During a temporary closing of the herbarium of The New York Botanical Garden, I worked in the United States National Herbarium at Washington, D. C., and in the Herbarium of Harvard University at Cambridge, Mass. To the officers of these institutions I am deeply grateful.

The plates in color are from my own photographs, except for three kindly contributed by Vicki Love, of Columbia, Missouri: *Belamcanda chinensis* (PLATE 3), *Baptisia leucantha* (PLATE 6), and *Erigenia bulbosa* (PLATE 9); and *Silene virginiana* (PLATE 5) and *Lithospermum canescens* (PLATE 11), by David B. Dunn, also of Columbia.

Finally, the manuscript could not have been prepared without the valued help of Carol Helen Woodward, editor of botanical and horticultural books. To her also I render sincere thanks.

HAROLD WILLIAM RICKETT

CONTENTS

*The color plates appear as
a group after page 32*

INTRODUCTION

The purpose of this book is to enable one who has no botanical training to identify wild flowers.

The area covered, the northeastern and north-central sections of the United States, extends from Maine westward to and including Minnesota and southward to Virginia, the Ohio River, and Missouri. This large region embraces many tyes of vegetation, from swamps to mountain forests, from sand dunes to prairies; and each type has its own kinds of wild flowers, besides many that are common to the entire range. Adjacent regions, especially in eastern Canada, also have many of the same wild flowers, and this book will serve to identify much of their flora. Current technical manuals list nearly 5,000 species of flowering plants for the area. These include many trees and shrubs and the grasses and sedges: plants not always thought of as wild flowers. Only a few low shrubs that may be taken for wild flowers are included in this book; grasses and sedges are omitted; so are such little-loved plants as the pigweeds, cockleburs, and ragweeds. Many other species, which enter our range only at its margins but really belong in other parts of the country, are also omitted or only briefly mentioned. The number of wild flowers here treated is thus pruned to 980.*

Identification is not easy. There are two methods. One—which should not be decried—is to turn the pages until a drawing or photograph appears that resembles the unknown plant. Some 750 species are here illustrated, 95 in full color. The second method is more tedious but more sure. On page 31 the reader will find the beginning of a guide to the classes and families of flowering plants represented in the area.† Having identified the family, he will be led to a means of choosing a genus within the family. And finally within the genus he will find one or more species, the distinguishing characteristics of which are briefly described and usually illustrated. If this seems a formidable task, let him be reassured: after a little practice the reader will know many of the commoner families at sight—the rose family, the pea family, the mint family—and can turn at once to the appropriate part of the

---

*For a complete treatment of all species of flowering plants, the reader must turn to one of the current manuals or floras; the use of such books entails the mastery of a rather extensive technical language. Some works of this kind are listed at the end of the discussion of the names of plants.

†It must be emphasized that the "guides" to families and genera found here and there through the book are *good only for the herbaceous species of our area*. The statements that they contain are frequently untrue for other species or other areas.

book. See also "Shortcuts to Identification" at the end of the Introduction.

What sort of characteristics must one examine? Some have attempted to use color as a preliminary means of identification. Color is mentioned in the descriptions that follow, but it is too variable to be reliable. Some flowers change color with age; many species have several color forms. Size also may be misleading. The heights of plants stated in the following pages are in general the *greatest heights ordinarily attained* by the species in question; but plants of the same species may be very much smaller, even when mature, depending on soil, moisture, light, and other agencies; and occasional specimens may exceed the heights given. Most of the drawings in this book are one-half the size of the plants from which they were made. Other sizes are indicated by numerals: "× ⅓," for example, means "one-third natural size"; "× 1" means "natural size." Many details are shown enlarged, as they appear when viewed through a hand magnifier. Most of these are attached to the plant to which they belong by a line with an arrow point at each end.

The actual features used in pinning down an unknown plant are such peculiarities as the numbers of the various flower parts, their relative position, whether they are joined or separate; the shape of leaves and whether or not their margins are toothed; the presence or absence of hairs. To determine such points a hand magnifier is useful (though not essential); it should magnify not more than ten diameters ("10 ×"). Such a magnifier should be held close to the eye, and the flower or leaf should be brought up to within about an inch of the front of the lens (the magnifier should not be held down on the object as a reading glass is held down on a page of print).

After the brief characterization of each species there follows a statement of the time of year in which it blooms (persons in the northern states will of course take the later part of the season stated, those in the southern part of the area, the earlier part). Then comes the type of habitat (swamp, sand, woodland, or other) in which the species is usually found. Finally the range in which the species grows is given; this is expressed by the usual abbreviations for the states, going generally from the northeastern limit of the species to the northwestern and from these to the southern limits, so as to outline an area: the abbreviations "s.," "w.," "sw.," etc. are used for "south," "west," "southwest," and so on. For example, "Mass. to Ont., s. to Fla., Ala., and Ark." outlines the area in which a species of meadow-rue is at present known to grow. A species thus located may not occupy *all* the area specified; mountains, deserts, and other barriers may interfere. Too much space would be required to list in this book the exact occurrence of every species—even if it were known.

Every effort has been made to minimize the technical jargon

of the botanist. Certain more or less technical terms, however, are essential to accurate description; these are explained in the glossary that follows. The numbers in parentheses refer to the accompanying illustrations.

Most wild flowers are herbaceous, in our climate dying to the ground every winter. They may be annual, growing from seed and maturing within a year; biennial, forming leaves the first year, flowering, fruiting, and dying the second year; or perennial, each year forming new leaves, stem, flowers, and fruit, usually from some underground part such as a rhizome or tuber. Such terms have some importance in understanding and identifying wild flowers.

Leaves are of great variety in shape, arrangement, toothing, veining, and so forth, and some vocabulary to express such differences becomes necessary. It should be noted that the *stalk* of a leaf is part of the leaf, not of the stem, from which it is anatomically quite different. A divided leaf has several segments (or small blades) on one stalk, which may be distinguished from a branch bearing several leaves by the absence from its tip of a bud.

The parts of a flower are of the greatest importance in classifying plants. They are explained in the glossary and illustrated in the accompanying figures. The perianth, which in a complete flower consists of sepals and petals, protects the inner parts in the bud and may act as a lure and a landing place for insects which carry pollen. Pollen from the anthers of the stamens is transferred by one means or another to the stigma of the pistil, and there puts forth a delicate living thread which penetrates the style and ovary and accomplishes fertilization within an ovule. The ovule becomes a seed, the surrounding ovary becomes a fruit (with or without other parts of the flower). Fruits are of great variety. Succulent fruits are mostly called berries, except those that have an inner hard layer around the seed—the stone fruits. Many fruits, in the botanical sense, are dry and inedible. An achene, for example, contains one seed, and is itself generally mistaken for a seed. Such careful distinctions, involving a consistent but not necessarily technical use of words, are essential to the understanding and identification of wild flowers.

SHORTCUTS TO IDENTIFICATION

Some flower families, and even some genera, can be quickly identified by one or several easily visible characteristics. A glance through the following 20 paragraphs may make it unnecessary to use the more formal guides to families and genera in this book.

1. The Daisy Family has small flowers closely packed in heads which may be mistaken for single large flowers; the marginal flowers of a head may resemble the petals of a single flower. See the detailed description of the family.

2. The Cactus Family is represented in our range by plants that are composed of chains of what look like thick leaves end to end, often prickly.

3. Plants that catch insects: the Pitcher-plant Family has hollow leaves shaped like pitchers or vases; the Sundew Family has small round, oval, or narrow leaves covered with sticky hairs.

4. Plants that grow in water: try the Arrowhead, Pickerel-weed, and Water-lily Families; *Ranunculus* in the Buttercup Family; *Nasturtium* in the Mustard Family; *Chrysosplenium* in the Saxifrage Family; *Utricularia* in the Bladderwort Family; *Justicia* in the Acanthus Family.

5. Plants that lack green color are found in the Broom-rape Family; see also *Monotropa* in the Pyrola Family.

6. Prickly vines: see *Smilax* in the Lily Family.

7. Plants with rather thick, succulent, very smooth leaves: try *Portulaca* in the Purslane Family; the Stonecrop Family; *Glaux* in the Primrose Family.

8. Plants with milky juice: see the Spurge, Dogbane, and Milkweed Families.

9. If the flowers or berries are on a branch that grows halfway between the points on the stem where leaves are attached, see the Potato Family.

10. If the flowers are in a narrow, *coiled* inflorescence, see the Borage and Waterleaf Families.

11. For flowers so small that their parts are not easily seen, try *Chamaelirium* and *Stenanthium* in the Lily Family; the Parsley and Mint Families. If they consist apparently of stamens and/or pistil(s) with no perianth, try the Buttercup Family.

12. For plants with numerous stamens, see the Buttercup, Rose, and St.-John's-wort Families; if the stamens are joined so as to form a sheath around the style (a conspicuous column in the center of the flower), see the Mallow Family.

13. For flowers with six perianth parts, either three green sepals and three colored petals, or six segments all much alike, see the Lily, Amaryllis, and Iris Families; the Arrowhead Family; *Tradescantia* in the Spiderwort Family.

14. The Orchid Family has one petal, usually the lowermost, markedly different from the other parts of the perianth, which are generally all separate.

15. Flowers with four sepals, four petals, four or eight stamens: try the Evening-primrose, Dogwood, and Bedstraw Families.

16. Flowers with four sepals, four petals, six stamens (two shorter than the other four): see the Mustard Family.

17. Flowers in simple umbels: try the Lily and Primrose Families.

18. Flowers in compound umbels: try the Parsley Family.

19. For flowers with joined petals that form distinct upper and

lower lips, try the Mint and Snapdragon Families. The Mint Family generally has paired leaves on a square stem.

20. Flowers like sweet-peas, with one petal standing more or less erect behind the four others, or creased and folded around them, and the two lowest joined to form a "keel": see the Bean Family. Some of these are vines; some have tendrils; most have divided leaves singly attached.

GLOSSARY

The definitions that follow are intended to apply only to the plants described in this book. They should be used together with the illustrations (indicated by the numbers in parentheses).

Achene (54): a small dry fruit that does not open at maturity to discharge its one seed; often miscalled a seed.

Anther (51): the part of a stamen that produces pollen; usually borne on a slender or flat stalk.

Arrow-shaped (20): of leaves, shaped like an arrowhead, with pointed lobes extending backward away from the tip. (More technically, sagittate.)

Axil (12): the smaller angle between a leaf and the stem to which it is attached.

Berry (53): in the strict botanical sense, a fruit that is succulent throughout and formed from a single ovary.

Bilaterally symmetric (43): of a flower, so constructed that its upper and lower halves are different; like halves may be obtained only by dividing it vertically. (In botanical books often called irregular; compare radially symmetric.)

Blade (11): of a leaf, the expanded, more or less flat part.

Bracts (31, 32): leaflike parts in an inflorescence, or on the stalk of a solitary flower, differing in size, shape, or color, or any combination of these, from the other leaves of the plant.

Bristle: a thin projection from the surface of a plant, stiffer than a hair but not so stiff as a spine or thorn.

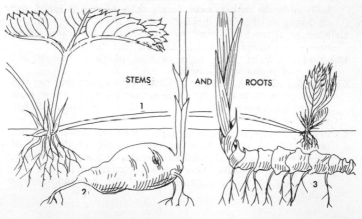

STEMS AND ROOTS

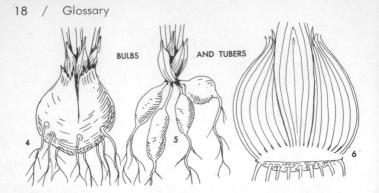

BULBS AND TUBERS

Bulb (6): a typically underground body, generally more or less spherical or pear-shaped, composed of a flattish, more or less disk-shaped stem which bears on its upper surface overlapping, usually succulent leaves that lack green color, and on its lower margin roots. (Compare tuber, corm.)

Calyx: the outer circle of parts (sepals) of a flower. These parts may be separate or joined into a more or less cuplike or tube-like envelope. The calyx encloses the other parts of the flower in the bud.

Capsule (55): a dry fruit that opens along two or more lines when mature. (Compare follicle. The fruit of the Bean Family, called a legume, also may open along two lines.)

Chaff: the bracts that adjoin the disk flowers of many *Compositae*.

Circle (9): used in this book of the disposition of leaves, when three or more are attached at one level. (More technically, a whorl.)

Cleft (26): of the blade of a leaf, the margin indented at least halfway to the midrib, more deeply than when it is lobed, not so deeply as when it is divided.

Column: in an orchid flower, the central structure composed of one or two stamens joined to the style and stigma.

Corm (4): a short, thick, more or less spherical, underground stem. (Often miscalled a bulb.)

Corolla: the inner circle of parts (petals) of a flower that has two circles of parts around the stamens and pistil(s). These parts may be separate or joined, and may be of any color (though green is rare).

Cyme: an inflorescence consisting typically of one flower with two lateral flowers arising from its stalk, usually in the axils of bracts (simple cyme, 33); from the stalks of the lateral flowers there may arise further lateral flowers (compound cyme, 34); and so on until a broad, more or less flat, complex cyme is formed.

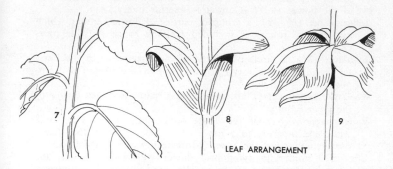

7   8   9

LEAF ARRANGEMENT

Discoid: of heads of *Compositae*, bearing disk flowers only.

Disk flower: in *Compositae* a tubular, radially symmetric flower; disk flowers may occupy the entire head or only the central part (disk).

Divided (25, 28): of leaves, composed of several apparent blades (segments or, more technically, leaflets) on one stalk or midrib; these segments are quite distinct. (Also called compound.)

Downy: possessing fine, short hairs, felt more easily than seen. (Compare hairy, woolly.)

False raceme (39): an inflorescence resembling a raceme but having flowers arranged alternately to right and to left along one side of the stem, which is often coiled; bracts when present are *opposite* the flower stalks.

Follicle (52): a dry fruit that opens along one vertical or lengthwise line when mature. (Compare capsule.)

Fruit (52–55): the body that normally contains the seed or seeds of flowering plants; it is developed from the ovary or ovaries with or without surrounding parts of the flower.

Glands (16): in this book, small bodies on the surfaces of plants, generally spherical and often stalked, which typically secrete oils or other substances.

Hairy (14): bearing easily visible hairs projecting more or less straight out from the surface. (Compare downy, woolly.)

Head (38): an inflorescence of flowers all close together, without stalks or with very short stalks, on a stem end (which in the *Compositae* is broad and disk-shaped or dome-shaped or conical).

Heart-shaped (19): of the blade of a leaf, shaped more or less like an inverted heart, with two rounded lobes at the base. A heart-shaped leaf may be pointed or blunt and of various shapes; the term refers more commonly to the base of the blade than to the whole blade. (More technically, cordate.)

Inferior ovary (49): an ovary surrounded by and inseparably joined with the basal parts of the flower or the expanded tip of the flower stalk. (Compare superior ovary.)

Inflorescence (33–39): a group or cluster of flowers among which no ordinary foliage is included (though bracts may be present).

Involucre (37): a circle of bracts; often conspicuous in the Parsley Family, and always present around the heads of *Compositae*.

Keel: the two lower petals, joined, of a papilionaceous flower of the Bean Family.

Lance-shaped (18): of the blade of a leaf, much longer than wide, and tapering to a more or less sharp point, the widest part being toward the base. (More technically, lanceolate.)

Lip: in a bilaterally symmetric flower with joined petals, the upper or lower part of the corolla; used also in the same way of a calyx of joined sepals. In an orchid flower, the one petal, usually the lowest, that differs in size, shape, or color, or any combination of these, from the other two petals.

Lobed (27): of the blade of a leaf, the margin indented so that several projections (lobes) are visible; the indentation does not extend so deeply as when a leaf is cleft.

Midrib (17–26): the central vein of an undivided leaf; the extension of the stalk of a pinnately divided leaf, to which the segments are attached.

Ovary (47): the basal part of a pistil, which contains the ovule or ovules in one or more chambers.

Ovate (17): of the blade of a leaf, longer than wide, the widest part being toward the base, and tapering to a sharp or blunt tip; wider than lance-shaped; the outline is that of an egg.

Ovule (48): the rudiment of a seed, contained within the ovary.

Paired (8): of the disposition of leaves, two attached at the same level on the stem, usually on opposite sides. (More technically, opposite.)

Palmately (30): of leaves, so divided, cleft, or lobed that the segments or lobes all radiate from one point or from one central part, somewhat as the fingers of the hand extend from the palm.

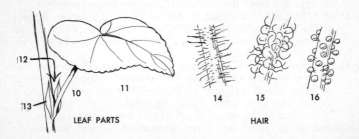

12
13
10
11
LEAF PARTS

14
15
16
HAIR

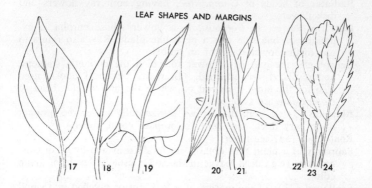

LEAF SHAPES AND MARGINS

17   18   19   20   21   22 23 24

Panicle: a loose inflorescence combining usually a number of cymes.

Papilionaceous: butterfly-like; a term used of flowers of the Bean Family (see the description of this family).

Pappus: in *Compositae,* the hairs, bristles, or scales that replace the calyx.

Parasite: a plant or animal that obtains food directly from another living organism; parasitic plants usually lack green color.

Perianth: the part of a flower that surrounds the stamens and pistil(s), composed of calyx and corolla, or of calyx only.

Petal (40): one of the parts that compose the corolla, within the sepals and surrounding stamens and pistil(s). They may be separate or joined, and of any color (though green is rare).

Pinnately (29): of leaves, so divided, cleft, or lobed that the segments or lobes are arranged along the sides of a midrib or central part.

Pistil (44): the central organ in a flower (there may be several), the ovary of which forms the fruit.

Plain (22): of the margin of a leaf, destitute of teeth, notches, or scallops. (More technically, entire.)

Pollen: minute grains, produced (in flowering plants) in an anther, which, when carried to an appropriate stigma, stimulate the formation of fruit and seed.

Pollinium: a mass of pollen grains shed as a unit from the anther.

Raceme (36): an inflorescence in which flowers or flower clusters are arranged along a common stem, in many species each growing from the axil of a bract. (Compare false raceme.)

Radially symmetric (42): of a flower so constructed that like parts radiate from the center; it may be divided in any direction through the center and still yield approximately like halves. (In botanical books often called regular; compare bilaterally symmetric.)

Radiate: of heads of *Compositae,* having both ray flowers and disk flowers.

Ray, ray flower: in *Compositae,* a flower whose corolla is expanded on one side into a petal-like blade. Ray also refers to one of the flower stalks of an umbel.

Receptacle: the part of a flower to which the perianth, stamens, and pistils(s) are attached. (In many botanical books, used also for the large stem end on which the flowers of a head of *Compositae* are situated.)

Rhizome (3): a stem that grows horizontally under the ground; often very thick and short. (Compare corm, tuber.)

Root-tuber (5): see tuber.

Saprophyte: a plant that obtains its food from non-living organic material (e.g., dead leaves in the soil); usually devoid of green color.

Scalloped (23): of the margin of a leaf, cut or notched into small round projections or teeth. (More technically, crenate.)

Sepal (41): one of the parts that compose the calyx, surrounding all other parts of the flower. They may be green and leaflike, or of any other color.

Singly attached (7): of the disposition of leaves, only one at any level of the stem. (More technically, alternate. Compare circle, paired.)

Spadix: the inflorescence in the Arum Family: a thick stem bearing small, crowded, stalkless flowers.

Spathe (32): a bract or several bracts that enclose or partially enclose a flower or flowers.

Spear-shaped (21): of the blade of a leaf, shaped like a halberd, with pointed lobes extending straight out on either side from

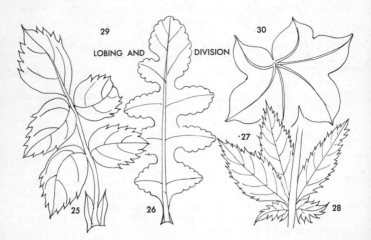

LOBING AND DIVISION

29

30

27

25

26

28

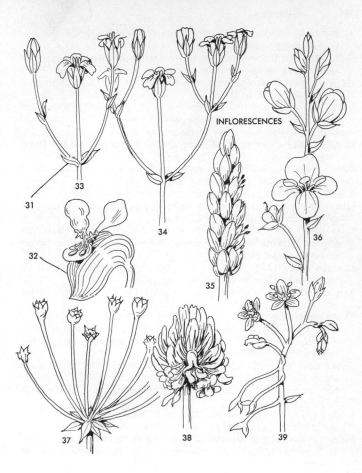

INFLORESCENCES

the base. (More technically, hastate. Compare arrow-shaped, heart-shaped.)

Spike (35): an inflorescence of flowers without stalks or with very short stalks arranged along a common stem.

Spine: a narrow projection from the surface, more rigid than a bristle; the same as thorn.

Stalk (10) of a leaf, the narrow part (often lacking) that bears the blade; of a flower, the supporting stem.

Stamen (50): the organ that forms pollen in a flower.

Standard: the upper petal of a papilionaceous flower of the Bean Family.

Stigma (45): a usually sticky part, generally at or near the tip of the style, which receives the pollen.

Stipules (13, 25): paired appendages at the base of a leaf.

Stolon (1): a stem that extends more or less horizontally over the ground, rooting at the tip; a runner.

Style (46): the part of a pistil above the ovary that bears the stigma (lacking in a few species, the stigma being then borne directly on the ovary).

Superior ovary (42): an ovary free from all surrounding parts of the flower. (Compare inferior ovary.)

Tendril: a slender branchlet, leaf, or part of a leaf that coils about or adheres to a support.

Thorn: see spine.

Toothed (24): of the margin of a leaf, bearing pointed teeth. (Technically the different kinds of teeth are indicated by the terms serrate, dentate, and others.)

Tuber (2): generally an enlarged subterranean stem; there is no sharp distinction among rhizome (3), corm (4), and tuber. Similar enlarged parts of roots are called tubers or root-tubers (5).

Umbel (37): an inflorescence of flowers on stalks that arise from the summit, or almost so, of the flowering stem.

Wing: a thin flange or membrane extending out from a seed, fruit, stem, or leaf stalk; also one of the two lateral petals of a papilionaceous flower of the Bean Family.

Woolly (15): bearing curled hairs which may be tangled together. (Compare hairy, downy.)

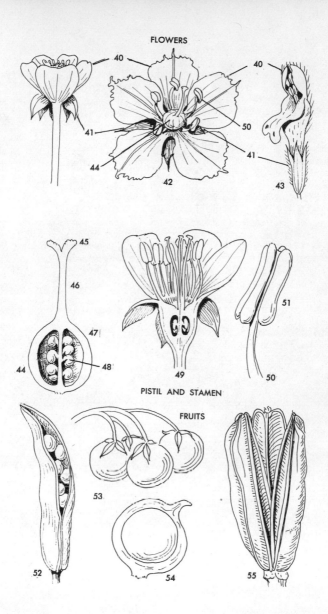

FLOWERS

PISTIL AND STAMEN

FRUITS

THE NAMES OF PLANTS

THE English names of plants are, of course, names given by people without botanical training. They are largely fanciful, relating to real or supposed characteristics and properties: fireweed comes up in burned woods; horse-mint has a mintlike odor but is larger and coarser than true mint; spring beauty—the name explains itself; lousewort was supposed to increase the infestation of cattle that ate it; such names as rose, lily, hyacinth, poppy are so old that they have lost all descriptive meaning—they are just names.

Unfortunately the use of English names has its drawbacks: (1) They are largely unintelligible to those whose language is not English. (2) The same names are applied to different plants in different parts of this country or in different English-speaking countries. "Bluebell" refers to two different plants of Britain, one of which grows also in North America; and to still a third unrelated plant of this country. (3) They do not indicate the relationships of different plants, and indeed are often misleading in this respect. "Virginia-cowslip" is not related to the English cowslip; "blue-eyed-grass" is not a grass. (4) And, worst of all for our purposes, many, perhaps most, of our wild species have never received English names.

For these reasons, those who want to name plants without danger of error—botanists, foresters, gardeners, druggists, and others—have maintained the Latin names given to plants in the eighteenth century, when Latin was still the everyday language of educated men. And names given to plants discovered since then have received similar names.

In these days, when Latin has become a dead language, such names seem formidable to most untrained persons. A very little practice in using them, however, soon overcomes this initial fear, and the amateur botanist learns to appreciate their value. The system that governs their use is not really difficult. The commonly recognized kinds of plants are *species*. All the wood lilies of the eastern United States compose a species. Similar species together form a *genus* (plural, *genera*). The wood lilies and the Canada lilies and the Turk's-cap lilies and others form the lily genus. (Or, if a species has no close relatives, as bloodroot has none, it is placed in a genus by itself.) Every genus is named by a single Latin word: *Lilium* (the lily genus), *Rosa* (the rose genus), *Sanguinaria* (bloodroot). Every species is named by two words,* of which the first is the name of the genus, the second a qualifying

*Or occasionally by three or more, in which case hyphens are used to make the name appear in two parts: *Aster novae-angliae*, the New England aster.

word, usually a Latin adjective, describing some characteristic of the species or commemorating the place where it was first found or the botanist who discovered it: *Lilium tigrinum, L. philadelphicum,*† *Rosa humilis, Sanguinaria canadensis, Gentiana andrewsii.* Similar genera are placed in the same family; the name of a family is formed from the name of a genus with the termination *aceae: Liliaceae, Rosaceae.* This is all that the amateur need know of botanical nomenclature.

In spite of the precision and simplicity of this system, it does happen that a plant will accidentally be given two or more names by two or more botanists, or that what at first seemed to be two species will prove on further study to be only one. In case of a conflict of names, the earliest is generally maintained. In this book the names generally accord with those used by the authors of the standard works listed below.

MERRITT LYNDON FERNALD, *Gray's Manual of Botany.* Eighth (Centennial) edition—illustrated. American Book Company, 1950.

HENRY ALLAN GLEASON, *The New Britton and Brown Illustrated Flora of the Northeastern United States and Adjacent Canada.* In three volumes. The New York Botanical Garden, 1952.

CHARLES CLEMON DEAM, *Flora of Indiana.* State of Indiana, Department of Conservation, Division of Forestry, 1940.

JULIAN ALFRED STEYERMARK, *Flora of Missouri.* [In preparation.]

†Note that the name of the genus, once used, may be abbreviated to its initial letter.

THE NEW FIELD BOOK OF
American Wild Flowers

GUIDE TO THE CLASSES OF FLOWERING PLANTS

ALL the families of flowering plants are placed in two classes: monocots and dicots. They may be distinguished by the following contrasting characteristics.

Seed leaves. The names of the two classes come from the number of seed leaves (*cotyledons*) of the embryo; the embryo is the miniature plant present in the seed. Monocots have one seed leaf, dicots two. These are generally, *but not always,* the first leaves to appear when the seed is planted.

Leaves. The veins of dicot leaves usually branch from one or more main veins; those veins again give off branches, and so on; many of the finer veins join, forming a network (see *Fig. 24*). The veins of many monocot leaves run from base to apex, straight in narrow leaves, curved in broad leaves, without giving off visible branches (see *Fig. 4*). Other monocots have a midrib from which branches run parallel with each other (*Fig. 9*). In general no network is found.

Flowers. The flower parts of monocots are generally in threes and sixes (*Fig. 1;* PLATE 1); those of dicots are frequently in fours and fives or in indefinite numbers (*Figs. 18, 28, 32;* PLATES 5, 6).

Stems. The conductive strands through which food and water pass are generally arranged, in dicots, in a cylinder in the stem (a ring in cross section). Those of monocots are generally scattered.

The stems of dicots, if they last for any time, become thicker through the activity of the cambium just beneath the bark. The older, lower part of the stem is consequently thicker than the younger, upper part. In most monocots there is no cambium. Their stems do not become thicker with age, and are of about the same thickness throughout their length.

There are exceptions to all the above distinctions. There are monocots with netted veins (*Fig. 8*), monocots with flower parts in fours (*Fig. 4*), dicots with flower parts in threes (PLATE 4), and so on. Classification of plants does not depend on single characteristics, but on *characteristics in combination*. When all the above points are considered, there is no difficulty in classifying a plant as a monocot or dicot.

DOGTOOTH-VIOLET
Erythronium americanum

WOOD LILY
Lilium philadelphicum

WAKE-ROBIN
Trillium erectum

CANADA LILY
Lilium canadense

ARGE-FLOWERED TRILLIUM
Trillium grandiflorum

 PLATE 1

STAR-OF-BETHLEHEM
Ornithogalum umbellatum

YELLOW STAR-GRASS
Hypoxis hirsuta

DWARF IRIS
Iris cristata

DAY-LILY
Hemerocallis fulva

YELLOW FLAG
Iris pseudacorus

BLUE FLAG
Iris versicolor

PLATE 2

BLUE-EYED-GRASS
Sisyrinchium angustifolium

BLACKBERRY-LILY
Belamcanda chinensis

STEMLESS LADY'S-SLIPPER
Cypripedium acaule

SPIDERWORT
Tradescantia virginiana

CALYPSO
Calypso bulbosa

PICKEREL-WEED
Pontederia cordata

 PLATE 3

SHOWY ORCHIS
Orchis spectabilis

WILD GINGER
Asarum canadense

MARSH-MARIGOLD
Caltha palustris

POKEWEED (IN FRUIT)
Phytolacca americana

LIVERLEAF
Hepatica nobilis

LESSER CELANDINE
Ranunculus ficaria

PLATE 4

RUE-ANEMONE
Anemonella thalictroides

COLUMBINE
Aquilegia canadensis

CELANDINE
Chelidonium majus

FIRE PINK
Silene virginica

DUTCHMAN'S-BREECHES
Dicentra cucullaria

BLOODROOT
Sanguinaria canadensis

PLATE 5

CRINKLE-ROOT
Dentaria diphylla

DAME'S ROCKET
Hesperis matronalis

MEADOW-SWEET
Spiraea latifolia

SAXIFRAGE
Saxifraga virginiensis

WILD STRAWBERRY
Fragaria virginiana

HARDHACK
Spiraea tomentosa

PLATE 6

FALSE INDIGO
Baptisia leucophaea

GROUND-NUT
Apios americana

SENSITIVE BRIER
Schrankia nuttallii

CROWN-VETCH
Coronilla varia

WILD GERANIUM
Geranium maculatum

VETCH
Vicia villosa

PLATE 7

MILKWORT
Polygala sanguinea

FLOWERING-WINTERGREEN
Polygala paucifolia

BIRD'S-FOOT VIOLET
Viola pedata var. lineariloba

TOUCH-ME-NOT
Impatiens pallida

COMMON BLUE VIOLET
Viola papilionacea

BIRD'S-FOOT VIOLET
Viola pedata

PLATE 8

LANCE-LEAVED VIOLET
Viola lanceolata

POPPY-MALLOW
Callirhoë involucrata

EVENING-PRIMROSE
Oenothera speciosa

FROSTWEED
Helianthemum canadense

WILLOW-HERB
Epilobium hirsutum

PURPLE LOOSESTRIFE
Lythrum salicaria

PLATE 9

HARBINGER-OF-SPRING
Erigenia bulbosa

PIPSISSEWA
Chimaphila maculata

CLOSED GENTIAN
Gentiana andrewsii

INDIAN-PIPE
Monotropa uniflora

BUTTERFLY-WEED
Asclepias tuberosa

PINESAP
Monotropa hypopithys

PLATE 10

COMMON MILKWEED
Asclepias syriaca

SPIDER MILKWEED
Asclepiodora viridis

VIPER'S-BUGLOSS
Echium vulgare

WILD SWEET-WILLIAM
Phlox divaricata

FORGET-ME-NOT
Myosotis scorpioides

JACOB'S-LADDER
Polemonium reptans

PLATE 11

YELLOW PUCCOON
Lithospermum canescens

BLUE VERVAIN
Verbena hastata

FALSE DRAGONHEAD
Physostegia virginiana

HORSE-MINT
Monarda fistulosa

MULLEIN
Verbascum thapsus

BEE-BALM
Monarda didyma

PLATE 12

MOTH MULLEIN
Verbascum blattaria

BEARDTONGUE
Penstemon digitalis

FALSE FOXGLOVE
Aureolaria flava

BEARDTONGUE
Penstemon hirsutus

TOADFLAX
Linaria vulgaris

TURTLEHEAD
Chelone glabra

PLATE 13

WOOD BETONY
Pedicularis canadensis

PAINTED-CUP
Castilleia coccinea

JOE-PYE-WEED
Eupatorium purpureum

GREAT LOBELIA
Lobelia siphilitica

WREATH GOLDENROD
Solidago caesia

IRONWEED
Vernonia noveboracensis

PLATE 14

NEW ENGLAND ASTER
Aster novae-angliae

WILD ASTER
Aster linariifolius

CONEFLOWER
Rudbeckia laciniata

DAISY FLEABANE
Erigeron philadelphicus

PRAIRIE CONEFLOWER
Ratibida columnifera

BLACK-EYED-SUSAN
Rudbeckia serotina

PLATE 15

SUNFLOWER
Helianthus divaricatus

WINGSTEM
Actinomeris alternifolia

BULL THISTLE
Cirsium vulgare

INDIAN-CUP
Silphium perfoliatum

STAR-THISTLE
Centaurea vochinensis

GOLDEN RAGWORT
Senecio aureus

PLATE 16

KING-DEVIL
Hieracium pratense

Monocots

(Monocotyledoneae)

(FOR DICOTS SEE PAGE 81)

GUIDE TO THE FAMILIES OF MONOCOTS*

THE families of monocots treated here are arranged in three groups.

GROUP I. Lilies and lilylike plants (p. 37).

The flowers here, with a few exceptions, are radially symmetric. (Some of the smaller orchids may seem to belong here if not closely observed; compare Group III.)

GROUP II. Aroids and other families with minute, tightly packed flowers (page 59).

Very small flowers crowded into cylindric or spherical masses are characteristic of this group (*Figs. 8, 9*). Lacking ornamental petals, they scarcely resemble flowers at all. In some species the entire flower cluster is enveloped by a special leaf, as in Jack-in-the-pulpit; this is sometimes mistaken for a single flower. Plants of this group grow mostly in moist places, some in water; a few are woodland inhabitants.

GROUP III. Orchids (page 64).

The orchid flower (*Figs. 10–13*) has two peculiar characteristics: (1) The lower petal generally differs from the others in size and shape and often in color; in a few species the upper petal is the distinctive one; in either case the conspicuous petal is called the *lip*. (2) The stamens, style, and stigma are united into a central structure called the *column*. The leaves vary from none at all to large glossy blades with prominent veins running unbranched from base to tip. Our species are plants of rich woods, moist meadows, and bogs.

Besides these there are the grasses and sedges, plants with mostly narrow leaves and small green or brown flowers which are not usually of interest to the amateur. They are families of considerable difficulty, not further described in this book. The two families, however, are fairly easily distinguished from each other. The leaves of the grasses (*Gramineae*) spring from a sheath that is open down one side. In the sedges (*Cyperaceae*) the sheath has no such opening, it completely encloses the stem. The stem of the grasses is usually hollow and round. That of the sedges is usually solid, and it may be triangular.

*See the second footnote in the Introduction.

GROUP I OF MONOCOT FAMILIES. LILIES AND LILYLIKE PLANTS

The perianth parts are mostly in threes and sixes, usually radially symmetric or nearly so. Most are perennial plants sending up flowering stems from underground rhizomes, bulbs, or corms, or from persistent fibrous roots. Here we include six families.

A. The **Lily Family** has a six-parted perianth (four-parted in the small flowers of *Maianthemum*), the segments in many species colored and shaped alike or nearly so; in others the two rings of three segments each are different. All colors occur in the flowers, but blue is rare. There are six stamens and one pistil; the stigma is generally three-lobed, or there may be three separate stigmas on a three-branched style. The ovary is superior. Fruits are generally three-chambered pods or berries.

B. The **Daffodil Family** resembles the Lily Family in number of parts but the ovary is inferior. The species here described have yellow or yellowish flowers.

C. The **Iris Family** is distinguished by the inferior ovary and by having only three stamens. The flowers of most of the native species within our range are blue or white; one introduced species has spotted orange flowers; another, clear yellow.

D. The **Spiderwort Family** has three petals, generally blue or purple but often of another color, three green sepals, and six stamens. The flowers of the common spiderworts (*Tradescantia*) are radially symmetric, those of the dayflowers (*Commelina*) bilateral, with two large upper petals, one smaller lower one. Leaflike bracts are just beneath or partly enclose the flower clusters. The ovary is superior.

E. The **Arrowhead Family** has three green sepals and three white (or pinkish) petals. In most species the stamens and pistils are numerous; in some they are in separate flowers. The pistils usually contain but one ovule each. The leaves arise on long stalks from the base of the stem. The plants grow in water or mud.

F. The **Pickerel-weed Family** has a six-parted bilateral perianth all of one color, generally blue, around six (sometimes three) stamens of unequal length. The plants grow in water.

LILY FAMILY (*Liliaceae*)

The Lily Family is a large and familiar one, including, besides many of our finest wild flowers, such cultivated plants as asparagus, onions, tulips, hyacinths, and many kinds of garden lilies. Except for those in the genus *Lilium*, most of our native species flower in spring.

Guide to Genera of *Liliaceae*

Seven groups of genera may be conveniently distinguished in the family.

I. Flowers (white or yellow) growing singly on stems that bear no leaves (though they may be sheathed by leaves): *Erythronium*.

II. Flowers (yellow or yellowish) hanging singly from the tips of leafy stems, which often fork (*Fig. 1*): *Uvularia*.

III. Flowers (not yellow) growing singly just above three net-veined leaves (*Fig. 1*): *Trillium*.

IV. Flowers (white, greenish, yellow, orange, pink, or red) mostly in umbels (in a few species singly) at the tips of stems which may or may not bear leaves. Several genera:

Allium (*Fig. 2*) has mostly narrow leaves with the odor of onions when crushed.

Nothoscordum (*Fig. 2*) has a similar aspect but no odor.

Medeola (*Fig. 2*) has two circles of leaves on the stem, the upper circle of three small leaves (*Fig. 3*).

Lilium (PLATE 1) has leaves in circles or scattered; the flowers are large, yellow to orange or red, sometimes arising from the axils of leaves as well as from the summit of the stem, sometimes single at the summit.

Clintonia (*Fig. 3*) has broad leaves rising from the ground, none on the stem.

V. Flowers (white, greenish, or pinkish) hanging singly or in twos and threes from the axils of the leaves; none in umbels: *Polygonatum* and *Streptopus* (*Figs. 3, 4*).

VI. Flowers (white, yellow, orange, blue, or lavender) in spikes, racemes, or much-branched clusters. Numerous genera:

Smilacina has white flowers in a raceme (simple or branched) at the end of a leafy stem, generally arching (*Fig. 4*).

Maianthemum has flower parts (white) in fours. The flowers are in a small raceme on a stem that bears two or three leaves (*Fig. 4*).

Ornithogalum has a green streak in the center of each perianth part, which is otherwise white, and grasslike leaves; the flowers are in a raceme (PLATE 1).

Camassia has bluish or lavender flowers in simple racemes (*Fig. 5*).

Melanthium has yellowish flowers in narrow, branched racemes. They turn brown (*Fig. 5*).

Veratrum has greenish flowers in large branched racemes, and large leaves which are plaited lengthwise (*Fig. 5*).

Chamaelirium has very numerous white flowers tightly crowded in a very long, narrow spike (*Fig. 6*).

Stenanthium has numerous small white flowers in a branched spikelike inflorescence. The leaves are grasslike, from the lower part of the stem (*Fig. 6*).

Hemerocallis has large lilylike flowers, orange or yellow, in a forking inflorescence, each flower lasting only a day (PLATE 2).

VII. Flowers in umbels from the axils of leaves on generally climbing, twining stems, prickly in many species. Individual flowers lack either stamens or pistil: *Smilax* (*Fig. 6*).

DOGTOOTH-VIOLETS (*Erythronium*) WHITE, LAVENDER-TINGED, OR YELLOW / The smooth leaves of these low-growing plants (4–8 in.) are rather thick and often mottled with brown or purple. The flowers droop on their stalks, the perianth parts more or less curled back. Both leaves and flower stalks arise from small bulbs deep in the earth. Because several years are required for the production of flowers, one often finds large flowerless patches of leaves, each leaf from a separate bulb.

E. americanum, the yellow dogtooth-violet, has a yellow perianth often tinged outside with lavender. § Early spring: rich moist woods and meadows, N. S. to Minn., s. to Fla. and Okla.; commoner eastward. PLATE 1.

E. albidum, the white dogtooth-violet, has a white perianth with yellow at the base inside and often a tinge of lavender outside. § Early spring: moist ground, Ont. to Minn., s. to Ky. and Okla.; rare eastward.

BELLWORTS (*Uvularia*) YELLOW OR CREAM-COLORED
Bell-like flowers about an inch long or less hang from the tips of the branches. Later flowers may arise opposite the leaves. The leaves are without stalks. The generally forked stem arises from a short, thick rhizome, and continues its growth after the fruit is formed.

U. perfoliata (2 ft.) has smooth green leaves, each encircling the stem, and yellow flowers. § Late spring: open woodlands, Mass. and s. Vt. to Ont., s. to Fla. and La. *Fig. 1.*

U. grandiflora (30 in.) has slightly larger yellow flowers. The leaves "clasp" the stem by lobes that project on either side; they have whitish hairs on the under side. § Late spring: rich woods, Que. to N. D., s. to Ga. and Okla.

U. sessilifolia, wild oats (18 in.), has leaves which are whitish but not hairy on the under side; they have no stalks, but do not embrace the stem. The flowers are pale yellow or cream-colored, usually less than an inch long. § Late spring: woodlands and clearings, N. B. to N. D., s. to Ga. and Ark. *Fig. 1.*

TRILLIUMS or WAKE-ROBINS (*Trillium*) VARIOUS COLORS
A circle of three broad leaves in which the veins branch and form a network is a distinguishing mark for *Trillium*. Above these grows a single three-petaled flower (the stalk of one species bending so as to carry the flower beneath the leaves). The fruit is a

podlike berry. The stem grows from a tuber or rhizome. All our species flower in spring.

I. Species with stalked flowers (compare II).

A. Species with stalked flowers and stalked leaves; the fruit three-lobed (compare B).

T. *undulatum,* painted trillium (20 in.), is a beautiful species with wavy-edged, recurved petals of white with purple or pink streaks. § Rich dark woods, e. Que. to Man., s. to Ga., Tenn., and Wis. *Fig. 1.*

T. *nivale,* dwarf white trillium (6 in.), has petals less than an inch long, white or sometimes pink-striped. § Rich woods, shady places, Pa. to Minn., s. to Ky. and Mo.

B. Species with stalked flowers and stalkless (or almost stalkless) leaves; the fruit six-ribbed.

T. *erectum,* purple trillium (1–2 ft.), known also as squawroot and stinking Benjamin, has ill-smelling flowers with petals of purple, maroon, brownish, yellowish, or white. The flower stalk may be erect, horizontal, or bent downward. § Rich woods, e. Que. to Mich., s. to Ga. and Tenn. and farther in the mountains. PLATE 1.

T. *grandiflorum,* large-flowered trillium (18 in.), has white, pink, or even green petals, which may exceed 3 inches in length (though oftener half that size). The flowers are usually erect. White flowers tend to turn deep pink as they age. § Rich woods, s. Que. and Me. to Minn., s. to Ga. and Ark. PLATE 1.

T. *cernuum,* nodding trillium (18 in.), has white or pinkish flowers which hang ("nod") below the leaves. The petals are about 1 inch long. The anthers are pink. § Damp woods, Nfld. to Wis., s. to Ga. and Ala. *Fig. 1.*

T. *flexipes* is similar to T. *cernuum,* but the flowers are larger, the petals often 2 inches long. The anthers are cream-colored and longer than their stalks. § Woodlands, N. Y. to Minn., s. to Md. and Mo.

II. Species with stalkless flowers.

T. *sessile,* toadshade (1 ft.), has petals which vary from maroon or purple to greenish or yellowish; they taper toward their base. The leaves are stalkless ("sessile"). § Open woods, N. Y. to Mo., s. to Ga. and Ark. *Fig. 1.*

T. *recurvatum* resembles T. *sessile,* but each petal is contracted at the base to a stalklike part. The leaves also are stalked. § Rich woods, Mich. to Wis. and Nebr., s. to Ala. and Ark. *Fig. 1.*

THE ONIONS (*Allium*)   WHITE, ROSE, OR PURPLISH

Besides the cultivated onions, leeks, and garlic, and a few attractive garden flowers, the genus *Allium* includes a number of

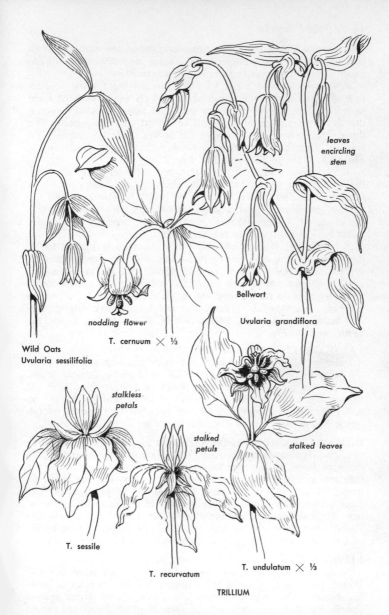

leaves
encircling
stem

nodding flower

Bellwort

Uvularia grandiflora

T. cernuum × ⅓

Wild Oats
Uvularia sessilifolia

stalkless
petals

stalked
petals

stalked leaves

T. sessile

T. recurvatum

T. undulatum × ⅓

TRILLIUM

FIGURE 1

wild species native in North America. These are commonest in the midwestern and western states. Some are difficult to distinguish without recourse to technical characteristics.

A. canadense, wild garlic (1–2 ft.), is notable for the production of small aerial bulbs instead of flowers in its umbels; there may be a few flowers (white or pink) or none. It is so common that it sometimes forms a grasslike sward in light woods. The flower stalk rises slightly above the leaves. § Early summer: all sorts of situations, sometimes covering the ground under trees, Me. to S. D., s. to Fla. and Tex. *Fig. 2.*

A. cernuum, wild onion (1–2 ft.), has a flower stalk bent near the tip so that the umbel extends sideways or downward (it is "cernuous"). The flowers are rose or purplish. The stem and the narrow leaves grow from a short rhizome on which several bulbs are clustered. § Late summer: rocky places, especially in mountains, N. Y. to B. C., s. to Ga. and Ariz.

A. stellatum, also called wild onion (2 ft.), is similar to *A. cernuum,* but has only one or two bulbs and the stem is straight. § Summer: rocky slopes, w. Ont. to Sask., s. to Ill. and Tex.

A. tricoccum, wild leek or ramp (18 in.), has much larger leaves (up to 10 inches long and 2 inches broad). An umbel of greenish-white flowers appears after the leaves have disappeared. The bulbs are clustered. § Summer: N. B. to Minn., s. to Ga., Tenn., and Ia. *Fig. 2.*

FALSE GARLIC (*Nothoscordum bivalve*) WHITE

False garlic (6–16 in.) has the aspect of some species of *Allium,* but lacks the characteristic odor of the wild garlic or wild onion. Its stem and grasslike leaves grow from an underground bulb. At the summit of the stem is an umbel of small whitish flowers on stalks of unequal lengths. § Spring: grasslands and open woodlands, Va. to Nebr., s. to Fla. and Tex. *Fig. 2.*

INDIAN CUCUMBER-ROOT (*Medeola virginiana*) GREENISH-YELLOW / Indian cucumber-root (1 ft.) is easily recognized by its circle of from five to nine leaves halfway up the stem. Near the tip there are three much smaller leaves, and, just above them, an umbel of a few small flowers, followed by purple berries. The stem grows from a white tuber which has the taste of a cucumber. *Medeola* may be confused with *Trientalis* of the Primrose Family; but *Trientalis* has only one circle of leaves. § Late spring and summer: deep woods, Que. to Minn., s. to Fla. and La. *Fig. 2.*

LILIES (*Lilium*) YELLOW, ORANGE, OR RED

Some of our best-known cultivated lilies come from the Old World, but North America has a number of wild species of striking beauty. Our native species are distinguished from related genera by their perianth of six spreading or backward-curved parts, all colored alike or nearly so, and variously mottled. The flat seeds are in two columns in each chamber of the pod. The

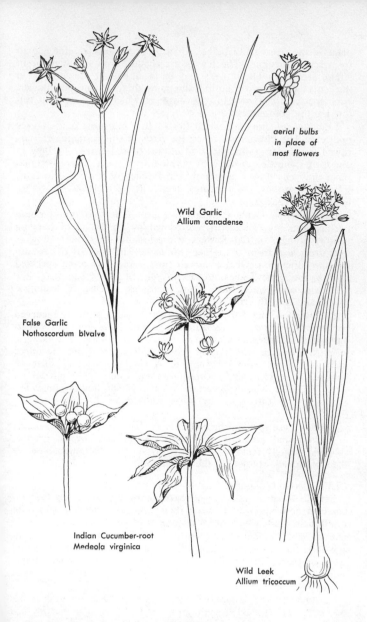

aerial bulbs
in place of
most flowers

Wild Garlic
Allium canadense

False Garlic
Nothoscordum bivalve

Indian Cucumber-root
Medeola virginica

Wild Leek
Allium tricoccum

FIGURE 2

plants grow from scaly bulbs, which in some species elongate to form scaly rhizomes. The leaves are scattered on the stem or in circles around it. The flowers may be in umbels at the summit, in the axils of leaves, or both; sometimes there is but one flower. Nine species are known in our range, of which the four that follow are the commonest.

L. philadelphicum, the wood lily (3 ft.), has most of its leaves in circles. The flowers are erect; the parts of the perianth are narrowed to slender stalks; they are orange or red-orange (yellow in one form), mottled inside with purple-brown spots. There is sometimes only one flower at the tip, but frequently from two to four. § Summer: woods and clearings, Me. to B. C., s. to N. C., Nebr., and N. M. PLATE 1.

L. canadense, Canada or meadow lily (6 ft.), is the common northeastern lily. The stem is crowned by an umbel of hanging yellow, orange, or red flowers (occasionally only one); flowers may grow also from the upper leaf axils. The six-parted perianth has spreading, somewhat recurved tips; inside it is often speckled with brown. The leaves are mostly in circles. § Summer: low fields and open woodlands, moist roadsides, e. Que. to Minn., s. to Va. and Ala. PLATE 1.

L. superbum, the Turk's-cap lily (8 ft.), has a strongly recurved perianth like that of the tiger lily of gardens. The stem bears scattered leaves below and a circle of leaves near the top. The flowers, which are orange with purple spots inside, grow from the upper axils as well as from the summit. A single plant may bear 40 flowers. § Late summer: wet meadows and woods, N. B. to Minn., s. to Fla. and Ala. Midwestern plants, which flower somewhat earlier, are distinguished by some authors as *L. michiganense. Fig. 3.*

Besides these species, the common garden tiger lily (*L. tigrinum*) is often found growing wild. It is recognizable by its orange, spotted, strongly recurved perianth, by its roughish stem, and by the small black bulblets in the axils.

CLINTONIA (*Clintonia*)   YELLOWISH OR WHITE

Several broad, shining, oval leaves grow directly from the rhizome in both species. Between them appears a leafless stem, up to 10 inches tall, which bears an umbel of small flowers.

C. borealis, bluebead or corn-lily, is the commoner. The greenish-white flowers number not more than eight in an umbel, sometimes only one. The berries are blue, or occasionally white. § Early summer: rich woods, Lab. to Minn., s. to Ga., Ind., and Wis. *Fig. 3.*

C. umbellulata has smaller flowers, up to 30 in an umbel, the perianth white speckled with green and purple. The berries are black. § Early summer: rich woods, N. Y. to O., s. in the mountains to Ga. and Tenn.

Solomon's-seal
Polygonatum biflorum

Turk's-cap Lily
Lilium superbum × ⅓

Bluebead
Clintonia borealis

FIGURE 3

SOLOMON'S-SEAL (*Polygonatum*)   WHITISH
The common name comes from the marks left by the scales on the underground stem (rhizome). In late spring this stem sends up a leafy stem which usually arches. The leaves, which arise alternately from opposite sides of the stem, are without stalks, oval, pointed at each end. From their axils flowers hang on slender stalks in early summer. These are followed by blue or black berries.

P. canaliculatum is the largest species (2–6 ft.). The leaves have mostly three or more prominent veins running from base to tip on each side of the midrib. Flowers are generally from two to ten in each axil. § Damp open places, N. E. to Man., and s. to S. C. and Okla.

P. biflorum (1–3 ft.) has generally one or two prominent leaf veins (best observed on the under side) on each side of the midrib. One or two flowers hang from each axil. § Open woods and banks, Conn. to Mich. and Nebr., s. to Fla. and Tex. *Fig. 3.*

P. pubescens (1–3 ft.) is similar to *P. biflorum* but has hairs along the veins on the under side of the leaves. § Woods, Que. to Man., s. to S. C., Ky., and Wis.

TWISTED-STALK (*Streptopus*)   PINK OR GREENISH
Twisted-stalks have much the aspects of Solomon's-seal, but the flower stalks arise *opposite* each leaf instead of in the axil. Each stalk is bent or twisted near the middle. The flowers, barely ½ inch long, appear singly or in pairs in summer. The berries are bright red. Our species are wide-ranging but less common than Solomon's-seal. Both grow in cold damp woods.

S. amplexifolius (3 ft.) has leaves that are heart-shaped at the base. The flowers are greenish. § Greenl. to Alaska, s. to N. Y. and Wis., and in mountains to N. C. and Ariz.

S. roseus (2 ft.) has leaves that are blunt at the base. The flowers are pink. § Lab. to Man., s. to N. J. and Wis., and in mountains to Ga. and Ky. *Fig. 4.*

FALSE SOLOMON'S-SEAL (*Smilacina*)   WHITE
In leaf *Smilacina* closely resembles *Polygonatum,* but the flowers are borne in a raceme at the tip of the stem instead of in the leaf axils. The stem, which grows from an underground rhizome, is often zigzag. The flowers are minute; the berries at first brownish and speckled, at maturity red or almost black.

S. racemosa (1–3 ft.), our commonest species, sometimes called false spikenard, has flowers in a branched raceme, followed by translucent red berries. § Early summer: rich woods, Que. to B. C., s. to Ga. and Ariz. *Fig. 4.*

S. stellata (2 ft.) has fewer flowers in a simple raceme. The berries become nearly black. § Early summer: moist open situations, Nfld. to B. C., s. to Va., Ariz., and Calif. *Fig. 4.*

S. trifolia (8 in.) is easily distinguished by seldom having more

Smilacina stellata × ⅓

Twisted-stalk

Streptopus roseus

Wild Spikenard
Smilacina racemosa × ⅓

Wild Lily-of-the-valley
Maianthemum canadense

FIGURE 4

than three leaves. The flowers are in a simple raceme; the berries dark red. § Summer: boggy woods, Lab. to B. C., s. to N. J., Ill., and Minn.

WILD LILY-OF-THE-VALLEY (*Maianthemum canadense*)
WHITE / This low-growing plant, which sometimes forms broad mats of green in woodlands, usually bears two oval leaves, each pointed at the tip and embracing the stem in its notched base. The minute, fragrant flowers grow in small racemes; each has four perianth parts and four stamens. The berries are at first speckled, then pale red. Canada Mayflower, a direct translation from the Latin, is another name. § Spring: woods and moist crevices, Lab. to B. C., s. to Ga., Tenn., and Ia. *Fig. 4.*

STAR-OF-BETHLEHEM (*Ornithogalum umbellatum*)   WHITE
Grasslike leaves and a green stripe on the outside of each perianth part characterize the star-of-Bethlehem, which often escapes from cultivation. The flowers are not in an umbel, but in a simple raceme on a stalk up to 10 inches tall. § Spring and early summer: Nfld. to Nebr., s. to N. C., Mo., and Kan. PLATE 1.

WILD HYACINTH (*Camassia scilloides*)   LAVENDER OR BLUE
The stem (2 ft.) bears flowers ½ inch long in a raceme. (True hyacinths belong to the genus *Hyacinthus,* of the Mediterranean region.) The generic name comes from the American Indian word "quamash," applied to the edible bulbs. A tuft of narrow leaves, rising from a bulb, surrounds the flowering stem. § Late spring and early summer: fields, roadsides, open woodlands, Ont. to Wis., s. and sw. to Ga. and Tex. *Fig. 5.*

CAMASS (*Zygadenus*)   WHITE
Plants of *Zygadenus* must be carefully distinguished from those of *Camassia,* for the bulbs are highly poisonous. The grasslike leaves are somewhat similar, but the flowers differ, being small, whitish, sometimes tinged outside with bronze or green. Most species grow in the South or West, but two, both called white camass, are found in our area.
Z. *glaucus* (3 ft.) has flowers in a branched raceme. § Late summer: rocky cliffs and bogs, Que. to Minn., s. to N. Y., O., and Ill., in mountains to N. C.
Z. *elegans* (2 ft.) has flowers in a simple, narrow raceme. § Summer: meadows, Minn. to Alaska, s. to Mo. and Ariz.

BUNCHFLOWER (*Melanthium virginicum*)   CREAM-COLORED, GREEN, OR PURPLISH / A coarse plant (3–5 ft.), with long, narrow, roughish leaves growing from the base. The numerous small flowers in the narrow, branched raceme are at first cream-colored, but change to green or purplish (the name of the genus means "black flower"). The fruit is a three-lobed pod. § Summer: wet woods and meadows, N. Y. to Minn., s. to Fla. and Tex. *Fig. 5.*

Bunchflower
Melanthium virginicum × ⅓

Wild Hyacinth
Camassia scilloides

Indian Poke
Veratrum viride × ¼

FIGURE 5

INDIAN POKE or **FALSE HELLEBORE** (*Veratrum viride*)
GREEN OR BROWN / Plants of *Veratrum* (to 7 ft.) are easily known by their large shining leaves which are deeply veined and plaited lengthwise. There are several leaves on the stem, which is topped by a branched raceme of small greenish flowers. Both leaves and flowers turn brown as they age ("Veratrum" means, in part, "black"). All parts of the plant, especially the roots, are extremely poisonous (but this species is not to be confused with the pokeweed, *Phytolacca americana,* which is also poisonous). § Early summer: wet places, Que. to Minn., s. to Md., and in the mountains to Ga. and Tenn. *Fig. 5.*

FAIRY-WAND or **DEVIL'S-BIT** (*Chamaelirium luteum*)   WHITE
These plants (1–4 ft.) have the sexes separated. The white male flowers have stamens and a rudimentary pistil; the greenish-white female flowers, on another plant, have a pistil and rudimentary stamens. The flowers are arranged in a long, slender, tightly packed spike; the staminate spike usually droops at the tip; the pistillate spike is shorter and blunter. Individual flowers are very small. The fruits are small pods. At the base of the stem is a tuft of flat, smooth, spreading leaves. § Summer: meadows and moist woods, Mass. to Mich. and Ill., s. to Fla. and Ark. *Fig. 6.*

DAY-LILIES (*Hemerocallis*)   ORANGE OR YELLOW
The day-lilies somewhat resemble the true lilies (*Lilium*), but are easily distinguished by their manner of growth and flowering. Swordlike leaves grow in dense clusters from the ground. The flowering stem, which is leafless, forks and usually forks again, each branch bearing a succession of flowers which remain open only a few hours before withering. ("Hemerocallis" means "beautiful for a day.") The perianth parts are bilateral in symmetry, and the style and stamens curve upward instead of being straight and evenly disposed within the perianth.

There are several species in the Old World. Two that have escaped from cultivation here are probably hybrids rather than true species. Both kinds develop thick masses of plants.

H. fulva (2–5 ft.), which is especially noticeable along roadsides in summer, has orange flowers about 6 inches long. § Summer: throughout. PLATE 2.

H. flava, the lemon day-lily, is slightly smaller and has yellow flowers. § Late spring: occasionally around old dwellings, N. E. to Mich. and Pa.

FEATHERBELLS (*Stenanthium gramineum*)   WHITE
From the lower part of the stem (5 ft.) of featherbells grow grasslike leaves which are folded lengthwise. The very small flowers are in a loose, slender, branched raceme; those on the side branches usually lack pistils. The fruits are small pods. § Late summer: woods and thickets, Pa. to Ill. and Mo., s. and sw. to Fla. and Tex. *Fig. 6.*

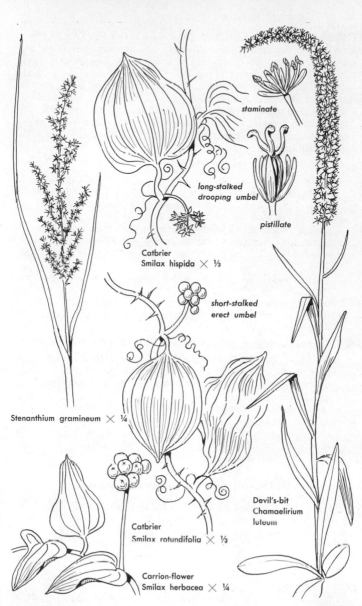

staminate

long-stalked
drooping umbel

pistillate

Catbrier
Smilax hispida × ⅓

short-stalked
erect umbel

Stenanthium gramineum × ¼

Catbrier
Smilax rotundifolia × ⅓

Carrion-flower
Smilax herbacea × ¼

Devil's-bit
Chamaelirium
luteum

FIGURE 6

CATBRIERS, GREENBRIERS, and CARRION-FLOWER (*Smilax*) GREEN / Scrambling over thickets or climbing into trees, the species of *Smilax* are often such vicious, entangling, prickly pests that in the South some are called "tramp's-trouble" and "hell-fetter." The tendrils by which they climb arise in pairs on the leaf stalks. The leaves are mostly up to 3 inches broad, shining, and with conspicuous veins. The flowers, small and greenish, appear in early summer in umbels of separate sexes in the leaf axils. The fruits are berries, generally black. The species are often difficult to distinguish.

I. Woody vines with prickly stems (compare II).

    S. rotundifolia, greenbrier or horsebrier, is a widespread pest, most common in the Southeast. The leaves are green on both sides. The umbels are on short stalks. § Moist thickets, N. S. to Mich., s. and sw. to Fla. and Tex. *Fig. 6.*

    S. glauca, sawbrier or wild sarsaparilla, has leaves less than 2 inches long, whitish on the under side. § Wastelands, open and wooded, in wet and dry places, Mass. to Kan., s. to Fla. and Tex.

    S. hispida has black prickles which are narrower and less stiff than those of other species. The leaves are prickly on the whitish veins beneath. The long stalks of the umbels droop from the axils. § N. Y. to Minn. and Nebr., s. to Fla. and Tex. *Fig. 6.*

II. Herbaceous plants without prickles, the flowers ill-scented.

    S. herbacea, carrion-flower, has leaves from 1 to 2 inches long, pale on the under side; the umbels are on long stalks. § Meadows and low woods, Que. to Minn. and Wyo., s. to Ga., Ala., and Okla. *Fig. 6.*

    S. pulverulenta is similar, but with leaf veins downy beneath. § Rich woods, R. I. to Mo., s. to Va. and Okla.

    S. ecirrhata is more or less erect, to 2 feet tall, with few or no tendrils. The leaves are pale beneath and narrow. § Woods, Ont. to Minn. and S. D., s. to Ala. and Mo.

DAFFODIL FAMILY (*Amaryllidaceae*)

Some amaryllids may be mistaken for members of the Lily Family; the main difference is that the ovary is inferior (*Fig. 10*). Species of several genera are grown in gardens: *Narcissus* (including daffodils and jonquils), *Galanthus* (snowdrops), *Leucojum* (snowflakes); some of these may occasionally be found growing wild.

YELLOW STAR-GRASS (*Hypoxis hirsuta*) YELLOW
From within a tuft of slightly hairy, grasslike leaves rises a slender stem (to 2 ft.), bearing from two to seven yellow flowers, the perianth flaring like a six-pointed star. The fruit is a small pod.

§ Spring and summer: moist woods and meadows, Me. to Man., s. to Fla. and Tex. PLATE 2.

FALSE ALOE (*Agave virginica*)　　YELLOW

Along the southern margins of our range grows one species of *Agave*. A better known species is the century-plant of the southwestern states. There are many others throughout the warmer parts of the Americas, some cultivated in Mexico and Central America under the name of maguey. (The true aloes are natives of South Africa.) *A. virginica* has a tuft of long, thick, swordshaped leaves, from the center of which rises a many-flowered stem (to 6 ft.). The flowers are yellowish, fragrant, up to an inch long. § Summer: dry places, Va. and O. to Mo., s. and sw. to Fla. and Tex.

IRIS FAMILY (*Iridaceae*)

Wild irises resemble the cultivated species and are easily recognized. The relation of other genera of this family to the irises is not easily seen until the three stamens and the inferior ovary are noticed. The narrow, long-pointed leaves appear as if folded lengthwise, each embracing the next younger in the fold. Some familiar garden and greenhouse flowers, besides irises, belong here: crocus, montbretia, gladiolus, freesia. Only three genera are commonly found wild in our range (and the third is an escape from cultivation).

IRISES and FLAGS (*Iris*)　　BLUE, LAVENDER, OR YELLOW

Iris flowers have three spreading sepals of petal-like texture and color, generally curved downward, and three erect petals. The three-branched style has the appearance of three more petals in the center, lying over the sepals. The three stamens are hidden beneath the style branches, and the stigmas are small flaps on their under side. Each flower grows from a spathe of two bracts.

There are many species, identification of which is sometimes made difficult by hybridization. The following are the commonest.

I. versicolor, blue flag (4 ft.), often forms a mantle of blue across a wet field. One flower opens at a time from the papery spathe. The sepals are 2 inches or more long, blue, usually with a yellow base and darker veins; the petals are from half to two-thirds as long. § Early summer: wet fields and marshes, Lab. to Man., s. to Va., O., Wis., and Minn. PLATE 2.

I. prismatica, slender blue flag (3 ft.), is distinguished by the very narrow leaves (usually less than ¼ inch wide) and the three sharp angles of the pod which resembles a three-sided prism. The sepals are less than 2 inches long, pale blue with deep violet veins; the petals are pale blue. The rhizome lies on the surface of the ground or nearly so, forming ropelike, scaly running stems (stolons) from the ends of which the new leaves grow. The flowering stem grows from the end of last year's stolon, surrounded by remains of the old leaves. § Summer: brackish or fresh coastal marshes, sands, and meadows, near the coast, N. S. to Ga.

I. cristata, crested iris (8 in.), is a dwarf species. The leaves may reach a height of 15 inches and a width of 1 inch. The name comes from the three lengthwise orange ridges (crests) on each sepal; they end in a white patch. The rest of the perianth is pale blue or lavender; its base forms a slender 2-inch tube. § Late spring: rich woods, Md. to Mo. and Okla., s. to Ga. and Ala. PLATE 2.

I. pseudacorus, yellow flag (3 ft.), is a European species naturalized along streams and in other wet places in this country, especially in the Atlantic states. The flowers are large, showy, yellow, in branched clusters. § Summer: Nfld. to Minn. and s. PLATE 2.

One northeastern species, *I. hookeri,* has bristle-tipped petals. The southern *I. virginica* resembles *I. versicolor. I. brevicaulis* has a flat, bent stem. *I. fulva* has red-orange flowers.

BLUE-EYED-GRASS (*Sisyrinchium*)   BLUE, WHITE, VIOLET, OR YELLOW / The leaves of *Sisyrinchium* are stiff, narrow, grasslike, growing in erect tufts from a small bulb. The flowering stem is two-edged. The flowers grow in a small cluster more or less enclosed by a spathe; there may be several spathes on one stem. The six spreading perianth parts are all alike, usually blue, each commonly tipped with a small sharp point.

S. campestre (20 in.) has white- and yellow-flowered forms as well as the typical blue-flowered type. The tall stem is two-edged, winged; it bears but one flower cluster. § Spring and early summer: grasslands, Wis. to Man., s. to Ill. and Tex.

S. angustifolium (20 in.) has narrow leaves which turn black when dry. The flowering stem is winged, usually branched, and bears one or more spathes. § Summer: damp open places, Nfld. to Minn., s. and sw. to Fla. and Tex. PLATE 2.

S. atlanticum (30 in.) has a wiry, flexuous stem and pale leaves. The flowers are violet. § Early summer: mostly wet meadows, N. S. to Mich., s. to Fla. and Miss.

S. montanum (24 in.) has a single straw-colored spathe. The flowers are blue. The ripe seedpods are also of a pale straw color. § Summer: damp open places, from Nfld. across Canada, s. to N. J., Ill., and Ia., in mountains to N. C., N. M., etc.

BLACKBERRY-LILY (*Belamcanda chinensis*)   RED-ORANGE
The reddish-orange flowers, up to 2 inches across, have flaring perianth parts, all alike, mottled with purplish spots. The English name comes from the fruit, which splits open when ripe, disclosing black seeds which cohere in a mass that suggests a blackberry. The plant grows much like an iris, with a tall (to 3 ft.) leafless flowering stem arising among sword-shaped leaves. This is an Asiatic species which has made itself at home in the United

States. § Summer: woods and fields, often in dry places, Conn. to Ia. and Nebr., s. to Ga. and Mo. PLATE 3.

SPIDERWORT FAMILY (Commelinaceae)

The spiderworts and dayflowers belong to a family that is mainly tropical. Our few species include bad weeds and attractive wild flowers, some of which have been developed for garden use.

SPIDERWORTS (*Tradescantia*)   BLUE, PURPLE, ROSE, OR WHITE
These plants have lilylike, radially symmetric flowers with three petals, three green sepals, six stamens, and a pistil with two or three chambers. The green sepals distinguish the flowers from all in the Lily Family except *Trillium,* which is easily recognized by its three spreading net-veined leaves. The foliage of *Tradescantia* is somewhat grasslike.

The common name comes from the aspect of the upper leaves, which are narrow and spread out around the flowers. The flowers are generally in clusters above leaflike bracts, the unopened buds drooping, the open flowers, each an inch or more across, erect and lasting only a short time. In most species the stamens are covered with blue hairs. Four species are widespread in our area; others are confined to our southern and western borders. The plants are often found along roadsides, gravelly banks, and railroad embankments. All are flowers of late spring and summer.

T. virginiana (18 in.) has smooth leaves which are scarcely longer than the two unequal bracts. The flower stalks and sepals are hairy. § Me. to Minn., s. to Ga. and Mo. PLATE 3.

T. bracteata (18 in.) has long bracts and very hairy flower stalks and sepals; some of the hairs, as seen through a magnifier, are tipped with small glands. The petals are usually rose. § Prairies, Ind. to Minn. and Mont., s. to Mo. and Kan.

T. ohiensis (3 ft.) has smooth flower stalks and sepals. It is often grown in gardens and has probably escaped from cultivation in the East. § Prairies and thickets, Mass. to Minn., s. and sw. to Fla. and Tex.

T. occidentalis (2 ft.) bears glands on all the hairs of the flower stalks and sepals. § Prairies, Wis. to Mont., s. to La. and Mexico.

DAYFLOWERS (*Commelina*)   BLUE OR VIOLET
Of the three petals two are more prominent, the lower one being smaller and often of a different color. Only three of the six stamens bear pollen, the others being smaller and sterile. The ovary may have only two chambers; or, when the upper one also is present, it may lack an ovule. The single bract forms a curved spathe which conceals the unopened buds. Flowers appear continuously through summer and early autumn.

C. communis, a troublesome weed, has bright blue upper petals and a small white lower petal. The stem lies on the ground, the flowering ends curving up. This is a native of eastern Asia. § Widespread in yards, gardens, and roadsides, Mass. to Wis., s. to N. C., Ala., and Ark. *Fig. 8.*

C. virginica (3 ft.) has three blue petals, the lower one only slightly smaller. It is a perennial with a rhizome. § Woodlands, N. J. to Kan., s. to Fla. and Tex.

C. erecta has a very small white lower petal; otherwise it is much like *C. virginica.* § Sandy soil, open or wooded, N. Y. to Mich. and Wyo., s. to Fla. and Mexico; Cuba.

ARROWHEAD FAMILY (*Alismataceae*)

The arrowheads and their relatives are generally found in shallow water or wet mud or sand. While the leaves of some species are shaped like an arrowhead, those of others vary from oval to long and narrow.

WATER-PLANTAIN (*Alisma*)   WHITE OR PINK

The small flowers of *Alisma* have a ring of minute pistils on a flat base surrounded by six stamens, these in turn by three petals, and these by three green sepals. The flowers occur often in groups of three or more on the branches of a tall raceme.

A. triviale has the largest flowers of our species, the petals being up to ¼ inch long. The leaf blades are broad, more or less ovate, often heart-shaped, on long stalks. The racemes may extend 3 feet above the water. (This species was formerly thought to be the European *A. plantago-aquatica.*) § Summer: from Que. across Canada, s. to Md. and Mexico. *Fig. 7.*

A. subcordatum is similar; the petals are much smaller (1⁄12 inch long). § Summer: N. E. to Minn., s. to Fla. and Mexico.

A. gramineum has grasslike leaves up to 3 feet long submerged in the water, or somewhat broader blades on slender stalks which carry them above the surface. § Summer and autumn, rather rare, Que., N. Y., Wis., and western states.

ARROWHEADS (*Sagittaria*)   WHITE

The flowers grow in circles, usually of three, at several levels on a leafless stem. In many species the lower flowers have no stamens, only pistils; in others the pistillate and staminate flowers are on different plants; in still others the flowers, or some of them, have both stamens and pistils. The pistils form a more or less spherical mass on a rounded base. The three petals are round; the stamens are indefinite in number. Botanists differ in their opinions of the characteristics and even the names of the species, which differ only in small details. The plants flower in ditches and on wet banks of ponds and streams in summer.

S. latifolia, wapato (to 4 ft.), has leaves of the characteristic arrowhead shape, but greatly varied in width. It is the commonest species. § Throughout North America. *Fig. 7.*

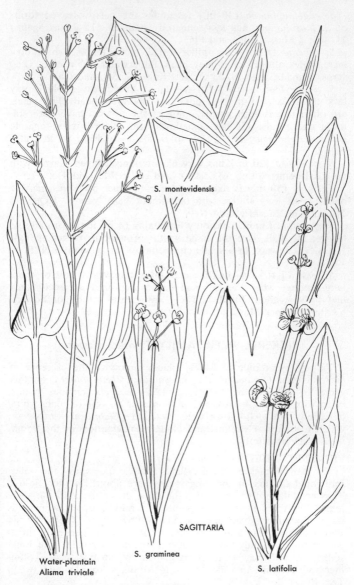

S. montevidensis

SAGITTARIA

Water-plantain
Alisma triviale

S. graminea

S. latifolia

FIGURE 7

S. engelmanniana (30 in.) resembles the narrow-leaved forms of *S. latifolia* but has less numerous stamens (15–25 as against 25–40). § Mass. to Pa. and Fla.

S. cuneata (8 in.) has rather broad, short leaves, which may lack blades altogether if they grow underwater. § From e. Que. across Canada, s. to N. J., O., Ill., Kan., N. M., and Calif.

S. montevidensis (to 5 ft.) has large, broad leaves which may lack the backward-directed points of the arrowhead. The petals are often tinged with purple; some of the flowers have both stamens and pistils. (It has sometimes been placed in a separate genus, *Lophotocarpus*.) § Del. to S. D., s. to Fla., w. to Calif. *Fig. 7.*

S. graminea (20 in.) has very narrow lance-shaped leaves, with no basal points. § Lab. to Sask., s. and sw. to Fla. and Tex. *Fig. 7.*

S. rigida (30 in.) is likely to have both types of leaves, narrow or oval, on long stalks, with or without basal points. § Que. to Minn., s. to Va., Mo., and Nebr.

S. spatulata (30 in.) has only leaf stalks (4 in. long), usually no blades; the stalks are the same width throughout, rather spongy. It has few flowers, in a single circle, on a spongy stem. § N. B. to Va.

S. teres (1 ft.) has hairlike or quill-like leaves a foot or more long (spongy when they grow in deep water; they are really only leaf stalks without blades). There are several circles of flowers. § Late summer: Mass. to Md.

PICKEREL-WEED FAMILY (*Pontederiaceae*)

Tall spires of blue in watery places announce the presence of pickerel-weed (*Pontederia*) in midsummer. *Heteranthera,* another genus in this aquatic family, contains less conspicuous plants, often with floating leaves, and with smaller flowers of blue, white, or yellow. The well-known water-hyacinth (*Eichhornia crassipes*), which has choked streams and hindered navigation in the South, is also in this family.

PICKEREL-WEED (*Pontederia cordata*)   BLUE

The stem of pickerel-weed extends about a foot above the water. Individual flowers in the long raceme are about an inch across. They are bilaterally symmetric: the three upper perianth parts are joined, the three lower are separate; the middle upper segment is larger than the others and has two yellow spots. There are six stamens, three long and three short. The ovary is generally three-chambered, but only one chamber contains an ovule. The long-stalked leaves vary from heart-shaped to lance-shaped. § Summer and autumn: in water, N. S. to Minn., s. to Fla. and sw. to Tex. PLATE 3.

There are many other aquatic plants, in several families. Water-weed (*Elodea canadensis*). is rarely seen in flower. Eel-grass (*Vallisneria spiralis*) has grasslike leaves which may grow yards long under water, and pistillate flowers on long stalks which coil spirally as the fruit develops. (These two are in the *Hydrocharitaceae*.) The tiny duckweeds (*Lemna*) that cover quiet waters are also flowering plants, though the flowers are rare. They form a family (*Lemnaceae*) related to the Calla Family. The Pondweed Family (*Naiadaceae*) contains several genera that grow submerged, some of them (*Potamogeton*) thrusting spikes of greenish flowers above the surface.

GROUP II OF MONOCOT FAMILIES. AROIDS AND OTHER FAMILIES WITH MINUTE, TIGHTLY PACKED FLOWERS

These are plants whose flowers lack the form and the showy parts usually considered characteristic of flowers. They have stamens and pistils (often in separate flowers) and some have sepals; many flowers are so tightly crowded in a cylindrical or spherical mass that they may be mistaken for one large flower. The two families that follow are not closely related, botanically. Most of their species grow in wet places.

The **Cat-tail Family** is known by the velvety brown cylinders borne on tall stalks.

The **Calla Family**, often referred to as "the aroids," bears its flowers in a rather thick cylindrical or club-shaped spike, generally with a large leaflike or petal-like spathe growing from its base and partly or wholly enclosing it.

CAT-TAIL FAMILY (*Typhaceae*)

The cat-tails may not at first impress one as flowering plants. They grow from 3 to 10 feet tall, with long, narrow, erect leaves and a stiff stem that ends in a compact cylindrical inflorescence— the familiar "cat-tail." There is but one genus.

CAT-TAILS (*Typha*)   BROWN

The velvety brown inflorescence is formed of thousands of tiny female flowers packed together, containing pistils and no other parts. The ovary develops into a minute achene borne on a stalk from which grow long, soft hairs—the most conspicuous part of the fruit. The staminate flowers, each consisting only of several stamens, grow in a mass above the pistillate flowers, forming a more slender and lighter-colored "tail." This disappears after the pollen is shed, leaving only the central stalk, more or less withered. Both our species flower in summer in swamps, wet ditches and meadows.

T. latifolia, with leaves up to an inch broad, has the staminate part of the spike directly above the pistillate part. § Throughout North America. *Fig. 8.*

T. angustifolia, with leaves scarcely ½ inch broad, has an inch or two of bare stalk between the staminate and pistillate flowers. § N. S. to Ont. and s. and sw. to Va. and Mo.; Calif.; most abundant in the coastal states.

CALLA FAMILY (*Araceae*)

The aroids are characterized by minute flowers crowded on a rather thick cylindric or club-shaped stem, called a spadix (*Fig. 9*), at the base of which, in most genera, grows a leaf of special form, a spathe. The spathe may enfold the spadix, partly or wholly concealing it, or may stand away from it. A familiar example is the calla-lily, which is unrelated to the true lilies. In this, the single white or colored petal-like structure is the spathe; the yellow column within it is the spadix. The family is very large and mainly tropical, but a few species grow in temperate North America, some being very common.

SKUNK-CABBAGE (*Symplocarpus foetidus*) GREEN AND PURPLISH-BROWN / The large, almost globular spathe (4–8 in.) of mottled purple, brown, and green that encloses the flowers of skunk-cabbage signals the advent of spring through much of our range. Enough heat is developed by the spathe in its growth to thaw the soil around it and to enable it to push up even through ice and snow. The large leaves develop later, appearing first as a pale, tightly wrapped, elongated cone; becoming by midsummer by far the largest leaves in swampy places, the blades often a foot or more broad and twice as long, on stalks of the same length which rise directly from the ground. They are unusual for monocots in having a network of veins. All parts have the characteristic skunk-like odor, especially when broken.

The small flowers which cover the nearly spherical spadix have four thick sepals, all packed together, and four stamens which project above them; after these wither, the stigma emerges. The fruit is formed from the whole mass of flowers, the spathe withering. § Early spring: swampy ground, running water, Que. to Man., s. to Va., O., Ill., and Ia. *Fig. 8.*

JACK-IN-THE-PULPIT and GREEN-DRAGON (*Arisaema*)

GREEN AND PURPLISH-BROWN / *A. triphyllum,* Jack-in-the-pulpit (2 ft.), has a pulpitlike spathe surrounding and arching over the top of the spadix, which is "Jack." The spathe is streaked and mottled in tones of purple, brown, and green; it is generally 3 or 4 inches tall. The flowers are at the base of the spadix, the upper ones staminate, the lower pistillate; but in many plants only staminate or pistillate flowers are found. The withering of the spathe in autumn discloses a group of brilliant scarlet berries,

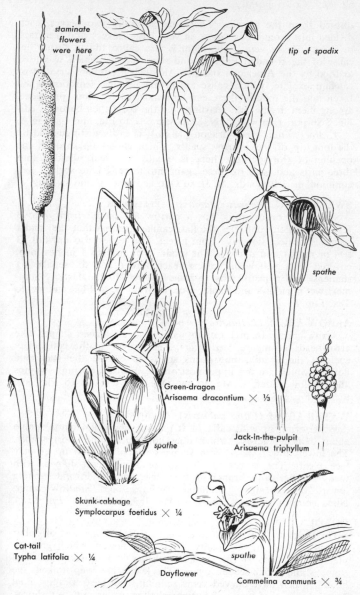

staminate flowers were here

tip of spadix

spathe

Green-dragon
Arisaema dracontium × ⅓

spathe

Jack-in-the-pulpit
Arisaema triphyllum

Skunk-cabbage
Symplocarpus foetidus × ¼

spathe

Cat-tail
Typha latifolia × ¼

Dayflower
Commelina communis × ¾

FIGURE 8

formed from the ovaries. There are generally two leaves, each divided into three lobes (more in very large leaves) and traversed by a network of veins. The plant is also called Indian turnip because of the rounded underground stem (corm) which was used as food by the American Indians. Although it contains crystals of calcium oxalate, which cause an intense burning sensation when taken into the mouth, these can be removed by various processes, among them drying and roasting, and the corm then becomes edible. § Spring: rich woods, N. S. to Minn., s. to Fla. and La. *Fig. 8.*

A. dracontium, green-dragon (18 in.), is easily distinguished by the long tip of the narrow spadix, which curves up through the opening of the spathe. There is usually one leaf, divided into three parts and each of these again into three. § Late spring: less common, in rich woods, N. H. to Ont. and Wis., s. and sw. *Fig. 8.*

SWEET-FLAG (*Acorus calamus*)   YELLOWISH

Sweet-flag, or calamus, has a narrow flat spathe from 1 to 3 feet long which continues the flat leaflike stem, so that the spadix seems to project sideways from a leaf. The leaves also are tall (3 feet or more) and narrow. The spadix is from 1 to 3 inches long, covered with yellowish flowers; each flower has six sepals, six stamens, and a pistil. The rhizome is sweet to the taste. § Summer: wet meadows and banks, Que. to Minn., s. to Fla., and sw. to Tex. *Fig. 9.*

ARROW-ARUM (*Peltandra virginica*)   GREEN

Arrow-arum (16 in.) gets its name from its leaves, shaped like arrowheads (compare *Sagittaria*). The narrow spathe completely encloses the spadix, but opens so as to expose the staminate flowers, which are the uppermost on the spadix. § Spring: swamps and shallow water, s. Me. to sw. Que. and Ont., s. to Fla., sw. to Tex. *Fig. 9.*

WATER-ARUM (*Calla palustris*)   WHITE

Water-arum or wild calla (1 ft.) has a nearly flat white spathe about 2 inches across, which does not conceal the short spadix. The lower flowers have both stamens and pistils, the upper may lack pistils. The leaves are broad, somewhat heart-shaped, with many parallel veins branching from the central vein and running toward the margins. § Summer: swamps, bogs, shallow water, Nfld., across Canada, s. to N. J., Pa., Ind., and Minn. *Fig. 9.*

GOLDEN-CLUB (*Orontium aquaticum*)   YELLOW

Golden-club (1 ft.) has no evident spathe, only a sort of collar around the base of the spadix. The yellow flowers which give the plant its name cover the spadix; each has four or six sepals and stamens and a one-seeded ovary. The leaves are long-stalked; the blades, which have curved veins running from base to apex, float on the surface of water. § Spring: shallow water and wet shores, Mass. to Fla. and La. *Fig. 9.*

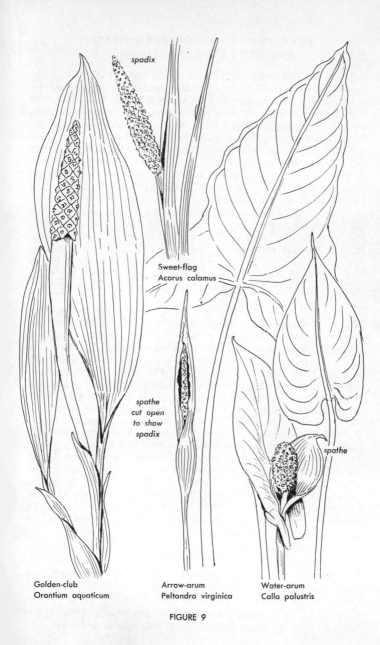

spadix

Sweet-flag
Acorus calamus

spathe
cut open
to show
spadix

spathe

Golden-club
Orontium aquaticum

Arrow-arum
Peltandra virginica

Water-arum
Calla palustris

FIGURE 9

GROUP III OF MONOCOT FAMILIES.
ORCHID FAMILY (Orchidaceae)

The flowers of many orchids are very striking in both form and color. This is particularly true of the orchids of the tropics, the plants grown by fanciers the world over. Some of our native orchids are showy, too; others have small greenish or whitish flowers which may not reveal the intricacy of their structure unless they are seen through a magnifier.

Many tropical orchids (including some in southern Florida) grow perched on the branches of trees. Our native northeastern orchids, in contrast, all grow on the ground. Most have green leaves and make their own food; a few have no green parts and live, as fungi do, on organic matter in the soil. The roots of all our orchids are associated with fungi. This is one reason for the difficulty of transplanting and cultivating them; the fungus as well as the orchid must be able to tolerate the new surroundings. Wild orchids are protected by law in many states. It is a temptation, when one finds a rare and beautiful plant, to take it home. The temptation should be resisted, for almost certainly the plant will die, especially if it is an orchid; and nature is thereby despoiled.

The flower of an orchid is somewhat on the same plan as that of a lily, in that there are six perianth parts. But there the resemblance ends. The three outer parts are sepals, often (not always) colored differently from the three petals. The flower is bilateral; usually the lowest petal differs in size, form, and color from all other parts of the perianth. This is the *lip*. It forms a landing place and often a lure for the insects on which pollination depends. (In a few of our species the lip is the uppermost part.) The other two petals are the *lateral petals*. The one stamen or pair of stamens, the style, and the stigma are all joined in a central structure called the *column*. The pollen grains adhere to each other in two small masses which are attached to a sticky base. The head of an intruding insect of a certain size and shape can scarcely avoid coming in contact with this base. Accordingly, when the insect withdraws from the flower, it bears the pollen masses, or *pollinia,* stuck to its head and carries them to other flowers, which are thus fertilized. The ovary is inferior; though generally narrow it may contain thousands—even millions—of ovules; orchid seed is dustlike.

Guide to Native Orchid Genera

I. One genus, *Cypripedium,* distinguished by its large slipperlike lip (*Fig. 10;* PLATE 3). The leaves are generally broad. There are two fertile stamens. (Compare II and III.)

II. Genera that have the lip uppermost in the flower (*Fig. 11*)—the reverse of the usual position. Only one stamen is fertile.

Calopogon has a raceme of fairly large pink or magenta flowers and one or more narrow leaves near the base of the stem.

Malaxis has a spike or spikelike raceme of very small greenish flowers and one or more ovate leaves near the base of the stem or sheathing it halfway up.

III. Genera that have the lip lowermost in the flower. These have but one fertile stamen.

A. Genera that have usually only one flower to a stem, rarely two or three (compare B).

Isotria has five or six leaves in a circle, just below the flower stalk. The sepals are very narrow (*Fig. 10*).

Calypso has one broad leaf at the base, none on the stem. The lip is shoe-shaped with a white "apron" at the end (PLATE 3).

Arethusa has one narrow leaf on the stem, besides one or more small scales. The lip bears a purple and yellow fleshy projection (*Fig. 11*).

Cleistes has one or two leaves on the stem. The lip is narrow, the edges curled to make a trough, the lateral petals lying along the top of this (*Fig. 11*). The sepals are narrow, nearly erect.

Pogonia has one or sometimes two rather narrow leaves on the stem (not counting the bract behind the flower). The lip is flat, fringed, and has three rows of fleshy yellow projections on the surface (*Fig. 11*).

B. Genera that have several or many flowers on the stem.

1. Genera that have several or many flowers and no green leaves (or one that soon withers) at the time of flowering (compare 2 and 3).

Aplectrum bears a single green leaf after flowering; it lasts over winter, but usually withers just before the next flowering (*Fig. 11*). The lip is white with violet or magenta streaks.

Corallorhiza has no green parts at any time. The lip is white spotted with purple, or entirely purple (*Fig. 12*).

2. Genera that have several or many flowers and fully developed leaves on the stem.

Epipactis has many greenish-white flowers in a tall raceme; there are several narrow leaves attached singly on the stem (*Fig. 12*).

Listera has small greenish flowers in a spike and a pair of ovate leaves halfway up the stem (*Fig. 12*).

Triphora has usually three drooping flowers, white or pink with green veins, growing from the axils of small leaves singly attached on the stem (*Fig. 12*).

3. Genera that have several or many flowers on the stem but whose leaves (not counting a few scales) are all at or near the base.

Malaxis has small greenish flowers in a spike and one or two ovate leaves near the base of the stem or sheathing it half-way up (*Fig. 10*).

Orchis has a white lip, projected downward at the base in a "spur" (hollow tube). At least the upper sepal and the lateral petals form a purplish or rose hood over the column (PLATE 3).

Habenaria has flowers of various colors, the lip of the same color as the other parts; the lip is flat, in some species fringed, prolonged downward at the base in a "spur" (hollow tube; *Fig. 13*).

Liparis has a madder-brown, purplish, or yellowish flat lip; the other petals are threadlike, the sepals also narrow (*Fig. 14*).

Goodyera has ovate or oblong basal leaves usually marked with a network of white lines (*Fig. 13*), and a spike of small white or greenish flowers, with saclike lip.

Spiranthes has a spike of small white flowers, in some species forming a spiral, in others all on one side of the stem or in several vertical rows (*Fig. 12*); the lip is flat. The leaves are mostly narrow and basal.

LADY'S-SLIPPERS or MOCCASIN-FLOWERS (*Cypripedium*)

PINK, YELLOW, OR WHITE / The lady's-slippers are perhaps our best-known and most striking native orchids. The leaves are mostly broad, shining, with conspicuous lengthwise folds in which lie the veins. The two lower sepals are united in most species. One generally narrow petal extends to either side. The third is the lip, saclike or slipper-shaped. Of the five species in our range, all except one bear leaves on the flowering stem and have a roundish opening in the pouch formed by the lip. The exception is the first one described below.

C. acaule, the stemless lady's-slipper (16 in.), is so called because the stem that bears the leaves does not appear above the ground; the two leaves spring from the ground at the base of the flowering stem, which bears a single flower. The sepals and lateral petals are yellowish or brownish. The lip, up to 2 inches long, is pink with red veins, or, in one form, white. The opening in the lip is a cleft with inrolled edges which touch. § Late spring: dry woods, bogs, and swamps, Nfld. to Alta., s. to Ga. and Ala. PLATE 3.

C. calceolus, the yellow lady's-slipper (2 ft.), has usually from three to five leaves and one or two flowers on the stem. The sepals and lateral petals are purplish-brown or greenish-yellow, the petals twisted; the lip is yellow. The species is quite variable, and has been divided into several varieties. § Late spring: bogs and most

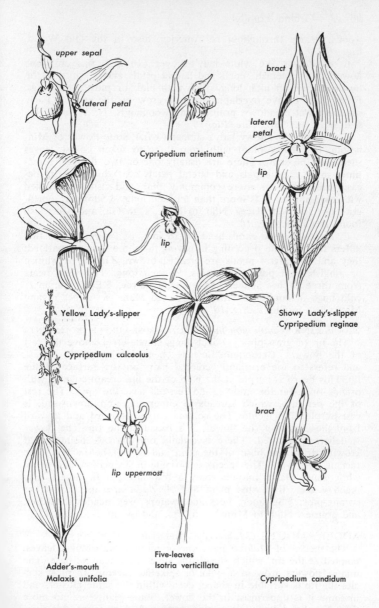

upper sepal

lateral petal

Cypripedium arietinum

bract

lateral petal

lip

Yellow Lady's-slipper

Cypripedium calceolus

lip

Showy Lady's-slipper
Cypripedium reginae

Adder's-mouth
Malaxis unifolia

lip uppermost

bract

Five-leaves
Isotria verticillata

Cypripedium candidum

FIGURE 10

woods, nearly throughout N. America; also in the Old World. *Fig. 10.*

C. candidum, the white lady's-slipper (16 in.), has only one flower, with greenish sepals and lateral petals and a white lip up to more than an inch long, often with pink or purple markings. From three to five overlapping leaves grow on the stem. § Early summer: wet meadows, prairies, and woodlands, N. Y. to N. D., s. to N. J. and Mo.; rare. *Fig. 10.*

C. reginae, the showy lady's-slipper (3 ft.), state flower of Minnesota, is a hairy plant with from three to seven coarse leaves sheathing the stem. There are usually one or two flowers, sometimes more. The sepals and lateral petals are white, the lip occasionally white or more commonly pink and usually streaked with rose-purple; it is more than an inch long. § Summer: northern bogs and wet places, Nfld. to Man., s. to Ga. and Mo.; also found in China. *Fig. 10.*

C. arietinum, the ram's-head (4–16 in.), is a rare species that differs from all the preceding in having the three sepals separated; they and the lateral petals are greenish-brown. The lip is whitish or pinkish with purple-red veins, ½ inch long. The stem bears from three to five leaves and a single flower. § Early summer: cold bogs in coniferous forests, Que. to Man., s. to N. Y. and Mich.; also in China. *Fig. 10.*

GRASS-PINK (*Calopogon pulchellus*)   ROSE-PURPLE OR MAGENTA

The lip of grass-pink, ½ inch long, stands erect above the rest of the flower. "Calopogon" means "beautiful beard" in Greek, and refers to the brilliantly colored hairs on the surface of the lip. This beard is purple at the base of the lip, cream-colored with orange tips near the middle, and rust-red near the apex. The rest of the perianth, which spreads to either side and downward, is rose-purple or magenta. The column curves outward and upward from the center of the flower; it is broad at the tip. The flower is delicately scented. There is usually one narrow, pointed leaf growing from the base of the stem and ending below the loose raceme of flowers. The species is variable in size, color, and form; while some plants may be only a few inches tall, others may reach 4 feet. Both this plant and *Arethusa* are also known as swamp-pink. § Summer: bogs and swamps, wet meadows, ditches, and prairies, Nfld. to Minn., s. to Fla. and sw. to Tex. *Fig. 11.*

ADDER'S-MOUTH (*Malaxis*)   GREENISH

The species of *Malaxis* have one or more ovate or oval leaves, pointed at the tip, which sheath the stem from near its base. The minute flowers grow in a spike or spikelike raceme. In most species the lip is variable in shape, even within the same cluster, and in some it is uppermost in the flower. Some plants are no more than 2 inches tall, but they may reach a foot or more. All grow in wet woods and bogs, flowering mostly in late summer.

M. unifolia, green adder's-mouth, has green flowers in a relatively broad spike. The lip is about ⅛ inch long, three-pronged; at first it is uppermost, then by a twisting of the flower stalk it is brought into the lower position as the flower matures. § Nfld. to Man., s. to Fla. and La. *Fig. 10.*

M. brachypoda, white adder's-mouth, has greenish flowers. The lip, which is narrowed into a pointed tongue, is regularly lowermost in the flower. (Some botanists consider this a variety of the Old-World *M. monophyllos,* in which the lip is uppermost in the flower.) § Nfld. to Man., s. to Pa., Ind., Mich., Wis., Tex., and Calif.

FIVE-LEAVES (*Isotria verticillata*)   YELLOWISH AND PURPLE
Isotria (15 in.) is distinguished by the circle of five or six leaves near the summit of the stem. The single flower has yellowish-green petals and long, narrow, purplish sepals. The lip is less than an inch long; it is yellowish-green streaked with purple. § Late spring: sandy pine woods, damp forests, and boggy places, Me. to Wis., s. to Fla., and sw. to Tex. *Fig. 10.*

CALYPSO or FAIRY-SLIPPER (*Calypso bulbosa*)   PURPLISH AND WHITE OR YELLOWISH / The single flower of *Calypso* grows at the tip of a leafless stem (8 in.). The sepals and lateral petals are purplish, nearly an inch long. The lip forms an elaborate "slipper" about the same length; it is whitish or yellowish, marked with reddish spots and streaks. In front of the cavity of the slipper is a white "apron" which bears near its base three rows of hairs, golden spotted with purple. The column forms a hood over the opening in the lip. This may well be the most beautiful of our native orchids. The single broad but pointed, deeply veined leaf arises late in the season directly from the underground corm; it lasts over winter, withering soon after the plant flowers. § Spring: in moss of cold coniferous forests, often at high altitudes, from Lab. and Que. across Canada, s. to N. Y., Wis., Minn., Ariz., and Calif. PLATE 3.

DRAGON'S-MOUTH or BOG-PINK (*Arethusa bulbosa*)   MAGENTA AND PURPLE / This is one of the loveliest of our native orchids. The stem (1 ft.) bears a single exquisite flower (rarely two) at its summit. The magenta-pink sepals stand nearly erect, slightly spreading; the lateral petals curve forward over the column. The lip, about an inch long, is larger than the other parts. It curves downward, and on its purple-blotched upper surface bears a fleshy tissue covered with thick, yellow, purple-tipped hairs (the "beard"). On the apparently leafless flower stalk are two or three sheathing scales, from within the uppermost of which the one leaf grows, after the flower has passed. The leaf is perhaps 6 inches long, ½ inch wide, sharp-pointed. § Late spring: bogs, generally in peat moss, Nfld., across Canada, s. to N. J., Ind., and Minn.; farther s. in the mountains. *Fig. 11.*

ROSEBUD ORCHID (*Cleistes divaricata*)   PURPLISH, PINK, OR
WHITE / The rosebud orchid has conspicuously long and narrow
sepals which flare away from the other perianth parts. They are
brownish or purplish, 2 inches long or more, curved and spreading. The lateral petals vary from purplish or pink to white; with
the narrow, trough-shaped lip they form a tube, inside which is the
column. The lip is greenish with purple veins and a lengthwise
"crest." The one leaf, midway on the stem like that of *Pogonia,*
contributes to its other name of spreading pogonia. The leaf is
narrowly lance-shaped, from 2 to 4 inches long. The slender stem
may reach more than 2 feet in height. § Summer: damp pine barrens, prairies, swamps, bogs, dry upland woods, N. J. to Fla. and
Miss. *Fig. 11.*

SNAKE-MOUTH (*Pogonia ophioglossoides*)   ROSE OR WHITE
Snake-mouth (2 ft.) usually has one leaf (sometimes two)
about halfway up the stem, and a single flower (sometimes two
or three) at the summit, with a bract just behind it. The leaf is
lance-shaped, sharp-pointed, up to 5 inches long; occasionally
there are also long-stalked leaves from the base. The flower,
which may vary from rose-pink to white, is very fragrant. The
perianth is about an inch long, the sepals quite broad and more
or less enclosing the petals. The lip hangs down. Its three rows
of yellowish projections, like coarse hairs, have given rise to the
name of beard-flower. § Late spring and early summer: bogs, Nfld.
to Minn., s. and sw. to Fla. and Tex. *Fig. 11.*

PUTTY-ROOT or ADAM-AND-EVE (*Aplectrum hyemale*)   GREEN-
ISH OR WHITE / Putty-root (20 in.) may seem a leafless plant, for
its one leaf (oval, up to 7 inches long) comes from the corm in
autumn, lasts over winter, and withers just before the flowers appear. The plant owes its names to the whitish corms (generally
two: Adam and Eve), from which the leaf and the flowering stem
arise. The flowers are greenish or whitish with madder-purple
markings. The lip flares from a narrow base and is three-lobed;
it is about ½ inch long, marked with magenta. § Late spring:
wet, muddy soil in creek bottoms, bogs, and swamps, and in low
woodlands, Que. to Sask., s. to Ga. and Ark. *Fig. 11.*

THE CORAL-ROOTS (*Corallorhiza*)   YELLOWISH, BROWNISH, OR
PURPLE / The coral-roots are of the small company of flowering
plants that lack green color and live as mushrooms do on dead
organic material in the soil—decaying leaves and other plant
detritus. They are not parasites, since they do not feed on living
organisms; they are saprophytes. The "coral root" is really an
underground stem, a rhizome, much branched. The flowers are in
a spikelike raceme on a leafless stem which generally does not
exceed 18 inches in height; they are small, yellowish, brownish,
or purple. Five species are known in our area.
 C. maculata (6–30 in.) is the largest; it is also the most wide-

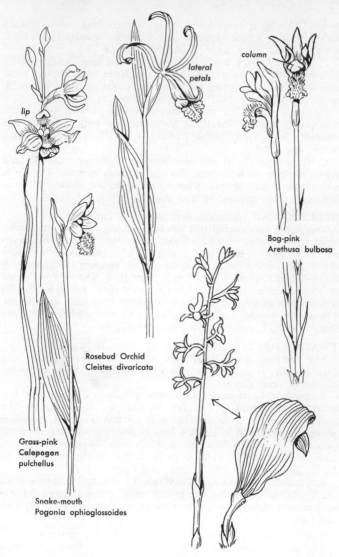

lip

lateral
petals

column

Bog-pink
Arethusa bulbosa

Rosebud Orchid
Cleistes divaricata

Grass-pink
Calopogon
pulchellus

Snake-mouth
Pogonia ophioglossoides

Putty-root
Aplectrum hiemale

FIGURE 11

spread. The lip is three-lobed, ⅕ to ⅓ inch long, white spotted with crimson. § Late summer and autumn: woods, from Nfld. across Canada and s. to N. J. and Ind. *Fig. 12.*

C. trifida (12 in.) has a lip about ⅕ inch long, white usually without spots. The lateral petals and the upper sepal form a hood over the column. § Spring and summer: moist woods, from Nfld. across Canada, s. to N. J., Ind., Colo., and Ore. *Fig. 12.*

C. striata (12 in. or more) has a pinkish or whitish perianth with purple stripes. The lip is about ½ inch long. § Spring and summer: from Que. across Canada, s. to N. Y., Mich., Wis., Minn., and Calif.

C. wisteriana (4–16 in.) has very small flowers, the lip and sepals scarcely ⅓ inch long, the lateral petals shorter. The lip is white spotted with purple. § Spring and summer: woods, N. J. to Mo., s. to Fla., and sw. to Tex. *Fig. 12.*

HELLEBORINE (*Epipactis helleborine*)   GREENISH
This is the only orchid that has been introduced (no one knows how) from Europe and has spread like a weed through this country. The stem (3 ft.) bears a number of leaves which are very variable in outline, ovate or lance-shaped, clasping the stem by a heart-shaped base or attached by a short stalk. The flowers, borne in a tall raceme, are greenish tinged with rose or purple; the lip is somewhat fleshy and saclike, with the tip bent back underneath. § Summer: woods, wooded roadsides and waste places, Que. to Ont., s. to N. J. and Pa.; Wis.; Mo. *Fig. 12.*

TWAYBLADES (*Listera*)   GREENISH, PURPLISH, OR RED
The common name, twayblade, means "two leaves" (see also *Liparis*). The stem bears a pair of ovate leaves halfway to the raceme of small flowers.

L. cordata, heart-leaved twayblade (10 in.), has more or less heart-shaped ("cordate") leaves; so also do other species. The purplish-green lip is distinctive: it is divided into two spreading prongs; altogether it is ¼ inch long or less; the sepals and lateral petals are smaller. § Summer: mossy woods, bogs, swamps, etc., from Nfld. across Canada, s. to N. J. and in the mountains to N. C., and to Mich., Wis., Minn., and Calif. *Fig. 12.*

L. australis, the southern twayblade (1 ft.), has a deeply cleft, red lip, ⅓ inch long, the two prongs more or less parallel. § Early spring to summer: rare in e. Canada, s. through N. E. to Fla. and La.

THREE-BIRDS (*Triphora trianthophora*)   PINK OR WHITE
The three flowers resemble those of *Pogonia,* and since they hang from their stalks the plant is also called the nodding pogonia. The leaves are very small, scattered along the fragile stem (9 in.); the flowers come from the upper axils. They vary from pink to almost white, with a tinge of purple. The slender sepals are longer than the lip; the upper one arches. The lip has three

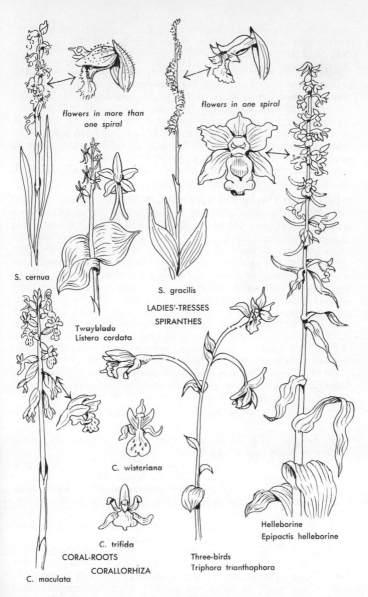

flowers in more than
one spiral

flowers in one spiral

S. cernua

S. gracilis

LADIES'-TRESSES
SPIRANTHES

Twayblade
Listera cordata

C. wisteriana

C. trifida

CORAL-ROOTS
CORALLORHIZA

C. maculata

Three-birds
Triphora trianthophora

Helleborine
Epipactis helleborine

FIGURE 12

greenish ridges running lengthwise. § Late summer and autumn: rich humus and leafmold, even rotten logs, Me. to Wis., s. to Fla., Ala., and Ark.; uncommon. *Fig. 12.*

SHOWY ORCHIS (*Orchis spectabilis*) PURPLE OR ROSE AND WHITE / The showy orchis (1 ft.) is comparable in size to some of our cypripediums—a large plant as our native orchids go. The two smooth basal leaves may be 8 inches long and half as wide. Between them rises the stem bearing from two to 15 flowers in a raceme. The sepals and lateral petals together form a purple or pinkish hood over the column. The lip is usually white, about ½ inch long, with a hollow tube or "spur" extending backward at one side of the stalk. § Early summer: rich wooded slopes, N. B. to Minn., s. to Ga. and Kan. PLATE 3.

REIN ORCHIDS and FRINGED ORCHIDS (*Habenaria*) VARIOUS COLORS / The general aspect of the species of *Habenaria* is most varied. Some have leaves on the flowering stem, either broad leaves or narrow; others have leaves only at the base, perhaps with scales on the stem. The flowers are individually not large, but are borne in tall racemes and in some species make a conspicuous show with sepals and petals of orange, yellow, magenta, purple, or white; in others they are green. The sepals and petals are more or less alike, in many species forming a hood. The lip is generally flat, in several species beautifully divided and fringed, with a hollow tube or "spur" which extends backward alongside the flower stalk. The spur of some species is so long and slender that it yields nectar only to large moths; these emerge from feeding with the stalked pollen masses fastened to their eyes by sticky disks.

Many species are common, particularly in damp places. Identification is not always easy without a technical manual; some species interbreed, with confusing results.

I. Species with the lip three-lobed or fringed or both (compare II).

    A. Species with three-lobed, fringed lip, magenta or purple flowers (compare B and C).

        H. psycodes, the purple fringed orchis (3 ft.), has long, relatively narrow, pointed lower leaves; the upper ones are very small. § Summer: wet upland meadows, open woodlands, bogs and swamps, Nfld. to Ont., s. to Ga., Tenn., and Ia. *Fig. 13.*

    B. Species with lip fringed or lobed or both, greenish or white flowers.

        H. lacera, the ragged orchis (2 ft.) has a lip with three very deeply fringed lobes, the middle lobe being long and narrow. The lateral petals are also narrow. The upper leaves are small, bractlike. § Summer: open swamps, meadows, woodlands, Que. to Minn., s. and sw. to Fla. and Tex. *Fig. 13.*

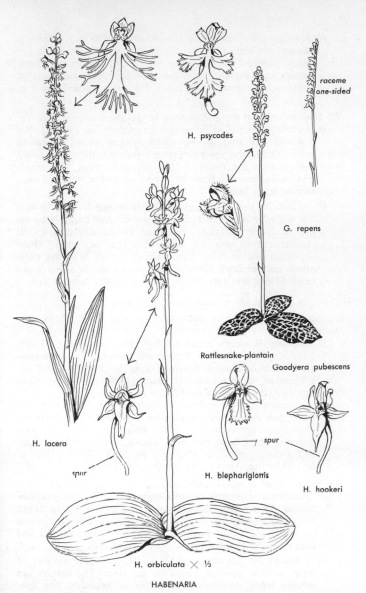

H. psycodes

raceme one-sided

G. repens

Rattlesnake-plantain

Goodyera pubescens

H. lacera

spur

H. blephariglottis

spur

H. hookeri

H. orbiculata × ⅓

HABENARIA

FIGURE 13

H. *blephariglottis,* the white fringed orchis (30 in.), has white flowers; the sepals are broad, almost round; the lip is un-lobed, copiously fringed; the spur is up to an inch long, slender and curved. § Late summer: acid swamps and bogs, Nfld. to Ont. and Mich., s. to Fla., Ala., and Miss. *Fig. 13.*

C. Species with lip fringed, orange or yellow flowers.

H. *cristata,* the crested or golden fringed orchis (30 in.), has a flower like that of the white fringed orchis except in color. The leaves are narrow and pointed, the upper much smaller than the lower. § Late summer: bogs, low mead-ows, moist barrens, from N. J. to Fla. and w. to Tex.; once known from Mass.

H. *ciliaris,* the yellow fringed orchis or orange-fringe (30 in.), has a flower much like that of the crested orchis (the lip not so deeply fringed), but may be distinguished by its slender, curved spur, up to an inch long or longer. There are from one to three lance-shaped leaves near the base, much smaller ones above. § Late summer: in many types of situations, but rare, N. E. to Wis., s. to Fla. and Tex.

II. Species with the lip neither lobed nor fringed.

A. Species with unlobed, unfringed lip, and basal leaves only (compare B).

H. *hookeri,* Hooker's orchis (1 ft.), has two broad, bluntly pointed leaves which lie flat on the ground. The yellowish-green flowers have a narrow, tapering, blunt-pointed lip. § Summer: woods and wet places, Nfld. to Minn., s. to W. Va., Ill., and Ia. *Fig. 13.*

H. *orbiculata,* the round-leaved orchis (2 ft.), has two almost round leaves lying on the ground. The flowers are greenish-white; the lip is narrow with almost parallel sides and rounded tip. § Late summer: woods, occasionally in bogs and swamps, Nfld. to Minn., s. to N. J., W. Va., and n. Ill.; Mont. to Alaska and Wash. *Fig. 13.*

B. Species with unlobed, unfringed lip and leaves on the stem.

H. *flava,* the tubercled or rein orchis (2 ft.), has greenish-yellow flowers; the sepals and lateral petals are of about the same length; the lip is oblong with a tooth or tubercle on either side near the base. § Summer: open woods and meadows, Nfld. to Minn., s. to Fla. and Tex.

H. *dilatata,* the tall white orchis (3 ft.), bears a number of long, narrow, pointed leaves on the stem. The flowers are usually white, sometimes yellowish or greenish. The spur about equals the narrow tapering lip. The upper part of the perianth forms a hood over the column. § Summer and autumn: wet places from near sea level to the slopes of high mountains, across Canada and s. to N. J., Wis., S. D., N. M., and Calif.

H. clavellata, the club-spur or small green orchis (18 in.), bears only one full-sized leaf. The blunt lip is barely ¼ inch long, the markedly curved spur more than twice as long. The plant pollinates itself and produces more seedlings than other orchids; thus it may become quite common. § Summer: wet places, even in water, Nfld. to Minn., s. to Fla. and Tex.

H. hyperborea, the tall green orchis (3 ft. or more), may bear stem leaves 10 inches long. The greenish lip tapers toward the tip; the spur is of about the same length—less than ¼ inch. § Summer: subarctic bogs, across Canada, s. to Pa., Nebr., N. M., and Ore.

H. viridis, the bracted orchis (2 ft.), has a blunt lip, a very short spur, and narrow lateral petals. It is a stout plant with a leafy stem and a long bract under each flower. § Summer: in many situations, from open meadows to dense forests, often at high altitudes, across the continent in the north, s. to N. J., O., Ill., Ia., Colo., and B. C. A variety occurs in the Old World.

TWAYBLADES (*Liparis*)   MADDER-BROWN, PURPLE, OR YELLOW-ISH / Like the other plants called twayblade (*Listera*), *Liparis* has two leaves, but at the base of the stem, not halfway up. The color of the broad flat lip is distinctive. The flowers grow in an open raceme; the sepals and lateral petals are narrow.

L. liliifolia, large twayblade or purple scutcheon (10 in.), has a madder-brown or purple lip, ½ inch long. § Spring and early summer: woods and clearings, N. H. to Minn., s. to Ga., Ala., and Mo. *Fig. 14.*

L. loeselii, olive scutcheon or russet-witch (8 in.), has a yellowish-green lip, ¼ inch long, or less. § Early summer: wet woods, Que. to Sask., s. to Md., Ala., Mo., and N. D.

THE RATTLESNAKE-PLANTAINS (*Goodyera*)   WHITE
Most of the small orchids of the genus *Goodyera* may be recognized by their rather broad basal leaves, which are generally marked with a pattern of white lines on a dark green ground. The flowers are small, whitish, crowded in a spikelike raceme which may be one-sided or spiral. The lateral petals with the upper sepal form a hood over the column and lip. The lip is rather fleshy, and forms a sac at its base. These are plants of coniferous or mixed forests, all blooming in summer.

G. repens, creeping rattlesnake-plantain (10 in.), has a one-sided raceme. § Across Canada and s. to N. C., Mich., Wis., Minn., S. D., etc. *Fig. 13.*

G. tesselata, checkered rattlesnake-plantain (16 in.), has a downy stem, leaves up to 3 inches long, and a one-sided or spiral, rather loose raceme. § Nfld. to Man., s. to N. Y., Mich., Wis., and Minn.

G. oblongifolia, green-leaved rattlesnake-plantain (18 in.), has dark green leaves which may have a white midrib but lack the white network of other species. The raceme is often one-sided or spiral. § From Que. across Canada, s. to Me., Mich., Wis., and in the western mountains.

G. pubescens, downy rattlesnake-plantain (16 in.), is named for its downy stem. The raceme is densely flowered, cylindrical. § Que. and Ont. and s. to Fla. and Mo. *Fig. 13.*

LADIES'-TRESSES (*Spiranthes*) WHITE

Ladies'-tresses are small, inconspicuous orchids which bear a spike of small white flowers. In most species the flowers form a spiral around the stem, whence the name of the genus; but in some species the flowers are all on one side, in others in a cylindric spike (made up apparently of several spirals together). The leaves are basal or nearly so, grasslike in many species. The stems vary in height from a few inches to 2 feet or more; the usual height is about a foot. The base of the lip more or less surrounds the column; the outer part is spreading and variously lobed, toothed or waved. There are some three hundred species of *Spiranthes,* at least eight in our range. It is not difficult to recognize the genus, but the species are variable and interbreed, and so are difficult to identify.

I. Species with a densely flowered spike, the flowers in several spirals (compare II).

  S. cernua (2 ft.) is one of the tallest. The leaves are basal, lance-shaped with the narrower end down. The flowers are sweet-scented; they tend to curve downward (they are "cernuous"). The perianth is nearly ½ inch long; the lip is delicately crisped at the margin. § Autumn: bogs, swamps, wet meadows, thickets, woodlands, Nfld. to Minn. and S. D., s. to Fla. and Tex. *Fig. 12.*

  S. romanzoffiana (20 in.) is distinguished by the narrowing of the lip near the middle. The flowers are scarcely more than ¼ inch long; they are hooded. The leaves are basal, grasslike. § Late summer: wet places, also dry woods, from Lab. across Canada, s. to Pa., Mich., S. D., and Colo.

  S. ovalis (12 in.) is a slender plant, with almost grasslike basal leaves and with stem leaves diminishing upward. The flowers are less than ⅕ inch long. § Autumn: moist shady woods, thickets, wet grassy places, Va. to Mo., s. to Fla. and Tex.

II. Flowers in a single row, vertical or spiraling.

  S. gracilis (2 ft.) has tiny flowers. The lip curls up at the sides to form a tube with the rest of the perianth and is fringed at the end; it has a green stripe down the middle. The leaves, at the base of the stem, are relatively broad. § Late summer: open woods, barrens, etc., across Canada, s. to N. C., Tenn., Wis., and Minn. *Fig. 12*.

S. vernalis (to 3 ft.) is easily identified by the red down in its inflorescence. § Spring and summer: wet pastures, coastal and inland marshes, pine barrens, Que. (?) and N. E., s. to Fla., on the Coastal Plain to Tex. and n. to Mo.

S. grayi is variable in habit (to 2 ft.), the tiny flowers (up to ⅙ inch long) spiraling on some plants, not on others. The stem rises from a slender underground tuber. § Spring to autumn: dry, well drained, open land, Mass., s. to Va.; Mich.

S. lucida (10 in.), whose small flowers (¼ inch long) are so crowded that they may seem to be in two rows, has a lip marked with a central yellow stripe and fine green lines. § Late spring and early summer: sandy and gravelly banks, wet meadows, bogs, and open wooded slopes, N. S. to Minn., s. to N. C., Tenn., and Mo.

S. praecox (to 30 in.) has flowers ⅖ inch long, their parts conspicuously veined with green. The leaves are grasslike or even threadlike. § Spring and summer: wet coastal areas, N. J. to Fla. and w. to Tex.

Dicots

(Dicotyledoneae)

GUIDE TO THE FAMILIES OF DICOTS

The families of dicots are here arranged in six arbitrary groups. On the page indicated for each, a guide will be found to the families included in that group. Note that since these guides make use of the most obvious characteristics possible, it is not always possible to arrange the families in them in the same order that they occupy in the text.

The Six Groups

I. Flowers with a perianth that consists of only one circle of parts (sepals), p. 84.

The perianth may be green or of other colors; it may resemble the petals of other flowers.

To determine the number of circles in the perianth it is often necessary to examine unopened buds. Some species have both sepals and petals, but the sepals fall as the flower opens (see *Sanguinaria*). Also in some families the sepals are minute and easily overlooked (see the Parsley Family).

Groups II to VI contain families characterized by two circles of perianth parts, sepals and petals; but a few species in these lack petals; see *Alchemilla, Sanguisorba, Ludwigia, Glaux, Lepidium, Draba, Cardamine, Chrysosplenium.*

II. Flowers with both sepals and petals, the petals not joined; the ovary or ovaries superior, p. 107.

In some flowers, as those of *Dodecatheon* and *Veronica,* the petals may seem to be separate, but are actually joined at the base; if one is pulled off, the others come with it (see IV and V).

III. Flowers with both sepals and petals, the petals not joined; the ovary inferior, p. 209.

See the note under II. When the pistil is inferior there is often a swelling (containing the ovary) beneath the sepals.

IV. Flowers radially symmetric, with joined petals and superior ovary (or ovaries), p. 239.

The petals may form a tube or bell, or they may be joined at the base only (see the note under II).

If there is even a slight difference in size or shape among the petals, the plant belongs in V (see *Veronica*).

V. Bilaterally symmetric flowers with joined petals and superior ovary (or ovaries), p. 279.

See notes under II and IV.

VI. Flowers with joined petals and inferior ovary, p. 326.
See notes under II and III.

GROUP I OF DICOT FAMILIES. FLOWERS WITH A SINGLE CIRCLE OF PERIANTH PARTS (SEPALS)

A. Plants with three sepals to a flower (compare B and C).

The **Birthwort Family** has sepals joined in their lower parts to form a tube (*Fig. 14*). There are six or twelve stamens. The ovary is partly or wholly inferior.

The **Buttercup Family** includes one genus, *Hydrastis,* classed here; the sepals fall as the flower opens.

B. Plants with more than three sepals to a flower, and one pistil.

The **Sandalwood Family** is represented in this book by one genus, which has sepals united to form a cup with five teeth (*Fig. 14*). The ovary is inferior. There are five stamens.

The **Smartweed Family** is distinguished by the tubular sheath around the stem where a leaf is attached (*Fig. 15*). The parts of the flower vary from three to nine. The ovary is superior.

The **Pokeweed Family** has one species in our range, with small white or pink flowers in an erect raceme, and purplish-black berries in a drooping raceme (PLATE 4). The number of flower parts varies. The ovary is superior.

The **Four-o'clock Family** is represented with us by plants that have small pink flowers contained in an involucre.

The **Buttercup Family** has species in this group, distinguished by divided or lobed leaves and numerous stamens (*Figs. 18, 19*).

C. Plants with more than three sepals and more than one pistil to a flower.

The **Buttercup Family** has species in this group (*Figs. 19–22*).

BIRTHWORT FAMILY (*Aristolochiaceae*)

This is a family that suggests the monocots in having a three-parted calyx. There are usually six or 12 stamens and a six-chambered ovary. The calyx is reddish or brownish. The leaves are generally stalked and heart-shaped, without marginal teeth.

In our range there are three genera: *Asarum,* with inferior ovary, flowers near the ground, 12 stamens; *Hexastylis,* with partly inferior ovary, flowers near the ground, 12 stamens; *Aristolochia,* with partly inferior ovary, flowers generally near the ground but on the leafy stem, six stamens, the calyx formed into a curved tube.

WILD GINGER (*Asarum canadense*)   REDDISH-BROWN
Wild ginger has soft, downy, heart-shaped leaves about 4 inches wide; their stalks, about 3 inches long, grow from a rhizome

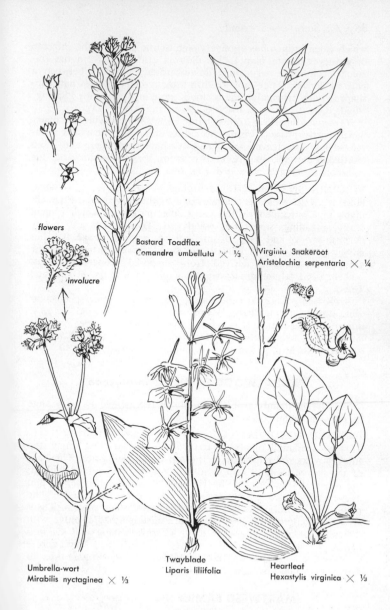

flowers

involucre

Bastard Toadflax
Comandra umbellata × ⅓

Virginia Snakeroot
Aristolochia serpentaria × ¼

Umbrella-wort
Mirabilis nyctaginea × ⅓

Twayblade
Liparis liliifolia

Heartleaf
Hexastylis virginica × ⅓

FIGURE 14

which when broken has a gingery smell (true ginger is the rhizome of a very different plant). The flowers also grow from the rhizome, each on a very short downward-curving stalk between a pair of leaves. They are reddish-brown, hairy, somewhat cup-shaped, with triangular calyx lobes pointing outward. § Spring: woods, Que. to Man., s. to N. C., Ala., and Ark. PLATE 4.

Hexastylis, heartleaf, differs from *Asarum* in having an ovary which partly projects inside the calyx, and which bears six separate styles. The leaves are generally smaller, glossier, and often mottled. Four species are known from Virginia southward, the commonest being *H. virginica. Fig. 14.*

VIRGINIA SNAKEROOT (*Aristolochia serpentaria*)   MADDER-PURPLE / *Aristolochia* is characterized by the curved tube ("Dutchman's pipe") formed by the calyx, the margin of which is generally spreading, sometimes widely so. The flowers are mostly purplish-brown and very ill-smelling. *A. serpentaria* (2 ft.) has narrowly heart-shaped leaves; the small flowers grow near the ground. Its name is derived from supposed properties against snakebite. § Early summer: woods, Conn. to Kan., s. to Fla. and Tex. *Fig. 14.*

Aristolochia is a vast genus in the tropics, with some spectacular vines among its members. Within our area (in Pa. and Va.) *A. durior* may be found. It is a fast-growing vine with large rounded leaves. The small pipelike flowers grow in the leaf axils. *A. tomentosa* (Ind. to Mo., s. and sw.) is similar but downy.

SANDALWOOD FAMILY (*Santalaceae*)

This large, mainly tropical family is represented in our range by only one genus of herbaceous plants.

BASTARD TOADFLAX (*Comandra*)   GREENISH-WHITE
These are small plants (1 ft.) with leaves attached singly; the small flowers are clustered at the top in simple cymes. The base of the flower forms a cup around the ovary and joined with it; the ovary is inferior. On the rim of the cup are five sepals and five stamens, each stamen opposite the center of a sepal. The plants are parasitic on the roots of various other species. There are two common species which are distinguishable only, with difficulty, by small characteristics: *C. richardsiana* and *C. umbellata.* § Late spring and summer: (*C. richardsiana*) Nfld., across Canada and s. to N. Y., Ind., and Mo.; (*C. umbellata*) Me. to Mich., s. to Ga. and Ala. *Fig. 14.*

SMARTWEED FAMILY (*Polygonaceae*)

The Smartweed Family is easy to recognize, because at every point where a leaf is attached to the stem there is a tubular sheath

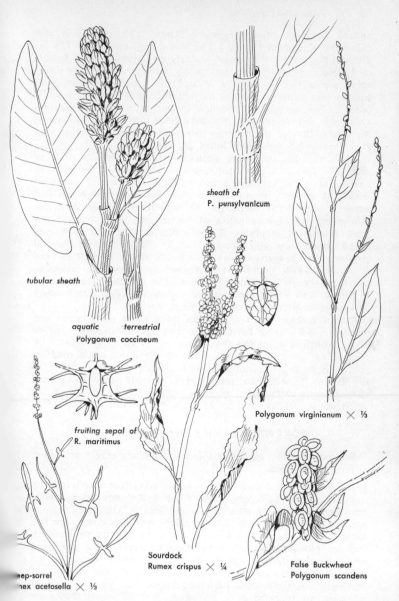

sheath of
P. pensylvanicum

tubular sheath

aquatic   terrestrial
Polygonum coccineum

fruiting sepal of
R. maritimus

Polygonum virginianum × ⅓

Sourdock
Rumex crispus × ¼

ep-sorrel
nex acetosella × ⅓

False Buckwheat
Polygonum scandens

FIGURE 15

around the stem, often forming a "knot." (The family is also called the Knotweed Family.) The stems may be zigzag. The individual flowers are very small, scarcely qualifying as wild flowers in the ordinary sense. They lack petals, have from three to six or seven sepals (which may be colored like petals), mostly from four to nine stamens, and one pistil. The fruit is a small grainlike achene. Two genera are common in our area: *Polygonum,* the knotweeds and smartweeds, including the tear-thumbs; and *Rumex,* the docks. Besides these weeds the family includes rhubarb and buckwheat, both sometimes found growing wild.

Polygonum has the sepals mostly petal-like, generally white or pink. The flowers are in tight spikes or clustered in the axils. *P. coccineum,* water smartweed, has handsome spikes of scarlet or deep pink flowers; it grows on or near the shores of ponds and streams, often partly submerged, throughout our range. *P. orientale,* prince's feather, a native of Europe and Asia, has escaped from cultivation in places. It has spikes of rose-colored flowers which often droop, and broad-bladed, long-stalked leaves. Several species (as *P. pensylvanicum*) have pretty spikes of pink flowers. *P. scandens,* false buckwheat, is a vine; its sepals bear conspicuous flaps ("keels") on their backs. In the woods *P. virginianum* is found, with broad lance-shaped leaves and very small white flowers in clusters along a tallish stem. *Fig. 15.*

Rumex has six green sepals, the three inner ones larger and enclosing the achene. In the mass they are unattractive, but as seen through a magnifier the sepals are often quite beautifully fringed (as in *R. maritimus*). One of the commonest roadside species is *R. crispus,* sourdock, with crisped and wavy edges to the leaves. *R. acetosella,* sheep-sorrel, a small plant with spear-shaped leaves and slender spikes of reddish flowers, is one of our worst weeds of lawns and fields; it came from Europe. *Fig. 15.*

POKEWEED FAMILY *(Phytolaccaceae)*

We have but one species in this family; many others are found in tropical America.

POKEWEED (*Phytolacca americana*)   GREENISH-WHITE OR PINK
Pokeweed (or pokeberry) (to 9 ft.) is a weedy plant, widely branched, with singly attached stalked leaves. The small flowers are in long, erect racemes that are paired with the leaves. The five sepals assume the aspect of petals. There are usually ten stamens, and ten pistils which cohere to make apparently one pistil and which together develop into the single purple-black berry. The red juice of the berry has been used as a pigment. The racemes of berries droop, their stems becoming bright red. Various parts of the plant are reported to be poisonous, but the young shoots are eaten as cooked greens. § Summer and autumn: Que. to Minn., s. and sw. to Fla. and Tex. PLATE 4.

FOUR-O'CLOCK FAMILY (Nyctaginaceae)

In our range this family is represented only by the genus *Mirabilis*. The flowers consist of a tubular calyx which resembles a corolla; there are no petals; one or more flowers are surrounded by bracts joined in a cuplike involucre. *Mirabilis jalapa* is cultivated; the calyx surrounded by an involucre is easily mistaken for a corolla surrounded by a calyx.

Bougainvillea is another well-known cultivated genus.

Mirabilis nyctaginea.   PINK

This rather weedy plant (3 ft.) has paired, more or less ovate and cordate, stalked leaves. Many involucres are clustered at the summit of the stem, each containing from one to five small flowers. § Late spring and summer: Mass. to Man., s. to La. and Tex. *Fig. 14.*

BUTTERCUP FAMILY (Ranunculaceae)

The buttercups and their relatives form a large family, almost entirely of herbaceous plants native in the North Temperate Zone. (One genus, *Clematis*, consists of woody vines, which are not treated here.) The group includes many of our common and familiar flowers of spring and early summer. Some are medicinal plants; some are poisonous. In general they can be recognized by their numerous stamens and pistils, the latter usually on a knob or column ("receptacle") in the center of the flower. In the buttercups themselves the flowers have both sepals and petals. In most genera the sepals have the appearance of petals and the petals are small, often stamenlike, or lacking. The pistils mature into small berries or pods or achenes; the pods ("follicles") split open when ripe; the achenes remain unopened.

Guide to Genera of *Ranunculaceae*

I. Genera with radially symmetric flowers (compare II).

A. Genera with both sepals and petals, the petals lacking spurs (hollow projections) (compare B and C).

Ranunculus has green sepals and yellow or white petals (*Figs. 16, 17;* PLATE 4).

Myosurus has an extremely long receptacle projecting from the center of the flower and covered with small pistils (*Fig. 18*). The petals are very small; the sepals are spurred.

Actaea has small white petals; the sepals fall early. The flowers are in a close cluster a short distance above the large divided leaves (*Fig. 18*).

Hepatica may be mistakenly sought here; it has three small green bracts below the flower, but these are not sepals (PLATE 4); the apparent petals are the sepals.

B. Genera that have no visible petals; the sepals commonly resemble petals.

1. Genera with no petals and yellow sepals (compare 2 and 3).

Caltha has round leaves (PLATE 4); it grows in wet places.

Trollius has leaves cut into sharp segments (*Fig. 19*).

2. Genera with no petals and sepals that fall as the flower opens, leaving only stamens and/or pistils.

Hydrastis, a low plant, has one flower, one basal leaf, two leaves on the stem (*Fig. 19*).

Cimicifuga is known by its very tall, slender raceme (*Fig. 19*).

Thalictrum is much branched. The long-stalked leaves are much divided into small notched or lobed segments (*Fig. 20*).

3. Genera with no petals and white or lavender petal-like sepals.

Hepatica (PLATE 4) has three sepal-like bracts below each flower; the basal leaves are three-lobed, live over winter, and are brown and flaccid at flowering time.

Anemone is known by the leaves that grow from one point some distance below the first flower. These and the basal leaves are palmately lobed or divided (*Figs. 21, 22*).

Anemonella has two or three leaves beneath the flower cluster; each of these and each basal leaf is divided into three long-stalked leaflets, each *notched* at the end (PLATE 4 and *Fig. 21*).

Isopyrum resembles *Anemonella;* the segments of the leaves are more deeply three-lobed with *rounded* gaps between (*Fig. 21*); the stalks of the stamens are white.

Coptis bears its flower or flowers on short, slender, leafless stalks growing from the ground; the fruits are stalked follicles (*Fig. 22*).

Myosurus may lack petals; see above, under A.

C. Genus with both sepals and petals, the petals extended upward into long spurs: *Aquilegia* (PLATE 5).

II. Genera with bilaterally symmetric flowers.

Delphinium has one spur, on the upper side; our species are mostly blue or purple (occasionally pink, white, or greenish) (*Figs. 22, 23*).

Aconitum has an upper sepal shaped like a hood or helmet, in our species blue or white (*Fig. 23*).

BUTTERCUPS and CROWFOOTS (*Ranunculus*)   YELLOW OR WHITE / Buttercups, in general, are familiar flowers of fields, woods, and wet places, many of them known by the glossiness of their petals. Most of them have five green sepals, five petals (yellow unless otherwise indicated here), a mass of stamens, and a knob-

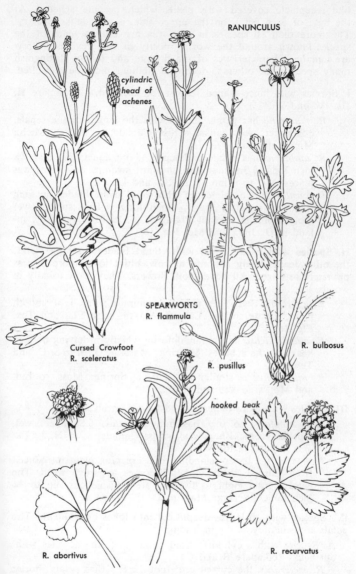

RANUNCULUS

cylindric head of achenes

SPEARWORTS
R. flammula

Cursed Crowfoot
R. sceleratus

R. pusillus

R. bulbosus

hooked beak

R. abortivus

R. recurvatus

FIGURE 16

like receptacle covered with pistils which become achenes. At the base of each petal, on the upper side, is a scalelike nectary. The more than 30 species in our area are only a tenth of the species known around the world, mostly in cool regions. A few are aquatic. Characteristics of the flowers and foliage distinguish many species; for others a technical manual must be consulted.

I. Species with lance-shaped leaves; the spearworts (compare II, III, IV, and V).

R. *flammula* has petals about twice the length of the sepals. § Summer: wet banks, across Canada, s. to Pa., Mich., Minn., and Ore. *Fig. 16.*

R. *ambigens* has petals and sepals about equal, less than ½ inch long. § Summer and autumn: swamps and other wet places, Me. to Minn., s. to Ga. and La.

R. *pusillus* has basal leaves with small ovate blades on long stalks. The petals are 1/12 inch long. § Late spring: wet ground on the Coastal Plain, N. Y. to Fla. and Tex.; inland in O., Ind., and Mo. *Fig. 16.*

II. Species with basal leaves with round blades on long stalks, the other leaves being cut into narrow, blunt lobes more or less pinnately arranged. All have small flowers. They grow usually in woods.

R. *abortivus* (2 ft.), in places a common weed, is a smooth plant. § Late spring: Lab. to Alaska, s. to Fla. and Tex. *Fig. 16.*

R. *allegheniensis* is similar, differing chiefly in having hooked beaks on the achenes. § Spring: Mass. to O., s. to S. C. and Tenn.

R. *micranthus* is similar but hairy. § Spring: Mass. to Ind. and Mo., s. to Va. and Ark.

III. Species with more or less round blades on all leaves.

R. *cymbalaria* (6 in.) has minute petals. § Summer: wet, especially brackish places, across Canada, s. to N. J., Ill., and Ia., and in the West.

R. *ficaria,* the lesser celandine, is a creeping plant introduced from Europe; it sometimes becomes a garden weed. The petals (from eight to twelve) are conspicuous, up to ¾ inch long. § Spring: Mass to D. C. PLATE 4.

IV. Species with all leaves deeply cut into lobes or segments. The petals are generally ¼–½ inch long.

A. Species with a cylindric head of achenes, the achenes without beaks (compare B and C).

R. *sceleratus,* the cursed crowfoot (2 ft.), has petals shorter than the sepals. The stem is smooth, somewhat thick; its

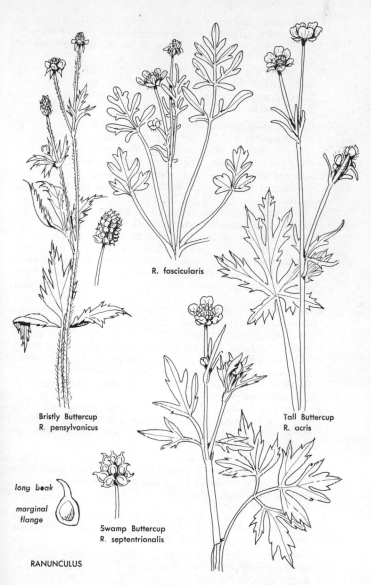

R. fascicularis

Bristly Buttercup
R. pensylvanicus

Tall Buttercup
R. acris

long beak

marginal
flange

Swamp Buttercup
R. septentrionalis

RANUNCULUS

FIGURE 17

juice causes blisters. § Summer: across Canada, s. to Fla., Ark., and Calif.; also in Europe and Asia. *Fig. 16.*

B. Species with a sort of bulb formed by the dilated bases of leaf stalks.

> *R. bulbosus,* the bulbous buttercup (1 ft.), has a flower an inch across; the petals usually number more than five. § Spring and summer: fields, a native of Europe widely established here. *Fig. 16.*

C. The remaining species of the group with cut leaves are not easy to distinguish without the help of a technical manual.

> *R. repens,* the creeping buttercup, has more or less hairy erect flowering stems. The leaves may have white markings, and the flowers may be double. § Spring and summer: naturalized from Europe in fields and wet places, Lab. to Minn., s. to N. C. and Mo.; in the West.

> *R. recurvatus* (2 ft.) has pale yellow petals, shorter than the sepals. The achenes have hooked beaks. § Late spring: woods, Nfld. to Man., s. to Fla. and Tex. *Fig. 16.*

> *R. pensylvanicus,* the bristly buttercup (2 ft.), has petals shorter than the sepals and a rather large head of achenes. Its stems are hairy. The achenes are sharply beaked. § Summer: wet places, Lab. to Alaska, s. to Del., Ia., Colo., and Ore. *Fig. 17.*

> *R. septentrionalis,* swamp buttercup, has long weak stems that come to lie on the ground. The achenes have a strong marginal flange and a long beak. § Late spring: moist woods, banks, and fields, Lab. to Man., s. to Va. and Ark. *Fig. 17.*

> *R. hispidus* is similar to the swamp buttercup, but more erect. The achenes lack flanges. The stem is more or less hairy. § Spring: dry woods and moist soil, Mass. to N. D., s. to Ga., Ala., and Mo.

> *R. fascicularis* (10 in.) has pale yellow petals, twice the length of the sepals. The leaves are cut into narrow blunt lobes. § Spring: prairies and other dry places, Mass. to Minn., s. to Ga., La., and Tex. *Fig. 17.*

> *R. acris,* the tall buttercup (to 3 ft.), has petals about twice as long as the sepals. § Spring to autumn: introduced from Europe and common in fields and roadsides in many places, especially eastward. *Fig. 17.*

V. Aquatic species, the water crowfoots. All grow in ponds or other quiet waters, flowering in summer. Some or all of their leaves are divided into threadlike segments.

> *R. flabellaris* has yellow flowers slightly earlier than the others (from April on). Me. to B. C., s. to N. C., La., Kan., and Calif.

> *R. aquatilis* has white flowers. The leaves are stalked. Greenl.

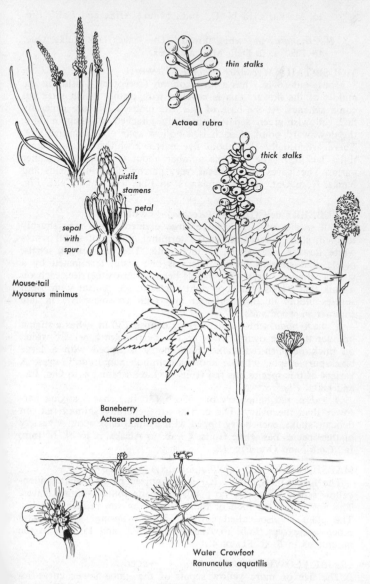

thin stalks

Actaea rubra

thick stalks

pistils
stamens
petal

sepal
with
spur

Mouse-tail
Myosurus minimus

Baneberry
Actaea pachypoda

Water Crowfoot
Ranunculus aquatilis

FIGURE 18

to Alaska, s. to N. C., Ind., Minn., Ariz., and Calif. *Fig. 18.*

R. circinatus has white flowers. The leaves lack stalks. Que. to Ore., s. to Del., Mo., and Tex.

MOUSE-TAIL (*Myosurus minimus*) WHITE

Mouse-tail (6 in.) has a long column (receptacle) rising in the middle of the flower; this is covered with pistils, which later become achenes. At the base of this, the mouse's tail, are generally five yellowish-green sepals apparently attached by their middle; the downward point of each is a hollow spur of diminutive size. There are usually also about five narrow, whitish petals (sometimes lacking). The stamens number about ten, but the number varies. The leaves are all basal, very narrow. § Spring: fields and banks, from Ont. across Canada, s. to Fla., Tex., and Calif. *Fig. 18.*

BANEBERRY or COHOSH (*Actaea*) WHITE

Both species of *Actaea* have large divided leaves with sharply toothed, stalked segments and a terminal cluster of small ivory-white flowers, the petals ⅛ inch long. The number of sepals, petals, and stamens varies. There is one pistil, terminated by a stigma without a style. The pistils become showy berries, each on a stalk that stands almost at right angles to the central stem. Both species bloom in early summer and fruit conspicuously in late summer in woodlands.

A. pachypoda, white baneberry or cohosh (30 in.), has a stigma broader than the ovary below it. The berries are generally white, on thick purplish-red stalks. Each berry is tipped with a large black-purple spot, whence another common name: doll's-eyes. A variety of this species has red fruits. § Que. to Man., s. to Ga., La., and Okla. *Fig. 18.*

A. rubra, red baneberry or cohosh (30 in.), has a stigma narrower than the ovary. The berries are generally shining red, on delicate stalks, each berry tipped with a small dark spot. A variety of this species has white fruits. § Lab. to Alaska, s. to N. J., Ind., Ia., Colo., and Ore. *Fig. 18.*

MARSH-MARIGOLD (*Caltha palustris*) YELLOW

The marsh-marigold (2 ft.) is recognized by its bright golden-yellow sepals (there are no petals) and the round, shining leaves. The flowers are an inch or more across, on few-branched stalks. The plant is also called cowslip. § Early spring: swamps and other wet places, Lab. to Alaska, s. to Va. and Ia. and in the mountains to S. C. PLATE 4.

GLOBE-FLOWER (*Trollius laxus*) YELLOW

The five or more yellow sepals of the globe-flower curve inward to form a sort of sphere about ¾ inch across. Within there are very small petals, resembling stamens without anthers. The

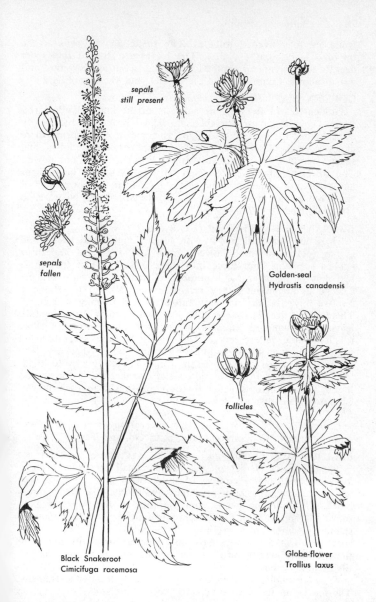

sepals
still present

sepals
fallen

Golden-seal
Hydrastis canadensis

follicles

Black Snakeroot
Cimicifuga racemosa

Globe-flower
Trollius laxus

FIGURE 19

fruits are many-seeded follicles. The single flower opens at the tip of a leafy stem (20 in.). The leaves are divided into from five to seven pointed, toothed segments. § Spring: swamps and wet meadows, Conn. to Mich., s. to Del. and O.; rare. *Fig. 19.*

GOLDEN-SEAL (*Hydrastis canadensis*)   GREENISH
Golden-seal (1 ft.) gets its name from the knotty, yellow rhizome. Gathering these for their medicinal properties has nearly exterminated the species. From the rhizome in early spring there arises a single basal leaf; it is roundish but deeply lobed and sharply toothed. The stem bears two similar leaves and one flower. The flower has three sepals which fall as they open. The stamens and pistils are numerous. The pistils later form a tight cluster of small red berries. § Spring: woods, Vt. to Minn. and Nebr., s. to Ga., Ala., and Ark. *Fig. 19.*

BUGBANE or RATTLETOP (*Cimicifuga*)   WHITE
These are very tall plants with large, long-stalked leaves and a long raceme of small flowers. Each leaf is divided into three stalked segments, and these into three again, so that the whole leaf may be mistaken for a number of small leaves on a branch. The petals are minute; they resemble the stalks of the stamens, but are forked at the tip; they fall early and so may be lacking. The four or five sepals are petal-like, white; they also soon fall, leaving the numerous stamens to give a feathery or hairy effect to the whole inflorescence. The pistils become several-seeded follicles which make a rustling or rattling sound when dry. The Latin name means the same as the English: putting bugs to flight.
  C. racemosa (8 ft.), also called black snakeroot, is widespread in our area. There is generally only one pistil in each flower. § Summer: woodlands, Mass. to Ont., s. to Ga., Tenn., and Mo. *Fig. 19.*
  C. americana (4 ft. or more) has several pistils in each flower. § Late summer: woodlands, s. Pa., s. to Ga. and Tenn.

MEADOW-RUE (*Thalictrum*)   WHITE, YELLOWISH, OR PURPLISH
The species of *Thalictrum* are in general tall, somewhat branching plants with ample clusters of small fuzzy flowers. The leaves are much divided, usually by threes, the ultimate segments three-lobed. There are no petals, and the four or five sepals usually soon fall. The color of the flowers·is chiefly that of the numerous stamens—white, green, yellow, or purplish. In several species some or all of the flowers have only stamens or pistils, not both; the two kinds may be on the same or on separate plants. The pistils become achenes.
  T. polygamum, tall meadow-rue (3–5 ft.), has white stamens. The leaves on the stem may have very short stalks or none, so that the three main divisions of each leaf may be mistaken for three separate leaves; each of these divisions is itself divided.

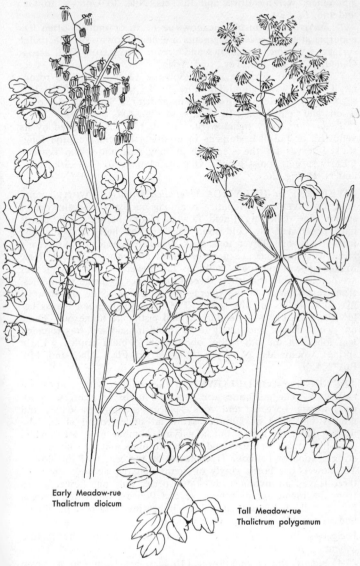

Early Meadow-rue
Thalictrum dioicum

Tall Meadow-rue
Thalictrum polygamum

FIGURE 20

§ Summer: wet meadows and thickets, Nfld. to Ont., s. to Ga. and Ind. *Fig. 20.*

T. dasycarpum, purple meadow-rue (3 ft. or more), often has a purple stem. The leaf segments are finely downy on the under surface. § Summer: meadows and stream banks, from Ont. across Canada, s. to O., La., Tex., and Ariz.

T. revolutum, wax-leaved meadow-rue (3 ft.), may be recognized by the waxy glandular hairs on the under side of the leaf segments (to be seen with a hand magnifier). § Summer: dry open woods and fields, Mass. to Ont., s. to Fla., Ala., and Ark.

T. dioicum, early meadow-rue (1–2 ft.), is distinguished by its yellowish or purplish stamens in drooping flowers, and the long-stalked leaves on the stem which may rise above the flowers. § Early spring: moist woods, Que. to Man., s. to Ga., Ala., Mo., and N. D. *Fig. 20.*

LIVERLEAF or HEPATICA (*Hepatica nobilis*) WHITE, BLUE, PINK, OR LAVENDER / Hepatica is among our best-loved flowers of spring. The delicately tinted flowers bloom before other plants have penetrated the cold soil. They rise on hairy stalks a few inches high, one flower to a stalk, from the cluster of last year's basal leaves, which are now brownish and usually flaccid. New foliage appears on hairy stalks as the flowers wither. The leaves are unmistakable with their three broad lobes (whence the names, from resemblance to the liver). What appear to be the flower's five to 12 petals are the sepals. The three small green leaves below them are bracts. The stamens and pistils are numerous. There are two varieties: one, likely to be found in acid soil, has rounded leaf lobes; in the other the lobes taper to blunt points. § Early spring: woodlands, N. S. to Man., s. to Fla., Ala., and Mo. PLATE 4.

ANEMONE or WINDFLOWERS (*Anemone*) WHITE, BLUE, OR LAVENDER / The anemones are perennial herbs of prairies, meadows, woods, barrens, and rocky places, sending up leaves and flowers in spring or summer from an underground stem. The flowers have no petals but a varying number of mostly white petal-like sepals. Stamens and pistils are numerous, the latter covering a knob or cylinder (receptacle) in the center of the flower. The flowers are borne singly on stems that rise above a circle of three leaves, an involucre. In some species only one flower grows from the involucre; in others, several flowers; often one finds a flower stalk and beside it a branch bearing a second involucre, and so on. The pistils become achenes.

I. Species with styles more than an inch long on the mature achenes (compare II).

A. patens, the pasque-flower (16 in.), has from five to seven large sepals each 1–1½ inches long, varying from white to blue

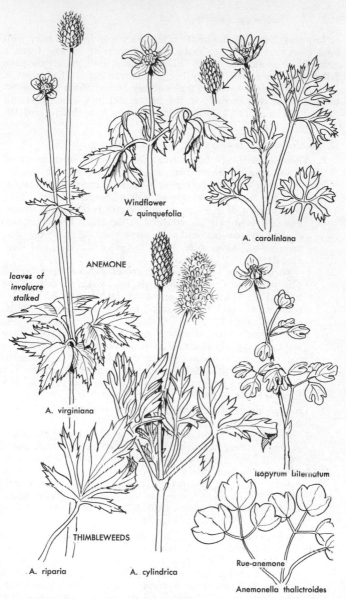

Windflower
A. quinquefolia

A. caroliniana

ANEMONE

leaves of
involucre
stalked

A. virginiana

Isopyrum biternatum

THIMBLEWEEDS

A. riparia

A. cylindrica

Rue-anemone

Anemonella thalictroides

FIGURE 21

or lavender, hairy on the under side. The whole plant is silky with long hairs, the flower in early spring appearing to rise from a nest of silvery fur. Often no foliage is seen until the sepals have fallen. The leaves are deeply cut into narrow lobes. The plant is later made conspicuous by the feathery styles which remain attached to the ovaries and, on the mature achenes, reach a length of an inch or more. § Spring: dry prairies, from Mich. and Ill. w. and nw. *Fig. 22.*

II. Species with styles no more than ¼ inch long.

A. Thimbleweeds, so called from the shape of their heads of fruit. (See also *A. caroliniana,* in C.) The achenes are woolly. The leaves below the flowers are stalked, their segments cut nearly to the base. The plants are tall. (Compare B and C.)

   A. virginiana (30 in.) has an involucre of two or three leaves. The leaf segments are rounded at the base. The "thimble" is oval in outline, about ½ inch thick. § Summer: dry, open woods, Que. to N. D., s. to Ga., Ala., Ark., and Kan. *Fig. 21.*

   A. riparia (30 in.) has an involucre of two or three leaves. The leaf segments are more or less wedge-shaped at the base. The "thimble" is about ⅓ inch thick. § Summer: open woods and rocky banks, from Nfld. across Canada, s. to Md. *Fig. 21.*

   A. cylindrica (3 ft. or more) may have from three to ten leaves in the involucre. The leaf segments are narrow at the base, their points blunter than in the two preceding species. The "thimble" is about ⅓ inch thick, up to 1½ inches long. § Summer: dry open woods and prairies, Me. to w. Canada, s. to N. J., O., Mo., and Ariz. *Fig. 21.*

B. Low plants with a slightly rounded receptacle and long-stalked leaves in the involucre.

   A. quinquefolia, wood anemone (8 in.), is a delicate plant. A single flower with usually five white sepals, each about ½ inch long, rises on a fragile stem above the involucre. Because the leaf blades are very deeply cut, they may be mistaken for five separate leaves. The single basal leaf is similar but larger. § Spring and early summer: moist woodlands, from Que. across Canada, s. to N. J., Ga. in the mountains, Ill., and Ia. *Fig. 21.*

C. Species with low rounded receptacle and three-parted leaves without stalks in the involucre, the basal leaves long-stalked.

   A. caroliniana (16 in.) has from 10 to 20 sepals, white, pink, red, or purplish, nearly an inch long. The flower stalk is woolly. The receptacle becomes longer as the achenes mature, forming a "thimble." § Late spring: dry places, Ind. to Wis. and N. D., s. to Fla. and Tex. *Fig. 21.*

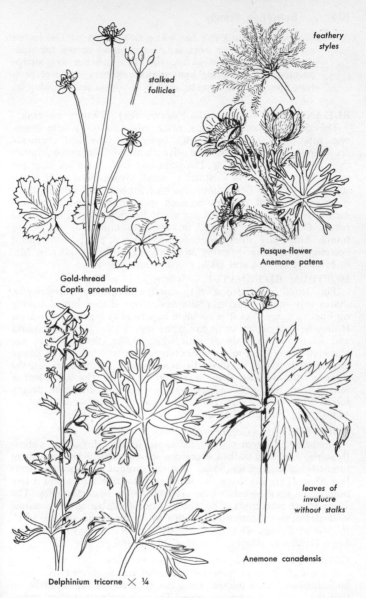

stalked
follicles

feathery
styles

Gold-thread
Coptis groenlandica

Pasque-flower
Anemone patens

leaves of
involucre
without stalks

Anemone canadensis

Delphinium tricorne × ¼

FIGURE 22

A. canadensis (to 3 ft.) has white flowers up to 1¾ inches across. The five or more sepals are broad across the middle, bluntly pointed at the tip. The achenes are sharp-pointed. § Late spring and summer: shores and wet prairies, Que., across Canada, s. to N. J., Mo., and N. M. *Fig. 22.*

RUE-ANEMONE (*Anemonella thalictroides*)   WHITE OR PINK

This delicate plant (6–8 in.), often mistaken for a true anemone, may also be confused with *Isopyrum*. The leaf segments are merely notched at the end, like those of *Thalictrum,* rather than lobed as in *Isopyrum*. The stem and leaf stalks are like fine wires. They grow from a cluster of small pink tubers, each at the summit of a root. Below the cluster of long-stalked flowers there is an involucre of two leaves, each with three long-stalked segments. The five to ten sepals are about ½ inch long; there are no petals. Occasionally "double" flowers with numerous sepals are found. There are many stamens and several pistils; each pistil becomes an achene. § Spring and early summer: woodlands, Me. to Minn., s. to Fla. and Okla. PLATE 4 and *Fig. 21.*

ISOPYRUM BITERNATUM   WHITE

This small plant (to 1 ft.), closely resembling *Anemonella,* shares with many American wild flowers the distinction of having no English name. Yet it is common in woods in much of our area. It may be recognized by its five white sepals (there are no petals) and its numerous stamens with white stalks. Small tubers are scattered along the roots, not clustered. The leaf below the flower has no main stalk; its three divisions appear as three leaves; the same is true of most of the leaves on the stem. The basal leaf is long-stalked. The ultimate segments are stalked and quite deeply lobed, with rounded gaps between. § Spring: moist woods, Ont. to Minn., s. to Fla. and Tex. *Fig. 21.*

GOLD-THREAD (*Coptis groenlandica*)   WHITE

Gold-thread (5 in.) owes its name to the threadlike yellow rhizome. The long-stalked evergreen leaves are divided into three toothed segments. Each flower is at the summit of a separate leafless stem. There are from five to seven petal-like sepals and a like number of small petals which are little more than nectaries. The stamens are numerous. The pistils, from three to seven, become stalked follicles. Some consider this to be the same species as *C. trifolia* of Europe and Asia. § Early summer: mossy woods and bogs, Greenl. to Alaska, s. to N. C., Ind., and Ia. *Fig. 22.*

COLUMBINE (*Aquilegia*)   RED AND YELLOW

Columbine flowers have five beautiful petals shaped like vases and attached at the middle. Each flower droops from its stalk, so that the "vases" are upside down. The tubular part that is uppermost is the spur of each petal. Nectar is secreted in its bulbous

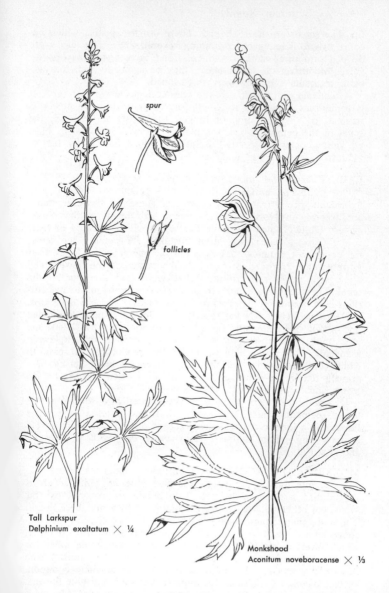

spur

follicles

Tall Larkspur
Delphinium exaltatum × ¼

Monkshood
Aconitum noveboracense × ⅓

FIGURE 23

tip. The sepals are heart-shaped. There are five pistils, which become five follicles, each containing several seeds. The leaves are divided into three stalked segments, and these again may be divided into three; the lower leaves may be again divided; the ultimate segments are irregularly three-lobed.

A. canadensis (1–3 ft.) is the common species in our area. It is sometimes known as rock-bells or honeysuckle. The flower is from 1 to 2 inches long, or longer; the sepals are reddish; the spurs of the petals are red, the blades yellow. (Some forms have all yellow or white petals.) § Spring: woods and rocky ledges, Nfld. to Sask., s. to Fla. and Tex. PLATE 5.

LARKSPUR (*Delphinium*) BLUE, PINK, OR WHITE

Our cultivated annual and perennial delphiniums are largely hybrids of species from many countries. There are, however, many wild species in North America; some half-dozen in the northeastern United States. All have five sepals which, because of their colors (mostly blue), are often mistaken for petals. One sepal, the uppermost, extends backward into a spur. The petals are four (rarely two), forming the "bee" in the center of the flower. The upper two petals are prolonged backward into the spur of the sepal. The stamens are numerous. There are from one to five pistils which become follicles with several seeds.

D. tricorne (to 3 ft.) has mostly basal leaves, which are divided into about five segments, these cut into long narrow lobes; the lobes may be sharp-pointed or blunt. The flowers, only a few in a raceme, vary from blue or violet through occasional pink to white (or variegated), and are 1–1½ inches long. § Spring: dry gravelly banks or—apparently in the East—rich woods, Pa. to Minn. and Nebr., s. to Ga., Ala., and Okla. *Fig. 22.*

D. exaltatum (to 6 ft.) has leaves divided into several rather broad segments which are deeply cleft into pointed lobes. The flowers, in a long, often branched raceme, are blue or white, rarely an inch long. § Late summer: rich woods, Pa. to O., s. to N. C. and Ala. *Fig. 23.*

MONKSHOOD or ACONITE (*Aconitum*) BLUE OR WHITE

In aconite the uppermost of the five blue or white sepals is shaped like a hood or helmet. Two petals are covered by this sepal; the other petals are much smaller, if they are there at all. There are many stamens and from three to five pistils which become follicles with several seeds. The plants grow from a tuber, which forms a lateral branch, at the end of which the tuber for the next year develops. These tubers contain a deadly poison. The three native species all grow in woods, but are nowhere common.

A. uncinatum (3 ft.) has a smooth flower stalk and blue flowers. § Late summer and autumn: Pa. to Ind., s. to Ga. and Ala.

A. noveboracense is similar but has a hairy stalk. § Summer: N. Y. to Wis. and Ia. *Fig. 23.*

GROUP II OF DICOT FAMILIES. PETALS SEPARATE; OVARY OR OVARIES SUPERIOR

A. Plants rooted underwater, the leaf blades floating or rising above the surface (compare B, C, D, E, and F).

The **Water-lily Family** has a number of radiating stigmas on the upper surface of the ovary.

B. Land plants with numerous stamens and more than one pistil in a flower.

The **Buttercup Family** includes some genera classed here. They have leaves without stipules (the stalks sometimes expanded at the base). The stamens are attached just beneath the dome or knob of the receptacle on which the pistils are borne.

The **Rose Family** has leaves with conspicuous stipules. The stamens are attached near the margin of an expanded disk, the receptacle, from which the perianth also arises. The pistils are borne in the cuplike receptacle, or on a hump in the middle much as in the Buttercup Family.

C. Plants with two sepals, four or more stamens, and one pistil in a flower.

The **Purslane Family** has generally five petals and the same number of stamens.

The **Poppy Family** has four, eight, or other numbers of petals and stamens more numerous than the petals (PLATE 5).

The **Bleeding-heart Family** has four petals in two unlike pairs, forming a bilaterally symmetric flower. One or both of the outer petals extend backward, near the stalk, into a tube or sac ("spur") (*Fig. 30* and PLATE 5).

D. Plants with radially symmetric flowers that have more than two sepals and not more than ten stamens. Twelve families are included here.

The **Barberry Family** has (as represented in this book) four or six sepals, six, eight, or nine petals, and (except in *Podophyllum*) as many or twice as many stamens as petals (*Fig. 25*).

The **Pink Family** has four or five petals, usually the same number of stamens or twice as many, from two to five styles on the one ovary (*Figs. 26–29;* PLATE 5).

The **Mustard Family** has generally four sepals, four petals, six stamens of which two are shorter than the other four, one pistil (*Fig. 31;* PLATE 6).

The **Sundew Family** has leaves covered with sticky hairs (*Fig. 37*). There are in our species usually three styles.

The **Stonecrop Family** has four or five petals and as many stamens or twice as many, and several pistils. Most species are succulent (*Fig. 37*).

The **Saxifrage Family** has generally four or five sepals and petals, four, five, or ten stamens, and two styles (*Fig. 38*) except in one genus which has four stigmas on the ovary and no styles; the ovary is often cleft, and gives rise to a two-beaked capsule. The leaves are generally basal.

The **Geranium Family** has five sepals and petals, ten stamens, a five-lobed ovary with one style, a long-beaked fruit which splits into five parts (*Figs. 56, 57;* PLATE 7). The flowers are mostly lavender or rose.

The **Wood-sorrel Family** has five sepals and petals, ten stamens joined at the base of their stalks, one ovary with five styles (*Fig. 58*). The flowers are yellow, violet, pink, or white.

The **Flax Family** is composed of very slender plants with short, narrow leaves, and blue or yellow flowers (*Fig. 57*).

The **Spurge Family** is included with the above families by botanists, although most of its species have no petals and many lack sepals. See the description of the family (*Fig. 61*).

The **Bean Family** (see below) includes some genera with radially symmetric flowers (*Fig. 56*).

The **Loosestrife Family** has (as represented in this book) from four to six sepals and petals, as many stamens or more, paired narrow leaves without teeth. The joined sepals form a cup or tube (*Fig. 66*).

E. Plants with bilaterally symmetric flowers that have more than two sepals and not more than ten stamens.

The **Bean Family** mostly has flowers that contain five, nine, or ten stamens which in many species are joined by their stalks into one or two groups, and one pistil. The leaves are singly attached, mostly divided (*Figs. 46–55;* PLATE 7).

The **Milkwort Family** has flowers mostly in spikes or heads; in our species there are five sepals (two of which resemble the petals), three petals joined to each other and to the eight stamens. The lowest petals are often fringed (*Fig. 58;* PLATE 7). The leaves are not divided.

The **Touch-me-not Family** has five very unequal petals, of which the lowest and largest extends backward into a hollow orange or yellow sac ending into a bent tube ("spur"; PLATE 8). There are five stamens and one pistil.

The **Violet Family** has five approximately equal petals, the lowest of which generally extends backward in a "spur." The five stamens closely invest the pistil so that only the beaklike end is seen (PLATE 8).

F. Plants with more or less radially symmetric flowers, more than two sepals, more than ten stamens, one pistil.

The **Barberry Family** (see above under D) has one genus, *Podophyllum,* with numerous stamens. The leaf blades are attached to their stalks by their middle.

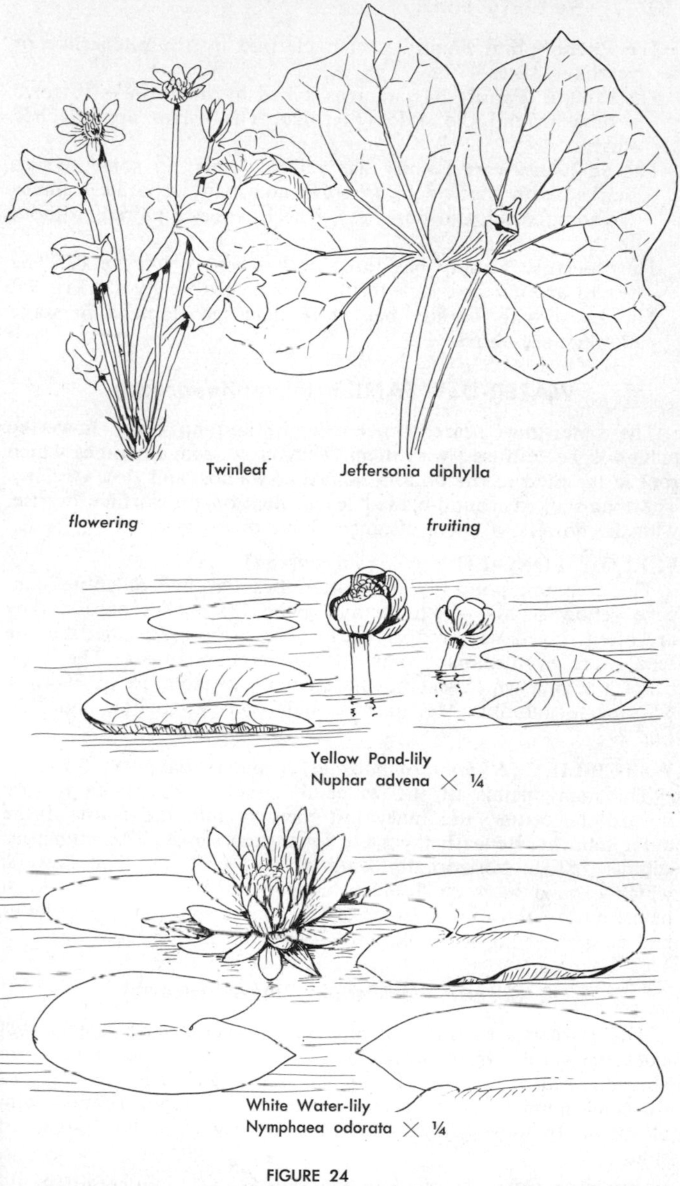

Twinleaf   Jeffersonia diphylla

flowering   fruiting

Yellow Pond-lily
Nuphar advena × ¼

White Water-lily
Nymphaea odorata × ¼

FIGURE 24

The **Pitcher-plant Family** is characterized by the pitcherlike or vaselike leaves (*Fig. 37*).

The **Mallow Family** has stamens joined by their stalks to form a tube around the style (*Fig. 62*). The leaves are attached singly.

The **St.-John's-wort Family** has yellow petals (in some species marked with black dots; *Fig. 64*) and many separate stamens (in some species in bunches). The leaves are paired, without teeth.

The **Rockrose Family** has three or five sepals, five petals. The leaves are narrow, lack teeth, are attached singly (PLATE 9).

The **Loosestrife Family** has more than ten stamens in some flowers; see above.

WATER-LILY FAMILY (*Nymphaeaceae*)

The water-lilies scarcely need description; no other flowering plant will be confused with them. They grow from rhizomes which root in the mud at the bottom of lakes, swamps, and slow streams. The long-stalked, round-bladed leaves float on the surface or rise, with the flowers, a short distance above it.

YELLOW POND-LILY (*Nuphar advena*) YELLOW

The common pond-lily or spatter-dock has five or more concave yellow sepals which form a globe 1½ inches across; they are often tinged with red or green. The petals, concealed by the sepals, are even shorter than the numerous stamens. The pistil bears a stigma which extends horizontally in from 15 to 30 rays. § Spring to autumn: Me. to Wis. and Nebr., s. to Fla. and Tex. *Fig. 24.*

WATER-LILY (*Nymphaea odorata*) WHITE OR PINK

The many petals of the water-lily gradually diminish in size toward the center, the innermost merging into the form of the outer stamens. Beneath them are four green sepals. The numerous stigmas radiate horizontally, ending in curved tips. The flowers, which expand to 4 or 5 inches across, are very fragrant. Each opens during the mornings of several successive days. § Summer and autumn: Nfld. to Man., s. to Fla. and Tex. *Fig. 24.*

BARBERRY FAMILY (*Berberidaceae*)

The Barberry Family contains several herbaceous species besides the shrubs from which it takes its name. The flowers are characterized by four or six sepals, six or eight petals, stamens of the same number as the petals (except in May-apple), and a single pistil. In most genera the stamens open by a lid instead of splitting.

BLUE COHOSH (*Caulophyllum thalictroides*) YELLOWISH

Small flowers in a cluster terminate the nearly 3-foot stem of

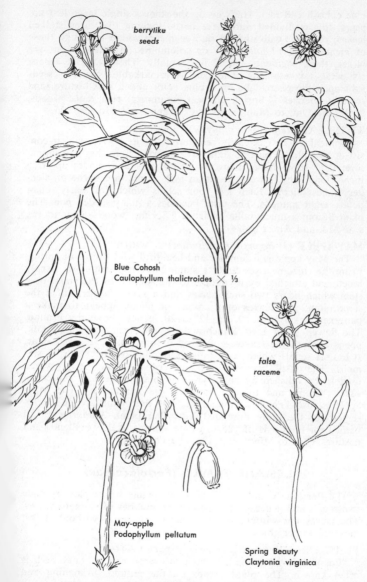

berrylike
seeds

Blue Cohosh
Caulophyllum thalictroides × ⅓

false
raceme

May-apple
Podophyllum peltatum

Spring Beauty
Claytonia virginica

FIGURE 25

blue cohosh (40 in.). Halfway up the stem a single large leaf appears; this is divided into three parts, looking like three stalked leaves; each is again divided into segments which look like those of meadow-rue (*Thalictrum*) or columbine (*Aquilegia*) but are larger; these segments spread horizontally. There are six sepals, six petals, six stamens. The fruit is remarkable: the two seeds split open the pistil, take on a blue color and a soft texture, and resemble berries. § Spring and early summer: rich moist woods, N. B. and Ont. to Man., s. to S. C., Tenn., and Mo. *Fig. 25.*

TWINLEAF (*Jeffersonia diphylla*) WHITE

Twinleaf (8 in.) is easily recognized by its leaves, which consist of two blades on one stalk. At flowering time they are immature; later some have stalks 20 inches long and blades up to 6 inches long. The flowers, about an inch across, are borne on slender leafless stems. Each has four sepals which fall early, eight petals, eight stamens. The pistil becomes a many-seeded pod. The plant becomes much taller in fruit. § Spring: woods, Ont. to Ia., s. to Md. and Ala. *Fig. 24.*

MAY-APPLE (*Podophyllum peltatum*) WHITE

The May-apple is a familiar and beautiful wild flower of spring. From the rhizome rises either a single large leaf, roundish, deeply lobed, and attached by its middle to the summit of the stalk; or a stem which bears two such leaves and a single flower, all at the same point. The leaves of a colony of plants appear to make a patterned, level carpet from 12 to 20 inches above the ground. The flower, from 1 to 2 inches wide, on a short arching stalk, opens beneath the leaves, giving off a somewhat oversweet odor. It has six sepals which soon fall, six or nine petals, 12 or 18 stamens. The pistil becomes a many-seeded yellow berry, which used to be relished by countryfolk in marmalade and preserves. (The rhizome and foliage, however, are poisonous.) The May-apple is also known as mandrake, but this name should be reserved for the quite unrelated European plant, *Mandragora,* so named for hundreds of years. § Late spring: open woodlands and pastures, Que. to Minn., s. to Fla. and Tex. *Fig. 25.*

PURSLANE FAMILY (Portulacaceae)

The Purslane Family contains small plants whose flowers have two sepals and generally five petals; the number of stamens varies. The leaves are without marginal teeth, generally without stalks; they are rather thick.

PURSLANE (*Portulaca oleracea*) PALE YELLOW

"Pussley" is the name by which this weed and culinary herb is often known. The plant creeps on the ground, branching and forming mats which are hard to kill even when uprooted; it will survive exposure to the sun and take root again. The leaves are succulent. The flowers are small, stalkless, in the leaf axils. § Summer: waste ground and gardens, throughout. *Fig. 26.*

SPRING BEAUTY (*Claytonia*)   PINK OR WHITE
Spring beauty has a pair of smooth leaves halfway up the flowering stem (about 12 in.). The flowers are in a false raceme, their stalks projecting to one side of the stem, with usually one bract opposite the lowest flower. The unopened flowers droop at the tip. The petals are pink or white with veins of deeper pink. There are five stamens.

C. virginica (8 in.) has very narrow, pointed leaves. § Early spring, N. S. to Minn., s. to Ga. and sw. to Texas. *Fig. 25.*

C. caroliniana (8 in.) has blunt leaves, wider across the middle, on short stalks. § Early summer: Nfld. to Sask., s. to N. E., Ill., and Minn.; farther s. in the mountains.

PINK FAMILY (Caryophyllaceae)

The pinks and their relatives (including the cultivated carnations and sweet-Williams) form a large family of herbaceous plants mostly of the North Temperate Zone. The leaves are usually attached in pairs (but in some species occur in circles or tufts), and in many species they are small and narrow, even needlelike. The flowers of many genera are arranged in compound cymes. Most species have five petals and twice as many stamens; but some have four petals, others none, and the number of stamens may vary. There is one pistil with from two to five styles. The fruit is usually a small round capsule which splits from the top down.

Guide to Genera of *Caryophyllaceae*

I. Genera with united sepals which form a tube from which the petals emerge (compare II).

A. Genera with united sepals and two styles on each ovary (compare B and C).

Saponaria has broad leaves and dense clusters of large pink-and-white flowers (*Fig. 26*).

Dianthus has very narrow leaves and, in our commonest wild species, small pink or red flowers (*Fig. 26*).

B. Genus with united sepals and three or four styles on each ovary: *Silene* (*Figs. 26, 27;* PLATE 5).

C. Genera with united sepals and four or five styles on each ovary.

Lychnis generally has several flowers (white, pink, or red) to a stem, with calyx teeth that do not spread (*Fig. 28*).

Agrostemma has one large purplish-red flower at the top of a long stem, with five long narrow teeth on the calyx extending beyond the petals (*Fig. 28*).

II. Genera with separate sepals; the plants are generally small.

Stellaria and *Cerastium* have five petals, notched, or in some species so divided that they appear as ten (*Fig. 29*).

Arenaria has five petals notched (not divided to the base), and generally two styles to each pistil (*Fig. 29*).

BOUNCING-BET (*Saponaria officinalis*)   WHITE AND PINK

Bouncing-Bet (2–3 ft.) is a native of the Old World that is very much at home in the New, growing abundantly along roadsides, on railroad embankments, and in other waste places. The flowers, about an inch across, form ragged-looking cymes. Each petal has a sharp-pointed appendage, like a horn, where the broad, spreading part joins the slender stalklike part. The leaves are smooth, fairly broad across the middle, pointed at the tip, 3 or 4 inches long. The Latin name is derived from a property of the juice: it lathers in water like soap. For this reason the plant is sometimes called soapwort. The same peculiarity is true of a number of species in this family. § Summer and early autumn: waste places, throughout. *Fig. 26.*

PINKS (*Dianthus*)   ROSE

Several species of *Dianthus* brought from the Old World have established themselves in our area. They only remotely resemble the carnations, which are also in this genus.

D. armeria, Deptford pink (2 ft.), is a very slender plant, with paired needlelike leaves about 2 inches long. At the summit is a cluster of small flowers of pink or deep rose, opening one at a time. § Summer: from Que. westward, s. to Ga. and Mo. *Fig. 26.*

THE CAMPIONS and CATCHFLIES (*Silene*)   WHITE, PINK, RED, OR LILAC / The catchflies are named from the sticky substance found on the stems and elsewhere in some species; small insects are thus caught. The campions, also called wild pinks, are handsome flowers. The genus is much like *Lychnis* (also known as campion), being distinguished chiefly by the number of its styles, which is almost always three. The many-seeded capsule opens at the top, splitting into three or six teeth. The petals have a blade (usually notched or cleft) borne at the end of a slender stalklike part; in some species there is a scale on the upper surface at the base of the blade.

I. Species with large white flowers, the stems not sticky (compare II and III).

   S. stellata, starry campion (2 ft.), has a delicate fringe on the ends of the petals; scales are lacking. The leaves are often in circles of four. § Late summer: woods and clearings, Mass. to Mich. and N. D., s. to Ga. and Tex. *Fig. 26.*

   S. nivea, white or snowy campion (1 ft.), is similar but lacks the fringe; the petals are merely notched, the flowers rather few. The leaves are all in pairs. § Summer: rich woods, Pa. to S. D., s. to Md. and Mo. *Fig. 27.*

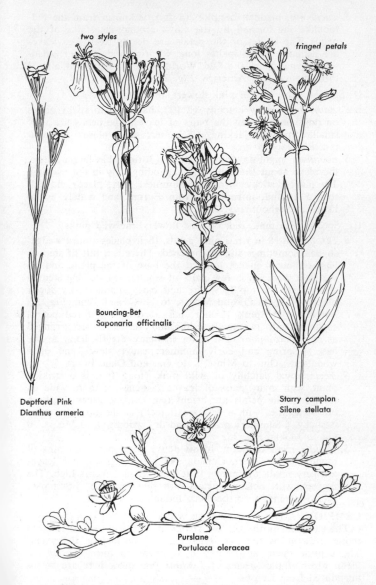

two styles

fringed petals

Bouncing-Bet
Saponaria officinalis

Deptford Pink
Dianthus armeria

Starry campion
Silene stellata

Purslane
Portulaca oleracea

FIGURE 26

S. cucubalus, bladder campion (2 ft.), is known from the balloonlike sac formed by the calyx around the stalks of the petals. The blades of the petals are deeply cleft. The leaves are paired, up to 3 inches long. § Spring and summer: roadsides; a native of the Old World, widely established almost throughout North America. *Fig. 27.*

II. Species with white or pink flowers, the stems sticky.

S. antirrhina, sleepy catchfly (2 ft.), has blackish sticky zones on the stem between the pairs of leaves. The petals are very small, sometimes lacking. § Summer: waste places, throughout. *Fig. 27.*

S. noctiflora, night-flowering catchfly (30 in.), has larger petals, the blade about ¼ inch long, expanding only in the evening. The plant is sticky all over. § Summer: waste places and cultivated ground; introduced from Europe and widely established throughout. *Fig. 27.*

III. Species with pink, red, or lilac flowers; the wild pinks.

S. caroliniana (8 in.) has pink petals, their blades almost wedge-shaped, sometimes slightly notched. There is a tuft of smooth leaves about 4 inches long at the base of the plant, and on the stem there are a few pairs of smaller leaves. The stem is sticky near the top. § Spring and early summer: dry rocky places, N. H. to O. and Mo., s. to N. C. and Tenn. *Fig. 27.*

S. virginica, fire pink (2 ft.), has narrow, bright red petals, each split into two teeth at the end. Its leaves are arranged as in *S. caroliniana,* but differ in being slightly hairy at the base. § Spring and early summer: rocky slopes and open woodlands, Ont. to Minn., s. to Ga. and Okla. PLATE 5.

S. regia, royal catchfly or wild pink (to 5 ft.), is a striking plant, with many pairs of leaves 2 inches or more wide on the stem. The petals are bright red, narrow, generally sharp but sometimes with a few small teeth at the tip. The calyx is sticky. § Summer: prairies and dry woods, O. to Mo.; s. to Ga. and Okla. *Fig. 28.*

S. acaulis, moss campion, forms dense tufts on the summits of mountains in eastern Canada and New England. The leaves are very small, the plants little more than 2 inches high. The flowers, with notched petals, are pink or lilac. § Summer: rocky barrens in northeastern mountains. *Fig. 28.*

CAMPION (*Lychnis*)   ROSE OR WHITE

The campions in the genus *Lychnis* are to be distinguished from those in *Silene* by the five styles that are normal on the ovary. The capsule opens at the top by splitting to form five or ten teeth. Most of the species of *Lychnis* that grow here are weeds introduced from Europe.

L. flos-cuculi, ragged-Robin (2 ft.), has deep rose-pink petals (occasionally white) cut into several long teeth and so giving the

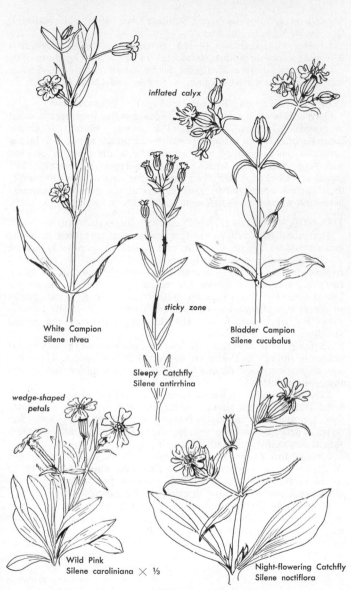

White Campion
Silene nlvea

inflated calyx

sticky zone

Sleepy Catchfly
Silene antirrhina

Bladder Campion
Silene cucubalus

wedge-shaped petals

Wild Pink
Silene caroliniana × ⅓

Night-flowering Catchfly
Silene noctiflora

FIGURE 27

flower a ragged appearance. § Summer: wet fields and roadsides, Que. to N. Y., s. to Pa. *Fig. 28.*

L. alba, white campion (4 ft.), is so like *Silene noctiflora* that it is often confused with it. It has leaves up to 4 inches long. The calyx becomes enlarged, almost as in *Silene cucubalus.* § Summer: from Que. across Canada, s. to Ga. and Calif. *Fig. 28.*

CORN COCKLE (*Agrostemma githago*)   PURPLISH-RED
Corn cockle (3 ft.) is so called because it has long been a weed in grainfields ("corn" in England is usually wheat). It comes from Europe. It has a single purplish-red flower about 1½ inches across at the summit of each stem. The whole plant is covered with short hairs. The leaves are very narrow and pointed. The sepals are joined for half their length, forming a ten-ribbed tube; their narrow upper halves project beyond the petals. § Summer: fields and waste places, throughout. *Fig. 28.*

THE CHICKWEEDS (*Stellaria* and *Cerastium*)   WHITE
The group of small weeds frequently seen spreading near the ground in lawns, gardens, fields, and roadsides, commonly known as chickweeds, comprises two genera, distinguished by rather inconspicuous details. They are all plants with slender stems which carry pairs of small leaves and small white flowers mostly on long stalks. The five petals are notched or cleft, in some species so deeply that there appear to be ten. There are generally ten stamens, but sometimes fewer. The differences between the genera are these:

Stellaria, some of whose species are called starworts, has plants generally smooth and likely to be found in wet places. There are usually three styles. The capsules open by splitting lengthwise into three or six parts.

Cerastium, some of whose species are called mouse-ear chickweeds because of the shape and texture of their leaves, has plants that are generally downy, often sticky. There are usually five styles. The capsules open only at the top, splitting into ten teeth (small but easily seen with a magnifier).

Most of the species flower from spring to summer, some longer. At least one (*S. media*) is a winter-growing annual, likely to be found in flower at any favorable time of year. Nearly all the chickweeds are widespread throughout our range.

S. media is the commonest of the chickweeds and extremely variable: the stamens may number from two to ten and the petals may be lacking. The stem usually (but not always) bears lines of short hairs. It may be recognized chiefly from its leaves, which are about an inch long or less and generally on distinct stalks. The sepals are at least as long as the deeply cleft petals. *Fig. 29.*

S. pubera (to 16 in.) is a native woodland species, growing more or less erect. It is distinctly downy. Its leaves may be 4 inches long and quite broad.

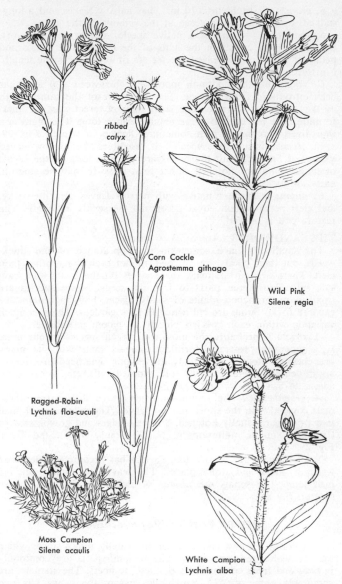

ribbed
calyx

Corn Cockle
Agrostemma githago

Wild Pink
Silene regia

Ragged-Robin
Lychnis flos-cuculi

Moss Campion
Silene acaulis

White Campion
Lychnis alba

FIGURE 28

S. graminea, stitchwort (20 in.), has narrow leaves and a long-stalked, branched inflorescence at the summit of the stem.

S. longifolia (18 in.) is a native species similar to stitchwort, but forming its cymes in the axils of the leaves. The sepals and petals of both narrow-leaved species are of about the same length. *Fig. 29.*

C. vulgatum, the common mouse-ear chickweed (20 in.), has been introduced from Europe. The petals are of the same length as the sepals or shorter. The stem may be erect, lax, or mat-forming. The paired leaves are about ¾ inch long. The plant is a short-lived perennial which sometimes flowers in winter. *Fig. 29.*

C. arvense is a native species. It resembles the narrow-leaved species of *Stellaria,* but the petals are twice as long as the sepals or longer, and are notched rather than cleft. It may be smooth, hairy, or sticky. *Fig. 29.*

C. nutans is another native with narrow leaves, usually sticky, and cleft petals which equal or exceed the sepals in length. The mature pod is curved.

THE SANDWORTS (*Arenaria*)   WHITE
The sandworts have somewhat the appearance of the chick-weeds, but their petals are notched, or not even that, rather than cleft. There are ten stamens, three styles on the ovary; the capsule splits into three parts to free the seeds. Many species are small, wiry, branched plants of sandy places, high mountains, or exposed rocks. Some are cultivated in rock gardens. There is much variation within each species. Nearly all bloom in summer.

A. stricta is probably the most widespread species in our area. It is generally prostrate, forming compact mats with its many branches; the stems are up to 16 inches long. The needlelike leaves are in dense clusters. § Rocky soil, exposed cliffs, etc., across Canada, s. to S. C., Ark., and Tex. *Fig. 29.*

A. groenlandica, the mountain sandwort (6 in.), forms dense mats covered with the short, narrow leaves. The petals are ¼ inch long or longer, usually notched. § Rocky ledges and gravel, eastern Canada, s. in the mountains to N. Y., Conn., N. C., and Tenn. *Fig. 29.*

The European *A. serpyllifolia* (8 in.) has become a widespread weed in sandy and stony places. The leaves are ovate, only ¼ inch long. The sepals are about ⅛ inch long, the petals even shorter. *Fig. 29.*

POPPY FAMILY (*Papaveraceae*)

The Poppy Family is noted for its usually milky juice, which may be white, red, or yellow. The perianth parts are commonly in twos and fours or multiples of these numbers. The stamens are commonly numerous. In our native species the ovary has two chambers and becomes a narrow capsule. Both herbs and shrubs

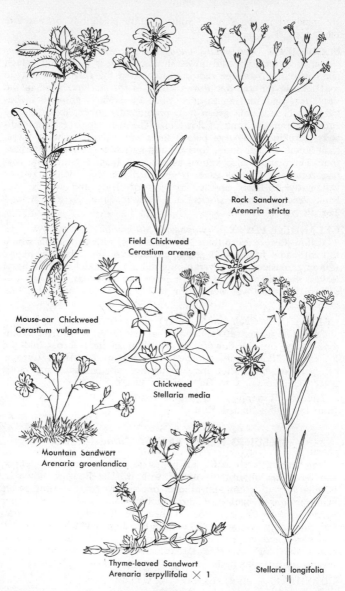

Mouse-ear Chickweed
Cerastium vulgatum

Field Chickweed
Cerastium arvense

Rock Sandwort
Arenaria stricta

Mountain Sandwort
Arenaria groenlandica

Chickweed
Stellaria media

Thyme-leaved Sandwort
Arenaria serpyllifolia × 1

Stellaria longifolia

FIGURE 29

are included in the family. Some contain poisonous or narcotic substances.

BLOODROOT (*Sanguinaria canadensis*)   WHITE
Our most familiar wild flower in this family is bloodroot, which takes its name from the red-orange color of the rhizome (*not* the root). From this the one flower grows in spring, enveloped in the single leaf and starting to open when the stalk is about 6 inches tall. The broad, pale green leaf, prominently lobed, expands and enlarges after the time of flowering. The two sepals fall immediately, revealing the large petals; there are usually eight of these, each about ¾ inch long, four usually narrower than the alternate four. The plant is also known as puccoon, from a name that certain American Indians gave to several plants that yield a red or yellow dye. § Early spring: margins of fields and woods, wet banks, rocky wooded slopes, etc., Que. to Man., s. to Fla. and Tex. PLATE 5.

CELANDINE-POPPY (*Stylophorum diphyllum*)   YELLOW
Yellow flowers more than 2 inches across, with two sepals which fall early and four broad petals, characterize the celandine-poppy (20 in.). Besides the several long-stalked, pinnately lobed basal leaves, there is a pair of similar leaves on the stem. The juice is yellow. § Spring: wet woods, Pa. to Wis., s. to Va. and Ark. *Fig. 30.*

CELANDINE (*Chelidonum majus*)   YELLOW
Celandine plants (30 in.) somewhat resemble those of the celandine-poppy, but the flowers are less than an inch across and the leaves are often singly attached. It is an invader from Europe, escaped from cultivation here. § Summer: shady banks and moist places, Que. to Ia., s. to Ga. and Mo. PLATE 5.

The prickly poppies (*Argemone*) of the West may also escape from cultivation in the East.

BLEEDING-HEART FAMILY (*Fumariaceae*)

This family is close to the poppy family in technical details, and by some botanists is united with it. The flowers, however, have a very different appearance, one or two of the four petals being prolonged backward into a hollow spur, and the two inner petals adhering to each other at their tips. The flowers are therefore bilaterally symmetric. There are two sepals which do not fall, one pistil, and six stamens. Our species all have flowers in racemes, dangling on short, slender stalks. The fruits are mostly several-seeded slim pods.

CORYDALIS   PINK, PURPLISH, OR YELLOW
There are many species of *Corydalis* around the world, mostly in Europe and Asia. Six or seven are known from our area. The

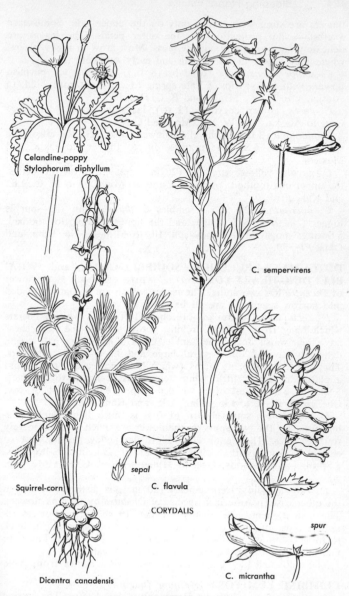

Celandine-poppy
Stylophorum diphyllum

C. sempervirens

sepal

C. flavula

CORYDALIS

Squirrel-corn

Dicentra canadensis

spur

C. micrantha

FIGURE 30

flowers are slim, with a spur only on the upper side. Some have a crest—a flat projection—on the outer petals. The leaves are delicately cut into many narrow parts. Most grow in rocky places, where they flower in late spring and early summer.

C. sempervirens, pale corydalis (3 ft.), has pink or purplish flowers with yellow tips. § Late spring to early autumn: Nfld. to Alaska, s. to N. Y., Minn., and B. C. *Fig. 30.*

C. aurea, golden corydalis (2 ft.), lacks the crest. § Summer: Que. to Alaska, s. to W. Va., Mo., and Calif.

C. montana (2 ft.), with yellow flowers, also lacks the crest. The spur is longer. § Spring: prairies, Ill. to Ida., s. to Okla. and Mexico.

C. flavula, yellow corydalis (20 in.), has crests on the petals, the upper one toothed. § Spring: Conn. to Minn., s. to N. C., La., and Kan. *Fig. 30.*

C. micrantha (20 in.) resembles *C. flavula,* but the spur is longer ($\frac{1}{10}$ to $\frac{1}{6}$ inch long), and the upper crest is not toothed. § Spring: moist, often sandy soil, Ill. to Minn., s. to Tenn. and Okla. *Fig. 30.*

DUTCHMAN'S-BREECHES, SQUIRREL-CORN, and WILD BLEEDING-HEART (*Dicentra*) WHITE OR PINK / Each flower

of *Dicentra* has two spurs. The leaves, which are pinnately divided into narrow segments, are all basal.

D. cucullaria, Dutchman's-breeches (1 ft.), has whitish flowers which hang from slightly arching stems, so that the "breeches" have their waists down, their ankles up. The leaves are pale green, delicately divided into several large and many small segments. They and the flowering stems (which have no leaves) grow from a cluster of many little white tubers just beneath the surface. § Spring: woods and open wooded slopes, either moist or dry, Que. to N. D., s. to Ga., Ala., Ark., and Kan. PLATE 5.

D. canadensis, squirrel-corn (1 ft.), is much like Dutchman's-breeches, but the two spurs on the flower are much shorter, merely rounded sacs. The "squirrel-corn" is the yellow tubers, not so closely packed as the white "grains" of Dutchman's-breeches. § Spring: moist woods, Que. to Minn., s. to N. C. and Mo. *Fig. 30.*

D. eximia, wild bleeding-heart (20 in.), is distinguished from the other eastern American species of *Dicentra* by its pink flowers. The leaf segments are slightly broader. In shape the flowers resemble those of squirrel-corn. It has no tubers, but a short, thick rhizome. § Summer: mountain woods, N. Y., N. J., and Pa., s. to Ga. and Tenn.; elsewhere escaped from cultivation.

The cultivated bleeding-heart, *D. spectabilis,* comes from Asia.

CLIMBING FUMITORY (*Adlumia fungosa*) PINK

In its first year, *Adlumia* forms only a few leaves. The second year the stem may climb to a height of 10 feet, or ramble over

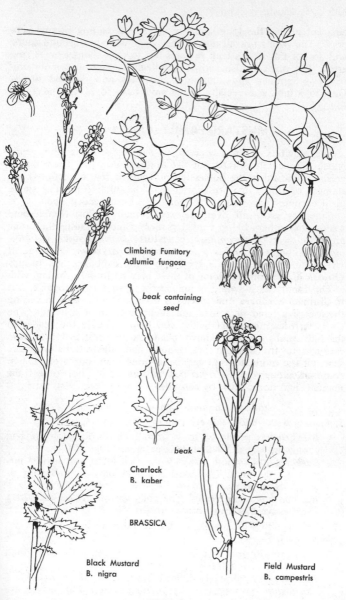

Climbing Fumitory
Adlumia fungosa

beak containing
seed

beak –

Charlock
B. kaber

BRASSICA

Black Mustard
B. nigra

Field Mustard
B. campestris

FIGURE 31

adjacent plants, the long stalks of the leaves coiling around supports. The petals are all united; they bear two short round spurs, and do not fall as the fruit matures but form a spongy outer covering. The plant is also known as Allegheny vine and mountainfringe. § Summer and autumn: wet woods and wooded slopes, Que. to Minn., s. especially in the mountains to N. C. and Tenn. *Fig. 31.*

MUSTARD FAMILY (Cruciferae)

The crucifers or cross-bearers are named for their four petals which are usually spread out flat to form a cross. Their distinguishing feature is the possession of (with a few exceptions) six stamens of which two are shorter than the other four. The single pistil becomes a usually narrow or flat, several-seeded pod.

Crucifers grow all over the world, many being troublesome weeds, and others being valued garden plants. Among the latter are wallflower (*Cheiranthus*), candytuft (*Iberis*), stock (*Matthiola*), rock cress (*Arabis*), *Aubrieta,* and *Alyssum;* also radish (*Raphanus*), horseradish (*Armoracia*), the cabbages and turnips (*Brassica*), and others. Some of these may be found growing wild.

The family as a whole is among the easiest to recognize, but to distinguish genera and species is often difficult, often requiring the use of a hand magnifier and attention to minute details. The characteristics mentioned below *may* help to guide the reader to the right genus for an unknown plant; but he must probably have recourse to the detailed descriptions and illustrations to make sure. Of the more than 40 genera reported from our area, 17 are common enough to be described in this book. For others the manuals and floras must be consulted.

Guide to Common Genera of *Cruciferae*

I. Genera with yellow flowers (but see also II).

   Brassica has petals ¼ to ½ inch long, or longer. The pod ends in a beak ¼ inch long or more (*Fig. 31*).

   Barbarea has smooth leaves with basal lobes that nearly surround the stem. The pod has a beak only ⅛ inch long or less (*Fig. 32*).

   Rorippa has ovate sepals. The pods are mostly ½ inch long or less, rather oval, often curved (*Fig. 32*).

II. Genera with white, pink, or purple flowers (in a few species pale yellow).

   A. Genera with more or less slender pods generally more than ½ inch long (compare B, C, and D).

      Dentaria has palmately divided leaves (*Fig. 32;* PLATE 5).

      Nasturtium grows in or by running water. The leaves are pinnately divided (*Fig. 32*).

      Arabis has long, very slender, flat pods, in several species curved and drooping, in others erect against the stem (*Fig. 33*).

Cardamine has basal leaves either with round blades on long stalks, or pinnately divided (*Fig. 34*). The flowers of some species are tiny. The pods are not flat.

Hesperis is tall with relatively broad leaves, toothed at the edges, and large, purple, pink, or white flowers; the petals are about an inch long (PLATE 6).

B. Genera with oval or elliptic pods generally less than ⅔ inch long.

Draba has usually a tuft of small, undivided basal leaves, few or none on the stem (*Fig. 35*). The pods are mostly from three to six times as long as wide.

Berteroa has cleft petals, leaves on the stem. Pods are only about twice as long as wide (*Fig. 35*).

C. Genera with flat pods about as wide as long.

Capsella has heart-shaped pods tapering to the base (*Fig. 35*).

Lepidium has round pods containing only two seeds (*Fig. 36*).

Thlaspi has round pods notched at the top, containing eight seeds (*Fig. 36*).

D. Genera with thick, inflated pods.

Armoracia has short pods (if any mature) shaped like footballs. The basal leaves have long, coarsely toothed blades on long stalks (*Fig. 36*).

Cakile has thick, succulent, narrow leaves. It grows on beaches. The pods are in two sections of different shapes (*Fig. 36*).

MUSTARDS AND THEIR RELATIVES (*Brassica*)   YELLOW

The most important genus in the mustard family (economically speaking) is *Brassica,* for cabbages, cauliflower, broccoli, Brussels sprouts, turnips, and other familiar vegetables, as well as mustard, are species and varieties in it. Several troublesome weeds also belong to *Brassica,* all introduced from the Old World. The most abundant ones are mentioned below. Some of the weedy wild forms are closely related to the cultivated plants. All are widely established throughout our range and bloom in summer, often into autumn. The flowers are mostly in simple racemes.

B. nigra, black mustard (5 ft.), is bristly with a sparse growth of sharp hairs, especially on the lower parts. The lower leaves are stalked; the blades have a broad tip with several small lobes below. The pods stand nearly straight up, alongside the main stem. *Fig. 31.*

B. kaber, charlock (2 ft.), is also more or less bristly. The conspicuous beak of the pod is flat and usually contains a seed. *Fig. 31.*

B. juncea (1–3 ft.) in contrast is quite smooth. The lower leaves are pinnately cut into a number of lobes.

B. campestris, field mustard (3 ft.), may be recognized by the small leaves with projecting lobes which clasp the stem. The large basal leaves are stalked and deeply lobed. *Fig. 31.*

Several other weedy genera with yellow flowers are known as mustards: *Sisymbrium,* hedge-mustard and tumble-mustard; *Erysimum,* wormseed-mustard; *Descurainia,* tansy-mustard. These unattractive weeds of barnyards and roadsides are not here described.

YELLOW ROCKET, WINTER CRESS (*Barbarea vulgaris*)

YELLOW / This is a very common and conspicuous weed (to 3 ft.), with tall branching racemes of flowers which resemble those of the mustards. The "ears" on the leaves together with the shortness of the beak on the pod will distinguish it from *Brassica.* Late in the season winter cress grows a basal rosette of leaves, which stays green through the winter. § Spring: fields and roadsides, throughout; originally from Europe. *Fig. 32.*

THE YELLOW CRESSES (*Rorippa*)   YELLOW

The yellow cresses, some of which grow in water, are much like water cress except for their color. They have generally pinnately cut leaves and mostly short pods which are rounded or curved.

R. islandica (to 3 ft.), generally much branched, is a common and very variable species. At least some of its varieties came from Europe. Its pods are round. § Late spring to autumn: wet soil, throughout. *Fig. 32.*

R. sinuata is similar to *R. islandica,* but shorter; its pods are curved; it is found in sandy instead of wet soil. § Late spring and summer: Ont. to Wash., s. to Ill., Tex., and Calif. *Fig. 32.*

R. sylvestris (20 in.) has more sharply toothed leaves and slightly longer pods, to ⅔ inch long. § Late spring and summer: wet soil, Nfld. to N. D., s. to N. C. and La.; introduced from the Old World. *Fig. 32.*

THE TOOTHWORTS (*Dentaria*)   WHITE OR PURPLISH

Unlike many species of the mustard family, the toothworts are handsome spring flowers with petals nearly an inch long. They grow from thick rhizomes which have a pleasant radish-like taste. The name refers to the "teeth" on these underground stems. All are plants of rich moist woods, growing from 8 to 16 inches tall.

D. laciniata has three leaves on the stem, each leaf divided palmately into three long narrow segments and these generally toothed or cut along their margins. It is the commonest species. § Que. to Minn. and Nebr., s. to Fla. and La. *Fig. 32.*

D. diphylla, crinkle-root, has two leaves on the stem, each divided into three broad segments. § N. B. to Minn., s. to Pa. and O., in the mountains to Ga. and Ala. PLATE 5.

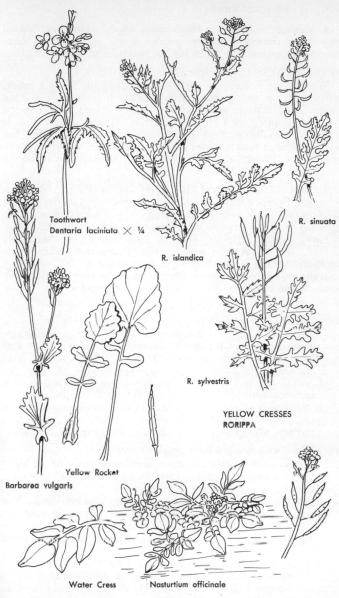

Toothwort
Dentaria laciniata $\times$ ¼

R. islandica

R. sinuata

R. sylvestris

YELLOW CRESSES
RORIPPA

Yellow Rocket

Barbarea vulgarls

Water Cress   Nasturtium officinale

FIGURE 32

D. heterophylla has two small leaves on the stem, each divided into three narrow segments, besides basal leaves which have broader segments. § N. J. to Ind., s. to Ga. and Ala.

WATER CRESS (*Nasturtium officinale*) WHITE
Water cress is common everywhere in and by running water, particularly in spring water. It is a smooth plant with trailing stems, small flowers, and pinnately divided leaves with rounded lobes. It is often used in salads, and in Europe especially it is cultivated for that purpose. The common name "nasturtium" has been applied to a well-known garden plant, *Tropaeolum,* to which water cress is quite unrelated. § Summer: throughout; originally from Europe. *Fig. 32.*

THE ROCK CRESSES and SICKLE-PODS (*Arabis*) WHITE OR PINKISH / Except for the Eurasian species that are familiar in rock gardens, the rock cresses are mostly rather weedy plants. The genus is large. In general its members are known by their long, narrow, usually flat pods, which in some species are noticeably curved. The flowers are mostly white (sometimes yellowish or pinkish), seldom as much as ½ inch in diameter. Although certain details of the pods must often be seen for sure identification, some of our common species are easily recognized.

I. Species with curved fruits, the plants mostly tall: the sickle-pods (compare II and III).

    A. laevigata (3 ft.) is conspicuous for its pale grayish-green, very smooth leaves; those on the stem clasp it by two rounded lobes. § Early summer: woods, Que. to S. D., s. to Ga., Ala., and Okla. *Fig. 33.*

    A. viridis (20 in.) is similar, has flowers ⅓ inch long. § Summer: wooded ledges, Me. to Pa. and Ga.; Mich.; Ind. to Okla.

    A. canadensis (3 ft.) has stem leaves that are more or less hairy and toothed; they have short stalks. § Summer: woods and thickets, Me. to Minn., s. to Ga. and Tex. *Fig. 33.*

II. Species with straight pods, more or less erect.

    A. drummondi (3 ft.) has leaves similar to those of *A. laevigata.* § Summer: ledges, gravels, etc., Lab. to B. C., s. to Del., Ill., Ia., Ariz., and Calif.

    A. virginica (1 ft. or less) has pinnately divided leaves. The pods are an inch long or less. This may be easily confused with the smaller species of *Cardamine;* but these have even shorter pods, which are not flat. § Spring: fields, roadsides, Va. to Kan., s. to Fla. and Tex. *Fig. 33.*

    A. lyrata (1 ft. or more) has very narrow leaves on the stem; the basal leaves are usually pinnately lobed. § Late spring and summer: chiefly in sandy soil, Vt. to Alaska, s. to Ga., Mo., and Wash. *Fig. 33.*

    A. hirsuta (30 in.) is a hairy plant (though there is a smooth

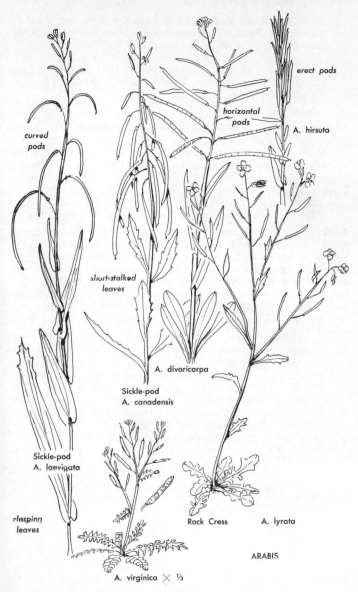

curved pods

erect pods

horizontal pods

A. hirsuta

short-stalked leaves

A. divaricarpa

Sickle-pod
A. canadensis

Sickle-pod
A. laevigata

clasping leaves

Rock Cress

A. lyrata

ARABIS

A. virginica × ⅓

FIGURE 33

variety) with flat pods that stand erect, parallel and close to the stem. § Summer: limestone ledges, Que. to Alaska, s. to Ga., Ala., Ark., Ariz., and Calif. *Fig. 33*.

A. glabra (4 ft.) also has pods that parallel the stem, but they are not flat. The plant is smooth except near the base. § Late spring and early summer: ledges and fields, Que. to Alaska, s. to N. C., O., Ark., and Calif.

III. Species with horizontal pods.

A. divaricarpa (3 ft.) may have pinkish flowers. The pods, about 3 inches long, stand out more or less straight from the stem. The leaves are narrow and pointed, smooth on the edges. § Summer: sandy and rocky places, across Canada, s. to N. Y., Ia., Colo., and Calif. *Fig. 33*.

A. patens is a shorter, somewhat hairy plant, with flowers ½ inch across. The long-stalked pods are 1½ inches long. § Spring: rocky places, Pa. to Ind., s. to N. C. and Tenn.

THE BITTER CRESSES (*Cardamine*)   WHITE SOMETIMES TINGED WITH ROSE OR PURPLE / The bitter cresses come in a large variety of forms and sizes, some with round-bladed leaves on long stalks, some with pinnately divided leaves. Most grow in wet places. Some of the smallest species may be mistaken for *Draba;* but the pods are longer and narrower. Some may be confused with *Arabis;* this, however, is more likely to be hairy. Only minute details of fruit and seeds can distinguish all species of these genera with certainty.

I. Species that have some leaves with round blades (compare II).

C. bulbosa, spring cress (18 in.), is quite smooth. The basal leaves are long-stalked; the stem leaves are mostly narrow. The stem and basal leaves grow from a cluster of small round corms. The white petals are about ½ inch long. § Spring and early summer: wet meadows and banks and shallow water, Que. to S. D., s. to Fla. and Tex. *Fig. 34*.

C. douglassii (1 ft.) is similar, but hairy. The petals are usually tinged with rose or purple. § Spring: rich woods and springs, Conn. to Ont. and Wis., s. and sw. to Va. and Mo.

C. rotundifolia, mountain water cress, is a weak plant with round leaves on the stem, which grows from a thin rhizome. The petals are less than ½ inch long, white. § Early summer: near springs and brooks, N. Y. to O., s. to N. C. and Ky. *Fig. 34*.

C. longii is similar to *C. rotundifolia* but has no petals. § Summer and early autumn: tidal estuaries near the coast, Me. to Va.

II. Species with pinnately divided leaves.

C. pratensis, cuckoo-flower (2 ft.), has white or rose petals nearly an inch long. This is a very variable species. Pods are

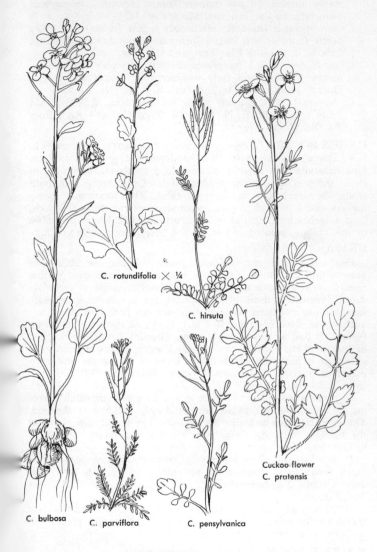

C. rotundifolia × ¼

C. hirsuta

C. bulbosa

C. parviflora

C. pensylvanica

Cuckoo flower
C. pratensis

CARDAMINE

FIGURE 34

rarely formed. § Early summer: moist meadows, throughout Canada, s. to Va., Ind., and Minn. *Fig. 34.*

C. pensylvanica (to 2 ft., often only a few inches) has white petals about ⅙ inch long. § Spring and summer: moist places, Lab. to B. C., s. to Fla., Tex., and Ore. *Fig. 34.*

C. parviflora (8 in.) has leaves divided into very narrow segments. § Spring and early summer: dry woods and ledges, Que. to Minn., s. to Fla. and Tex.; B. C. to Ore. *Fig. 34.*

C. hirsuta (1 ft.) has tiny petals $\frac{1}{12}$ inch long. § Spring: old fields and roadsides, N. Y. to Ill., s. to Ga. and Ala.; from the Old World. *Fig. 34.*

DAME'S ROCKET (*Hesperis matronalis*)   WHITE, PINK, OR PURPLE / Dame's rocket (3 ft.) is a handsome escape from gardens, now naturalized in colorful masses along roadsides, especially in moist shady places, in the northern half of our range and south along the coast and in the mountains. The numerous showy flowers, about ¾ inch across, are in terminal racemes. The pods, 2 to 4 inches long, spread in all directions. The leaves are more or less oblong, pointed and toothed. § Early summer. PLATE 6.

DRABA   WHITE

Draba is a large genus of small plants. Eighteen or 20 species grow within our limits (64 in North America). Like most of this family, they are hard to distinguish without recourse to technical details. However, most of our species are northern, some only touching our northern borders; these are not here considered.

D. verna, whitlow-grass (to 6 in.), is one of the smallest spring flowers. It has no leaves on the stem. The tiny petals are notched or forked at the ends. It comes from Europe, where it is so variable that it has been made into a number of species and even placed in a genus of its own. § Spring: fields, etc., Vt. and Ont. to Ia., s. to Ga., Ala., and Mo. *Fig. 35.*   .

D. reptans is similar, but there is usually a pair of small leaves on the stem, and the petals are not deeply notched at the end. The stem and flower stalks are smooth. The leaves are plain on the margins, with no teeth. § Spring: dry soil, Mass. and R. I. to Ont. and Minn., and s. and sw. *Fig. 35.*

D. brachycarpa (8 in.) is a plant of our southern borders. Its name refers to its short pods, no more than ⅕ inch long, and quite smooth. § Spring: dry places, Va. to Kan., s. to Fla. and Tex. *Fig. 35.*

D. cuneifolia (10 in.) has toothed basal leaves, and a few leaves on the stem. It is roughly hairy. § Spring: dry places, Ill. to Colo., s. to Fla. and Mexico. *Fig. 35.*

HOARY ALYSSUM (*Berteroa incana*)   WHITE

This is a small weed (1–2 ft.) that came from Europe. It has somewhat the aspect of a *Draba,* but there are more leaves on the stem. The stem and leaves are hoary with a fine whitish down.

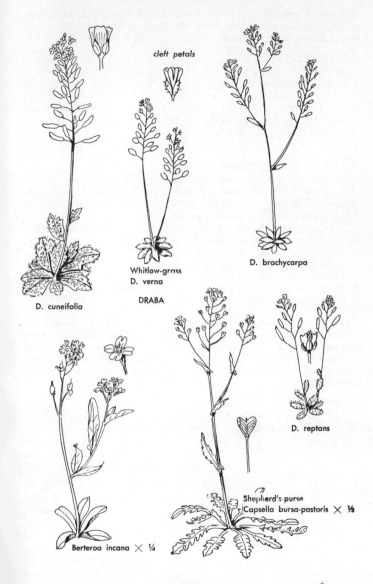

cleft petals

DRABA

D. cuneifolia

Whitlow-grass
D. verna

D. brachycarpa

D. reptans

Berteroa incana × ¼

Shephard's-purse
Capsella bursa-pastoris × ⅓

FIGURE 35

The leaves are pointed, often lance-shaped. The petals are white, notched at the end. The pods are short. § Summer: fields and waste places, N. S. to Mont., s. to N. J. and Kan. *Fig. 35.*

SHEPHERD'S-PURSE (*Capsella bursa-pastoris*)   WHITE

Anyone who has tended a lawn knows shepherd's-purse, a troublesome little weed from the Old World. It is very variable, the basal leaves pinnately cut or divided or merely toothed, the stem hairy or smooth. The narrow leaves on the stem have sharp basal extensions, one on either side of the stem. It is easily known by its heart-shaped pods, notched at the top and tapering to the base. § Spring to autumn: lawns, waste places, throughout. *Fig. 35.*

PEPPER-GRASS (*Lepidium*)   WHITE

Species of *Lepidium* are weeds of roadsides and waste places. The common species described below flower in spring and early summer. The name is from the peppery taste of the pods. There is one seed in each half of the pod.

L. virginicum (20 in.) is our commonest species. The round, flat pod is notched at the end. § Throughout. *Fig. 36.*

L. densiflorum (20 in.) is similar. The flowers are more crowded and have no petals or very minute ones. § Throughout.

L. campestre (20 in.) has narrow leaves with basal lobes which embrace the stem. The pod is longer than broad, notched. § Throughout.

PENNY CRESS (*Thlaspi arvense*)   WHITE, PINK, OR BLUE

Penny cress is a stray from the Old World, recognizable by its flat round pods—the "pennies"—often ¾ inch across, notched at the top. The leaves on the stem have two sharp points at the base, like an Indian arrowhead. § Spring and early summer: throughout. *Fig. 36.*

HORSERADISH (*Armoracia rusticana*)   WHITE

Horseradish is a tall, coarse plant (3 ft. or more), known by its long-stalked, toothed basal leaves; also by its pods, which are thick and short, egg-shaped or football-shaped (but they soon fall, and apparently never contain good seeds). The plant was brought from Europe and escaped from cultivation in many places. § Summer: moist or dry soil, throughout. *Fig. 36.*

SEA ROCKET (*Cakile edentula*)   PALE PURPLE

This bushy succulent plant (to 1 ft.) is found on sea beaches along the Atlantic Coast and on the beaches of the Great Lakes. The peculiar pods each consist of two sections, the upper or end one pointed, the lower one narrower; there may be one seed in each part, or the lower may be seedless. The young foliage has the flavor of horseradish. The plants are cooked for greens by some shore dwellers. § Summer. *Fig. 36.*

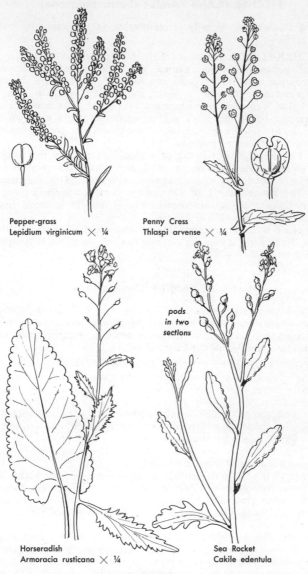

Pepper-grass
Lepidium virginicum × ¼

Penny Cress
Thlaspi arvense × ¼

pods
in two
sections

Horseradish
Armoracia rusticana × ¼

Sea Rocket
Cakile edentula

FIGURE 36

PITCHER-PLANT FAMILY (*Sarraceniaceae*)

The Pitcher-plant Family is represented in our range by only one genus.

PITCHER-PLANTS (*Sarracenia*)   PURPLISH-RED OR YELLOW
The pitcher-plants are named for their remarkable leaves, shaped like vases or pitchers and holding water. Small insects drown and decompose in the water, some of the products of their dissolution furnishing nourishment to the plant. The flowers also are remarkable for the large, umbrella-like end of the pistil which bears the five small stigmas on the under side. There are five sepals, five petals, and many stamens.

S. purpurea (20 in.) is the only species in most of our range. The pitcher-shaped leaves, up to 8 inches tall, are curved and broadened above the middle, somewhat contracted at the opening. The flowers are 2 to 2½ inches across. § Summer: bogs, across Canada, along the coast to Fla., inland to northern Ind., Ill., and Minn. *Fig. 37.*

S. flava is a tall southern species that extends north to Virginia. It is distinguished by its long yellow petals and trumpet-shaped pitchers.

SUNDEW FAMILY (*Droseraceae*)

The *Droseraceae* are a small family of small insect-catching plants which inhabit bogs and other wet places. In our range their only representatives are in the genus *Drosera*. Farther south the Venus' fly-trap (*Dionaea muscipula*) occurs.

SUNDEWS (*Drosera*)   WHITE, PINK, OR PURPLE
The sundews have leaves covered with gland-tipped hairs which exude a sweet sticky material attractive to insects. The insects become entangled by some of the hairs; other hairs bend in over them and complete their capture. The sticky secretion contains a digestive substance which converts the insect body to nutrients; these are absorbed by the plant. The small flowers open one or two at a time on a curved false raceme. The sepals, petals, and stamens are in fives; there are usually three styles.

D. rotundifolia (1 ft.) is the commonest species; the blades of the leaves, on long stalks, are about ⅜ inch across. The flowers are white or pink, about ¼ inch across. § Summer: peaty and boggy soil, across Canada, s. to Fla., Ala., Minn., and Calif. *Fig. 37.*

D. filiformis (8 in.) has narrow leaves up to 10 inches long. The flowers are purple, less than ½ inch across. § Late summer: near the coast, Mass. to Del.; N. C. to Fla. and La. *Fig. 37.*

D. intermedia (10 in.) has oval blades about ¼ inch wide on

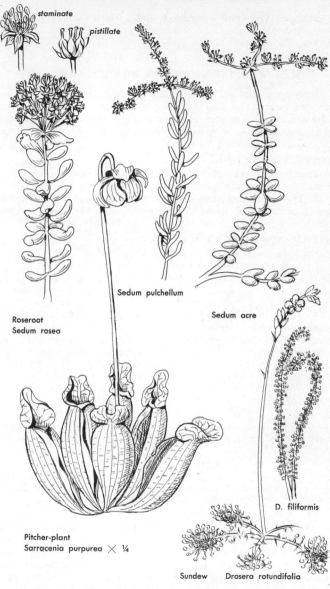

staminate

pistillate

Roseroot
Sedum rosea

Sedum pulchellum

Sedum acre

Pitcher-plant
Sarracenia purpurea × ¼

D. filiformis

Sundew   Drosera rotundifolia

FIGURE 37

long stalks. The small flowers are white. § Late summer: wet peat and sand, along the coast, Nfld. to Tex., and around the Great Lakes.

SEDUM OR STONECROP FAMILY (Crassulaceae)

Most species of the *Crassulaceae* are succulent plants with undivided leaves. The flower parts are generally in fours or fives. The species of our area are mostly small plants. The family is well represented among house plants and in rock gardens, and several of these escape from cultivation.

DITCH STONECROP (*Penthorum sedoides*)   YELLOWISH-GREEN
This curious plant (3 ft.) has five sepals, no petals, ten stamens, and five pistils joined at the base. The fruit is a five-horned pod. The leaves are not succulent. § Summer and early autumn: moist ground, Que. to Minn. and Nebr., s. to Fla. and Tex. *Fig. 38.*

STONECROPS and LIVE-FOREVER (*Sedum*)   WHITE, PUR-PLISH, ROSE, YELLOW / *Sedum* is a large and difficult genus, but only three native species are at all common in our area. There are four or five sepals and the same number of petals and pistils; the stamens are twice as many as the sepals. The leaves are smooth and rather thick.

S. rosea, roseroot (16 in.), has greenish-yellow or purplish flowers in a close cluster at the tip of the stem. The leaves are frequently in fours. The flower parts are usually in fours, and either stamens or pistils are lacking. § Spring and summer: cliffs and ledges, subarctic Canada, s. to Me. and Pa., and farther in the mountains; Colo. and B. C. *Fig. 37.*

S. ternatum (8 in.) has white flowers in an inflorescence composed of several spreading false racemes. The stems lie on the ground, the flowering branches curving upward. Some of the leaves are usually in circles of three. § Spring and summer: damp cliffs, mossy banks, etc., Conn. to Mich., s. and sw. to Ga. and Ark.

S. pulchellum has white or rose flowers on several spreading false racemes. The leaves on the flowering branches are numerous and narrow. § Late spring and summer: moist or dry rocks and rocky soil, W. Va. to Kan., s. to Ga. and Tex. *Fig. 37.*

The European *S. acre* (*Fig. 37*) is a common escape from cultivation, becoming a troublesome weed in gardens. Its creeping stems form a mat covered with small, thick leaves and at times bearing yellow flowers. *S. telephium,* live-forever, is also found growing wild in many places. The leaves have slightly notched margins. It grows up to 2 feet tall. The flowers are reddish-purple, in close, rounded clusters. Variegated forms occur.

pods

Ditch stonecrop
Penthorum sedoides

Grass-of-Parnassus
Parnassia glauca × ⅓

Saxifraga pensylvanica × ⅓

FIGURE 38

SAXIFRAGE FAMILY (*Saxifragaceae*)

Many of the *Saxifragaceae* grow in clefts where they become a factor in the weathering and splitting of rock. The plants mostly have their principal leaves in a tuft or rosette at the base of a slender flowering stem; the leaves commonly have rounded blades with toothed edges. Most of the species have small flowers. The parts are in fours or fives or a multiple thereof, except the pistils: there may be one pistil with two styles or with four stigmas, or two pistils partly united by their ovaries. There is generally a cup at the base of the flower which may be joined to the lower half of the ovary; the ovary is then said to be half-inferior.

I. Genera with ten stamens in each flower (compare II and III).

   A. Genus with a branched inflorescence: *Saxifraga*.

   B. Genera with simple racemes (which may be spikelike).

   Tiarella has small petals and sepals from which the stamens project. The flowering stem is generally leafless.

   Mitella has small petals finely cut, feather-fashion. There may be one or two leaves, without stalks, on the flowering stem.

II. Genus with four to eight stamens, no petals; aquatic: *Chrysosplenium*.

III. Genera with five stamens in a flower, five petals.

   A. Genus with a single flower on each stalk: *Parnassia*.

   B. Genus with flowers in inflorescences: *Heuchera*.

THE SAXIFRAGES (*Saxifraga*)   WHITE, GREENISH, YELLOWISH, OR PURPLISH / *Saxifraga* is a large genus, with many species in the far north and on high mountains. Besides the two common ones mentioned below, a number of northern species may be found in northern New England (especially in the mountains) and in Michigan; and several southern species may be found in the Appalachians near our southern limits. These must be sought in the manuals. The genus is recognized by the five sepals, five petals, ten stamens, and two-parted capsule; most species have a cluster of basal leaves around a single flowering stem.

S. virginiensis (4 in. increasing to 1 ft.) has leaves only 2 or 3 inches long, rather coarsely toothed or scalloped, nearly half as broad as they are long. The whole plant is usually hairy. The flowers are in tight clusters on a branched stalk. The petals are white, about ¼ inch long. § Spring: rock ledges and open woodlands, Que. to Man., s. to Ga. and Okla. PLATE 6.

S. pensylvanica (4 ft.) has leaves often 6 or 8 inches long, more or less lance-shaped, much less than half as broad as they are long, rather shallowly toothed. The flowers are dull greenish, yellowish, or purplish, the petals very small. § Early summer: bogs and wet meadows, Me. to Minn., s. to Va. and Mo. *Fig. 38.*

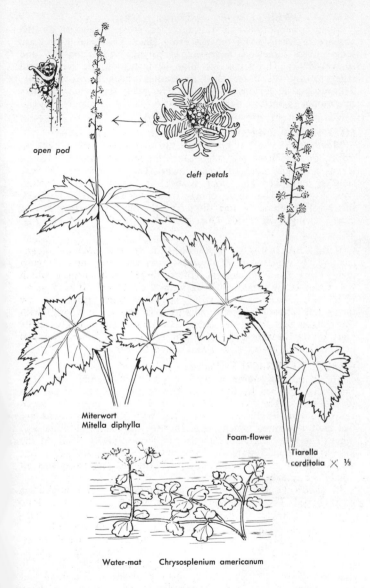

open pod

cleft petals

Miterwort
Mitella diphylla

Foam-flower

Tiarella
corditolia × ⅓

Water-mat   Chrysosplenium americanum

FIGURE 39

FOAM-FLOWER (*Tiarella cordifolia*) WHITE

Foam-flower (1 ft.) is distinguished from miterwort by the absence of leaves from the flowering stem. The basal leaves are long-stalked, somewhat heart-shaped, slightly lobed, toothed, and sparsely hairy. The petals, less than ¼ inch long, are narrow and taper toward the base. The ten stamens project conspicuously. The seedpod is curiously lopsided. The plant forms long runners in summer. § Spring: rich woods, N. S. to Ont., s. to N. E. and Mich., and in the mountains to Ga. and Ala. *Fig. 39.*

MITERWORT, BISHOP'S-CAP (*Mitella diphylla*) WHITE

Miterwort (18 in.) is known by the two leaves, which have no stalks, on the flowering stem near the inflorescence. The basal leaves resemble those of foam-flower. The inflorescence is very slender, spikelike. The chief beauty of miterwort is its small, fringed petals. The name comes from the two-beaked seedpod; this breaks open at the top, disclosing the black seeds in a sort of cup. § Spring: rich woods, Que. to Minn., s. to S. C. and Mo. *Fig. 39.*

GOLDEN-SAXIFRAGE, WATER-MAT (*Chrysosplenium americanum*) YELLOWISH / *Chrysosplenium* gets its names (English and Latin) from its flowers (often tinged with purple) which sometimes cover shallow waters with their bloom. It is a small plant with a creeping stem which sends up erect branches a few inches tall. These bear small paired leaves (not an inch long) with short stalks and roundish blades. The flowers grow singly at the ends of the branches. § Spring: in springs and other cool wet places, Que. to Minn., s. to Ga., O., and Ia. *Fig. 39.*

GRASS-OF-PARNASSUS (*Parnassia*) WHITE

This is not, of course, a grass, nor does it resemble one. It is easily distinguished by the pretty flowers borne singly at the tips of tall stems. The five petals are white with conspicuous green veins running lengthwise. Alternating with the five stamens are five cleft structures which represent the rudiments of other stamens. The flowering stem usually bears one stalkless leaf. At the base of the stem is a small cluster of smooth, long-stalked leaves, also with prominent veins running lengthwise. The parnassias all inhabit wet places.

P. glauca (2 ft.) has broad leaf blades that are sometimes heart-shaped. The rudimentary stamens, which are nearly as long as the true stamens, are deeply cleft into three prongs. § Late summer: Nfld. to Man., s. to N. J., Ind., Ia., and S. D. *Fig. 38.*

P. palustris (16 in.) has heart-shaped blades on its basal leaves. The rudimentary stamens look almost like fringed inner petals. § Summer: Lab. to Alaska, s. to N. Y., Minn., and Ore.

P. parviflora (1 ft.) is also a northern resident. The basal leaf blades taper at both ends. The rudimentary stamens are short. § Summer: across Canada, s. to Ont., Wis., and Utah.

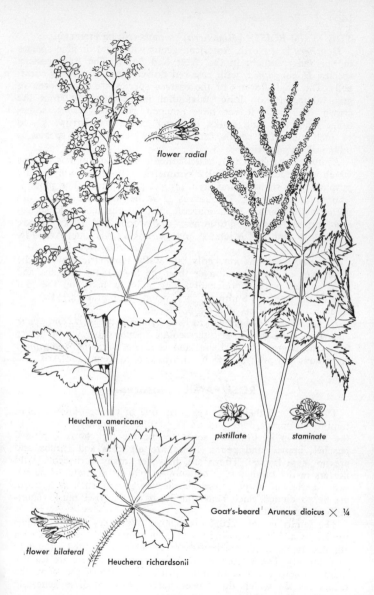

flower radial

Heuchera americana

pistillate   staminate

flower bilateral

Heuchera richardsonii

Goat's-beard Aruncus dioicus × ¼

FIGURE 40

THE ALUM-ROOTS (*Heuchera*)   GREENISH OR PURPLISH

Heuchera is a North American genus with eight or nine species in our range, others in the West and South. The southwestern species, *H. sanguinea,* with rose-red flowers, is cultivated as coral-bells. The small flowers of the eastern species are often borne in great abundance on long stalks that rise successively from the crown. The basal leaves have notched, roundish blades, sometimes lobed, on long stalks. The five petals are narrow, $\frac{1}{12}$ to $\frac{1}{8}$ inch long. The sepals form a cup which in some species is bilaterally symmetric.

H. americana (to 3 ft.), often called rock-geranium, has flowers which are practically radially symmetric. The petals are usually purplish. The stamens and style project prominently. The plant is smooth or nearly so. The leaves, 2 inches or more broad, are occasionally marked with maroon. This is our most widespread and variable species. § Summer: dry woods and rocky slopes, Conn. to s. Ont. and Mich., s. and sw. to Ga., Ala., and Ark. *Fig. 40.*

H. richardsonii has markedly bilaterally symmetric flowers (the upper part of the calyx longer than the lower); the stamens and style do not project noticeably. The plant is hairy on the leaf stalks and stems. § Summer: dry woods and prairies, Mich. to Alta., s. to Ind., Kan., and Colo. *Fig. 40.*

H. hirsuticaulis is believed to be a hybrid between *H. americana* and *H. richardsonii.* It is intermediate between the two in flower form and degree of hairiness, and is highly variable. § Summer: dry woods and prairies, Mich. to Minn., s. to Tenn. and Ark.

ROSE FAMILY (Rosaceae)

The roses and their relatives form one of the best-known plant families in our gardens and on our tables, especially if one takes the family in its broadest sense to include the cherries, plums, peaches, apples, and pears. These are all trees and shrubs and are not here treated. There are, however, many herbaceous wild flowers in the family. It is sometimes difficult to draw a line between herbs and shrubs; some borderline genera, such as *Spiraea,* are here included. Such beautiful shrubs as the roses must, regrettably, be omitted.

The family is not hard to recognize. With very few exceptions the leaves are attached singly and each is generally provided with stipules. In many genera the leaves are cleft or divided, pinnately or palmately. The flowers are radially symmetric; there are usually many stamens and one or more pistils. The end of the stem, the receptacle, on which the flower parts are situated, is generally expanded into a disk, a cup, or a dome.

In this family especially the word "fruit" is hard to define. In ordinary speech we apply the word to that which follows the flower, no matter what its exact origin or structure. A straw-berry is the enlarged receptacle on the surface of which are the matured pistils; these are not seeds, but each contains a seed. Each matured pistil corresponds in origin to a grape or an orange; it is a fruit itself, an achene. The urnlike receptacle of a rose becomes the succulent "hip"; within are a number of achenes (not seeds), each containing a seed. In other genera no succulent fruit develops; the flower yields merely a mass of achenes, or larger, several-seeded follicles.

Guide to Common Herbaceous Genera of *Rosaceae*

I. Genera that form follicles, which split open at maturity. The flower has several pistils, not enclosed by the receptacle. (Compare II, III, and IV.)

> *Aruncus* has pinnately divided leaves; the numerous small flowers have either stamens or pistils, not both; they are in a panicle (*Fig. 40*).
>
> *Spiraea,* which is rather woody, has undivided leaves lacking stipules. The numerous flowers are in narrow panicles (PLATE 6).
>
> *Gillenia* has palmately divided leaves; the petals are narrow. The flowers are comparatively few, in a loose panicle (*Fig. 41*).

II. Genera that form achenes, not enclosed in the receptacle, mostly on a projection in the middle of the flower. There is generally a circle of bracts just outside the sepals, looking like extra sepals (see also *Dalibarda* in IV).

> A. Genera with yellow flowers (compare B).
>
> > *Potentilla* has leaves divided pinnately or palmately (*Figs. 41, 42*).
> >
> > *Geum* has pinnately divided leaves, the end segment usually the largest; small segments are usually mixed with larger ones. The styles mostly have a crook in the middle (*Fig. 43*); they form "tails" on the achenes (*Fig. 43*).
>
> B. Genera with white or pink flowers.
>
> > *Geum* has some species with white flowers (see II A above).
> >
> > *Fragaria* has leaves divided into three, on stalks growing from the base (PLATE 6).
> >
> > *Filipendula* has pinnately divided leaves on the stem. The flowers are small, very numerous (*Fig. 44*).

III. Genera that form one or several achenes more or less enclosed in the receptacle.

> *Agrimonia* has yellow petals. The leaves are pinnately divided. The receptacle is cone-shaped with the point down, covered with hooked bristles (*Fig. 44*).
>
> *Alchemilla* has four green sepals, no petals, palmately lobed

leaves. The conical receptacle encloses usually one achene. *Sanguisorba* has four white or purple petal-like sepals, no petals, pinnately divided leaves. The four-angled receptacle usually holds one achene (*Fig. 45*).

IV. Genera that form fruits composed of small cherrylike, more or less succulent units grouped together, each containing a stone. The stem is woody or creeping.

> *Rubus* is generally woody and prickly. The pistils, later the small units of the fruit, are on a hump in the center of the flower (*Fig. 45*).
> *Dalibarda* is not prickly. The fruits are rather dry at maturity. The leaves are undivided, long-stalked (*Fig. 44*).

GOAT'S-BEARD (*Aruncus dioicus*)   WHITE

The second word of the botanical name—*dioicus*, "in two households"—refers to the separation of stamens and pistils in the flowers of different plants. The flowers are minute, tightly pressed against long spreading branches that bear no leaves. There are 15 or more stamens in the male flowers, three or four pistils in the female. The leaves are pinnately divided, the lower segments again divided into three. The plants grow from 3 to 6 feet tall. § Late spring and early summer: rich woods especially in the mountains, Pa. to Ia., s. to Ga., Ala., and Okla. *Fig. 40.*

SPIRAEA (*Spiraea*)   WHITE OR PINK

The numerous species of *Spiraea* (many of which are cultivated) are known by their undivided leaves which lack stipules and their dense clusters of small white or pink flowers. The flower has a cup-shaped base and several pistils (usually five) which form as many follicles. They are shrubby plants which bloom in summer.

S. tomentosa, hardhack or steeplebush (3 ft.), is known by its terminal spire of small flowers, usually a deep pink, below which are several spreading lateral spikes, the whole forming a showy inflorescence. The follicles are downy. The leaves are woolly and whitish on the under side. § Wet meadows, N. S. to Minn., s. to Ga. and Ark. PLATE 6.

S. latifolia, meadow-sweet (to 5 ft.), has white flowers in small round clusters, the lower clusters on longer stems, so that the inflorescence is more or less pyramidal. The leaves are smooth; the branches are reddish or purplish. § Wet meadows and rocky uplands, Nfld. to Mich., s. to N. C. PLATE 6.

S. alba, also called meadow-sweet (to 6 ft.), is distinguished by the downy stems on which the flowers are borne. § Wet meadows and swamps, Que. to Alta., s. to N. C., O., Mo., and S. D.

INDIAN PHYSIC (*Gillenia*)   WHITE OR PINK

The leaves of *Gillenia* are palmately divided into three sharply toothed segments. They have no noticeable stalks. Both of our

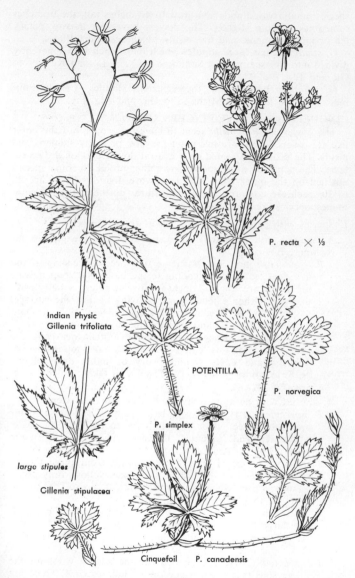

P. recta × ⅓

Indian Physic
Gillenia trifoliata

POTENTILLA

P. norvegica

large stipules

Gillenia stipulacea

P. simplex

Cinquefoil   P. canadensis

FIGURE 41

species inhabit woodlands and grow to 40 inches tall, the branches sometimes arching slightly. The flowers have five narrow petals, ten or more stamens, and five pistils which become follicles.

G. stipulacea has large stipules which make each leaf apparently divided into five segments. § Summer: N. Y. to Ia. and Kan., s. to Ga. and Tex. *Fig. 41.*

G. trifoliata has narrow, inconspicuous stipules. § Early summer: N. Y. to Ont. and Mich., s. to Ga. and Ala. *Fig. 41.*

CINQUEFOILS or FIVE-FINGERS (*Potentilla*) YELLOW

The flowers of *Potentilla* seem to have ten sepals, but the outer five are bracts. There are five petals, several or many stamens and pistils. The pistils are seated on a central dome, part of the receptacle. The petals of most species are rather broad, in some species notched on the outer edge. The leaves are divided. There are 25 or 30 species in our area, some of them far northern; the ten commonest species are treated here.

I. Species with palmately divided leaves (compare II).

A. Species with palmately divided leaves and creeping stems (compare B).

P. canadensis has leaf segments that are wedge-shaped, the marginal teeth not extending to the base. The erect flowering stems are about 3 inches tall. The plant is hairy with the hairs either extending out or lying against the surface. § Spring and early summer: dry open places, N. S. to Ont., s. and sw. to S. C. and O.; Mo.; mainly eastern. *Fig. 41.*

P. simplex has leaf segments generally toothed nearly to the base. The stem is hairy, the leaves not noticeably so. § Spring and early summer: dry or moist open places, N. S. to Minn., s. to N. C., Tenn., and Okla.; chiefly western. *Fig. 41.*

B. Species with palmately divided leaves and erect stems.

P. norvegica (3 ft.) is a very hairy plant. The leaf segments are only three; their margins are toothed to the base. § Summer and autumn: thickets, clearings, and waste places, Lab. to Alaska, s. to N. C., Tex., and Ariz. *Fig. 41.*

P. rivalis (20 in.) is rather bushy, with from three to five segments per leaf. The flowers are pale yellow, only about ⅕ inch across. § Summer: riverbanks, damp soil, Minn. to B. C., s. to Ill., Mo., N. M., and Calif.

P. recta (to 3 ft.) has from five to seven segments per leaf. The large flowers (up to an inch across) are in a flat cluster. § Summer: dry soil, Nfld. to Minn., s. to N. C., Ky., Ark., and Kan.; introduced from Europe. *Fig. 41.*

P. argentea (20 in.) is named for the silvery wool on the under side of the leaves and on the inflorescence. There are five narrow, sharply toothed leaf segments. § Summer:

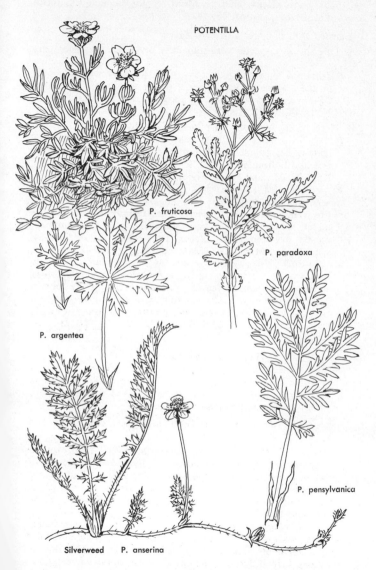

POTENTILLA

P. fruticosa

P. paradoxa

P. argentea

P. pensylvanica

Silverweed P. anserina

FIGURE 42

dry open places, Nfld. to Mont., s. to Va. and Ill.; introduced from Europe. *Fig. 42.*

II. Species with pinnately divided leaves.

A. One shrubby species with pinnately divided leaves (compare B).

   P. fruticosa, shrubby cinquefoil (3 ft.), has leaves usually silky on the under side and on some plants woolly on both sides. § Summer and autumn: meadows, Lab. to Alaska, s. to N. J., Ill., S. D., and Ariz. *Fig. 42.*

B. Herbaceous species with pinnately divided leaves.

   P. paradoxa (1–2 ft.) has from seven to 11 segments per leaf, rather coarsely and bluntly toothed. § Summer: prairies and bottomlands, Ont. to B. C., s. to N. Y., Pa., Mo., Kan., N. M., and Wash. *Fig. 42.*

   P. pensylvanica (20 in.) has a number of stems. The leaf segments are deeply cut into fingerlike lobes blunt at the tips. The leaves are grayish-green, usually woolly on the under side. This is a very variable species. § Summer: mostly dry and rocky places, from Que. across Canada, s. to N. H., Mich., Ia., Colo., and Calif. *Fig. 42.*

   P. anserina, silverweed, spreads by slender stolons, from which arise the leaves, up to a foot long, and the flower stalks which bear no leaves. The leaf segments are numerous, small ones often alternating with the larger ones, all silvery-silky on the under side. § Summer: stony or sandy shores, across Canada, s. to N. Y., Ind., Ia., N. M., and Calif. *Fig. 42.*

GEUM (*Geum*)   YELLOW, WHITE, OR PURPLISH

The species of *Geum* (known sometimes as avens) are recognized by their long slender styles which in most have a crook below the stigma. The upper part breaks off, and the lower part, with its hooked end, remains on the achene.

I. Species with yellow or cream-colored petals (compare II and III).

   G. vernum (2 ft.) has basal leaves that vary from round-bladed on a long stalk to pinnately divided. The cluster of achenes is raised above the sepals on a short but visible stalk, after the petals fall. The flowers are small, the petals only about ⅙ inch long. § Spring: rich woods, N. Y. to Mich. and Kan., s. to Md., Tenn., and Ark.

   G. macrophyllum (3 ft.) has basal leaves that are pinnately divided with a very large end segment and much smaller lateral segments. The plant is hairy or bristly. The flowers may be ¾ inch across. § Summer: moist woods, across Canada and s. to N. Y., Mich., Wis., Minn., and Calif.

   G. aleppicum (3 ft.) is a hairy plant. The leaves are very vari-

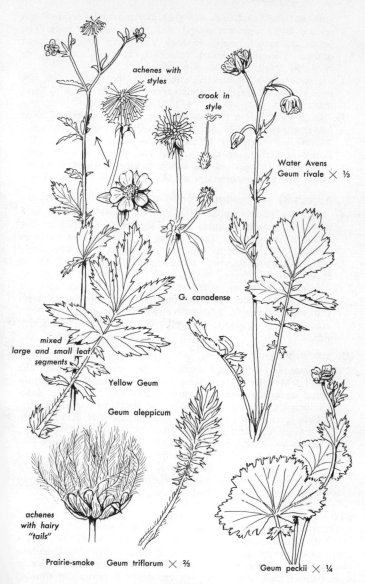

achenes with styles

crook in style

Water Avens
Geum rivale × ⅓

G. canadense

mixed large and small leaf segments

Yellow Geum

Geum aleppicum

achenes with hairy "tails"

Prairie-smoke   Geum triflorum × ⅔

Geum peckii × ¼

FIGURE 43

able, but the basal ones are generally pinnately divided into several large segments mixed with much smaller ones. The petals are broad, nearly ½ inch long, deep yellow or even orange. § Summer: moist meadows, across Canada, s. to N. J., Ill., Nebr., and Mexico. *Fig. 43.*

G. *virginianum* resembles G. *canadense* (see below), but has pale yellow or greenish petals shorter than the sepals. § Summer: woods, Mass. to Ind., s. to S. C. and Tenn.

G. *peckii* (1 ft.) is a mountain species with long-stalked basal leaves either round-bladed and undivided or with a few small lateral leaf segments below the large end segment. The flowers are about an inch across. The style is not obviously crooked as in most of the other species. § Summer: alpine slopes and cliffs, mountains of Me. and N. H. *Fig. 43.*

II. Species with petals purplish or yellow with a purplish tinge.

G. *triflorum,* prairie-smoke (16 in.), has basal leaves up to 8 inches long with as many as 17 segments. The flowers are about an inch across. The style is not crooked and becomes a hairy "tail" on the achene, up to 2 inches long. The whole plant is hairy. § Summer: prairies and rocky places, N. Y. to B. C., s. to Ill., Nebr., N. M., and Calif. *Fig. 43.*

G. *rivale,* water avens (4 ft.), has flowers that hang from the curved stalks. The sepals are purple and the petals yellowish suffused with purple. § Summer: swamps, wet meadows, bogs, etc., across Canada, s. to N. J., O., Ill., Minn., and Calif. *Fig. 43.*

III. Species with white petals.

G. *canadense* (4 ft.) is a slender, rather straggling plant. The basal leaves are long-stalked, the blade usually divided into three segments, sometimes into more. The petals are about ¼ inch long, about the same as the sepals or slightly longer. § Late spring and early summer: woodlands, N. S. to N. D., s. to Ga., Ala., and Tex. *Fig. 43.*

G. *laciniatum* (3 ft.) is a hairy plant. The basal leaves are pinnately divided with the segments usually deeply cleft. The petals are very small, only about ⅛ inch long, shorter than the sepals. § Summer: moist meadows and thickets, N. S. to Mich., s. to Md., Ind., and Mo.

STRAWBERRIES (*Fragaria*) WHITE

The strawberries are recognized by their leaves, which are divided into three sharp-toothed segments on long stalks. The leaves grow from a very short underground stem, from which stolons also grow and form new clusters of leaves. The flowers are in cymes on leafless stems. The numerous small pistils are situated on a dome-shaped projection of the receptacle in the middle of

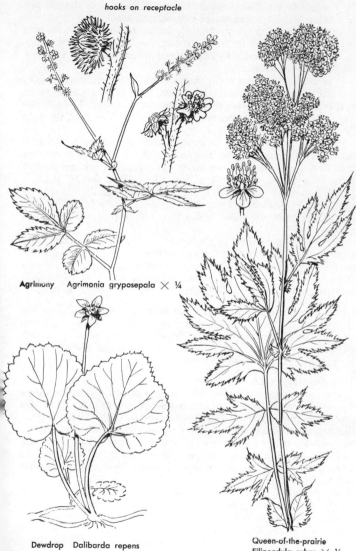

hooks on receptacle

Agrimony Agrimonia gryposepala $\times$ ¼

Dewdrop Dalibarda repens

Queen-of-the-prairie
Filipendula rubra $\times$ ⅓

FIGURE 44

the flower. This becomes the edible fruit, the "seeds" on its surface being really achenes, each containing a seed.

Two species, both very variable, occur in our area, blooming in spring and fruiting in early summer. Both are found in a variety of situations, mostly in dry upland woods and grassy slopes, but also on roadsides.

F. virginiana is the more common. The flower cluster is usually flat and does not rise above the leaves. The flowers are about an inch broad, the fruits less than an inch in diameter. The achenes are sunken in small pits on the mature fruit. § Lab. to Alta., s. to Ga. and Okla. PLATE 6.

F. vesca has its flowers generally raised above the leaves in a longer, not flat cluster. The flowers are about ½ inch across, the fruit less than ½ inch in diameter. The achenes are not sunken in the fruit. § Nfld. to Alta., s. to Va., Mo., Nebr., and N. M.

The cultivated strawberries are hybrids, originally derived in part from *F. virginiana*. They may occasionally be found growing wild. Their fruits are many times larger than those of the native species.

The so-called barren strawberry (*Waldsteinia fragarioides*) grows in woodlands mostly in the northern parts of our area and in the mountains. The plants somewhat resemble strawberry plants, but the petals are yellow. The receptacle is cup-shaped with from two to six pistils inside. The pistils become follicles.

QUEEN-OF-THE-PRAIRIE (*Filipendula rubra*)   PINK

Queen-of-the-prairie (7 ft.) has many small flowers in a dense cluster. The leaves are pinnately divided: the end segment is cleft into several sharp lobes. § Summer: meadows and moist prairies, N. Y. to Minn., s. to Ga., Ky., and Ia. *Fig. 44.*

THE AGRIMONIES (*Agrimonia*)   YELLOW

The agrimonies are known by the top-shaped receptacle below the sepals, which bears hooked hairs around its edge. The five petals are small, yellow. The flowers are in long, narrow, spikelike racemes. There are only two pistils, which become achenes enclosed by the bristly receptacle and the sepals. The leaves are pinnately divided, small segments often being mixed with the larger ones. These are all woodland plants, blooming in summer and early autumn.

A. gryposepala (to 5 ft.) has scattered, rather long hairs. A lens will reveal numerous small glands on the flowering stem. § Que. to N. D., s. to N. J., Tenn., and Kan., and in the mountains to N. C.; B. C. to Calif. *Fig. 44.*

A. striata (to 6 ft.) is downy. § Across Canada, s. to N. J., W. Va., Nebr., and Ariz.

A. pubescens (to 5 ft.) is hairy. § Me. to Nebr., s. to Ga., Tenn., and Kan.

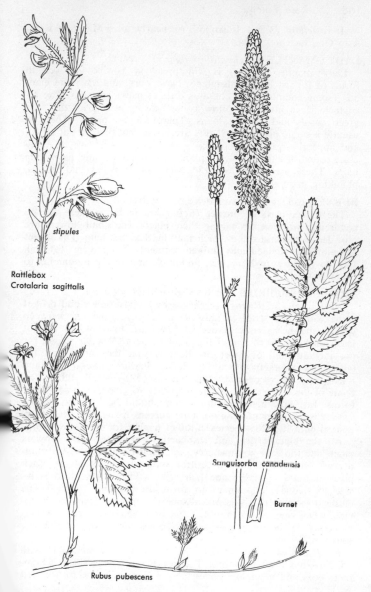

stipules

Rattlebox
Crotalaria sagittalis

Sanguisorba canadensis

Burnet

Rubus pubescens

FIGURE 45

A. rostellata (3 ft.) is smooth or nearly so. § Mass. to Kan., s. to Ga., La., and Okla.

LADY'S-MANTLE (*Alchemilla vulgaris*)   GREEN
Lady's-mantle (20 in.) is widespread in Europe and certain forms of it exist in New England, New York, and maritime Canada (some botanists treat these as distinct native species). The receptacle is an inverted hollow cone, bearing at its rim the four green sepals and four stamens. There are no petals. There is usually a single pistil. The leaves are broad, not divided but lobed, and appearing as if folded like a fan. The flowers are in many close roundish clusters. Some plants are smooth, some have long hairs. These are plants of cold, wet, rocky slopes and shores, blooming in summer.

BURNET (*Sanguisorba canadensis*)   WHITE
The flower parts of burnet (6 ft.) are in fours; there are no petals, the white sepals taking their place. The small flowers are crowded in a dense spike which may be 8 inches long. The leaves are pinnately divided into stalked segments. § Summer: wet soil, Lab. to Man., s. to N. J., O., and Ind., and in the mountains to Ga. *Fig. 45*.

THE BLACKBERRIES and RASPBERRIES (*Rubus*)
Most species of *Rubus* are shrubs or woody canes, and do not come within the scope of this book. However, the line between woody and herbaceous plants is very hard to draw, so that at least some species of *Rubus* find a place here. A better reason for not including all or most of them is that they are—even for botanists—extremely difficult to define. Perhaps several thousand forms may be recognizable in our range by small differences. Some of these breed true, some hybridize to give rise to still other forms. Just how many similar forms should be included in one species is a matter of opinion. One current manual of the northeastern flora lists 205 species; another has 24 for the same area!

All the blackberries and raspberries—brambles—have flowers much like those of a strawberry, with many stamens, and a number of pistils situated on a central knob of the receptacle. Each pistil becomes a small stone fruit, like a cherry (the seed is inside the stone); all cohere to form the familiar "berry." The cluster of succulent pistils of a raspberry separates from the receptacle when ripe, like a thimble; that of a blackberry adheres permanently to the receptacle, which comes away from the flower stalk.

R. chamaemorus, cloudberry (6 in.), has a creeping stem with one-flowered erect branches. The leaves are not divided. § Summer: bogs and mountain slopes, across Canada and s. to Me. and N. H.

R. pubescens, the dwarf blackberry (18 in.), has creeping stems from which rise erect leafy branches which bear several leaves and flowers. The leaves have three segments. The flowers are white or pink. § Late spring and summer: damp slopes and shores, across Canada and s. to N. J., O., Ind., Ia., and Colo. *Fig. 45.*

DEWDROP (*Dalibarda repens*)   WHITE
The dewdrops (2–4 in.) are woodland plants with somewhat downy, heart-shaped leaves on long stalks. The flowers are of two kinds: those with white petals usually bear no fruit; other flowers lack petals but each forms from five to ten small, rather dry fruits. The flower stalks rise from a creeping stem. Some but not all of the sepals are toothed. § Summer: wet woods, Que. to Minn., s. to N. J. and O., and in the mountains to N. C. *Fig. 44.*

BEAN FAMILY (*Leguminosae*)

The beans and their relatives form an enormous family which includes trees, shrubs, and herbs of all parts of the world from the tropics to the arctic. Some are familiar on our tables: peas, beans, soy beans, lentils. Others grace our gardens: lupines, sweet-peas, golden-chain, locust, wisteria. They include also plants of great importance as fodder and as sources of dyes, insecticides, etc.

Most botanists divide the family into three families or subfamilies; they are here held together for convenience. The feature common to all is the type of pod called a legume, which at maturity typically splits into two halves down two opposite lines; the seeds are in one row. But there are many exceptions to this description: one-seeded pods, pods that do not open at all, and others. The flowers of most genera are described as "papilionaceous"— butterfly-like. In such flowers there are five petals, one erect called the standard, two at the sides called the wings, and two joined along one edge to form a keel, which may be boat-shaped or variously coiled. The wings may be joined to the keel. The pistil and stamens are within the keel, but those of many species are suddenly revealed when an insect alights on the keel and "trips" the mechanism. There are usually ten stamens joined by their stalks in one or two groups. In some genera, however, the petals are more or less alike and distinct and the stamens may be less than ten or numerous. These are the genera classified separately as mentioned above. The leaves are singly attached, often divided, and usually provided with stipules. In this book only herbaceous species are described. Some of the native trees and shrubs also have handsome flowers; e.g. the black locust (*Robinia*) and redbud (*Cercis*).

Guide to Certain Genera of *Leguminosae*

I. Genera with papilionaceous flowers (they must sometimes be dissected to determine if the petals described above are actually present (compare II).

A. Genus with undivided leaves: *Crotalaria* (flowers yellow) (compare B, C, D, E, and F).

B. Genus with leaves divided palmately into from seven to 11 segments: *Lupinus* (flowers blue, sometimes white) (*Fig. 46*).

C. Genera with leaves divided palmately or pinnately into three, five, or seven segments; not climbing or twining plants.

Psoralea (flowers mostly blue, in spikes) has three or five leaf segments at the end of the stalk; at least the end segment is stalked (*Fig. 46*).

Lotus (flowers yellow to red, in a head) has what seem to be three segments (with plain margins) at the end of the stalk with two segments (appearing like large stipules) at the base of the stalk (*Fig. 47*).

Trifolium (flowers white to crimson or yellow, in heads or spikes) has three leaf segments without stalks (*Figs. 47, 48*).

Medicago (flowers yellow or blue, in heads or racemes) has three leaf segments, the end one stalked. The pods are tightly coiled (*Fig. 48*).

Melilotus (flowers yellow or white, in racemes) has three leaf segments, the end one stalked; the foliage is sweet-smelling (especially when crushed). The pod is short, round (*Fig. 48*).

Desmodium (flowers white to purple or green, in racemes) has three leaf segments with plain margins, the end one stalked. The pods are composed of "joints" separated by constrictions (*Fig. 49*); they easily adhere to clothing.

Lespedeza (flowers yellowish to purple, in heads or spikes) has three leaf segments with plain margins, the end one stalked. The pod is short, one-seeded (*Fig. 50*).

Stylosanthes (flowers orange-yellow, in short spikes) has three narrow leaf segments. The flower has a long, narrow base (*Fig. 51*). The pod is short, one-seeded, hooked at the end.

Baptisia (flowers white, yellow, or violet, in racemes) has three leaf segments with plain margins on a very short leaf stalk; the stipules may be large and simulate another pair of segments. The pod is thick, stalked, and ends in a beak or hook (*Fig. 51;* PLATE 6).

D. Genera with leaves divided pinnately into three or five segments; twining plants without tendrils.

Apios (flowers brown-purple) has five leaf segments. The keel is sickle-shaped (PLATE 7).

Strophostyles (flowers pink or greenish) has usually three-lobed leaf segments. There is a pair of narrow bracts at the base of the calyx (*Fig. 52*).

Clitoria (flowers pale blue) has a conspicuous, notched standard (*Fig. 52*).

Amphicarpaea (flowers pale purple or white) has very hairy stems and leaf stalks, the hairs often pointing backward (*Fig. 52*).

Phaseolus (flowers purple) has a coiled keel (*Fig. 52*).

E. Genera with leaves divided pinnately into more than seven segments. No tendrils.

Coronilla (flowers pink, in heads) has a narrow pod with several constrictions (PLATE 7).

Tephrosia (standard yellow, wings blue; flowers in racemes) has straight, narrow, hairy pods (*Fig. 53*).

Astragalus (flowers white to purple) has pods in some species thick and fleshy or woody, in others coiled or curved (*Fig. 53*).

F. Genera with pinnately divided leaves that bear tendrils (*Figs. 53, 54*).

Vicia (flowers from purple to white) has from eight to 20 leaf segments, besides a pair of small stipules (*Fig. 53*). The style has a tuft of hair on the end.

Lathyrus (flowers red, purple, blue, or cream-colored) has from two to 12 leaf segments, not counting the two large stipules (*Fig. 54*).

II. Genera with flowers not papilionaceous.

A. Genera with a standard but no true wings or keel (compare B).

Amorpha (flowers purple or white, in long tapering racemes) has ten projecting stamens, only one petal (*Fig. 54*).

Petalostemum (flowers rose-purple or white, in heads or short spikes) has five projecting stamens, four petal-like sterile stamens (*Fig. 55*).

B. Genera with five petals all much alike (very small in some).

Cassia (flowers yellow, in long or very short racemes) has five petals, five sepals scarcely joined, five or ten stamens (*Figs. 55, 56*).

Desmanthus (flowers greenish, in dense round heads) has five stamens in each flower (*Fig. 56*).

Schrankia (flowers pink, in dense round heads) has ten or more stamens in each flower. The stems are trailing, prickly (PLATE 7).

RATTLEBOX (*Crotalaria sagittalis*)   YELLOW

Rattlebox (16 in.) is a hairy plant with narrow undivided leaves; the stipules make an arrowhead pointing down. The petals are yellow. Under a lens the ten stamens may be seen to be all joined near the base of their stalks. There are five short anthers and five longer, alternating. The name comes from the pod, which becomes dry with the seeds loose within. § Summer: dry, sandy soil, Mass. and Vt. to Minn. and S. D., s. to Fla. and Tex. *Fig. 45.*

LUPINE (*Lupinus perennis*)   BLUE OR WHITE

The lupines form a large and very difficult genus. However, most American species are western; in the eastern states there is only one native, *L. perennis* (2 ft.). The sepals are joined but unequally, so that there are upper and lower "lips." The petals are blue, or sometimes white. The leaves are palmately divided into from seven to 11 narrow segments at the summit of a long stalk. The pods are flat and downy. § Late spring and early summer: dry soil, meadows, etc., sw. Me. to Minn., s. to Fla., O., Ind., and n. Ill. *Fig. 46.*

SCURF-PEAS (*Psoralea*)   BLUE, PURPLISH, OR WHITE

The genus *Psoralea* includes a number of attractive small plants of the plains and prairies of the Midwest, and some in open woodlands in the more eastern states. They are summer-flowering perennials with thick underground stems or tuberous roots. The leaves are palmately or pinnately divided into three or five segments, usually on a fairly long stalk. The flowers, about ⅜ inch long, are mostly blue or purplish (in some species white), in spikes.

P. onobrychis, sometimes called sainfoin (to 5 ft.), has leaves divided into three, the end segment on a stalk so that the division is called pinnate. The blades are covered with small black dots (glands). The flowers are blue or white. § Rich woods, clearings, and prairies, O. to Ia., s. to W. Va., Tenn., and e. Mo. *Fig. 46.*

P. psoralioides (3 ft.) is a slender plant with narrow leaf segments and long-stalked flower spikes. § Open woodlands and prairies, Va. to Kan., s. to Ga. and Tex. *Fig. 46.*

P. tenuiflora (3 ft.) is similar but the end leaf segment is not stalked; all three arise palmately from the same point. The spikes are rather loosely flowered. § Dry prairies and open woodlands, Ind. to Mont., s. to Mo., Tex., and Ariz. *Fig. 46.*

BIRD'S-FOOT TREFOIL (*Lotus corniculatus*)   YELLOW OR RED

The genus *Lotus* is no relative of the Egyptian lotus, which is a water-lily. *L. corniculatus* (1 ft.) has five leaf segments, two at the base resembling stipules, the other three at the end of a stalk-like midrib. The flowers are yellow or red. § Summer: fields and roadsides, Nfld. to Minn., s. to Va. and O.; native of Europe. *Fig. 47.*

THE CLOVERS (*Trifolium*)   VARIOUS COLORS

Of the 300 or more species of clover only four are native in our range. So many, however, have been used for fodder and pasture and for honey that a number of species have become natu-

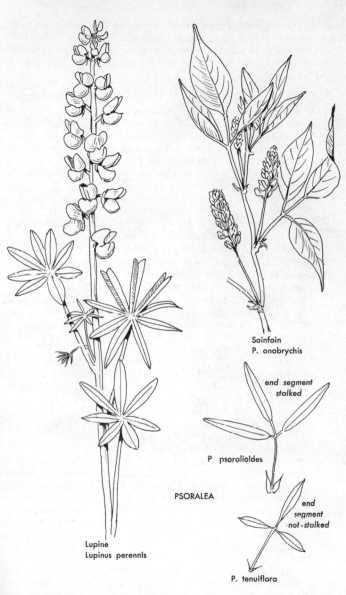

Sainfoin
P. onobrychis

end segment
stalked

P. psoralioides

PSORALEA

end
segment
not·stalked

P. tenuiflora

Lupine
Lupinus perennls

FIGURE 46

ralized. Twelve species are common enough to be mentioned here. They all have leaves divided into three and flowers in dense clusters. One mark of identification is in the sepals: they are united to form a cup, but their ends usually project from the rim as five slender teeth.

I. Species with red, pink, lavender, or white flowers (compare II).

    A. Creeping or reclining species (compare B).

        T. repens, white clover (6 in.), has a creeping stem from which the long-stalked leaves and the flowering stems arise. The flowers, in globular heads ¾ inch across, are on leafless stalks; they are white or pinkish, turning brown as they wither. § Spring to autumn: grasslands, open woods, etc.; often grown in lawns; throughout. *Fig. 47.*

        T. stoloniferum, one of two species called buffalo clover, has creeping stems which rise at the ends (1 ft.). The petals are white tinged with purple. The broad leaf segments are heart-shaped. § Late spring and summer: O. to S. D., s. to Tenn. and Kan.; a native of the western prairies. *Fig. 48.*

    B. Species with flowers from red to white, and growing more or less erect.

        T. pratense, common red clover (to 3 ft.), has leaves usually marked with a light "V." The pink or lavender flowers are on short stalks; the large head is closely invested by a pair of leaves, each three-divided and together creating the appearance of six leaves. § Spring to autumn: roadsides, fields, etc., throughout. *Fig. 47.*

        T. hybridum, alsike, bears individually stalked flowers in a long-stalked head. The flowers, which are spicily fragrant, are deep pink and white, turning brown in age. § Spring to autumn: roadsides, fields, etc., throughout. *Fig. 48.*

        T. medium, zigzag clover (20 in.), has purplish flowers in a round head. § Summer: fields, waste places, Que. to Mass. and elsewhere mostly in the eastern states.

        T. reflexum, buffalo clover (20 in.), has red-and-pink, red-and-white, or all-white flowers. The stems branch from the base. The leaf stalks are hairy. § Late spring and summer: sandy places and roadsides, w. N. Y. and s. Ont. to Kan., s. to Fla. and Tex.; native. *Fig. 48.*

        T. virginicum (6 in.) has a dense tuft of long-stalked leaves on a short stem; the leaf segments are very narrow. The flower heads are on short, hairy stems. The petals are white. § Spring and summer: rocky mountain slopes, Md., Pa., s. to Va. and W. Va.; native. *Fig. 48.*

        T. incarnatum, crimson clover (2 ft.), is silky-hairy; the crimson flowers are in oblong heads raised above the leaves. § Spring and summer: waste ground, roadsides, etc., throughout.

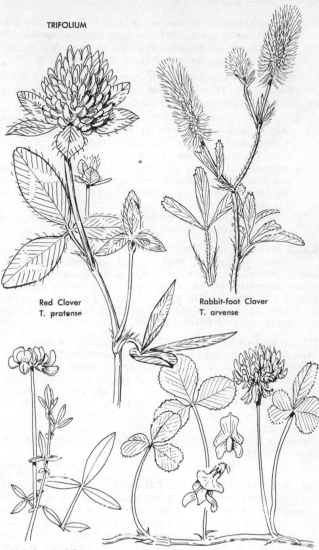

TRIFOLIUM

Red Clover
T. pratense

Rabbit-foot Clover
T. arvense

Bird's-foot Trefoil
Lotus corniculatus

White Clover   T. repens × ¾

FIGURE 47

T. arvense, rabbit-foot clover (18 in.), is downy. The short-stalked leaves are divided into very narrow segments. The flower heads are oblong, furry-looking, grayish. § Spring to autumn: dry roadsides and fields, throughout. *Fig. 47.*

II. Species with yellow flowers (all from the Old World). All are called hop clover. They are found in waste ground, lawns, etc. They should be compared with *Medicago lupulina* (*Fig. 48*).

T. agrarium is more or less erect (18 in.); the leaf stalks are only ½ inch long or less; the blades are divided into narrow, pointed segments. The flower heads may be ¾ inch long. § Across Canada, s. to S. C. and Ark.

T. procumbens lies on the ground. The short-stalked leaves are divided into rather broad segments. The flower heads are about ½ inch long. § Que. to N. D., s. to Ga. and Ark. *Fig. 48.*

T. dubium is similar but smaller. Each head contains usually not more than 15 flowers. § Throughout.

BLACK MEDICK (*Medicago lupulina*)   YELLOW
In general appearance black medick resembles the yellow-flowered clovers. The stem lies on the ground, sending up leaves divided palmately into three segments and branches which bear heads of small flowers. The pod is coiled and black, covered with raised veins. § Spring to winter: roadsides, lawns, waste places, throughout; native of Europe. *Fig. 48.*

THE SWEET-CLOVERS (*Melilotus*)   YELLOW OR WHITE
The sweet-clovers have flowers like those of the clovers but in slender spikelike racemes. They are bushy weedy plants often 5 or 6 feet tall, growing in all sorts of places, especially roadsides, throughout our area, blooming from late spring to autumn. The leaves and stems have a characteristic sweet odor, especially when crushed. The pod is round, only about ⅕ inch long, often with only one seed.

M. albus, white sweet-clover (reported up to 10 ft.), has white flowers. *Fig. 48.*

M. officinalis, yellow sweet-clover (5 ft.), has yellow flowers.

THE STICKTIGHTS or TICK-TREFOILS (*Desmodium*)   BLUE, PURPLISH, WHITE, OR GREEN / These common and mostly unattractive weeds of late summer get their various names from their pods, which are divided into "joints," each containing one seed (the botanical name comes from a Greek word for "chain"). At maturity the joints separate but do not split open; and, since they are generally covered with minute hooked hairs, they adhere to clothing and to the coat of animals, so that the seeds are scattered. The flowers are mostly rather small, in loose and slender racemes. The leaves are pinnately divided into three. In the main the plants are tall, some reaching a height of 6 feet; a few have stems that lie on the

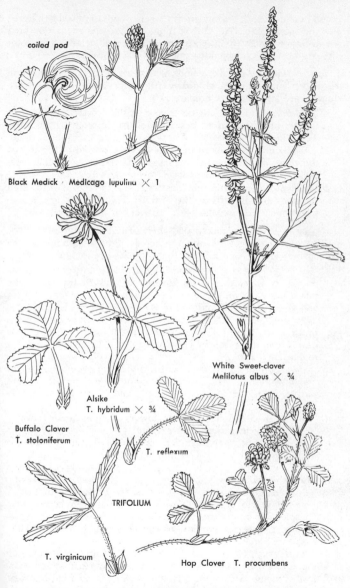

coiled pod

Black Medick · Medicago lupulina × 1

White Sweet-clover
Melilotus albus × ¾

Alsike
T. hybridum × ¾

Buffalo Clover
T. stoloniferum

T. reflexum

TRIFOLIUM

T. virginicum

Hop Clover T. procumbens

FIGURE 48

ground. The majority grow in dry open woods, roadside thickets, and the like places. The 20 or more species known in our area are distinguished by their pods and other small details. The commoner and more conspicuous ones are described below.

I. Species with long-stalked pods which are nearly straight along the upper edge, the joints nearly triangular (*Fig. 49*). The ten stamens are all joined. (Compare II.)

D. *nudiflorum* (1 ft.) has no leaves on the flowering stem. The flowers are purplish or rose. § Me. to Minn., s. to Fla. and Tex. *Fig. 49*.

D. *glutinosum* (2 ft. or more) has leaves crowded at the top of the stem, just below the racemes. The flowers are blue, purple, or rose. § N. S. to Sask., s. to Fla. and Tex.

D. *pauciflorum* (2 ft.) has scattered leaves, the few-flowered racemes growing from their axils. The flowers are white. § Summer: rich woods, N. Y. to Kan., s. to Fla. and Tex.

II. Species with short-stalked pods indented along both edges (the stalks scarcely project beyond the sepals; *Fig. 49*). Nine of the stamens are joined, one is free. Eight species are included here.

D. *sessilifolium* (to 5 ft.) has very narrow, blunt leaf segments on a very short stalk. The flowers are pink or lavender. The pod usually has only two or three joints. § R. I. to Ont., Mich., and Kan., s. to Pa. and Tex. *Fig. 49*.

D. *paniculatum* (3 ft.) has narrow, lance-shaped leaf segments up to 4 inches long. The raceme is much branched. The pods have from three to six joints. § Me. to Mich. and Nebr., s. to Fla. and Tex. *Fig. 49*.

D. *rotundifolium* (1 ft.) has nearly round leaf segments. Leaves and flower stalks rise from a creeping stem. The flowers are purple. § Vt. and Mass. to Mich., s. and sw. to Fla. and Tex. *Fig. 49*.

D. *canescens* (5 ft.) has pinkish flowers (turning green) nearly ½ inch long in a branched raceme. The stipules also are ½ inch long. The leaf segments are ovate, blunt. § Mass. to Minn. and Nebr., s. to Fla. and Tex.

D. *illinoense* (to 6 ft.) has long stipules, and usually a branched raceme. The leaf segments are ovate. The flowers are white. § Prairies, Ont. to Wis. and Nebr., s. to O., and sw. to Tex.

D. *canadense* (to 6 ft.) is bushy. The numerous racemes have conspicuous bracts under the flowers. The flowers are rose-purple. The leaf segments are ovate, blunt. § Que. to Alta., s. to S. C. and Okla. *Fig. 49*.

D. *viridiflorum* (3 ft.) has leaves covered with white wool on the under side. The flowers, at first pink, turn green. The leaf segments are blunt. § N. Y..to Okla., s. to Fla. and Tex.

D. *cuspidatum* (to 6 ft.) has ovate, pointed leaf segments and

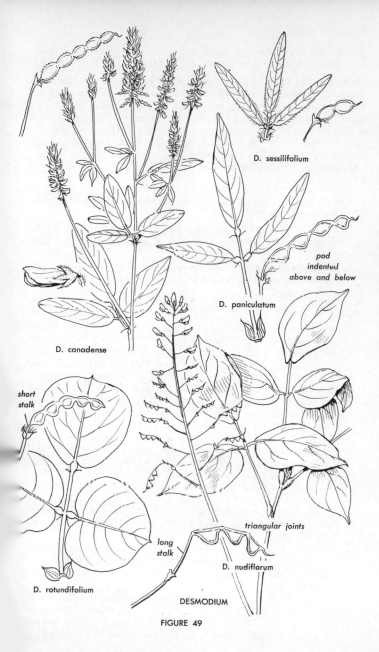

D. sessilifolium

pod
indented
above and below

D. paniculatum

D. canadense

short
stalk

D. rotundifolium

long
stalk

triangular joints

D. nudiflorum

DESMODIUM

FIGURE 49

rather triangular joints of the pod. The flowers are pink.
§ Rich woods, Mass. and N. H. to Minn., s. to Fla. and Tex.

THE BUSH-CLOVERS (*Lespedeza*) PURPLE, PINK, OR YEL-
LOWISH / The bush-clovers have leaves somewhat like those of the
true clovers, each divided into three segments. The flowers are
small; many species have, besides the ordinary flowers, clusters
of flowers that lack petals; these often form pods more abundantly
than the others. As in most of the tick-trefoils, nine of the ten
stamens are joined. The pod is very short, with one seed, and does
not open when ripe. The plants grow in dry soil of open woodlands and prairies.

I. Species with creeping or trailing stems, and erect flowering
branches (compare II).
  L. repens is smooth or nearly so. The flowers are purple. § Late
    spring to early autumn: Conn. to Kan., s. to Fla. and Tex.
    Fig. 50.
  L. procumbens is hairy. The flowers are purple. § Summer and
    autumn: Mass. to Ia. and Kan., s. to Fla. and Tex.

II. More or less erect species (some may partly recline on the
ground, with ascending tips). Eight species are included here.
  L. violacea (2 ft.) has scattered leaves; there are often leaves
    of two distinct sizes, those on the side branches much smaller
    than those on the main stems. The leaf segments are gen-
    erally ovate. The racemes are loosely flowered. The petals are
    purple; the wing petals are shorter than the keel. § Summer:
    Mass. and N. H. to Ia. and Kan., s. to Fla. and Tex. *Fig. 50.*
  L. virginica (3 ft. or more) has crowded leaves with narrow seg-
    ments. The flowers are purple, in short racemes which grow
    from the axils of leaves. § Summer: Mass. and N. H. to Ia.
    and Kan., s. to Fla. and Tex. *Fig. 50.*
  L. intermedia (2 ft.) is quite similar, with broader, ovate leaf
    segments. § Summer: sw. Me. to Ia. and Kan., s. to Fla. and
    Tex.
  L. hirta (3 ft.) is hairy. The leaf segments are oblong or ovate
    with the narrow end toward the stalk, blunt. The flowers are
    yellowish, in cylindric clusters on fairly long stalks. § Sum-
    mer and autumn: sw. Me. to Wis., s. and sw. to Fla. and
    Tex. *Fig. 50.*
  L. stuevei (3 ft.) is downy. The leaf segments are rather narrow.
    The flowers are purple, in dense clusters on short stalks.
    § Late summer: Mass. and Vt. to Kan., s. to Fla. and Tex.
    Fig. 50.
  L. capitata (5 ft.) is a bushy plant. It is very variable, usually
    silvery with silky hairs that lie flat, but often hairy with
    spreading hairs. The leaf segments are narrow. The flowers
    are cream-colored, rather large for this genus (½ inch long),

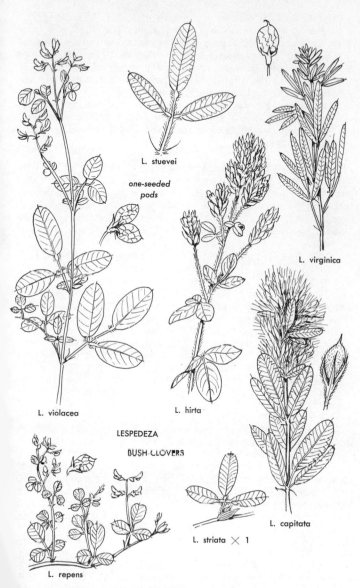

L. stuevei

one-seeded
pods

L. virginica

L. violacea

L. hirta

LESPEDEZA

BUSH-CLOVERS

L. capitata

L. striata × 1

L. repens

FIGURE 50

in dense hairy clusters in the axils of leaves. § Late summer: Que. to Minn. and Nebr., s. to Fla. and Tex. *Fig. 50.*

L. *striata* (1 ft.), Japanese-clover, is an introduced species common along roadsides. It is low, much branched, with small, almost stalkless leaves and pink or purple flowers in their axils. The stipules are conspicuous. § Summer and autumn: N. J. to Kan., s. to Fla. and Tex. *Fig. 50.*

L. *stipulacea,* Korean-clover, is similar but has broader leaf segments, more or less notched at the end, and flowers in dense clusters. It is cultivated in the South and is spreading northward as a weed.

PENCIL-FLOWER (*Stylosanthes biflora*)   ORANGE OR YELLOW
Pencil-flower is a small wiry plant (20 in.) with leaves divided into three narrow segments. Its names are derived from the peculiar long, hollow flower base or receptacle. The flowers are less than ½ inch long. The pod is short, one-seeded. Summer: dry woods and fields, N. Y. to Kan., s. to Fla. and Tex. *Fig. 51.*

WILD or FALSE INDIGOS (*Baptisia*)   BLUE, WHITE, OR YELLOW
The wild indigos are bushy, much-branched plants. The leaves, which are divided into three segments on a short stalk, usually turn black when dried. The calyx has upper and lower "lips," the upper in some species notched or two-lobed, the lower three-lobed. The ten stamens are separate. The pods are rather thick, papery or woody, stalked and sharp-pointed.

Some species of *Baptisia* have yielded an indigo-like dye; true indigo comes from another genus of the Bean Family. (Species of *Amorpha* are also called false indigo.)

B. *australis,* blue false indigo (5 ft.), has flowers about an inch long; the petals are dull blue. § Late spring and early summer: woods and thickets, usually moist, Pa. to Nebr., s. to Ga. and Tex.; also in N. Y. and Vt. *Fig. 51.*

B. *leucophaea* (3 ft.) is recognized by the large stipules which make the leaves seem to be divided into five. Another feature is the presence of large bracts with the flowers. The pod tapers to a short, thick stalk. § Late spring and early summer: prairies, Mich. to Minn. and Nebr., s. to Ky., Ark., and Tex. *Fig. 51* and PLATE 6.

B. *leucantha* (to 6 ft.) has leaf segments that tend to be broader toward the tip. The flowers are white. The pods are black, on a stalk up to ½ inch long. § Summer: prairies and woodlands, Ont. and O. to Minn. and Nebr., s. to Miss. and Tex. *Fig. 51.*

B. *tinctoria,* wild indigo (3 ft.), has smooth, bluish foliage when young. The leaf segments are usually less than an inch long, broader near the tip and usually notched. The flowers are small, yellow, in numerous racemes. The pods are less than ½ inch long, on long stalks. § Summer: Me. to Minn., s. to Fla. and La. *Fig. 51.*

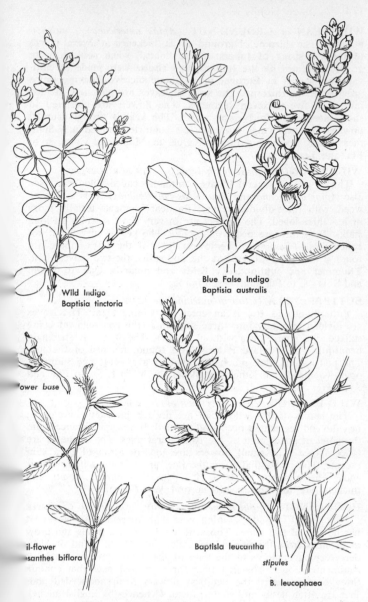

Wild Indigo
Baptisia tinctoria

Blue False Indigo
Baptisia australis

ower base

il-flower
esanthes biflora

Baptisia leucantha

stipules

B. leucophaea

FIGURE 51

WILD-BEAN or **GROUND-NUT** (*Apios americana*)   BROWN-PURPLE / The rhizome of ground-nut is thickened in several places to form a string of tubers. These "nuts," when cooked, were greatly esteemed by the Indians, and efforts were made to cultivate the species in Europe, but without success. Twining stems grow from the rhizome. The smooth leaves are pinnately divided into from five to seven segments. The flowers are clustered in short racemes on fairly long stalks. The keel is strongly curved upward, the two wings more or less contorted around it. § Summer: moist woods and thickets, Que. to Minn. and Colo., s. to Fla. and Tex. PLATE 7.

WILD BEAN (*Strophostyles helvola*)   PINK OR PURPLISH
This is one of several plants commonly called wild bean (see also *Apios americana* and *Phaseolus polystachios*). It is a twining weed, with three-divided leaves, the leaf segments usually more or less three-lobed. The flowers are in very short racemes on long stalks. They turn greenish as they age. The keel is curved but not coiled as in *Phaseolus*. The lowest lobe of the calyx (there are four) is much the longest. As the pod splits, the two halves twist. § Summer and autumn: dry fields and uplands, Que. to Minn. and S. D., s. to Fla. and Tex. *Fig. 52*.

BUTTERFLY-PEA (*Clitoria mariana*)   BLUE
Butterfly-pea (3 ft.) is an erect or twining plant. The leaves are divided pinnately into three segments (the end segment being stalked, the lateral ones without stalks). The flower is strikingly beautiful. The standard is large and round, notched at the top. The pod is long, flat, much like that of a sweet-pea. § Summer: open woodlands and other dry places, N. Y. to Ia., s. to Fla. and Ariz. *Fig. 52*.

WILD BEAN (*Phaseolus polystachios*)   PURPLE
The leaves of this wild bean are divided pinnately into three; i.e., the end segment is on a stalk or midrib at some distance from the point of attachment of the two lateral ones. The segments are lance-shaped. The small flowers are loosely arranged in a slim raceme. The petals that form the keel are spirally coiled at their ends. The pod also coils as it opens. § Summer: woods and thickets, Me. to Nebr., s. to Fla. and Tex. *Fig. 52*.

HOG-PEANUT (*Amphicarpaea bracteata*)   PALE LILAC OR WHITE
Hog-peanut is a low twining vine with three-divided leaves. It has flowers of two kinds. Those of one kind have petals and grow in racemes from the upper leaf axils. The others, found on slender creeping branches at the base of the plant, have no petals or rudimentary ones. The first type forms curved pods that contain three or four seeds; the petalless flowers form one-seeded pods that are often fleshy and subterranean (whence the English name) § Summer: woods and thickets, Que. to Mont., s. to Fla. and Tex. *Fig. 52*.

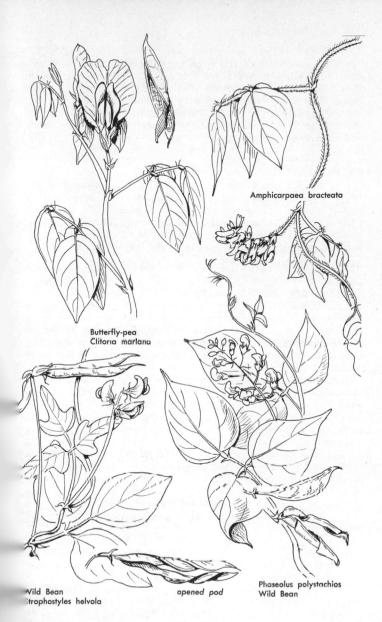

Amphicarpaea bracteata

Butterfly-pea
Clitoria mariana

Wild Bean
Strophostyles helvola

opened pod

Phaseolus polystachios
Wild Bean

FIGURE 52

GOAT'S-RUE (*Tephrosia virginiana*)   PINK- OR PURPLE-AND-YELLOW / Goat's-rue (2 ft.) is an attractive plant especially common in the Midwest, South, and Southwest. The leaves are pinnately divided into about 21 segments. The whole plant is hairy, in some places silky and silvery. The flowers are relatively large, with yellowish standard and pink or purple wings. Several flowers are crowded in a terminal raceme. § Summer: dry roadsides, fields and open woods, Mass. and Vt. to Minn., s. to Fla. and Tex. *Fig. 53.*

CROWN-VETCH (*Coronilla varia*)   PINK
Crown-vetch has a creeping stem which turns upward at the tip. The leaves are pinnately divided into about 21 segments; the petiole is short. The flowers are in a small head (really an umbel, since the flowers are stalked). The pods are constricted into a number of "joints." § Summer: roadsides, waste places, etc., N. E. to S. D., s. to Va. and Mo.; native of the Old World. PLATE 7.

THE MILK-VETCHES (*Astragalus*)   WHITE, YELLOW, VIOLET, OR PURPLE / The genus *Astragalus* is one of those difficult groups of species that need a knowledge of technical details and a manual for identification. There are certainly more than a thousand different kinds. As with the roses and brambles, opinions differ on the limits of species and consequently on the number of species in the genus; different authorities list from 19 to 25 in our area. It is impossible here to do more than mention a few of the more conspicuous species.
The American species of *Astragalus* grow mostly in the West. A number of species are poisonous, causing the behavior of livestock that gives these plants the name of locoweed. "Loco" means "crazy." Horses and other animals that have eaten *Astragalus* become very nervous and convulsive, often running around rapidly and aimlessly. Some of the western species absorb and retain the deadly mineral element selenium. The plants of our area are bushy, with pinnately divided leaves and white, yellowish, or purple flowers in racemes or heads. The pods are plump, in some species short and containing only one or two large seeds; these species are sometimes called ground-plums. The milk-vetches flower in spring and summer. They grow mostly in prairies and dry woodlands.
A. canadensis (to 5 ft.) has from 13 to 29 leaf segments. The flowers are white or yellowish. The pods are numerous, ½ inch long or longer. (This may be named *A. carolinianus* in some manuals.) § Que. to B. C., s. to Ga., Tex., and Colo. *Fig. 53.*
A. cooperi (3 ft.) has from 11 to 17 leaf segments. The flowers are white. The pods are less than ½ inch long, egg-shaped. (This is also called *A. neglectus*.) § N. Y. to Minn. and S. D., s. to O and Ia.
A. distortus (1 ft.) has from 13 to 25 leaf segments, each onl

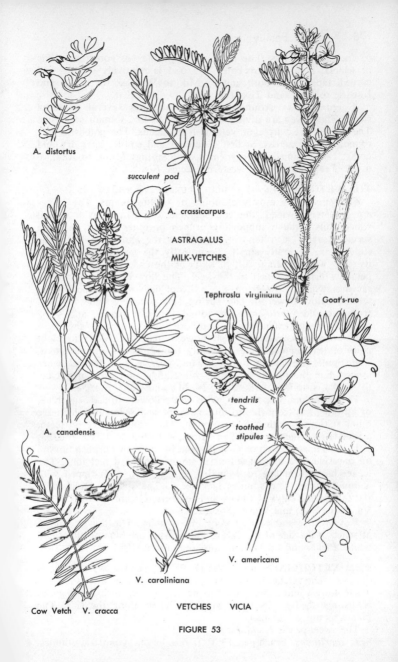

A. distortus

succulent pod

A. crassicarpus

ASTRAGALUS
MILK-VETCHES

Tephrosia virginiana   Goat's-rue

A. canadensis

tendrils

toothed
stipules

V. americana

V. caroliniana

Cow Vetch V. cracca   VETCHES VICIA

FIGURE 53

½ inch long or less. The flowers are purple (or sometimes lilac or white), in a short raceme. The pod is relatively slender and curved, tapering to both ends. § Md. to W. Va., Ill. to Ia. and Kan., s. to Miss. and Tex. *Fig. 53.*

A. crassicarpus, ground-plum (20 in.), has several clustered stems. The leaves are divided into from 15 to 23 small segments. The flowers are purple or yellowish, in heads. The pod is almost round, ½ inch across, at first succulent and edible, later dry and corky. (Also named *A. caryocarpus.*) § Spring: Minn. to Alta., s. to Ill., Tex., and Ariz.; a western species. *Fig. 53.*

THE VETCHES (*Vicia*)   BLUE, PURPLE, OR WHITE
The vetches are mostly climbing or trailing plants. The leaves are pinnately divided; the end segment is replaced by a tendril which coils about a supporting branch or other object; in some species several such tendrils appear at the end of a leaf. The stipules are generally small. Technically the genus is known by its style, which bears a tuft of hairs at the end; and by the wing-petals, which are joined to the keel. The flowers are generally in racemes which grow from the axils of leaves. The species described below flower in late spring and summer. Other species, from the Old World, may be found in waste places, and some southern species extend to the southern borders of our range.

V. americana, with purplish flowers, has from four to eight pairs of leaf segments, each usually tipped with a minute point. The stipules are sharply toothed. The lower teeth of the calyx are longer than the upper. § Shores, woodlands, and meadows, Que. to Alaska, s. to Va., Ark., Kan., N. M., and Calif. *Fig. 53.*

V. caroliniana, wood vetch, with white flowers tipped with blue, or all blue, has from five to nine pairs of leaf segments which are blunt at the tip, with a minute point. The stipules have no teeth. § Woods and thickets, N. Y. to Minn., s. to Fla. and Tex. *Fig. 53.*

V. cracca, cow vetch or Canada-pea, has blue or purplish flowers on one side of a long raceme. Its stems may be 6 feet long. The leaves have from five to 14 pairs of segments, each tipped with a minute point. The stipules lack teeth. The stalk is attached at the side of the calyx. § Fields and thickets, Greenl. to B. C., s. to Va., Ind., Wis., and Wash. *Fig. 53.*

V. villosa resembles *V. cracca* but is hairy. The flower stalk is attached at the side of the calyx. The flowers are blue or violet and white. Fields and thickets, throughout. PLATE 7.

THE VETCHLINGS and WILD PEAS (*Lathyrus*)   VARIOUS
COLORS / The vetchlings and wild peas resemble the vetches closely. Their flowers and stipules tend to be larger. Technically the genus is distinguished by its style which is hairy along the side. The plants bloom in summer.

The sweet-pea is *L. odoratus.*

L. maritimus, beach-pea (3 ft.), has large, symmetric stipules,

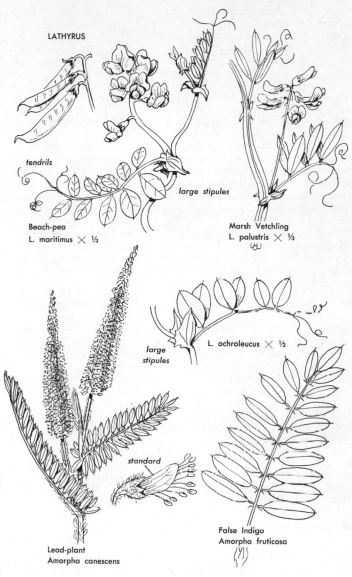

LATHYRUS

tendrils

large stipules

Beach-pea
L. maritimus × ⅓

Marsh Vetchling
L. palustris × ⅓

large stipules

L. ochroleucus × ⅓

standard

Lead-plant
Amorpha canescens

False Indigo
Amorpha fruticosa

FIGURE 54

shaped like arrowheads. There are a few large purple or blue
flowers in each long-stalked raceme. The species is extremely variable in size, in dimensions and texture of leaf segments, and in
hairiness. (Called *L. japonicus* by some authorities.) § Beaches,
in all countries around the North Pole, extending s. along our
coast to N. J. and inland to the Great Lakes. *Fig. 54.*

L. venosus is another variable species. The stem is angular. The
stipules are narrow or broad, asymmetric, seemingly attached at
their midpoints and pointed above and below. The purple flowers
are numerous and crowded in the racemes. § Woods and thickets,
Que. to Sask., s. to Ga., La., and Ark.

L. palustris, also very variable, has fewer leaf segments: from
two to four pairs. The stem often has two thin "wings" along its
length. The stipules vary from narrow to broad, in shape much
like those of *L. venosus,* but sometimes toothed. The racemes have
usually about six red-purple flowers. § Shores and moist thickets
and meadows, around the Pole and s. to N. Y., Mo., and Ore.
Fig. 54.

L. ochroleucus has from two to four pairs of leaf segments. The
stipules are large, toothed, with rounded base. The flowers are
yellowish-white, a few in each short-stalked raceme. § Woodlands,
across Canada and s. to N. Y., Ind., S. D., Ida., and Ore. *Fig. 54.*

LEAD-PLANT and FALSE INDIGO (*Amorpha*)   BLUE OR PUR-
PLE / The genus gets its Latin name, which means "without form,"
from its peculiar flowers. These have only one petal, the standard;
they lack the "form" characteristic of the family. The pod is short,
has only one or two seeds, and does not open. The plants are
shrubby with pinnately divided leaves. The blue or purple flowers
are crowded in long, tapering, spikelike racemes.

A. canescens, lead-plant (3 ft.), is covered with white hairs (it
is "canescent"). The leaf is divided into from 15 to 51 small segments, little more than ½ inch long. A number of racemes are
formed on the upper part of the plant. § Late spring and summer:
prairies and dry open woodlands, Mich. to Sask., s. to Ind., Ark.,
and N. M. *Fig. 54.*

A. fruticosa, false indigo (to 15 ft.), has from 13 to 35 leaf
segments, each up to 2 inches long. The species is very variable in
size and shape of leaf segments and the presence or absence of
hairs. Several racemes are clustered in a compound inflorescence.
(For another false indigo, see *Baptisia.*) § Late spring and summer:
riverbanks, thickets, moist woods, Pa. to Sask., s. to Fla., Tex., and
Mexico. *Fig. 54.*

THE PRAIRIE-CLOVERS (*Petalostemum*)   ROSE-PURPLE OR
WHITE / The flowers of these attractive plants are not typical of the
family. There is a standard. There are nine stamens, all joined;
but only five have anthers. The rose or white flowers are in dense
spikes or heads on thin wiry stems. In our commonest species the

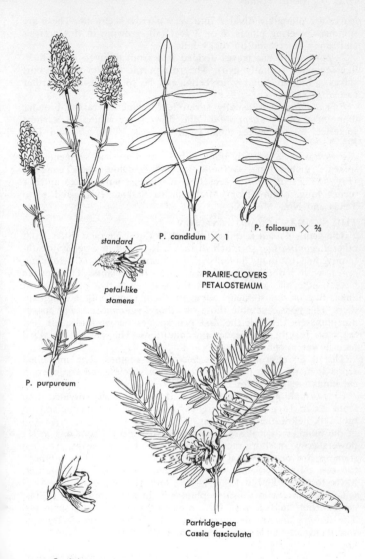

standard

petal-like
stamens

P. candidum × 1

P. foliosum × ⅔

PRAIRIE-CLOVERS
PETALOSTEMUM

P. purpureum

Partridge-pea
Cassia fasciculata

C. nictitans

FIGURE 55

leaves are pinnately divided into very narrow segments. These are summer-flowering plants, 2 or 3 feet tall, growing in dry prairies and sandy places and on rocky hills.

P. purpureum has leaves divided into from three to seven hairlike segments (usually five). The rose-purple flowers are in short spikes. § Ind. to. Alta., s. to Tenn. and N. M.; occasional farther east. *Fig. 55.*

P. candidum has usually seven leaf segments, rather broader than those of *P. purpureum*. The flowers are white, in a short spike less than 2 inches long. § Ind. to Sask., s. to Ala. and Tex. *Fig. 55.*

P. foliosum, a smooth plant with 11 or more leaf segments and spikes 2 inches long, is found in Illinois, Ohio, and Tennessee (*Fig. 55*). *P. villosum,* a densely hairy species with spikes up to 4 inches long, occurs from Michigan to Saskatchewan and s. to Texas and New Mexico.

THE SENNAS (*Cassia*)   YELLOW

The genus *Cassia* is quite different in floral characteristics from other *Leguminosae;* so much so that it is placed in a separate subfamily, and by many botanists, in a distinct family (*Caesalpiniaceae*), with redbud, honey-locust, and other plants. The flowers have five sepals, joined only at the very base, five petals almost alike, five or ten stamens, some of them commonly lacking anthers. The pods resemble those of other *Leguminosae*. The leaves are pinnately divided; the first two species below fold their leaf segments together under certain conditions. The species described here flower in summer.

This is an enormous genus in warmer regions. The medicinal senna is made from the leaves of certain species; and some tropical kinds are grown for ornament.

C. fasciculata, partridge-pea (3 ft.), has leaves divided into from six to 18 pairs of segments, with a saucer-shaped gland on the stalk below the lowest pair. The species is variable especially in the number of leaf segments and in hairiness. From one to six flowers grow in short racemes from the axils of leaves. The ten stamens are nearly equal in length, four having yellow anthers, the rest purple. § Sandy soil, old fields, roadsides, and prairies, Mass. to Minn. and S. D., s. to Fla. and Tex. *Fig. 55.*

C. nictitans, wild sensitive plant (20 in.), is similar to *C. fasciculata* but smaller, with from nine to 20 pairs of leaf segments. The flowers are smaller and have only five stamens. § Dry soil, woodlands, roadsides, etc., Mass. and Vt. to Ind. and Kan., s. to Ga. and Tex. *Fig. 55.*

C. marilandica, wild senna (to 6 ft.), has from three to six pairs of correspondingly large leaf segments, up to 3 inches long, more or less ovate. The leaf stalk bears a cylindric or domelike gland. The racemes of yellow flowers grow from the axils of leaves. The pod is flat, divided into sections that are wider than long. § Dry

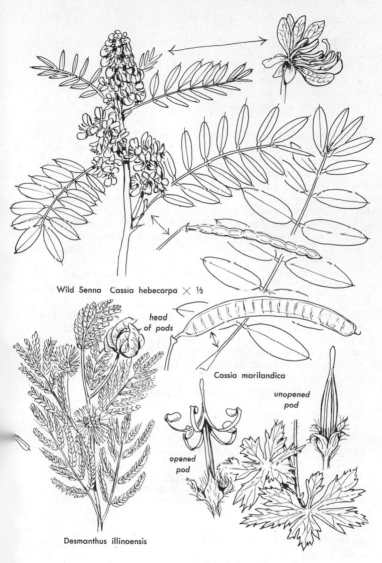

Wild Senna Cassia hebecarpa × ⅓

head
of pods

Cassia marilandica

unopened
pod

opened
pod

Desmanthus illinoensis

Geranium maculatum

FIGURE 56

roadsides and thickets, Pa. to Ia. and Kan., s. to Fla. and Tex. *Fig. 56.*

C. hebecarpa is similar to *C. marilandica,* with narrower, more sharply pointed leaf segments, from five to ten pairs, up to 2 inches long. The gland on the leaf stalk is club-shaped, the broader end uppermost. The flowers are numerous and crowded. The pods are somewhat hairy, divided into sections that are as long as wide or longer. § Moist open woods, N. E. to Wis., s. to N. C. and Tenn. *Fig. 56.*

PRAIRIE-MIMOSA (*Desmanthus illinoensis*)   GREENISH

Desmanthus and *Schrankia* (see below) represent the third subfamily or family (*Mimosaceae*) of the plants here called *Leguminosae.* The group is marked by having many small flowers in close clusters. The stamens are usually numerous, often long, so that the whole flower cluster has the appearance of a mass of colored hairs. Most of the genera include trees, especially in the tropics; the enormous genus *Acacia* belongs here. *Desmanthus illinoensis* (3 ft.) is not entirely typical of the group, for it has only five stamens to a flower. The plant is bushy. Each leaf is pinnately divided into five or more pairs of segments, and each of these is again divided into 20 or more narrow segments. § Summer: banks and prairies, O. to N. D. and Colo., s. to Ala. and Tex. *Fig. 56.*

SENSITIVE BRIER (*Schrankia nuttallii*)   PINK

This is a trailing, tangled plant (to 3 ft.) covered with hooked thorns. The leaves are much like those of *Desmanthus.* The stamens number ten or more to a flower. The pods are long and narrow, angular and covered with thorns. § Summer and early autumn: dry sandy soil, Ill. to Nebr., s. to Ala. and Tex. PLATE 7.

GERANIUM FAMILY (*Geraniaceae*)

The Geranium Family has flowers of great regularity, with all their parts in fives. There are five sepals, five petals, two sets of five stamens each (one set sometimes sterile), and a pistil that separates at maturity into five parts. The household geranium, named *Pelargonium,* belongs to this family; many of its varieties, like so many cultivated plants, do not have the precision of the above scheme. The leaves of our native species tend to be round in outline and lobed, cleft, or divided palmately.

THE CRANE'S-BILLS or WILD GERANIUMS (*Geranium*)

LAVENDER, PURPLE, PINK, OR WHITE / The name crane's-bill comes from the long beak of the pistil which bears the five stigmas. *Geranium* also is from a Greek word meaning "crane." When the fruit is ripe, this beak splits into five outer segments which curl up, each carrying a pod which contains a seed. The leaves are palmately lobed, cleft, or divided.

G. maculatum (2 ft. or more) has several long-stalked leaves

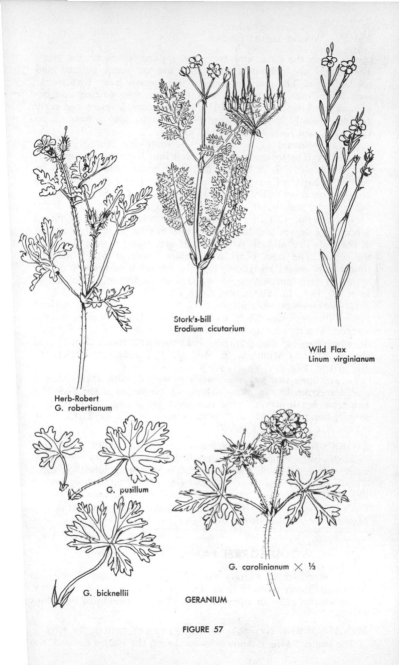

Stork's-bill
Erodium cicutarium

Wild Flax
Linum virginianum

Herb-Robert
G. robertianum

G. pusillum

G. bicknellii

G. carolinianum × ⅓

GERANIUM

FIGURE 57

arising from the base, and two short-stalked leaves on the stem. The blades are palmately cleft into five or seven pointed and toothed lobes. The plant is more or less densely hairy with rather long white hairs. The flowers vary from lavender to rose and occasionally white; they are 1 to 1½ inches across. § Spring and early summer: mostly in woods, also in open fields, Me. to Man., s. to Ga., Ark., and Kan. *Fig. 56* and PLATE 7.

G. carolinianum (2 ft. or more) is somewhat bushier than *G. maculatum*. The leaves are deeply cleft into from five to nine narrow, blunt parts. It is hairy with dense, rather short, whitish or yellowish hairs, often pointing downward. The pink flowers are crowded on short stalks, almost in a head. § Late spring and summer: on dry soil, waste places, etc., throughout. *Fig. 57.*

G. bicknellii (20 in.) somewhat resembles *G. maculatum* in aspect. The leaves are deeply cleft into five parts, mostly rounded at the end. The pink to purple petals are little or no longer than the sepals. The stem bears white hairs, some of which may be tipped with small dark glands (visible through a magnifier). § Late spring to early autumn: open woods and fields, across Canada, s. to N. Y., Ind., Ia., Colo., and Calif. *Fig. 57.*

G. robertianum, herb-Robert (2 ft.), has palmately divided leaves, the segments finely cleft pinnately. The foliage is strong-scented. The flowers are small (about ½ inch across), red-purple or sometimes white. § Spring and summer: rocky woods and shores, Nfld. to Minn., s. to Md., O., Ill., and Nebr.; from the Old World. *Fig. 57.*

G. pusillum (to 2 ft.) is much branched, with leaves deeply cleft into from five to nine parts which are lobed at the end. The numerous small flowers have red-violet petals only about ⅕ inch long. § Summer: fields and waste places, N. E. to B. C., s. to N. C., Ark., and Ore. *Fig. 57.*

STORK'S-BILL (*Erodium cicutarium*)   ROSE-PURPLE

Stork's-bill (16 in.) is distinguished from *Geranium* by its pinnately divided leaves; each segment is pinnately lobed or cleft. The flowers are less than ½ inch wide. The fruit is long-beaked like that of *Geranium*. Spring to autumn and sometimes in winter: fields, roadsides, etc., Que. to Mich., s. to Va., Tenn., Ark., and Mexico; native of Europe. *Fig. 57.*

WOOD-SORREL FAMILY (Oxalidaceae)

The Wood-sorrel Family resembles the Geranium Family in having its flower parts in fives. There are five styles on the ovary. Many species grow in tropical lands. Ours all belong to the genus *Oxalis.*

WOOD-SORREL (*Oxalis*)   YELLOW, VIOLET, WHITE, OR PINK

The genus *Oxalis* is known by its leaves, the blades divided into

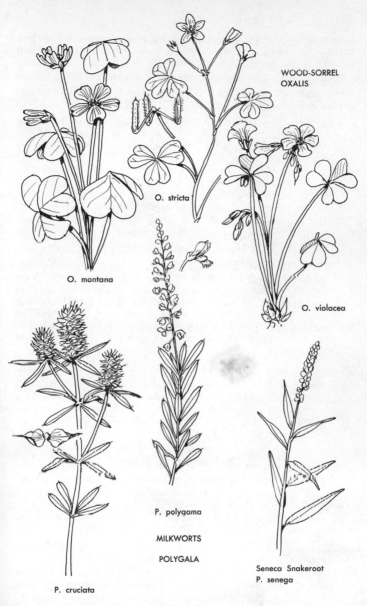

WOOD-SORREL
OXALIS

O. stricta

O. montana

O. violacea

P. polygama

MILKWORTS

POLYGALA

P. cruciata

Seneca Snakeroot
P. senega

FIGURE 58

three, on long stalks; the segments are heart-shaped and at first folded. The fruits are narrow pods, which may "explode" when handled, ejecting the numerous seeds.

I. Species with yellow flowers. These flower from spring to autumn, and are found throughout our range, in dry soil, waste places, etc. (Compare II and III.)

> *O. stricta* (to 20 in.) is known by the position of the pods. Their stalks are bent downward; at the end of each stalk the pod, an inch long, stands erect. The stems often tend to lie on the ground. *Fig. 58.*

> *O. europaea* (to 3 ft.) is extremely variable, and its forms may be found in many parts of the world. It may grow erect or reclining. The fruit stalks are not bent downward.

> *O. repens* sends its leaves and flowers up from a creeping stem. The stipules are broad. The flower stalks are more or less hairy. The fruit stalks are bent down as in *O. stricta.* This is a common weed in lawns and cultivated ground.

II. Species with violet flowers.

> *O. violacea* (8 in.) has leaves and flowering stems growing from a cluster of small bulbs. The under side of the leaves is crimson or violet. When the wind makes the leaves show this color, an expanse of the violet wood-sorrel is a beautiful sight. § Spring and summer: dry open woods, prairies, and old fields, Mass. and Vt. to N. D. and Colo., s. to Fla. and Tex. *Fig. 58.*

III. Species with white or pink flowers.

> *O. montana* is a low creeping plant. The petals are notched, usually white with pink or lavender veins, or all pink. (It is by some considered identical with the European *O. acetosella.*) § Summer: moist woods, chiefly in mountains, across Canada and s. to N. C., Tenn., Mich., and Minn. *Fig. 58.*

FLAX FAMILY *(Linaceae)*

The Flax Family is represented in our area by the genus *Linum.*

FLAX (*Linum*)   BLUE OR YELLOW

Our native species of flax are slender plants with narrow undivided leaves, and flowers in cymes. The flower parts are in fives; there are five styles.

I. Species with blue flowers (compare II).

> *L. lewisii* (2 ft. or more) is a native blue-flowered species, closely resembling garden flax (*L. perenne*), of which it may be a variety. The flowers are about an inch across. § Summer: grasslands and rocky places, Ont. to Wis. and Minn.; doubtfully in W. Va.

II. Species with yellow flowers.

L. virginianum (3 ft. or more) has threadlike branches, which often do not stand erect. § Summer: open woodlands, Me. to Ont. and Ia., s. to Ga. and Tex. *Fig. 57.*

L. medium (2 ft.) has leaves less than an inch long. The branches stand stiffly erect. § Summer: dry open places, Me. to Mich., s. and sw. to Fla. and Tex.

L. striatum (to 4 ft.) is distinguished by the narrow flanges or "wings" that descend, three from each leaf base, on the stem past the next leaf below. § Summer: bogs and moist woods, Mass. to Ont. and Mich., s. and sw. to Fla. and Tex.

MILKWORT FAMILY (*Polygalaceae*)

The *Polygalaceae* form a large family which grows all over the world; but we have only one genus, *Polygala.*

THE MILKWORTS (*Polygala*)   ROSE-PURPLE, PINK, WHITE, YELLOW, OR ORANGE / The flower of Polygala is generally small but complex. There are five sepals, of which the two lateral ones are much larger than the others and generally have the same color as the petals. There are three small petals more or less hidden by the two large sepals. The lowest of the three petals is commonly fringed or "bearded" with a tuft of hairs. There are six or eight stamens, more or less joined together and joined to the petals. The pistil develops into a small two-seeded pod. The flowers in most species are in heads or spikes. Several species have subterranean flowers which form pods without opening. Besides the species described below, several more may be found near our southern and western borders.

I. Species with rose, rose-purple, or magenta flowers (varying to white) (compare II and III).

A. Species with flowers in dense oblong heads (compare B).

P. cruciata (to 1 ft.; flowers purple to greenish-white) has its narrow leaves in fours (forming crosses, whence the name). § Summer and autumn: marshes, bogs, and sandy places, Me. to Minn., s. to Fla. and Tex. *Fig. 58.*

P. sanguinea (18 in.; flowers rose-purple to white and greenish) has leaves singly attached, narrow, bristle-pointed. Otherwise this might well be mistaken for a clover. § Summer and autumn: fields and open woods, N. S. to Minn., s. to S. C. and Okla. PLATE 7.

B. Species with rose, rose-purple or magenta flowers in slender racemes.

P. polygama (1 ft.; flowers pink to rose-purple) has flowers loosely arranged. The leaves are numerous, short, often broader toward the tip. § Summer: dry sandy soil, Que. to Minn., s. to Fla. and Tex. *Fig. 58.*

P. *incarnata* (2 ft.; flowers pale rose or rose-purple) has dense but narrow racemes. The leaves are very small and narrow, and soon fall. § Summer and autumn: barrens and prairies, N. Y. to Wis. and Nebr., s. to Fla. and Mexico.

P. *paucifolia,* flowering-wintergreen or fringed polygala (6 in.; flowers rose-purple), grows from a rhizome. The leaves are broad, and (except for a few scales) are clustered near the top of the stem. The few flowers are large (sometimes an inch long); the fringed lower petal is conspicuous. § Late spring and early summer: rich woods, Que. to Man., s. to Ga., Ill., and Minn. PLATE 8.

II. Species with flowers always white or greenish (or occasionally pale pink).

P. *senega,* seneca snakeroot (15 in.; flowers white), has a slender raceme at the summit of a leafy stem. The leaves are lance-shaped, singly attached. § Summer: rocky places, woods, prairies, etc., Que. to Alta., s. to Ga., Ark., and S. D. *Fig. 58.*

P. *verticillata* (16 in.; flowers white, greenish, or pinkish) has narrow leaves in circles. The flowers are in spikelike racemes on small branches. This is a very variable species. § Summer and autumn: moist sand, grasslands, open woods, Me. to Man., s. to Fla., Tex., and Utah.

III. Species with yellow or orange flowers.

P. *lutea,* yellow bachelor's-buttons (1 ft. or more), has flowers in dense heads. The more or less lance-shaped leaves are singly attached. § Late spring to autumn: moist sand and bogs of the coastal plain, from L. I. to Fla. and La. *Fig. 59.*

TOUCH-ME-NOT FAMILY (*Balsaminaceae*)

The touch-me-nots and their relatives have bilaterally symmetric flowers; one sepal is much larger than the others. There are five stamens and the pod splits into five parts. Most of the species are Asiatic. We have two native species, both inhabitants of wet places throughout our area, flowering all summer and into early autumn.

TOUCH-ME-NOT or JEWEL-WEEDS (*Impatiens*)   ORANGE OR YELLOW / The flower, about an inch long, hangs on a slender stalk; it is composed mostly of one large bell-like sepal which extends horizontally and has a tail-like hollow "spur" at its narrow end. The other two sepals are small and green. From the mouth of the large sepal three petals emerge, one above and two laterally; the lateral petals are two-lobed and may each be two petals joined. (The upper petal has by some been interpreted as a fourth sepal.)

The stamens and pistil are not seen until these parts fall. Both species have bluntly toothed leaves, attached singly. One English name is derived from the pod, which separates at a touch into its five parts, expelling the seeds as the walls curl.

I. capensis, common jewel-weed (to 5 ft.), has orange flowers spotted with reddish-brown. The spur is bent back along the large sepal and is about half its length. Summer: moist woods, Nfld. to Alaska, s. to Fla. and Okla.

I. pallida, pale jewel-weed (to 8 ft.), has yellow flowers, sometimes spotted with red. The spur is less than a third the length of the large sepal, and is bent down more or less at right angles. Wet places, Nfld. to Sask., s. to Ga. and Kan. PLATE 8.

VIOLET FAMILY (*Violaceae*)

The Violet Family contains (in our range) but two genera: *Viola,* the violets, and *Hybanthus,* the green violet. The latter, though unlike the violets in appearance, may be recognized by its pistil as soon as one is familiar with the flower of a violet.

THE VIOLETS (*Viola*)   VIOLET, PURPLE, YELLOW, OR WHITE

Fifty-one species of violets are reported from our area. Some are easy to recognize. Many are variable; and many hybridize, yielding forms that do not fit in any species. Of the difficult and confusing species, a few of the commoner are here described and pictured; for the others a more technical work must be consulted.

The flowers of all species are quite similar. There are five petals, the lowest extended back into a sac or "spur." The two lateral petals usually bear tufts of hair—"beards." Five stamens fit closely around the ovary and style. The style is thickened away from the ovary and ends in a head, which in many species bears a beak pointing downward; at its tip is the small stigma. The fruit is a capsule.

Besides the flowers that are usually seen, many species form others that do not open. These are usually formed later, often near or even under the ground; they form capsules more readily than the open flowers.

All our violets flower in spring (sometimes again in autumn when frosts hold off).

I. Species whose leaves and flower stalks grow from a rhizome (the so-called "stemless violets"; compare II).

A. *V. pedata,* the bird's-foot violet, is perhaps the most beautiful of all violets. The name is from the blades of the leaves, which are cleft palmately into narrow segments like the claws of a bird's foot. In one variety the flowers have the three lower petals of a lilac color (often splotched with purple), the two upper a dark purple (whence the local names velvets and wild pansies). The other variety has all petals lilac. The yellow-orange stamen tips project in the center, around the large beak of the pistil. The all-lilac variety is the commoner in the Atlantic states and the northern Midwest; in other regions the first variety predominates. Unlike most other violets, this species thrives in dry rocky places in the sun. § Mass. and N. H. to Minn. and Kan., s. to Fla. and Mo. PLATE 8.

B. The "blue stemless violets" (the flowers are sometimes white). The flowers are an inch across or more except as noted. (Compare C.)

   V. papilionacea, common blue violet, has heart-shaped leaves, smooth or nearly so. § Fields, woods, banks, etc., Me. to Wyo., s. to Ga. and Okla. PLATE 8.

   V. sororia is similar but downy or woolly. § Moist meadows and woods, Que. to Minn. and S. D., s. to N. C. and Okla.

   V. missouriensis has triangular leaves and flowers of a lighter blue with a white center. § Bottomlands, Ind. to Nebr., s. to Ky. and Tex. *Fig. 59.*

   V. cucullata bears its flowers on long stalks that overtop the leaves. The flowers are light blue or white, with darker veins. The flowers are generally not more than ¾ inch across. § Wet places, Nfld. to Ont., Minn., and Nebr., s. to Ga. and Ark.

   V. triloba has some of its leaves three-lobed. The first leaves of spring are apt to be unlobed, also those that are formed in summer; in summer it is woolly and is easily mistaken for *V. sororia.* One variety has leaves deeply cleft into more than three lobes, and this is almost indistinguishable from the following species. § Woodlands, Vt. to Mo., s. to Ga. and La. *Fig. 59.*

   V. palmata has *all* its leaves, at all seasons, deeply lobed or cleft. It is woolly. § Woodlands, Mass. and N. H. to Minn., s. to Fla. and Miss. *Fig. 59.*

   V. sagittata has spear-shaped leaf blades which are more or less toothed or lobed at the base. § Prairies, open woodlands, meadows, Mass. to Minn., s. to Ga. and Tex. *Fig. 59.*

   V. fimbriatula has rather narrowly ovate, blunt leaf blades, heart-shaped at the base. The flowers are less than an inch across. § Dry fields and slopes, N. S. to Minn., s. to Fla. and La.

C. "Stemless" violets with flowers not blue (but see under B); the petals may be white marked with blue or brownish lines, or yellow.

   V. pallens is a small violet with nearly round leaf blades. The flowers are white, less than ½ inch across. § Wet places, often along streams, across Canada, s. to S. C., Ind., Ia., N. D., and Colo. *Fig. 59.*

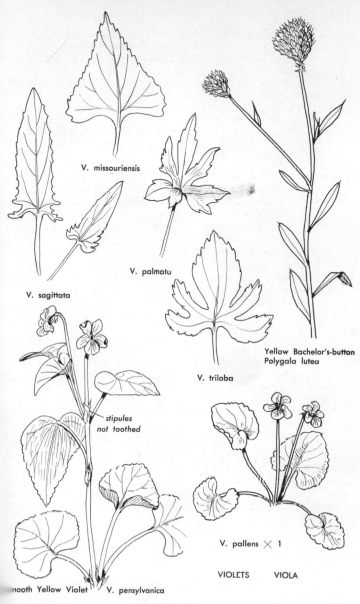

V. missouriensis

V. palmatu

V. sagittata

V. triloba

Yellow Bachelor's-button
Polygala lutea

stipules
not toothed

V. pallens × 1

Smooth Yellow Violet   V. pensylvanica

VIOLETS   VIOLA

FIGURE 59

V. blanda, sweet white violet, is a little larger than the preceding species, with fragrant white flowers about ½ inch across. § Cool, shady places, Que. to Minn., s. to Ga., Ind., and Wis.

V. rotundifolia has yellow flowers about ½ inch across. § Rich woods, Que. to Ont., s. to Ga. and O.

V. lanceolata has narrow lance-shaped leaf blades. The flowers are white with purple lines, about ¾ inch across, the lateral petals usually twisted and without beards. § Moist meadows and swamps, Que. to Minn. and Nebr., s. to Fla. and Tex. PLATE 8.

II. Species with erect stems that bear leaves and flowers.

V. rafinesquii, Johnny-jump-up, has long-stalked flowers, about ⅝ inch across or less, ranging from light blue to white. The stipules are cut into narrow segments. § Fields, etc., N. Y. to Mich. and Kans., s. and sw. to Ga. and Tex. *Fig. 60.*

V. canadensis, Canada violet, has bluish petals, white inside. § Woods, Nfld. to Sask., s. to S. C., Ala., Ia., and Ariz.

V. pensylvanica, smooth yellow violet, has several long-stalked basal leaves. The stipules are not toothed. The pods in one variety are woolly. § Damp woods and bottomlands, Que. to Man., s. to Ga. and Tex. *Fig. 59.*

V. pubescens, downy yellow violet, has generally a single basal leaf, or none. The stipules are scarcely toothed. § Rich woods, N. S. to N. D., s. to Ga. and Okla.

V. striata has cream-colored flowers marked with purple lines. The stipules are toothed. § Woodlands and banks, N. Y. to Minn., s. to Ga. and Ark.

V. conspersa is a very small plant with light blue flowers marked with dark lines and hardly more than ½ inch across. The stipules are toothed. § Woodlands and meadows, mostly in damp places, Que. to Minn., s. to Ga. and Mo.

GREEN VIOLET (*Hybanthus concolor*) GREENISH-WHITE
The green violet is a rather coarse plant (to 3 ft.) with more or less hairy leaves and small green flowers on short stalks hanging from the axils. The whitish petals are scarcely longer than the sepals. The stamens are joined in a sheath around the ovary. The head of the style is like that of a violet. § Spring and early summer: woods and ravines, sometimes in the open, Conn. to Ont. and Mich., s. and sw. to Ga., Ark., and Kan. *Fig. 61.*

SPURGE FAMILY (*Euphorbiaceae*)

The *Euphorbiaceae* are a vast and difficult family, mostly tropical. (Rubber, tapioca, and castor oil are obtained from plants in

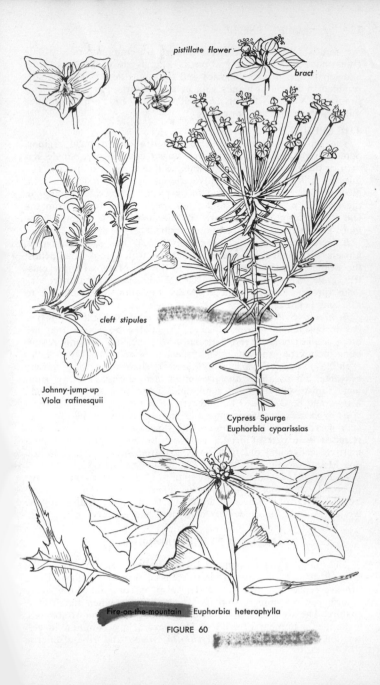

pistillate flower

bract

cleft stipules

Johnny-jump-up
Viola rafinesquii

Cypress Spurge
Euphorbia cyparissias

Fire-on-the-mountain Euphorbia heterophylla

FIGURE 60

this family.) In our species the flowers are staminate or pistillate (none have both stamens and pistils). Petals are generally lacking, and sepals also in some species; but the small flowers may be surrounded by bracts or glands with petal-like parts, the whole cluster simulating a single flower (*Fig. 60*). Many *Euphorbiaceae* have milky juice; many are poisonous.

THE SPURGES (*Euphorbia*)

The spurges are most numerous in dry and tropical regions. Some closely resemble cacti. Each flower consists of a single stamen or pistil, each on its own stalk, without sepals or petals. The juice is milky. Twenty-six native species are known in our area, most of which are weedy and inconspicuous, several creeping on the ground. Besides these about ten species have come from the Old World, some of them now troublesome weeds. A few of the more attractive species are here described.

E. corollata, flowering spurge (to 3 ft.), has each cluster of flowers surrounded by five white bracts which look like petals; the whole is easily mistaken for one flower. Many of these clusters grow in a broad, rather flat inflorescence. § Summer: dry fields, prairies, and woodlands, Mass. to Minn. and Nebr., s. to Fla. and Tex. *Fig. 61.*

E. heterophylla, fire-on-the-mountain, or painted-leaf (to 3 ft.), has inconspicuous flower clusters surrounded by leaves that are often colored pink or red, especially near the base (in this resembling poinsettia, to which this species is related). The leaves ("phylla") are of various ("hetero") shapes, in one variety grasslike, but usually with large blunt teeth or lobes. § Late summer: moist soil, often in sand, and waste places, Va. to Ind., Minn., and S. D., s. to Fla. and Ariz. *Fig. 60.*

E. cyparissias, cypress spurge (2 ft.), is known by its crowded, very narrow, pale green leaves. The flower clusters are each surrounded by a pair of broad, yellowish bracts. § Spring and summer, roadsides and old fields, Me. to Minn. and Colo., s. to Va. and Mo.; from the Old World. *Fig. 60.*

E. marginata, snow-on-the-mountain (2 ft.), is so named for its broad, white-margined leaves. Its flower clusters are surrounded by five petal-like bracts. § Summer: throughout; native to the western United States, widely cultivated and escaped in the East.

MALLOW FAMILY (*Malvaceae*)

The mallows are recognized by the hollow column around the style, formed of the numerous stamens all joined together. There are five sepals and five petals. The pistil is compound, the ovary ring-shaped, of numerous parts which separate when the fruit is mature. The style or styles project through the column of stamens.

Besides a number of wild species, several are common in cultivation, notably hollyhocks (*Althaea rosea*) and rose-of-Sharon

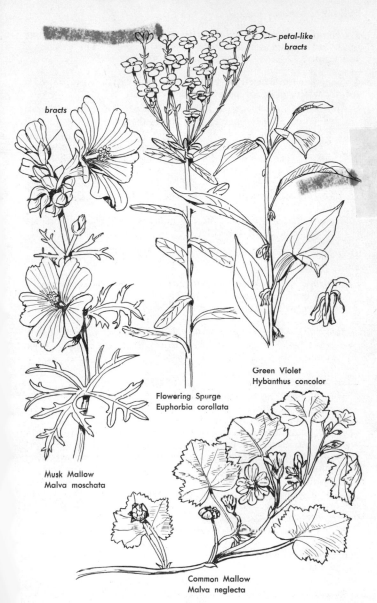

petal-like bracts

bracts

Green Violet
Hybanthus concolor

Flowering Spurge
Euphorbia corollata

Musk Mallow
Malva moschata

Common Mallow
Malva neglecta

FIGURE 61

(*Hibiscus syriaca*); many varieties of *Hibiscus rosa-sinensis* are cultivated farther south. Cotton and okra come from species of this family.

I. Genera with a circle of bracts below the calyx (*Figs. 61, 62*); mostly white, pink, or purple petals (compare II).

> *Malva* has three bracts to a flower. The petals are heart-shaped (notched at the outer edge). The anthers are at the summit of the column.
>
> *Callirhoë* has three bracts in most species. The petals are wedge-shaped (not notched). The anthers are at the summit of the column or on its sides.
>
> *Hibiscus* has generally about 12 bracts, and five united styles. The anthers appear along the sides of the column, not at the tip.
>
> *Althaea* has six or more bracts, many styles. The anthers are at the summit of the column.

II. Genera with no bracts below the calyx (*Fig. 63*); yellow or white petals.

> *Callirhoë,* with white, pink, or purple flowers, has some species with no bracts; see above.
>
> *Abutilon,* with yellow flowers, has broad, velvety leaves, un-lobed.
>
> *Sida,* with white or yellow flowers, has small, smooth leaves, not lobed, or sharply lobed leaves that are woolly when young.

THE MALLOWS (*Malva*)   WHITE, PINK, OR LAVENDER

The mallows have an ovary divided into from 10 to 20 parts. The styles are slender, with the stigma along the side of each, not at the tip. There are three bracts outside the calyx. The leaves of our species are round in outline but many are cut into narrow segments or lobes. All are from the Old World; some have become weeds in this country. The species described below flower in summer and autumn. They grow in waste places.

M. moschata, musk mallow (2–3 ft.), is the most beautiful species, with white to purple flowers 2 inches or more across. The leaves are cut into narrow, toothed segments. § Que. to B. C., s. to Va., Mo., and Nebr. *Fig. 61.*

M. rotundifolia, cheeses, creeps on the ground. The small petals, which project only slightly from the calyx, are pinkish or lavender, sometimes white, with darker lines. The English name applies to the flat, round fruits, which have a pungent taste. The leaves are generally about five- or seven-lobed. § Throughout.

M. neglecta, common mallow or cheeses, is similar to *M. rotundifolia.* It is distinguished by its larger, more conspicuous petals. § Throughout. *Fig. 61.*

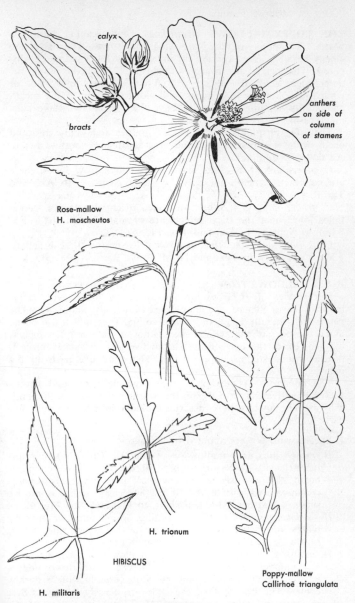

calyx

bracts

anthers
on side of
column
of stamens

Rose-mallow
H. moscheutos

H. trionum

HIBISCUS

H. militaris

Poppy-mallow
Callirhoë triangulata

FIGURE 62

THE POPPY-MALLOWS (*Callirhoë*)   RED-PURPLE, PINK, OR WHITE / The poppy-mallows are American natives. The leaves are chiefly basal, in most species cut into narrow lobes palmately disposed. The petals are nearly straight (not notched) along the outer edge, generally purple or red-purple (sometimes pink or white). The anthers may occur both along the sides of the sheath and at the summit. The styles have the stigma along the side, much as in *Malva*.

These are all plants of dry places, prairies and sandy soil, and occur in the western states of our area and thence southwestward. All flower in summer.

C. *alcaeoides* (1 ft.) has leaves cleft into narrow lobes; there are no bracts beneath the calyx. § Ill. to Nebr., s. to Ala. and Tex.

C. *triangulata* (2 ft.) has undivided, triangular leaves, sometimes lobed near the base. Bracts are present beneath the calyx. § Ind. to Nebr., s. to Ga. and Tex. *Fig. 62.*

C. *involucrata* (1 ft.) has deeply cut leaves and three bractlets. § Mo. to Wyo., s. to Tex. and N. M. PLATE 9.

ROSE-MALLOWS (*Hibiscus*)   PINK, WHITE, OR YELLOW

Our species of *Hibiscus* are mostly coarse plants with large, toothed leaves. There are many bracts, usually about 12. The petals are generally large, of various colors. The anthers are borne along the sides of the stamen sheath, not at the summit, which is toothed. From the end of the sheath five style branches project, bearing round stigmas at their tips. There are five parts to the ovary.

The numerous species of *Hibiscus* include herbs and shrubs (several cultivated), mostly of the warmer parts of both hemispheres. The species here described bloom in late summer and early autumn.

I. Species with flowers about 6 inches across.

H. *moscheutos,* rose-mallow or swamp-rose (to 6 ft.), has unlobed leaves which are smooth above, finely downy underneath with whitish hairs. The very large flower is usually cream-colored with a red or purple center. It has a musky smell. § Marshes, Md. to Ind., s. to Fla. and Ala. *Fig. 62.*

H. *lasiocarpus* (to 6 ft.), a similar rose-mallow of marshy places, has leaves that are downy on the upper side. § Ind. to Mo., s. to Fla. and Tex.

H. *palustris,* swamp-mallow or rose-mallow (to 7 ft.), has usually unlobed leaves which are whitened with down underneath. The flowers are pink or white, usually with a darker center. The branches of the style are densely downy. § Salt marshes and other wet places, Mass. to Mich., s. to N. C. and Ill.

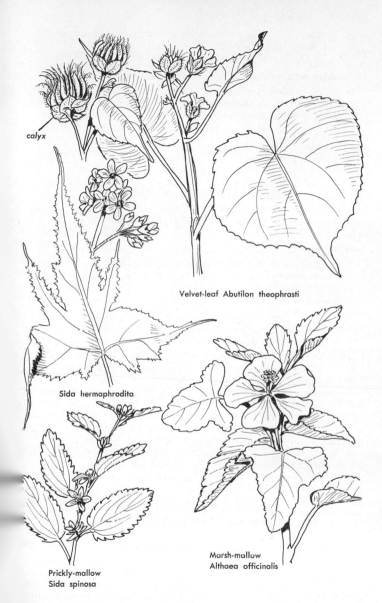

calyx

Velvet-leaf Abutilon theophrasti

Sida hermaphrodita

Prickly-mallow
Sida spinosa

Marsh-mallow
Althaea officinalis

FIGURE 63

H. militaris (to 6 ft.) has distinctive spear-shaped leaves. The pink flowers have dark centers. § Marshes and shallow water, Pa. to O., Minn., and Nebr., s. to Fla. and Tex. *Fig. 62.*

II. Species with flowers not more than 2 inches across.

H. trionum, flower-of-an-hour (2 ft.), has leaves divided into three narrow, toothed segments. The flowers are pale yellow with a purple center; they wither soon after opening. § Fields and roadsides, N. S. to Minn., s. to Fla. and Tex. *Fig. 62.*

MARSH-MALLOW (*Althaea officinalis*)   ROSE

This relative of the hollyhock has been introduced from Europe. The use made of its roots has given the name marshmallow to a popular confection. The plant (to 4 ft.) resembles *Malva* except in having six or more bracts. The flowers are a little over an inch across. The ovary has 16 or more parts, and there are as many styles. § Summer: edges of marshes, Mass. to Mich., s. to Va. and Ark. *Fig. 63.*

VELVET-LEAF (*Abutilon theophrasti*)   YELLOW

Velvet-leaf (3–4 ft.) has broad, heart-shaped leaves with long pointed tips and few or no teeth. Both stem and leaves are softly woolly. The flowers are about an inch wide. There are no bracts. § Summer and autumn: fields and waste places, throughout; native of Asia. *Fig. 63.*

SIDA   YELLOW OR WHITE

Sida is a genus of warm regions, with two species in our range. They have small, pale yellow or white flowers without bracts. The anthers are borne at the summit of the sheath. The five or more styles are tipped with round stigmas.

S. spinosa, prickly-mallow (3 ft.), has slender stems bearing small ovate or lance-shaped leaves with toothed margins, with a spine at the base of each. The yellow flowers are on short stalks in the axils. § Summer and autumn: fields and waste places, Mass. to Nebr., s. to the Gulf; a native of the tropics. *Fig. 63.*

S. hermaphrodita, Virginia-mallow (to 6 ft.), has large leaves deeply cut into from three to seven pointed lobes. The white flowers form a large cluster at the summit. § Summer and early autumn: moist soil, Pa. to Mich., s. to Md. and Tenn.; not common. *Fig. 63.*

ST.-JOHN'S-WORT FAMILY (*Hypericaceae*)

The St.-John's-worts and their relatives compose a small family marked by paired, undivided, toothless leaves which have translucent spots (glands). The petals are generally yellow; stamens are numerous; the ovary has from two to five parts, each with its own style and stigma. The fruit is a small many-seeded pod, generally pointed. *Ascyrum* has four yellow petals; *Hypericum* has five yellow petals; *Triadenum* has five pink or greenish ones.

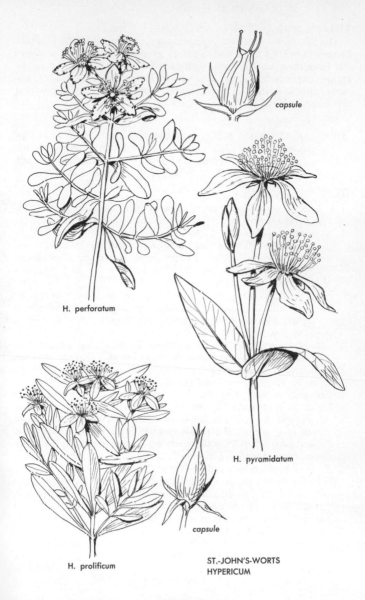

capsule

H. perforatum

H. pyramidatum

H. prolificum

capsule

ST.-JOHN'S-WORTS
HYPERICUM

FIGURE 64

THE ST.-JOHN'S-WORTS (*Hypericum*)   YELLOW

The St.-John's-worts have flower parts in fives and yellow petals. In several species the stamens are in groups or bundles. The ovary has from three to five parts, with as many styles. Separation of the species depends upon the number of styles, arrangement of stamens, characteristics of fruit, and other details. The commonest are here described.

I. Shrubby species.

    H. prolificum (to 6 ft.) is much branched, with a crown of golden flowers. The show of gold is due largely to the numerous erect stamens. § Summer: dry woodlands, open meadows, etc., N. Y. to Minn., s. to Ga. and La. *Fig. 64.*

II. Herbaceous species.

    A. Species with flowers more than ¼ inch across (compare B).

        H. pyramidatum, great St.-John's-wort (to 6 ft.), has flowers up to 2 inches across. As they age the petals roll up lengthwise. The stamens are very numerous, in five bundles. There are five styles. § Late summer: stream sides, moist meadows, and thickets, Me. to Man., s. to Md., O., and Kan. *Fig. 64.*

        H. punctatum (3 ft. or more) has leaves and petals conspicuously marked with black dots (glands). There are three styles. § Early summer: fields and woods, Que. to Minn., s. to Fla. and Tex.

        H. ellipticum (2 ft.) has narrow, flat leaves on usually unbranched stems; it grows from a rhizome. The flowers are about ½ inch across. § Summer: wet places, Nfld. to Man., s. to Md., O., Ia., and N. D.

        H. perforatum, common St.-John's-wort (2 ft. or more), is much branched. The leaves on the branches are about half as long as those on the main stem. The flowers are about an inch across; the petals usually have black dots on the margins. There are three styles. The stamens are in three or more bundles. § Summer: throughout; native of Europe, now a common weed in this country. *Fig. 64.*

    B. Herbaceous species with flowers less than ¼ inch across.

        H. canadense (30 in.) has flowers from ⅙ to ¼ inch across in clusters at the tip of the stem. The leaves are very narrow. § Summer: wet places, Nfld. to Man., s. to S. C., Ala., Ill., and Ia. *Fig. 65.*

        H. mutilum (30 in.) has flowers about ⅙ inch across in clusters at the tips of the stems. There are few stamens. The leaves are short, comparatively broad, with from three to five main veins. § Summer: wet places, Que. to Man., s. to Fla. and Tex. *Fig. 65.*

        H. gentianoides (2 ft.) has minute flowers (⅛ inch across) singly at the tips of numerous branches. The leaves are

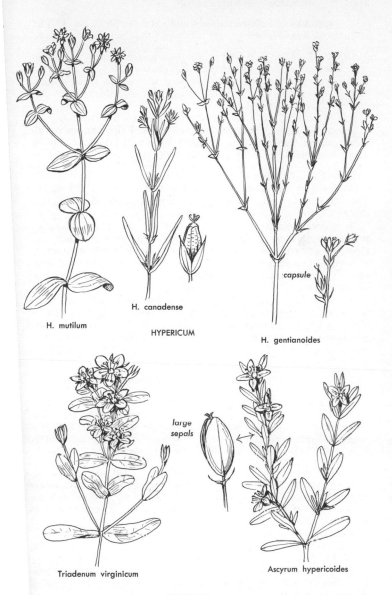

H. mutilum

H. canadense

HYPERICUM

capsule

H. gentianoides

Triadenum virginicum

large sepals

Ascyrum hypericoides

FIGURE 65

scalelike. § Summer: sandy soil, Me. to Minn., s. to Fla. and Tex. *Fig. 65.*

MARSH ST.-JOHN'S-WORT (*Triadenum virginicum*)   PINKISH
Triadenum is distinguished from *Hypericum* chiefly by the pinkish or greenish flowers which have nine stamens in three groups. The leaves are mostly without stalks. (Some authors unite this genus with *Hypericum.*)

T. virginicum (2 ft.) has numerous leaves, to 3 inches long, on a branching stem. The three bundles of stamens alternate with three orange glands. § Late summer: bogs and swamps, Lab. to Minn. and Nebr., s. to Fla. and Miss. *Fig. 65.*

ST.-PETER'S-WORTS (*Ascyrum*)   YELLOW
Ascyrum is distinguished by its four petals and paired sepals. The stamens are numerous and separate. The plants are rather shrubby.

A. hypericoides, St.-Andrew's-cross (3 ft.), has leaves about an inch long, tending to be broader at the end, with rounded tips. One pair of sepals is very small or even lacking. The other pair is large and surrounds the pod. There are two styles. § Late summer: dry, often sandy or rocky places, Mass. to Kan., s. to Fla. and Mexico. *Fig. 65.*

A. stans, St.-Peter's-wort, has leaves about 2 inches long, some of them extending partly around the stem at the base. One pair of sepals is broad, the other narrow. There are three or four styles. § Late summer: woodlands, meadows, and barrens, N. Y. to Mo. and s. to Fla. and Tex.

ROCKROSE FAMILY (*Cistaceae*)

The rockroses have only a superficial resemblance to roses. There are generally five sepals, two of them small or lacking, and three or five petals. The stamens are usually numerous. The fruit is a small pod with many seeds. Our species have small leaves, mostly singly attached, or scalelike and crowded.

FROSTWEED (*Helianthemum canadense*)   YELLOW
Frostweed (1 ft. or more) has a branched stem bearing singly attached leaves about an inch long. The flowers are usually single at the ends of branches, about an inch across. After these have bloomed, numerous flowers without petals are formed on short branches. Late in autumn crystals of ice may be seen in cracks of the stems. § Late spring and early summer: dry open places, N. S. to Minn., s. to N. C., Tenn., and Mo. PLATE 9.

H. bicknellii is a similar species with flowers in a raceme. Several species, with flowers of various colors, are in cultivation, especially in rock gardens.

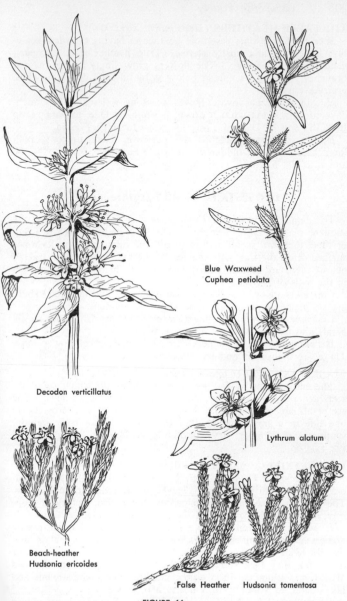

Blue Waxweed
Cuphea petiolata

Decodon verticillatus

Lythrum alatum

Beach-heather
Hudsonia ericoides

False Heather   Hudsonia tomentosa

FIGURE 66

THE FALSE HEATHERS (*Hudsonia*)   YELLOW

Species of *Hudsonia* resemble heather in having crowded, scale-like leaves on low bushy stems. (True heather is a European genus, in the *Ericaceae*.) The flowers grow singly at the ends of branches. The species named below grow on sand dunes, beaches, prairies, barrens.

H. tomentosa has ovate leaves reaching a length of ⅛ inch, covered by a dense whitish down. § Summer: Que. to Alta., s. to Ind., Ill., and N. D., and along the coast to N. C. *Fig. 66.*

H. ericoides, beach-heather, has narrower leaves up to ¼ inch long, green and not hidden by down. § Summer: Nfld. to N. H. and s. to Va. *Fig. 66.*

LOOSESTRIFE FAMILY (*Lythraceae*)

The petals and sepals of *Lythraceae* vary from three to six; the stamens may be more numerous. The base of the flower is a cup or tube, the pistil seated within it and the other parts on its inner surface or on the rim. Our species are herbs. Besides those treated below, there are several weedy genera with inconspicuous flowers in the axils of leaves.

Cuphea is sticky. The flower base is tubular and lopsided. There are six petals of unequal length, about 12 stamens.

Lythrum has a tubular flower base. There are from four to six petals and usually twice as many stamens.

Decodon has a cup-shaped, almost hemispherical flower base. There are five petals and ten stamens.

BLUE WAXWEED (*Cuphea petiolata*)   PURPLE

The entire plant (1 ft.) bears sticky hairs, to which small insects generally adhere. The flowers are in the axils of leaves. The six petals are unequal. The long tubular flower base projects on one side in a small sac, so that the flower is not truly radially symmetric. § Summer: dry woodlands, N. E. to Ia., s. to Ga. and La. *Fig. 66.*

LOOSESTRIFE (*Lythrum*)   PURPLE

Our species of *Lythrum* are tall slender herbs with usually red-purple flowers in the axils of leaves or in long terminal spikes. The English name may be misleading, being also, and more properly, applied to *Lysimachia* in the Primrose Family.

L. salicaria, common purple loosestrife (5 ft.), has red-purple flowers in long spikes; there are from four to six petals and usually twice as many stamens. The narrow leaves are paired or in circles; they lack stalks. § Summer: introduced from the Old World, now abundant in swampy meadows and along streams and lakes, Nfld. to Minn., s. to Va. and Mo. PLATE 9.

L. alatum (4 ft.) has four-angled stems. The leaves are paired or single, generally ovate. The flowers are in the axils of leaves. § Summer: wet open places, Ont. to B. C., s. to Ga., La., and Tex.; N. E. and N. J. *Fig. 66.*

WATER-WILLOW (*Decodon verticillatus*) LAVENDER
Water-willow is so named for the shape of its leaves, which are mostly in circles of three or four. The slender stem (to 8 ft.) usually arches. The flowers are crowded in the axils of the leaves. There are five petals and ten stamens rising from the almost globular flower base. § Summer: swamps and pools, N. S. to Minn., s. to Fla. and La. *Fig. 66.*

GROUP III OF DICOT FAMILIES. PETALS SEPARATE; OVARY INFERIOR

A. Succulent plants with one style to a flower and numerous stamens, sepals, and petals.
   The **Cactus Family** has one representative scattered through our range.

B. Plants with one style to a flower; flowers not in umbels; mostly four petals (some genera have two or five). (Compare C.)
   The **Melastome Family** has leaves with conspicuous lengthwise veins. Our species have eight stamens. The anthers open by pores in the end instead of by slits.
   The **Evening-primrose Family** has flowers in racemes or in the axils. The stamens are of the same number as the petals or twice as many. The anthers open by slits.
   The **Dogwood Family** (as represented by one herbaceous species in our range) has a head of small flowers surrounded by four petal-like white bracts. The flowers are succeeded by red stone fruits.

C. Plants with more than one style to a flower; the flowers in umbels; five petals.
   The **Parsley Family** has two styles. The leaves are mostly divided, attached singly, with wide membranes sheathing the stem. The fruit is a pod which splits into two halves.
   The **Ginseng Family** has two or five styles. Those with two styles have divided leaves in circles. The fruit is a berry.
   The **Saxifrage Family** includes some genera with a partly inferior ovary.

CACTUS FAMILY (*Cactaceae*)

This family is well known in the southwestern United States and Mexico, where some species reach great sizes. In our range only one species is widespread, though a few others may be found on our western borders.

PRICKLY-PEAR (*Opuntia compressa*)   YELLOW
The stem is composed of thick, oval joints, about 3 inches long; they are sometimes mistaken for leaves. Evenly spaced over these joints are tufts of small, brown, barbed hairs which are easily detached and become embedded in the skin at a touch, often leading to a painful inflammation. At the same points there may be one or two long, sharp spines, looking more dangerous but actually less so. The flowers are large and beautiful, 2 or 3 inches across, with bright petals and numerous stamens. The fruit is red, juicy and sweet, edible if the little barbed hairs are removed. § Early summer: rocky or sandy places, Mass. to Minn., s. to Ga., Miss., and Okla. *Fig. 67*.

MELASTOME FAMILY (*Melastomataceae*)

The melastomes form an enormous family, almost entirely tropical. They have four or five sepals and petals on a cup-shaped or tubular base, twice as many stamens, one pistil. The anthers open by a hole in the end. The leaves are characteristically marked with strong veins running from base to apex. We have but one genus in our range.

MEADOW BEAUTY (*Rhexia*)   CRIMSON, ROSE, OR WHITE
The species of *Rhexia* have four sepals, four petals, eight stamens, all seated on a tubular base which lasts into the fruiting stage with the ovary within it. The anthers are slim and curved, presenting a characteristic appearance.
R. virginica (3 ft.) has four "wings"—thin ridges—lengthwise on the stem. The leaves are bristly, stalkless, round at the base, sharply toothed, with generally three main veins. The petals are crimson. § Summer: moist sandy and peaty places, N. S. to Ont. and Wis., s. to Ga. and Okla. *Fig. 67*.
R. mariana (2 ft.) has a four-sided or almost round stem with no "wings." The leaves are narrow at the base, with short stalks, toothed and veined much as in *R. virginica*. The petals are rose or white. § Summer: wet sand and peat, mostly near the coast, Mass. to Va. and Fla.; se. Mo. to La. and Tex.; Ky. *Fig. 67*.

EVENING-PRIMROSE FAMILY (*Onagraceae*)

The *Onagraceae* have mostly four-parted flowers (in a few species they are two- or five-parted). The stamens equal or double the petals in number; the stigma may be two- or four-branched. The ovary is inferior, generally forming a narrow pod. The leaves are undivided and unlobed, mostly without stalks. Many species grow in wet places.

Some Genera of *Onagraceae*
I. Two genera have a hollow tube surmounting the inferior ovary

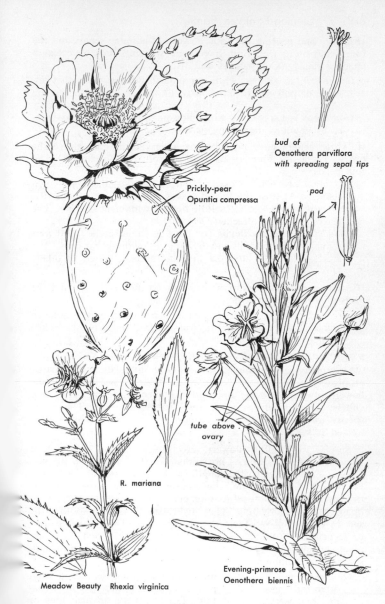

bud of
Oenothera parviflora
with spreading sepal tips

Prickly-pear
Opuntia compressa

pod

tube above
ovary

R. mariana

Evening-primrose
Oenothera biennis

Meadow Beauty Rhexia virginica

FIGURE 67

(*Fig. 67*) and bearing the four downward-pointing sepals and the four petals on its rim. Both have eight stamens. Both have leaves attached singly. (Compare II and III.)

> *Oenothera* has yellow, white, or pinkish flowers; those that are white or pinkish are quite large (2 inches across) (*Figs. 67, 68*).
>
> *Gaura* has red, pink, or white flowers with narrow petals generally about ¼ inch long or less (*Fig. 69*).

II. Three genera have no tube, or a very short one, above the ovary. There are four sepals (not sharply bent backward) and four petals.

> *Epilobium* has white, rose, or purplish petals; there are eight stamens. At least the lowest leaves are paired (*Figs. 69, 70*).
>
> *Jussiaea* (*decurrens*) has yellow flowers with eight stamens. The leaves are singly attached (*Fig. 70*).
>
> *Ludwigia* has yellow petals (or none in some species) and four stamens. The pod is usually angled, with four ridges. The leaves are singly attached in some species, paired in others (*Fig. 71*).

III. One genus has a short ovary with no tube above it, and the parts of the flower in twos.

> *Circaea* has two backward-pointing sepals, two deeply notched petals (looking like four), two stamens, and a two-branched stigma (*Fig. 71*).

EVENING-PRIMROSES and SUNDROPS (*Oenothera*)   YELLOW, WHITE, OR PINK / Evening-primroses bear no relation to the true primroses of the genus *Primula*. As their name indicates, the flowers of some species open in the evening, fading next day. Others, called sundrops, open only in the sunshine. The many species form several distinct groups, which some botanists have treated as separate genera.

I. Species with yellow flowers, erect buds, a long hollow tube above the inferior ovary, a horizontal position of seeds in the pod (i.e., at right angles to the length of the pod). (Compare II, III, IV, and V.) This group, the evening-primroses proper, is extremely complex; some of its members have been extensively used in experimental breeding. They hybridize in nature, so that the species cannot be satisfactorily distinguished. The following may be recognized, but intermediate plants may be expected. They are plants mainly of roadsides and waste places, blooming from midsummer into autumn.

> *O. biennis* (to 6 ft.), common evening-primrose, has a stem often red-tinged. The sepals have narrow tips that are separate but parallel in the bud. The petals are an inch long or less. § Throughout. *Fig. 67*.

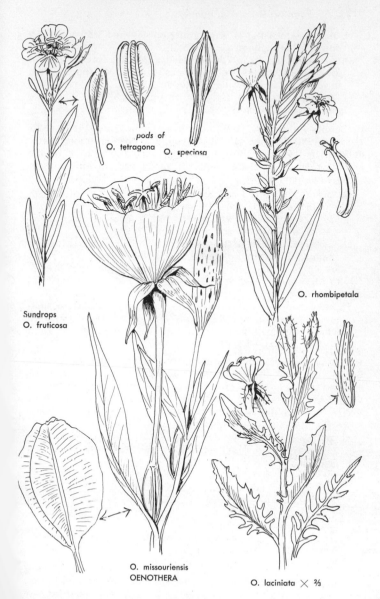

pods of
O. tetragona   O. speciosa

O. rhombipetala

Sundrops
O. fruticosa

O. missouriensis
OENOTHERA

O. laciniata × ⅔

FIGURE 68

O. strigosa (to 6 ft.) is very similar but covered with a grayish down. § Throughout.

O. parviflora (to 30 in.) has sepal tips that are spread apart in the bud. The petals are little more than ½ inch long. § Nfld. to Mont., s. to N. J. and Ill. *Fig. 67.*

O. cruciata (to 3 ft.) also has separate sepal tips. The very narrow petals form a cross. § N. E. to Mich.

II. Species with yellow flowers (some very pale), erect buds, seeds at an angle to the long axis of the pod. The pods are more nearly uniform in thickness throughout their length than those of the preceding group. All are plants of sandy soil, blooming from spring to autumn.

O. laciniata (1–2 ft.) has leaves with more or less prominent marginal teeth or lobes. The petals are typically less than ½ inch long, but one variety has petals over an inch long. § Mass. to N. D., s. to Fla. and Tex. *Fig. 68.*

O. rhombipetala (to 3 ft.) has narrow downy leaves with few or no teeth and many flowers in a terminal spike. The petals are up to an inch long. The pod is usually curved. § N. Y. to Minn. and S. D., s. to Fla. and Tex. *Fig. 68.*

O. humifusa (the spreading stems up to 15 inches long) is very densely downy with white hairs. The leaves may have shallow lobes or none. The petals do not exceed ½ inch in length. The pod is hairy, curved. § Along the coast from N. J. to Fla. and La.

III. Species with yellow petals mostly about an inch long, erect flower buds (but the entire flower cluster droops at first in *O. perennis*), a square pod ribbed at the corners, and seeds not in definite rows. The leaves are more or less lance-shaped, plain or nearly so along the edges. The plants grow in open woods and fields, flowering in summer. These are the sundrops.

O. tetragona (3 ft.) is very variable. The oblong pods bear hairs tipped with small glands. § Conn. to Mich., s. to Ga. and Tenn. *Fig. 68.*

O. perennis (2 ft.) has narrow leaves and petals less than ½ inch long. § Nfld. to Man., s. to N. C., O., and Mo.

O. pilosella (2 ft.) may be distinguished by its hairy stem. It has numerous flowers in a compact cluster. § Ont. to Mich. and Ia., s. to Va. and Ark.

O. fruticosa (spreading, to 3 ft.) usually has very short hairs lying more or less flat. The pod tapers downward to a sort of stalk. § N. E. to Mich., s. to Fla. and Okla. *Fig. 68.*

IV. Species with drooping buds and white or pink petals.

O. speciosa (2 ft.) has narrow sepals and delicately colored petals an inch or more long. The pod has eight ribs. § Summer: prairies and waste places, Mo. and Kan. to Tex. and

seed

four-lobed stigma

Fireweed
Epilobium angustifolium

Gaura biennls

FIGURE 69

Mexico; escaped from cultivation e. to Va. and Fla. *Fig. 68* and PLATE 9.

V. Species with yellow petals 2 inches long or more, erect buds.

O. *missouriensis* (to 20 in.) has erect buds, narrow sepals spotted with red in the bud, large yellow petals on a tube which may be 6 inches long. The pod is square in section with four thin "wings" projecting from the angles. § Summer: barrens and prairies, Ill. to Colo., s. to Tex. *Fig. 68.*

GAURA   RED, PINK, OR WHITE
This is a western genus with a few species in the eastern states. These are tall, straggly-branching plants with small leaves attached singly and small pink or white flowers in long spikes. There are four petals and eight stamens on the end of a tube which extends beyond the ovary. There are few seeds in the pod.

G. *biennis* (5 ft.) has petals about ¼ inch long. § Late summer: prairies and open woodlands, Que. to Minn., s. to N. C. and Tex. *Fig. 69.*

G. *parviflora* (to 6 ft.) is similar, softly downy all over, with very long spikes of flowers. The petals are only about $\frac{1}{12}$ inch long. § Summer: dry open places, Ind. to Wash., s. to Ia. and N. M.

G. *coccinea* (1 ft.) is branched from the base. The petals are up to ¼ inch long. § Summer: dry prairies, Ind. to Ia. and Alta., s. to Mo., Okla., Tex., and Calif.

THE WILLOW-HERBS and FIREWEEDS (*Epilobium*)   ROSE OR WHITE / The four petals of most species of *Epilobium* are rose-pink. The sepals may also be tinged with the same color. The pod is long and very narrow; it may be mistaken for a leafless and flowerless stalk. The ripened seeds have a tuft of hair at one end. The following are the commonest of the 15 or 20 species found in our area.

I. Species with stigmas divided into four branches (compare II).

E. *angustifolium,* common fireweed (to 6 ft.), has rounded petals about ½ inch long. The flowers are in an open, spike-like raceme. The English name is derived from the prevalence of the species in burned areas. § Summer: throughout Canada, s. to Md., O., Ill., Kan., S. D., Ariz., and Calif. *Fig. 69.*

E. *hirsutum* (3 ft.) branches widely. The petals are less than ½ inch long; each is notched so that there appear to be eight. The whole plant is softly hairy. § Late summer: usually in wet places, Que. to Ont. and Mich., s. to N. Y., O., and Ill.; introduced from Europe. PLATE 9.

II. Species with more or less club-shaped stigmas.

E. *strictum* (2 ft.) has narrow leaves without marginal teeth. The petals are less than ½ inch long. The plant is downy.

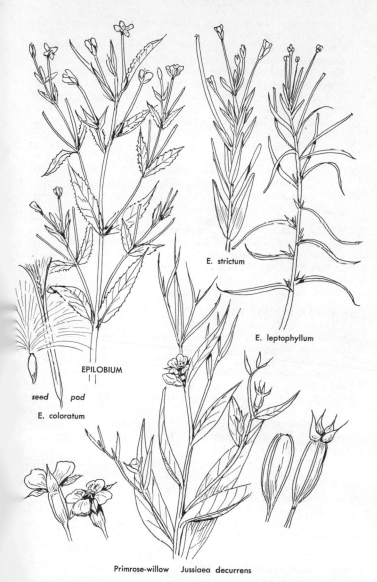

EPILOBIUM

seed   pod

E. coloratum

E. strictum

E. leptophyllum

Primrose-willow   Jussiaea decurrens

FIGURE 70

§ Summer to autumn: wet places, Que. to Minn., s. to Va., O., and Ill. *Fig. 70.*

E. leptophyllum (2 ft.) has very narrow leaves which are densely downy on the upper side; they have no teeth. There are often tufts of small leaves in the axils. The petals, usually white, are not more than ¼ inch long. § Summer to autumn: wet places, Que. to Alta., s. to Va., O., Kan., and Utah. *Fig. 70.*

E. coloratum (3 ft.) has sharply toothed leaves. The pink or white petals are less than ¼ inch long. The hairs on the seeds are cinnamon-colored. § Late summer: moist soil, Que. to Minn. and S. D., s. to Ga., Ala., Ark., and Kan. *Fig. 70.*

E. adenocaulon is distinguished from *E. coloratum* mainly by the seeds, which have whitish hairs, but also by the leaves, which generally have fewer teeth. § Summer: throughout except in the South.

PRIMROSE-WILLOW (*Jussiaea decurrens*)   YELLOW
This is neither a primrose nor a willow. *J. decurrens* (3 ft.) has square stems, the edges of the leaves running down ("decurrent") into the sharp corners. The leaves are narrow. The flowers grow on long stalks from the axils. § Summer: swamps or shallow water, Md. to Mo., s. to Fla. and Tex. *Fig. 70.*

THE FALSE LOOSESTRIFES (*Ludwigia*)   YELLOW
There are many species of this genus, which is distinguished mainly by four usually yellow petals (when there are any) and four stamens. Some are aquatic.

L. alternifolia, seedbox (3 ft.), has leaves singly attached. The small flowers, less than ¼ inch across, are on very short stalks in the axils. The English name describes the fruit, which is short and square. § Summer: swamps and other wet places, Mass. to Mich., s. and sw. to Fla. and Tex. *Fig. 71.*

L. sphaerocarpa (3 ft.) is similar but the leaves are narrower and there are usually no petals. § Summer: wet places, Mass., s. to Fla. and Tex.; Ind.; Mich.

L. polycarpa (3 ft.) has minute greenish petals or none. The flowers are without stalks. The leaves, which are narrow, are attached singly. § Summer: swamps and wet prairies, N. E. to Minn., s. to Tenn. and Kan.

L. palustris, water-purslane, has paired leaves on stems that tend to lie prostrate, often rooting at the joints. The petals are minute or lacking. § Summer and autumn: wet mud or shallow water, N. S. to Ore., s. to Fla. and Mex. *Fig. 71.*

ENCHANTER'S NIGHTSHADES (*Circaea*)   WHITE
These small plants are distinguished by having only two petals (white) and two sepals. The petals are deeply notched and so may be mistaken for four. The flowers are in racemes. The leaves

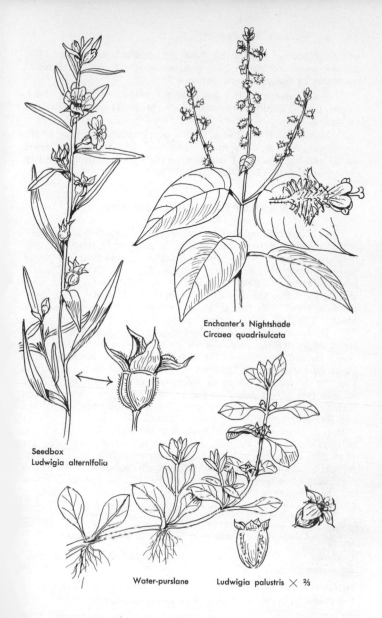

Enchanter's Nightshade
Circaea quadrisulcata

Seedbox
Ludwigia alternifolia

Water-purslane   Ludwigia palustris $\times$ ⅔

FIGURE 71

which are broad toward the base and pointed, are paired. The inferior ovary forms an oval pod covered with hooked bristles; the stalks of the pods turn downward.

C. quadrisulcata (3 ft.) has a round, two-lobed stigma, and a ridged pod. § Summer: woods, N. S. to N. D., s. to Ga. and Okla. *Fig. 71.*

C. alpina (to 1 ft.) has a stigma deeply cleft into two. There are fewer flowers than in *C. quadrisulcata.* § Summer: moist woods and bogs, across Canada, s. to N. Y., Ind., and Ia., and in the mountains to Ga., Utah, and Wash.

PARSLEY FAMILY *(Umbelliferae)*

The Latin name means "umbrella-carriers"; almost all the genera of this family bear their flowers in umbels. In most, the umbels are compound: the primary branches (rays) bear not single flowers but smaller, secondary umbels (*Figs. 73, 74*). The family may be recognized also by its leaf stalks, which embrace the stem usually by a thin sheath (*Figs. 75, 76*). The leaf blades are commonly divided. The five sepals are minute, sometimes practically absent. The five petals mostly curve inward at their tips (*Fig. 75*). There are five stamens, and two styles rising from the inferior ovary. (What looks like a superior ovary in the flower is really the swollen base of the style.) The genera are most accurately characterized by their small, generally flat or narrow fruits (see the drawings), which at maturity separate from the bottom up into two halves joined at the tip to a stalk that rises between them; each half contains one seed. The fruits are variously ribbed and through them run tubes which contain oil.

It is a large family, worldwide but most characteristic of the temperate zones. It includes a number of species cultivated for vegetables or herbs: parsley, parsnip, carrot, celery, dill, caraway, fennel; but some wild species are extremely poisonous. More than 50 genera have been reported in our area. Those described below are the commonest. For plants that do not fit any of the descriptions the more technical books must be consulted.

Guide to the Commoner Genera of *Umbelliferae*

I. Genus with flowers densely massed in heads instead of umbels: *Eryngium* (*Fig. 72*). (Compare II and III.)

II. Genus with round, undivided leaves on long stalks. Plants of wet places: *Hydrocotyle* (*Fig. 72*).

III. Genera with flowers in umbels and divided leaves. Most genera belong here (18 in this book).

A. Genera with white or greenish flowers (occasionally purple-tinged; see *Thaspium* under III B).

1. Genera with white or greenish flowers and palmately divided leaves, the segments toothed or cleft but not themselves divided (*Fig. 73*). (Compare 2 and 3.)

Sanicula has primary rays of various lengths in one umbel. The sepals are relatively long. The fruit is bristly.

Cryptotaenia has uniform rays. The sepals are practically lacking. The fruit is smooth.

2. Genera with white or greenish flowers and pinnately divided leaves, the segments not themselves divided (*Fig. 74*). More or less aquatic plants.

Berula has short, broad, scalloped segments on the lower leaves; those of the upper leaves are jagged. The fruit has very narrow ribs.

Sium has narrow segments on all leaves, evenly toothed. The fruit has conspicuous ribs.

Oxypolis has very varying leaves (*Fig. 74*). The fruit has flanges or "wings" at the edges. There are few or no bracts.

3. Genera with white or greenish flowers and leaves divided into segments that are themselves divided (*Figs. 75–79*). Nine genera are here treated.

Daucus has bracts divided into very narrow segments. The fruit is bristly (*Fig. 75*).

Conioselinum has parsley-like leaves, few or no bracts. The fruit is narrow, smooth (*Fig. 75*).

Heracleum has enormous leaves and may be 10 feet tall. The petals are notched and of various lengths (*Fig. 76*).

Osmorhiza has licorice-smelling roots. The narrow fruits have bristles which lie flat against the ribs (*Fig. 76*).

Erigenia flowers very early in spring, when the one or two basal leaves are only half-grown. The fruit is round and flat (*Fig. 77* and PLATE 9).

Chaerophyllum has parsley-like leaves. The umbel has only three or four primary rays which bear a few flowers on very short stalks (*Fig. 77*).

Cicuta has sharp-pointed, narrow leaf segments, with widely separated marginal teeth. The ribs of the fruit are thick and flat (*Fig. 77*).

Conium has parsley-like leaves and a few small bracts around the umbel. The fruits have wavy ribs at least when young (*Fig. 78*).

Angelica has leaf segments without stalks, seated on the very large sheaths around the stem; the uppermost leaves may consist of sheaths only. The plants may be 6 feet tall (*Fig. 78*).

B. Genera with yellow (or cream-colored) flowers.

Taenidia has long-stalked leaves, much divided, the ultimate segments without teeth (*Fig. 78*).

Zizia has a stalkless flower in the middle of each umbel. The leaf segments are toothed (*Fig. 79*).

Thaspium has all flowers stalked. The fruit bears thin "wings" instead of ribs (*Fig. 79*). One variety has greenish or purple flowers.

Pastinaca has leaves pinnately divided, the coarsely toothed segments perhaps cleft but not again divided (*Fig. 80*).

ERYNGO or RATTLESNAKE-MASTER (*Eryngium yuccifolium*)

GREEN / The species of *Eryngium* are *Umbelliferae* without umbels. The structure of flower and fruit places them in the Parsley Family, but the flowers are closely massed in heads which suggest some relative of the sunflower family. One sees only the green bracts. This species (3–4 ft.) is a stiff, usually prickly plant. The leaves are undivided, up to 3 feet long, narrow, usually with spinelike teeth on the margins. § Summer and autumn: open woodlands and prairies, s. Conn., N. J.; O. to Minn., s. to Fla. and Tex. *Fig. 72.*

THE WATER-PENNYWORTS (*Hydrocotyle*)   WHITE

They are called pennyworts ("penny-plants") from their round leaf blades. Our species grow in marshes and on wet soil, where the stems creep or float, sending up the long-stalked leaves and the flowering branches. The fruits are round and flat, with strong curved ribs.

H. americana has tiny flowers growing from the axils of leaves, with almost no stalks. The leaves are shaped much like those of the household geranium, *Pelargonium,* deeply notched at one side. § Summer and early autumn: Nfld. to Minn., s. to Va. and Tenn. and in the mountains to N. C. *Fig. 72.*

H. umbellata has usually simple umbels with sometimes as many as 100 flowers all forming a dome-shaped cluster. The round leaf blades are not deeply notched, and the stalks are attached to the middle of the disk. § Summer and early autumn: N. S. to Minn., s. to Fla. and Mexico. *Fig. 72.*

H. verticillata has leaves similar to those of *H. umbellata.* The inflorescence is in several stories: that is, from the center of an umbel rises a stem that bears another umbel, and so on. § Summer: near the coast from Mass. to Fla. and Tex.; Mo., Okla., Utah, and Ore. *Fig. 72.*

THE BLACK SNAKEROOTS (*Sanicula*)   GREENISH OR YELLOW

The genus *Sanicula* is characterized by small greenish-white or yellow flowers with narrow sepals as long as the petals; by irregular umbels, the rays being of different lengths; by the broad toothed leaf segments all arising palmately from the end of th stalk; and by round or oval, bristly fruits. Some of the flower have only stamens; others have both stamens and pistil. The fo

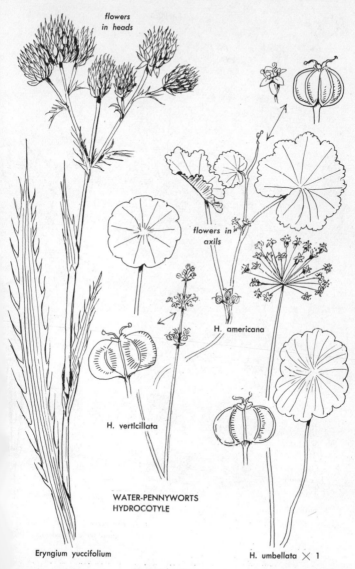

flowers
in heads

flowers in
axils

H. americana

H. verticillata

WATER-PENNYWORTS
HYDROCOTYLE

Eryngium yuccifolium

H. umbellata × 1

FIGURE 72

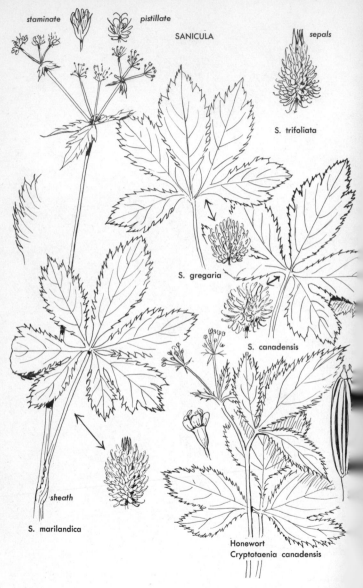

staminate   pistillate   SANICULA   sepals

S. trifoliata

S. gregaria

S. canadensis

S. marilandica

sheath

Honewort
Cryptotaenia canadensis

FIGURE 73

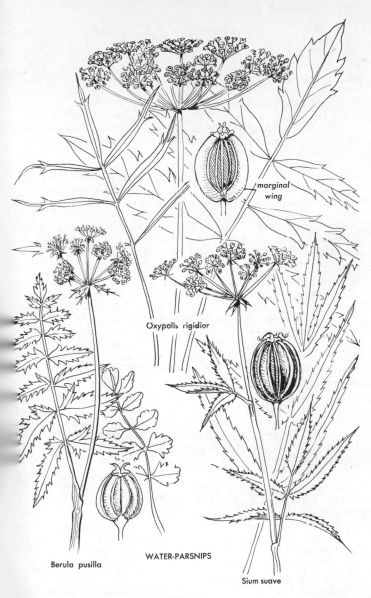

marginal
wing

Oxypolis rigidior

WATER-PARSNIPS

Berula pusilla

Sium suave

FIGURE 74

mer usually have much longer stalks than the latter (which may have none).

S. marilandica (to 5 ft.) has five leaf segments, the two at the base cleft so that there seem to be seven. The flowers are nearly white; those with pistils have no stalks. The styles on the fruits are longer than the bristles. § Late spring and summer: woodlands, Nfld. to B. C., s. to Ga., Kan., and N. M. *Fig. 73.*

S. gregaria (3 ft.) is very like *S. marilandica* but may have three or five leaf segments. The flowers are yellowish, those with pistils on short stalks. § Spring and summer: woodlands, Que. to Minn. and S. D., s. to Fla., La., and Kan. *Fig. 73.*

S. trifoliata (3 ft.) has leaves divided into three, the lateral segments cleft so that there seem to be five. The flowers are white; those with pistils have no stalks. The sepals remain on the fruit, forming a distinct beak which is longer than the bristles. § Summer: N. B. to Minn. and s. to N. C. and Tenn. *Fig. 73.*

S. canadensis (30 in.) has leaves and flowers like those of *S. trifoliata,* but the pistillate flowers have short stalks. The sepals are shorter than the bristles. § Late spring and summer: Mass. and N. H. to Minn., s. to Fla. and Tex. *Fig. 73.*

HONEWORT (*Cryptotaenia canadensis*)   WHITE
Honewort (30 in.) somewhat resembles *Sanicula* but is easily distinguished by the lack of visible sepals, the rays of uniform length, and the smooth, slim, dark fruit. The leaves are palmately divided into three; the segments are toothed on the edges. This has been known as wild chervil (see also *Chaerophyllum*) and used for seasoning as chervil is. § Summer and early autumn: woodlands, N. B. to Man., s. to Ga. and Tex. *Fig. 73.*

WATER-PARSNIP (*Berula pusilla*)   WHITE
Berula pusilla (3 ft.) is a slender plant. The leaves are pinnately divided, the segments of the lower leaves short and scalloped, those of the upper leaves unevenly and sharply toothed, some even cleft. The umbel is surrounded by rather leaflike bracts. The fruit is only about $\frac{1}{16}$ inch long, with narrow ribs. § Summer and early autumn: swamps and springs, N. Y. and Ont. to Minn. and B. C., s. to Mich., Tex., and Mexico. *Fig. 74.*

WATER-PARSNIP (*Sium suave*)   WHITE
Sium suave (to 6 ft.) has a furrowed or angled stem. The leaves are divided into very narrow segments which bear evenly spaced sharp teeth. The bracts around the umbel are narrow, small. The fruit is nearly $\frac{1}{8}$ inch long, with conspicuous thick ribs. § Summer and early autumn: swamps, muddy shores, often partly submerged in water, throughout. *Fig. 74.*

COWBANE (*Oxypolis rigidior*)   WHITE
Cowbane (5 ft.) is so named from its poisonous juice. Th leaves are pinnately divided into narrow segments which are ex tremely variable; they may be 6 inches long, very sharp-pointe

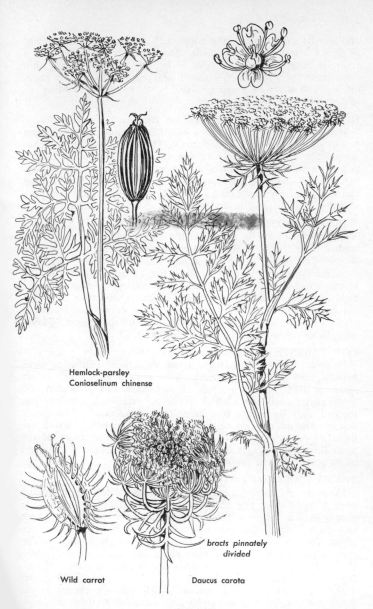

Hemlock-parsley
Conioselinum chinense

bracts pinnately divided

Wild carrot

Daucus carota

FIGURE 75

and usually jagged along the edges with only a few sharp teeth; or very narrow and without teeth. There are no bracts, or only a few very narrow ones. The fruit is flat, the margins bearing thin membranes or "wings." § Summer and early autumn: swamps, ditches, and wet woods and prairies, N. Y. to Ont. and Minn., s. to Fla. and Tex. *Fig. 74.*

HEMLOCK-PARSLEY (*Conioselinum chinense*)   WHITE
   Hemlock-parsley (to 5 ft.) somewhat resembles both poison hemlock and parsley, also wild carrot. The umbel is often 6 inches across. The leaves are finely divided. It is harmless, but no casualties will result from mistaking it for poison hemlock and abstaining from it—whereas the reverse error may be fatal. § Summer and early autumn: open places, often in moist soil, Lab. to Minn., s. to Pa. and Mo. and in the mountains to N. C. *Fig. 75.*

WILD CARROT, QUEEN-ANNE'S-LACE (*Daucus carota*)
WHITE / Wild carrot is related to the cultivated carrot and has a similar root. It is a familiar and troublesome weed from the Old World. The leaves are pinnately divided into narrow segments, these mostly again pinnately divided. It may be recognized by the bracts, which are pinnately divided into narrow segments and are about as long as the primary rays. The fruits bear rows of strong curved bristles. The flowers are white or sometimes pink; there is often a single purple flower in the center of the umbel. § Summer: fields, roadsides, etc., throughout. *Fig. 75.*

COW-PARSNIP (*Heracleum lanatum*)   WHITE
   In spite of the name, there is no danger of confusing cow-parsnip with the garden parsnip. Cow-parsnip is a much larger plant (to 10 ft.), with enormous leaves. Each leaf is divided into three parts; each part, which is broad and variously cut and toothed, may be over a foot long. The whole plant is downy or woolly. The umbel may be 8 inches across. The petals, which are white or purple-tinged, are notched or forked, and those of the outer flowers are larger than those toward the center. § Summer: moist places, almost throughout. *Fig. 76.*

SWEET CICELY (*Osmorhiza*)   WHITE
   Sweet Cicely is so called from its roots, which when broken have a sweet odor like that of licorice. The several species are closely similar. Their leaves are divided into three segments which are again divided; the final segments are bluntly toothed on the edges. The flowers are few and small, with no visible sepals. The fruit is narrow, tapering to both ends, and bears rows of short bristles that lie along the ribs. They are woodland plants, blooming in spring and early summer.
   O. longistylis (3 ft.) is usually nearly smooth except at the joints of the stem. The two styles are visible on the fruit as a two-pronged beak about ⅛ inch long. § Que. to Alta., s. to Ga. and Tex. *Fig. 76.*

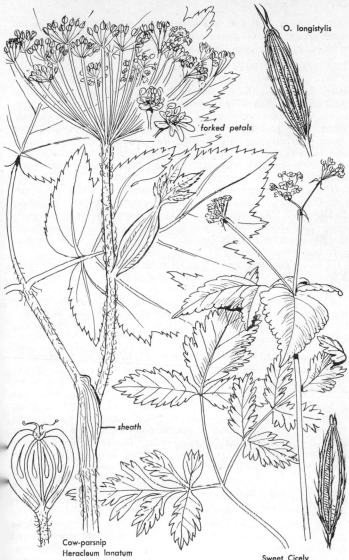

O. longistylis

forked petals

sheath

Cow-parsnip
Heracleum lanatum

Sweet Cicely
Osmorhiza claytoni

FIGURE 76

O. claytoni (3 ft.) is hairy or downy all over. The styles are much shorter, making two short points on the fruit. § Que. to Man., s. to N. C., Ala., Ark., and Kan. *Fig. 76.*

THE WATER-HEMLOCKS (*Cicuta*)   WHITE

The species of *Cicuta* are extremely poisonous; there have been many deaths of children and adults from chewing the leaves of these common plants. They are characteristically plants of swampy, marshy meadows and thickets, but are found also in wet ditches. Since it is impossible to specify an easy way to distinguish these plants from others of the family, it is the more important to be able to recognize the *Umbelliferae* in general and to regard them all (like toadstools) with caution until their identity is definitely known.

The water-hemlocks have flowers in an umbel which lacks surrounding bracts. The leaves (except the uppermost) are pinnately divided and the parts again divided and many of these parts again divided, the final segments being toothed at the margins, sharp-pointed, and rather far apart. The fruits are broad and flat, with thick, flat ribs.

C. maculata, cowbane (7 ft.), is the most widely distributed. § Summer: moist meadows, etc., Que. to Man., s. to Fla. and Tex. *Fig. 77.*

C. bulbifera (3 ft.) is named for the small bulbs in the axils of the upper leaves. The leaf segments are very narrow, with few teeth. § Summer: Nfld. to B. C., s. to Va., Ind., Ia., Mont., and Ore.

HARBINGER-OF-SPRING (*Erigenia bulbosa*)   WHITE AND BROWN

This delicate little plant (10 in.) is one of the first to flower in spring. From the white petals and brown stamens it is sometimes called pepper-and-salt. There are no visible sepals. The leaves (only one or two) are divided into three, and each segment is pinnately divided into narrow, blunt segments. Leaves and flowering stem grow from a small round corm. The leaves are only partly unfolded at flowering time. The bracts resemble the other leaves except in size. There are only three or four rays in the umbel. The fruit is flat and round. § Early spring: open woods and thickets, w. N. Y. and Ont. to Minn., s. to D. C., Ala., Miss., and Ark. PLATE 9 and *Fig. 77.*

WILD CHERVIL (*Chaerophyllum*)   WHITE

The leaves of *Chaerophyllum* are divided mostly into three parts, the parts pinnately divided, and the segments again divided or lobed or toothed. The fruits are smooth, tapering, with prominent ribs. The herb chervil is the European *Anthriscus cerefolium* The Latin name is from the same Greek word from which "chervil" is derived.

C. procumbens is a weak, spreading, branched plant, smooth or nearly so (stems to 2 feet long). § Spring: moist soil, N. Y. to

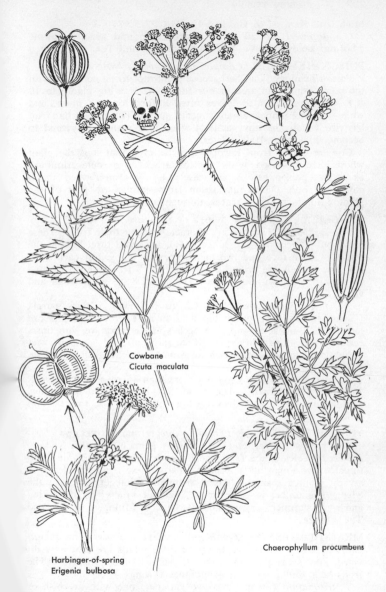

Cowbane
Cicuta maculata

Chaerophyllum procumbens

Harbinger-of-spring
Erigenia bulbosa

FIGURE 77

Mich. and Kan., s. to Ga. and La. *Fig. 77.*

C. tainturieri (to 30 in.) is more erect, and usually downy. § Spring: sandy soil, Va. to Kan., s. to Fla. and Tex.

POISON HEMLOCK (*Conium maculatum*)   WHITE

Poison hemlock is an herbaceous plant, not to be confused with the noble coniferous tree of our forests. It is a big plant (to 10 ft.), with much-divided leaves often a foot long or more, and white-flowered umbels about 2 inches across. The broad, flat fruit has ribs which are wavy at least when it is young; they tend to become thick and straight later.

Conium comes from Europe. It is believed that it is the plant whose juice was used by the ancient Greeks to execute criminals, as we use poison gas. In any case it is a common weed and a dangerous one. Death may result from eating any part of the plant. § Summer: waste places, throughout. *Fig. 78.*

ANGELICA (*Angelica*)   WHITE OR GREENISH

The species of *Angelica* are characterized by their fruits. These are about ¼ inch long or longer, oval, flat, with three ribs at the center of each face and two membranes or "wings" at each margin. The umbels are broad, many-flowered. The upper leaves may be sheaths only, without blades. The sheaths are very broad and veiny.

A. atropurpurea, alexanders (to 10 ft.), with a dark purple ("atropurpurea") or purple-blotched stem. The leaf sheaths are large. The umbels are up to 8 inches across and are sometimes composed of 45 primary rays. § Late spring to early autumn: wet bottomlands and swamps, Lab. to Minn., s. to Md., Ind., and Ia. *Fig. 78.*

A. venenosa (to 6 ft.) has not more than 35 rays in the umbel. The fruits are downy. The plant has been called poisonous. § Summer: woods and thickets, Mass. to Minn., s. to Fla. and Ark.

YELLOW PIMPERNEL (*Taenidia integerrima*)   YELLOW

The yellow pimpernel (3 ft.) differs from most other yellow-flowered species of the family in its leaves. These are divided into three or five long-stalked principal parts, these again divided into several pointed segments which are plain ("integerrima") at the edges. The umbel is quite ample, without bracts. § Late spring and early summer: dry woodlands, Que. to Minn., s. to Ga. and Tex. *Fig. 78.*

MEADOW-PARSNIPS (*Thaspium*)   YELLOW, PURPLE, OR GREEN-ISH / At least some of the leaves of these plants are pinnately divided into sharp-pointed segments with toothed margins. The fruits bear thin projecting membranes ("wings").

T. trifoliatum (30 in.) has two varieties: one with greenish or purple flowers, mostly southern and on the seaboard; the other with golden yellow flowers, more general in our range. § Spring

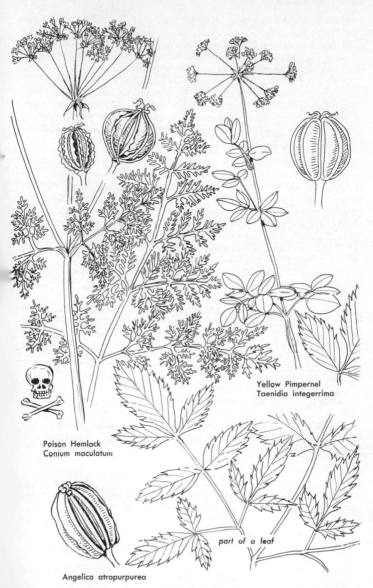

Yellow Pimpernel
Taenidia integerrima

Poison Hemlock
Conium maculatum

part of a leaf

Angelica atropurpurea

FIGURE 78

and early summer: woods and thickets, R. I. to Minn., s. to Ga., La., and Okla. *Fig. 79.*

T. barbinode (3 ft.) is easily distinguished by its pale yellow flowers and by the tufts of white hairs around the stem where a leaf begins. § Spring and early summer: woods and thickets, N. Y. and Ont. to Minn., s. to Fla. and Okla. *Fig. 79.*

There are few genera that contain species so easily confused as *Thaspium* and *Zizia*. *T. trifoliatum* resembles *Z. aptera* more than it resembles any other *Thaspium; T. barbinode* is like *Z. aurea*. For the actual distinction between the two genera, see under *Zizia*.

GOLDEN ALEXANDERS (*Zizia*)   YELLOW

These are delicate plants, usually 2 or 3 feet tall, with leaves mostly divided into three, the parts often again divided into sharp-toothed, pointed segments. At least one species is often confused with *Thaspium*. Two technical characteristics distinguish these genera; they are small but easily seen with a hand magnifier. In *Zizia* the central flower (or fruit) of each secondary umbel has no stalk; in *Thaspium* all flowers and fruits have stalks. In *Zizia* the ribs on the fruit are rounded, like pieces of string; in *Thaspium* they project as thin membranes ("wings").

Z. aurea (30 in.) has all its leaves divided, and usually more than ten rays to an umbel. § Late spring and early summer: open woodlands, Que. to Sask., s. to Fla. and Tex. *Fig. 79.*

Z. aptera (30 in.) has basal leaves with undivided blades on long stalks, and fewer principal rays. This is the species most like *Thaspium trifoliatum.* § Late spring and early summer: woods, thickets, and prairies, R. I. to B. C., s. to Ga., Ala., Mo., Utah, and Ore. *Fig. 79.*

PARSNIP (*Pastinaca sativa*)   YELLOW

This is our familiar vegetable run wild and forming a conspicuous weed (5 ft.) along our highways and in fields. The leaves are pinnately divided, the lower on long stalks; the segments are coarsely and irregularly toothed, but not again divided. The flowers are yellow, in wide umbels. § Summer: waste places, throughout. *Fig. 80.*

GINSENG FAMILY (*Araliaceae*)

The *Araliaceae* are most abundant in the tropics, where many of the species are trees and shrubs. The most familiar cultivated species of this family is English ivy, *Hedera helix.* A few species are herbaceous plants of our range. The family (with us) is distinguished by its five petals and stamens and inferior ovary; the leaves are divided and in some species the segments are again divided. The flowers are small, white or nearly so, in umbels. The fruit is a berry.

Panax has a single circle of three leaves a short distance below the umbel, each divided palmately.

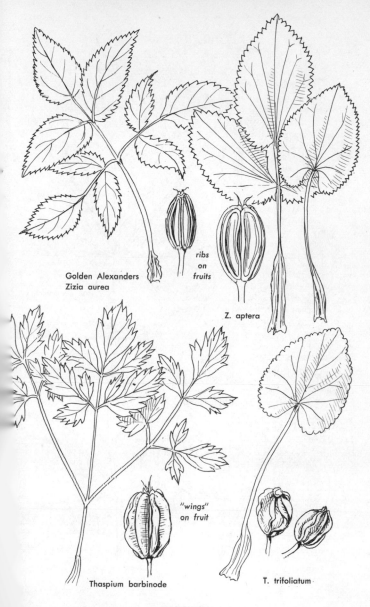

Golden Alexanders
Zizia aurea

ribs on fruits

Z. aptera

"wings" on fruit

Thaspium barbinode

T. trifoliatum

FIGURE 79

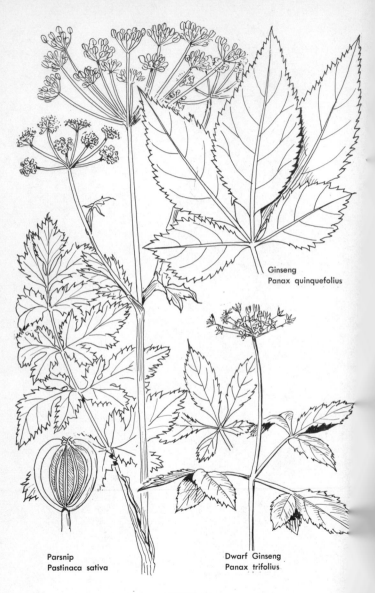

Ginseng
Panax quinquefolius

Parsnip
Pastinaca sativa

Dwarf Ginseng
Panax trifolius

FIGURE 80

Wild Sarsaparilla
Aralia nudicaulis

...rt of leaf of
...alia racemosa

Aralia hispida

FIGURE 81

Aralia has pinnately divided and redivided leaves growing either from the base of the stem or singly on the stem.

GINSENGS (*Panax*)   WHITE OR PINK

P. quinquefolius, ginseng (1–2 ft.), has each leaf divided palmately into usually five segments, each segment stalked. The flowers are greenish. The berries are red. This is the species for whose tuberous root the Chinese have paid large sums; with them it has a reputation as a potent medicine. § Summer: rich woods, Que. to Man., s. to Fla. and Okla.; now rare. *Fig. 80.*

P. trifolius, dwarf ginseng (8 in.), has each leaf divided into three or five segments which are not stalked. It grows only 6 or 8 inches tall. The flowers may be pink or white. The berries are yellow. § Spring: rich woods, Que. to Minn. and Nebr., s. to Ga., O., and Ia. *Fig. 80.*

ARALIA   WHITE

A. racemosa, spikenard (to 10 ft.), has leaves divided into three, each part again divided pinnately; the whole leaf may be nearly 3 feet long. The leaf segments are mostly indented (heart-shaped) at the base. The small white flowers are in numerous small umbels all gathered in a tall inflorescence. § Summer: rich woods, Que. to Man., s. to Ga. and Mexico. *Fig. 81.*

A. hispida, bristly sarsaparilla (3 ft.), resembles *A. racemosa,* but the stem is beset with slender spines. The leaf segments are not indented at the base. § Summer: open woodlands, across Canada, s. to N. J., W. Va., Ind., and Minn. *Fig. 81.*

A. nudicaulis, wild sarsaparilla (1 ft.), has a single leaf divided into three and each part again divided into three or five. The flowers are on a leafless stem shorter than the leaf, in several small umbels. § Late spring and summer: woods, Lab. to B. C., s. to Ga., Tenn., Nebr., Colo., and Ida. *Fig. 81.*

DOGWOOD FAMILY (Cornaceae)

The *Cornaceae* are almost all trees and shrubs. In our range only the bunchberry can pass for a wild flower.

BUNCHBERRY (*Cornus canadensis*)   WHITE

Bunchberry grows from a woody rhizome. The erect shoots (8 in.) bear what seems a circle of leaves, usually six. There is actually a pair of leaves, from the axils of which spring the other four. Above these is the head of small greenish-white flowers surrounded by four petal-like white bracts (a form with pink bracts is known). In this the bunchberry resembles the "flowering" dogwood, a tree or shrub; all dogwoods have flowers, but most lack the petal-like bracts around the flower clusters. The flowers of bunchberry are followed by a cluster of red stone fruits. § Late spring and summer: woods and generally boggy open places across Canada and s. to Md., O., Ind., Ill., Minn., and Calif. *Fig. 82.*

GROUP IV OF DICOT FAMILIES. PETALS JOINED; OVARY SUPERIOR; FLOWERS RADIALLY SYMMETRIC

These families are here arranged in eight groups (A to H below).

There are radially symmetric flowers (or flowers apparently radially symmetric) in families characterized by bilaterally symmetric flowers. See *Verbascum, Veronica, Aureolaria, Agalinis* in the Snapdragon Family; *Ruellia* in the Acanthus Family; *Mentha, Isanthus,* etc., in the Mint Family.

A. Small, erect plants, evergreen or completely lacking green color.

The **Pyrola Family** has ten stamens, five petals almost (or entirely) separate.

B. Creeping plants with evergreen leaves.

The **Heath Family** includes several herbaceous genera with radially symmetric flowers. The corolla is bell-shaped or has five pointed lobes at the end of a tube. There are five or ten stamens.

C. Creeping plants with crowded, needlelike leaves.

The **Diapensia Family** (as represented by the single species included in this book) forms mats covered with practically stalkless, five-parted flowers.

D. Erect plants with each stamen standing opposite the center of a petal.

The **Primrose Family** has parts in fives. The ovary has one chamber with many ovules attached to a central column or dome. There is one style.

The **Leadwort Family** (as represented by one herbaceous genus in our range) has stalked basal leaves and many scales on the much-branched stem. There are many small lavender flowers. There are three or five styles, one ovule. These are seaside plants.

E. Erect plants with two ovaries in one flower joined to a single stigma; two pods are formed from each flower.

The **Dogbane Family** has milky juice. The petals form a tube or bell. There is but one style for the two ovaries.

The **Milkweed Family** has milky juice in most species. The petals are joined at the base, and are in most species bent back along the stem; a crown of cuplike parts rises above them. There are two styles for the two ovaries, but the one stigma is joined to the stamens.

. Plants with one ovary, not lobed, bearing a single style with ne stigma (two-lobed in some species) or two stigmas.

The **Gentian Family** has paired leaves without stalks and without teeth. The ovary has one chamber containing many ovules.

The **Morning-glory Family** consists mostly of twining or trailing vines bearing leaves singly. The corolla forms a funnel with very shallow lobes, or a tube with a flaring disk. The ovary has two chambers, each with two ovules.

The **Waterleaf Family** (as represented here) has lobed or divided leaves attached singly. The ovary has one chamber containing several or many ovules. The flowers are in cymes or false racemes.

The **Potato Family** has leaves attached singly and flower clusters or single flowers in forks of the stem or between the points where leaves are attached. The ovary has two chambers and numerous ovules.

G. Plants with a three-branched style and a three-chambered ovary.

The **Phlox Family** has in most species a tubular corolla flaring at the end into five lobes; in others a bell-shaped corolla with five nearly separate petals. The leaves are undivided or pinnately divided.

H. Plants with a four-lobed ovary.

The **Forget-me-not Family** has five stamens. The plants are mostly hairy or rough. The flowers are in coiled false racemes.

PYROLA FAMILY (*Pyrolaceae*)

The Pyrola Family includes a number of small plants generally found in woodlands with conifers (hemlock, spruce, etc.). They are mostly evergreen, but some are delicate plants with no green coloring. The flowers generally hang down. There are usually five sepals, five petals (separate or nearly so), ten stamens, a pistil with five chambers but one style and stigma. The stamens shed their pollen through pores or slits in the end of the anther. The evergreen plants send up their erect flowering stems from woody rhizomes.

This group is sometimes called the Wintergreen Family, but true wintergreen (*Gaultheria*) is in the related Heath Family.

Four genera are here described.

Monotropa has no green color; the entire plant is white, pink, or red.

Chimaphila has leaves more or less in circles on the stem that bears the flowers; the flowers are almost in an umbel.

Pyrola has flowers in a raceme on a leafless stem. The leaves are all near the base, with stalks and broad blades (sometime leaves are lacking).

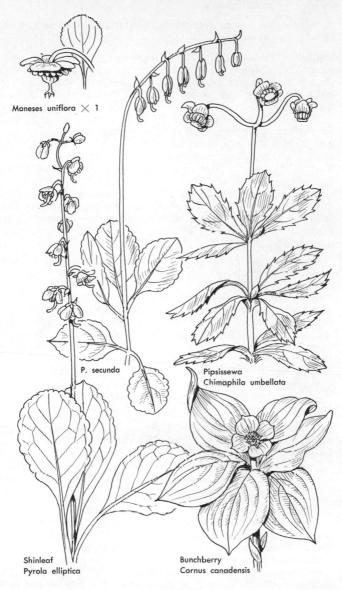

Moneses uniflora × 1

P. secunda

Pipsissewa
Chimaphila umbellata

Shinleaf
Pyrola elliptica

Bunchberry
Cornus canadensis

FIGURE 82

Moneses has leaves near the base, with a single flower at the tip of a leafless stem.

INDIAN-PIPE and PINESAP (*Monotropa*) WHITE, PINK, RED, OR YELLOW / *Monotropa* is one of the groups of plants that lack the green pigment chlorophyll. Though they bear flowers and reproduce by seeds, they obtain their food as mushrooms do, from the living or dead organic matter in the soil in which they grow.

M. uniflora, Indian-pipe (to 1 ft.), is familiar in rich, dark woods. The single flower hangs from its bent stalk. As the seed-pod matures the stalk becomes erect. The only leaves are scales along the stem. Most plants are waxy-white throughout, turning black as they dry; a bright red form occurs more rarely. § Summer: throughout. PLATE 10.

M. hypopithys, pinesap (to 16 in.), differs in having several flowers at the bent tip of the stem, and in being of various hues from tan or yellow to red. § Summer to autumn: throughout. PLATE 10.

CHIMAPHILA WHITE
Plants in *Chimaphila* have slender, persistent, somewhat woody stems bearing circles of evergreen leaves with a cluster of waxy flowers hanging above them.

C. umbellata, pipsissewa or Prince's-pine (10 in.), is a plant of dry woods, with dark green leaves broadest toward the tip and blunt. The white or pale pink flowers, each about ¾ inch across, are nearly in an umbel at the summit of the stem. § Summer: from Que. across Canada, s. to Ga., O., Minn., Utah, and Calif. *Fig. 82.*

C. maculata, pipsissewa or spotted-wintergreen (10 in.), differs in having leaves marked with white lines and tapering to a sharp point. The flowers are fragrant. § Summer: N. H. and Ont. to Mich. and Ill., s. to Ga. and Tenn. PLATE 10.

ONE-FLOWERED-WINTERGREEN (*Moneses uniflora*) WHITE OR ROSE / This plant (5 in.) looks like a diminutive *Chimaphila* or *Pyrola* but has only one flower. The stigma has five radiating branches. Its leaves are roundish. § Summer: moist northern woods and bogs, across Canada, s. to W. Va., Mich., Minn., Utah, and Ore. *Fig. 82.*

SHINLEAF (*Pyrola*) WHITE, PINK, OR CRIMSON
The species of *Pyrola* are composed of small, summer-flowering, woodland or mountain plants with evergreen leaves, mostly roundish, in a cluster at the base of the stem, and flowers spirally arranged around the stem except in one species.

P. secunda (8 in.) has flowers all on one side of the stem. The petals are white or greenish. § Moist woods and bogs, across Canada, s. to Va., O., Ia., N. M., and Calif. *Fig. 82.*

P. virens (1 ft.) has leaf stalks that are mostly longer than the blades they bear; some plants have no leaves at all and must get their food from organic matter, as does *Monotropa*. The flowers are white veined with green. § Dry woods, from Nfld. across Canada, s. to Md., Ind., Wis., Nebr., Ariz., and Ore.

P. asarifolia (14 in.) is distinguished by the indented (heart-shaped) base of the leaf blades. The petals are pink or crimson. § Wet woods, from Nfld. across Canada, s. to N. Y., Ind., Minn., Colo., and Ore.

P. elliptica (1 ft.) is probably our commonest shinleaf. The leaf blades are usually longer than their stalks, rounded at the end, slightly tapering to the stalks. The white petals are green-veined. This species and *P. rotundifolia* are sometimes called wild lily-of-the-valley, a name also applied to *Maianthemum canadense* in the Lily Family. § Dry woods, from Nfld. across Canada, s. to W. Va., Ill., S. D., and N. M. *Fig. 82*.

P. rotundifolia (1 ft.) is a larger plant with round leaves to 3 inches long and nearly as broad. The petals are white. § Damp thickets and bogs, Que. to Minn., s. to N. C. and Ky.

HEATH FAMILY (*Ericaceae*)

This is a large family of chiefly woody plants. In our country they are characteristic of acid soil, usually in bogs and on mountains; but many species are tropical or grow in the temperate Southern Hemisphere. Four of our native genera have herbaceous or nearly herbaceous species in our range. Such beautiful shrubs as mountain-laurel and the rhododendrons and azaleas are in this family but not treated in this book.

The parts of the flowers are mostly in fives and tens, except for the single pistil, which may have from two to ten chambers. The stamens discharge their pollen through pores at the tips of the anthers. Many species are evergreen.

I. Genera whose petals are almost completely joined, forming a cup or bell (compare II).

Kalmia has an open cup-shaped corolla, with ten small pouches projecting from the sides.

Gaultheria has a bell-like corolla. The berries smell and taste of wintergreen. The flowers and fruits are in the axils of leaves.

Arctostaphylos has a bell-like corolla. The flowers and fruit are in racemes.

II. Genus whose petals are joined only through about half their length, the tips being distinct.

Epigaea is composed of creeping plants.

THE LAURELS (*Kalmia*)   PINK OR CRIMSON

Our laurels are not those with which the ancient Greeks crowned their athletes; this was *Laurus*. The flowers of *Kalmia* are characterized by the ten pouches in the petals, in which the heads of the stamens are caught as the flower opens. A touch causes them to spring out, scattering their pollen on the intruding object. The leaves remain green through the winter.

These are more accurately classed as shrubs, but the following small species may be taken for an herbaceous wild flower.

K. *polifolia,* bog-laurel (to 2 ft.), has very narrow leaves, downy and white on the under side. The flowers are in a terminal cluster. § Late spring and summer: peat bogs, across Canada, s. to Pa., Mich., Minn., Ida., and Calif. *Fig. 83.*

WINTERGREEN and SNOWBERRY (*Gaultheria*)   WHITE

Our species of *Gaultheria* are composed of creeping plants with evergreen leaves. The parts of the flower are in fours or fives. Many other species occur in South America and in the Old World.

G. *procumbens,* wintergreen or checkerberry, has a creeping stem from which small erect branches (6 in.) grow, bearing the small flowers which droop from the axils of the leaves. The corolla forms a small urn which is five-toothed at the rim; there are five stamens. The fruit is a rather dry red berry which has the familiar flavor of wintergreen (as do the leaves when crushed). § Summer: cool damp woods and clearings, Nfld. to Man., s. to Ga., Ala., and Minn. *Fig. 83.*

G. *hispidula,* creeping snowberry, has much smaller leaves on its trailing stems. The corolla forms a more open cup, with four lobes; there are eight stamens. The berry is white, juicy, wintergreen-flavored. § Spring to summer: mostly in mossy coniferous woods and bogs, across Canada, s. to N. C., Minn., and Ida.

BEARBERRY (*Arctostaphylos uva-ursi*)   PINK OR WHITE

Bearberry is a somewhat shrubby trailing plant which grows in rocky and sandy places. The small blunt leaves are attached singly; they remain green through winter. The flowers, in terminal clusters, are pale pink or white (red in one form), the joined petals forming an egg-shaped body with tiny lobes at the mouth. The fruit is a dull red berry. Like trailing arbutus, bearberry is protected by law in some states. § Spring and summer: throughout northern Canada, s. to Va., Ind., Colo., and Calif. *Fig. 83.*

TRAILING ARBUTUS, MAYFLOWER (*Epigaea repens*)   ROSE OR WHITE / The beauty and fragrance of trailing arbutus have led to its near extinction in many places. One is tempted to transplant it to the garden; but it almost always disappears after a season or two. Even picking it is dangerous, as one may inadvertently take up yards of the creeping stems. Several states have laws against gathering it. It is at home in sandy soil, usually with conifers, through much of our area. The leaves remain green through winter; new leaves appear in summer. The old leaves are hairy and rather leathery. The petals form a short tube which flares into

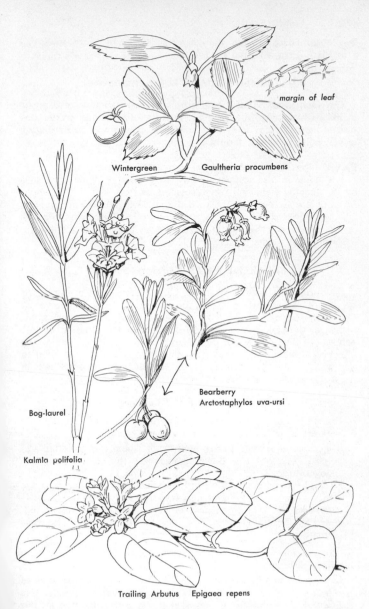

margin of leaf

Wintergreen   Gaultheria procumbens

Bog-laurel

Kalmla polifolia

Bearberry
Arctostaphylos uva-ursi

Trailing Arbutus   Epigaea repens

FIGURE 83

five lobes. There are ten stamens. § Early spring: Lab. to Sask., s. to Fla., Tenn., Ill., and Ia. *Fig. 83.*

DIAPENSIA FAMILY (*Diapensiaceae*)

The Diapensia Family is a group of inconspicuous evergreen plants with small white or pink flowers. Besides the pyxie, described below, *Galax aphylla,* a southern species with heart-shaped leaves, belongs in this family.

PYXIE (*Pyxidanthera barbulata*)   WHITE OR PINK
The pyxie is also known as flowering-moss, a name suggested by its creeping stem and tiny, crowded, narrow leaves, the whole forming a mat sometimes a yard across. The flowers are numerous, with five spreading lobes to the corolla. There are five stamens, joined to the corolla. The ovary has three chambers. § Spring: sandy pine barrens, N. J. to S. C. *Fig. 84.*

PRIMROSE FAMILY (*Primulaceae*)

Few primroses grow wild in the United States, but a number of species of the Primrose Family occur. The family is known by two somewhat technical characteristics: (1) Each stamen is attached at the center of a petal, instead of at the junction of two petals. (2) The ovary has one chamber, in which the ovules are attached to a stalk that rises from the floor and is not attached to the walls. There is a single style. In general the parts are in fives; the petals, when present, are joined, at least at the base.

Guide to Genera of *Primulaceae*

I. Genera whose leaves form a rosette at or near the ground; the flowers are in an umbel on a leafless stem (compare II).

Dodecatheon has its petals bent back, their tips pointing upward (*Fig. 84*); the flower hangs with the stamens pointing downward.

Primula has its petals forming a distinct tube, longer than the sepals, flaring at the end into five lobes (*Fig. 84*).

Androsace has very small flowers, the joined petals almost hidden by the sepals (*Fig. 84*). The basal leaves are also very small.

II. Genera whose flowering stem bears leaves also; the flowers are variously disposed.

Lysimachia and *Steironema* have yellow flowers in the axils of leaves or in terminal racemes (*Figs. 85, 86*).

Trientalis has a circle of leaves at the summit of the stem, just below the one or several flower stalks (*Fig. 86*). The flowers are white.

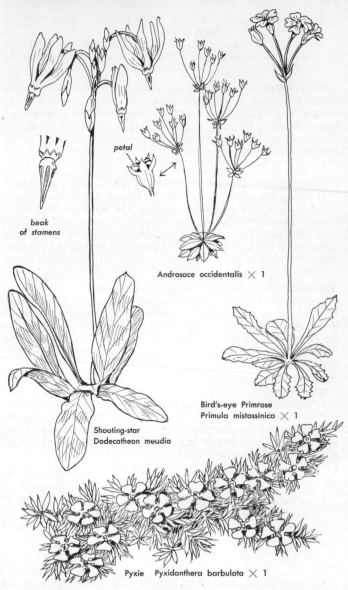

beak
of *stamens*

petal

Androsace occidentalis × 1

Bird's-eye Primrose
Primula mistassinica × 1

Shooting-star
Dodecatheon meadia

Pyxie Pyxidanthera barbulata × 1

FIGURE 84

Anagallis has scarlet, blue, or white flowers arising from the axils of paired, stalkless leaves.

Glaux is a succulent plant of salt places, with no petals but sepals that simulate petals (*Fig. 87*), the stamens arising between them. The flowers lack stalks.

SHOOTING-STAR (*Dodecatheon meadia*)   LAVENDER OR WHITE
The flowers of shooting-star hang in a drooping umbel at the summit of a leafless stem (to 2 ft.). The petals are bent sharply back. The stamens form a pointed beak in the center of the flower. The leaves are lance-shaped with the point down, numerous, very smooth. § Spring: prairies, open woods, D. C. to Wis., s. to Ga. and Tex. *Fig. 84.*

PRIMROSE (*Primula mistassinica*)   WHITE TO PINK OR PURPLE
The only true primrose that one is likely to find in our range is *P. mistassinica* of the northern borders. The petals are notched at the end. The flowers grow in an umbel at the summit of a leafless stem (6–8 in.). The leaves are smooth, but in some plants their lower side is covered with a yellow powder. § Spring and summer: rocks and shores, across Canada, s. to N. Y., Ill., and Ia.; not common. *Fig. 84.*

ANDROSACE (*Androsace occidentalis*)   WHITE
The plants of *Androsace* are tiny (3 in.), with a basal rosette of numerous leaves about ½ inch long. The flowers are in an umbel atop a leafless stem; the white petals barely protrude from the calyx. *A. occidentalis* is fairly common on exposed sandy and rocky places. § Spring: Ont. to B. C., s. to Ind., Ark., and Ariz. *Fig. 84.*

THE LOOSESTRIFES (*Lysimachia* and *Steironema*)   YELLOW
These two genera are not easily distinguished (indeed they have been merged into one by some botanists). Both have five stamens; in *Steironema* there are also five rudiments alternating with the stamens. In *Steironema* also each petal is curved around its stamen. For convenience all the loosestrifes (except purple loosestrife, in the *Lythraceae*) are here considered together.

I. Species with flowers in a raceme at the summit (compare II and III).

L. terrestris, swamp-candles (2 ft.), has long narrow leaves in pairs. The petals have dark markings. The stalks of the stamens are joined at the base. § Summer: wet places, Nfld. to Man., s. to Ga., Ky., and Ia. *Fig. 85.*

II. Creeping species with round, paired leaves and flowers in the axils.

L. nummularia, moneywort, has flowers borne singly in the axils of the leaves. § Summer: wet places, lawns, etc., throughout; native of Europe. *Fig. 85.*

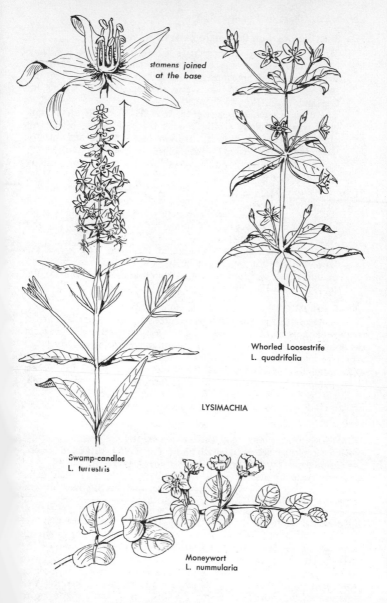

stamens joined
at the base

Whorled Loosestrife
L. quadrifolia

LYSIMACHIA

Swamp-candles
L. terrestris

Moneywort
L. nummularia

FIGURE 85

III. Erect species with flowers in axils of leaves.

L. *quadrifolia* whorled loosestrife (3 ft.), has most leaves in fours. The flowers are borne usually singly in the axils, on slender stalks. The stamens are joined at the base of the stalk. § Summer: woodlands and thickets, Me. to Wis., s. to Ga. and Tenn. *Fig. 85.*

S. *ciliatum,* fringed loosestrife (3 ft.), has leaves with a marginal fringe of hairs ("cilia") near the base of the blade and on the stalk. The flowers are on long stalks, and mostly hang facing the ground. The petals are toothed at the end. § Summer: swamps, wet meadows, banks of streams, nearly throughout. *Fig. 86.*

S. *quadriflorum* (2 ft.) is distinguished by its narrow, almost needlelike leaves. The flowers tend to be clustered toward the ends of the branches. The petals are toothed. § Late summer: wet open places, N. Y. and Ont. to Man., s. to Va. and Mo. *Fig. 86.*

S. *lanceolatum* (2 ft.) has stolons at the base. The leaves are lance-shaped but taper gradually toward the base, with no distinct stalk. § Summer: moist woodlands and prairies, Pa. to Wis., s. to Fla. and La. *Fig. 86.*

STAR-FLOWER (*Trientalis borealis*)   WHITE

Star-flower (10 in.) is easily recognized by its cluster of narrow leaves at the summit of a stem which is otherwise leafless (except perhaps for minute scales). (The plant may possibly be mistaken for *Medeola* in the Lily Family; but this has *two* circles of leaves.) The slender flower stalks grow from the same point as the leaves. The petals are from five to nine in number (commonly seven), pointed to form a star, and do not appear to be joined. § Late spring and summer: woodlands, across Canada, s. to Va., Ill., and Minn. *Fig. 86.*

PIMPERNEL (*Anagallis arvensis*)   VARIOUS COLORS

Scarlet pimpernel is a small plant (to 1 ft.) of waste places, an immigrant from Europe. The small leaves are paired. The flowers, typically scarlet, grow on slender stalks from their axils. There are also forms with purple, white, and bright blue flowers. § Spring and summer: throughout. *Fig. 86.*

SEA-MILKWORT (*Glaux maritima*)   WHITE, PINK, OR RED

Sea-milkwort (1 ft.) cannot easily be mistaken for anything else. Its leaves are thick, succulent, very small, in pairs. The flowers are seated in the axils of the leaves, with no stalks. There are no petals, but the round sepals are colored white or pink or even red. § Summer: salty beaches and marshes, Que. to Va.; inland on the northern shores of the Great Lakes; Alaska to Calif.; alkaline regions in the West. *Fig. 87.*

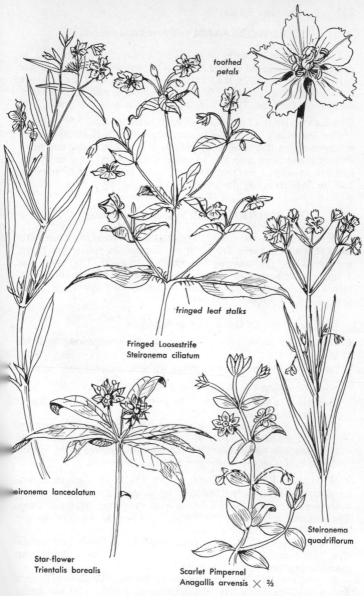

toothed petals

fringed leaf stalks

Fringed Loosestrife
Steironema ciliatum

Steironema lanceolatum

Steironema quadriflorum

Star-flower
Trientalis borealis

Scarlet Pimpernel
Anagallis arvensis $\times$ ⅔

FIGURE 86

LEADWORT FAMILY (*Plumbaginaceae*)

The Leadwort Family, a large family in the tropics and in deserts, is represented in our flora by the sea-lavender. The flower parts are in fives. As in the *Primulaceae,* the stamens are opposite the centers of the petals rather than alternating with them as they do in most families. There are five styles but only one ovule.

SEA-LAVENDER (*Limonium nashii*)   LAVENDER
The leaves are all at the base except for small scales on the much-branched flowering stem (nearly 2 ft.). The numerous small flowers grow along one side of each branch; they have no stalks, and are enveloped by thin bracts. § Late summer: salt marshes, Lab. to Mexico along the coast. *Fig. 87.*

GENTIAN FAMILY (*Gentianaceae*)

Flowers of *Gentianaceae* vary in the number of their parts from four to 12; there are as many stamens as petals; the petals are joined and the stamens are attached to them. The ovary has a single chamber, with many ovules. The leaves are commonly paired and without stalks, lobes, or teeth. The flowers of many species are bright and attractive.

Genus of *Gentianaceae*

I. Genus with petals joined only at the base, appearing separate (*Fig. 87*).

Sabatia has flowers varying from white to salmon-pink or rose.

II. Genera with a distinct tube of joined petals.

Bartonia is a slender plant with minute flowers and no leaves other than scales (*Fig. 87*).

Centaurium has small rose-purple flowers; five pointed lobes crown the corolla (*Fig. 87*).

Gentiana has comparatively large flowers colored blue, greenish, yellowish, or white (never pink) (*Fig. 88*).

THE MARSH-PINKS or ROSE-PINKS (*Sabatia*)   SALMON-PINK OR WHITE / The loosely clustered, handsome flowers have apparently separate petals which are joined in a ring by their bases. The number of flower parts varies from five to 12. The species named below all flower in summer.

S. dodecandra (2 ft.) has from eight to 12 petals and sepals The petals are pink or white, yellow at the base. § Brackish marshes near the coast, Conn. to Fla. and La.

S. campestris (1 ft.) has rose-pink flowers. There are usuall five petals. The calyx has ribs or wings. § Prairies and old fields Ill. to Kan., s. to La. and Tex. *Fig. 87.*

S. stellaris (2 ft.) has leaves usually broader above the middle

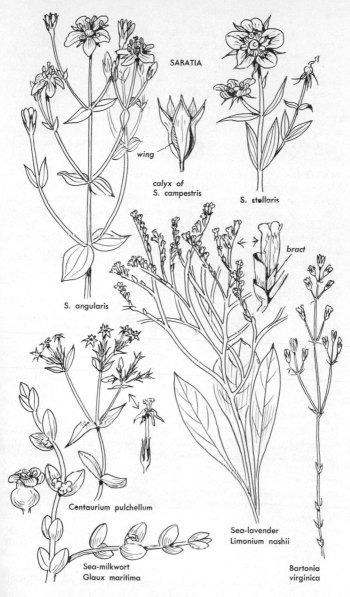

SABATIA

wing

calyx of
S. campestris

S. stellaris

S. angularis

bract

Centaurium pulchellum

Sea-lavender
Limonium nashii

Sea-milkwort
Glaux maritima

Bartonia
virginica

FIGURE 87

The flowering branches grow singly from the main stem. The corolla, of five petals, is pink with a yellow center. § Brackish marshes, Mass. to Fla. and La. *Fig. 87.*

S. *campanulata* is similar to S. *stellaris* and merges into it; the leaves taper upward from below the middle. § Damp soil of the coastal plain and Piedmont, Mass. to Ga. and Ala.; Ind.

S. *angularis* (1–3 ft.) is recognized by the angular branches with a thin "wing" along each angle, especially on the flower stalks. The flowering branches are paired. The corolla, usually of five petals, is pink with a green star-shaped center. § Moist soil, N. Y. and Ont. to Ia., s. to Fla., La., and Okla. *Fig. 87.*

BARTONIA   YELLOWISH, PURPLISH, OR WHITE

These insignificant plants of wet places have only scales for leaves. The stem (about 15 in.) may be yellow or purplish. The minute flowers, of much the same color, are in a long cluster at the summit. They flower in late summer.

B. *virginica* has mostly paired scales on the stem. § Bogs, etc., Que. to Minn., s. to Fla. and La. *Fig. 87.*

B. *paniculata* has mostly single scales. § Swamps, etc., near the coast, N. S. to Fla. and La., w. to Ky. and Okla.

CENTAURY (*Centaurium*)   PINK OR WHITE

The centauries are slender little plants with many minute flowers. The common species of our range are immigrants from Europe. They grow in fields and waste places, flowering in summer.

C. *umbellatum* (1 ft.) has flowers with almost no stalks, in cymes. The petals are purplish or rose. § Que. to Mich., s. to Ga. and Ind.

C. *pulchellum* (8 in.) has pink flowers on stalks about ⅛ inch long. § N. Y. to Va. and Ill. *Fig. 87.*

C. *spicatum* (1 ft.) has pink or white flowers in spikes. Margins of salt marshes, Nantucket; Md.; Va.

THE GENTIANS (*Gentiana*)   BLUE, VIOLET, WHITE, OR GREENISH / Some of our most beautiful wild flowers are gentians. The leaves are paired, without teeth, and without stalks or nearly so. The flowers may be in close terminal or axillary clusters, or single on long stalks. This is a large genus especially in mountains of all continents; there are many alpine species, prized by rock gardeners. We have 18 or 20 species, of which the following are the most widespread.

I. Species whose flowers do not open: the closed or bottle gentians. The flowers are in tight clusters. (*G. saponaria*—see II B below—opens only slightly.) (Compare II.)

G. *andrewsii* (to 3 ft.) is the commoner of these. The flowers, which have no stalks, are bright blue, in clusters at the summit and in the axils. If the petals are separated, their tips are seen to be joined by a fringed membrane wider than the petals. § Late summer: wet open places and road

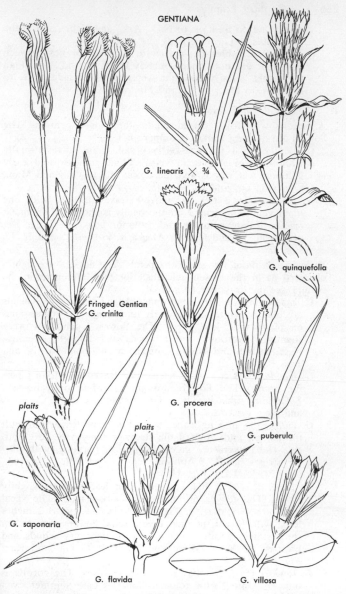

GENTIANA

G. linearis × ¾

G. quinquefolia

Fringed Gentian
G. crinita

G. procera

G. puberula

plaits

plaits

G. saponaria

G. flavida

G. villosa

FIGURE 88

sides, Que. to Sask., s. to N. J., Ark., and Nebr., and in the mountains to Ga. PLATE 10.

G. *clausa* resembles G. *andrewsii*. The membranes between the petals are not fringed, merely lobed, and no wider than the petals. § Early autumn: wet woods and fields, Me. to Minn., s. to Md., N. C., and Mo.

II. Species with open flowers.

A. Species with four fringed petals: the fringed gentians. The flowers are on long stalks. (Compare B.)

G. *crinita* (to 3 ft.) has fairly broad, ovate leaves, usually with three or five main veins. § Late summer and early autumn: wet woods and meadows, Me. to Ont. and Man., s. to Ga., O., and Ia. *Fig. 88.*

G. *procera* (to 2 ft.) has narrow leaves, usually with one main vein. The fringe on the petals is shorter than in G. *crinita.* § Late summer and autumn: bogs and other wet places, N. Y. and Ont. to Alaska, s. to O., Ia., and N. D. *Fig. 88.*

B. Species without fringe on the petals. The flowers are tightly clustered as in the closed gentians. For the differences in the corolla, see the drawings (*Fig. 88*).

G. *saponaria* (to 3 ft.) has lance-shaped leaves. The petals are blue or white, and scarcely longer than the membranes or plaits that join them. The flowers open only very slightly. § Autumn: moist woods and thickets, swamps, N. Y. to Ind. and Minn., s. on the coastal plain to Fla. and Tex. *Fig. 88.*

G. *flavida* (to 3 ft.) has lance-shaped leaves with long tapering points. The flowers are greenish-white or yellowish. § Autumn: open woods, s. Ont. to Man., s. to N. C., Ark., and Nev. *Fig. 88.*

G. *villosa* (18 in.) has lance-shaped or ovate leaves but with the narrow ends toward the stem; or some may be elliptical. The flowers are greenish-white or purplish, with purple stripes inside. § Autumn: open woods, N. J. to Ind., s. to Fla. and La. *Fig. 88.*

G. *puberula* (to 2 ft.) has stem and leaf margins slightly rough. The leaves are narrowly lance-shaped. The sepal lobes are very narrow. The corolla is blue, up to 2 inches long, with broad, pointed lobes. Some flowers may be on short stalks. § Late summer and autumn: dry woods and prairies, N. Y. to Minn. and N. D., s. to Ga. and Kan. *Fig. 88.*

G. *linearis* (to 2 ft.) has very narrow leaves. The corolla is blue or white, with rounded lobes. § Late summer: wet woods and meadows, Lab. to N. Y. and Minn., s. to Md. and W. Va. *Fig. 88.*

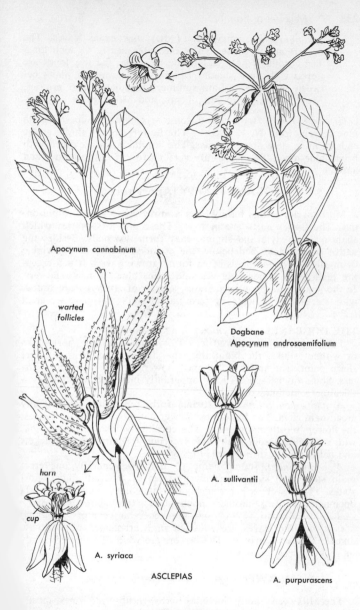

Apocynum cannabinum

Dogbane
Apocynum androsaemifolium

warted
follicles

horn

cup

A. syriaca

A. sullivantii

A. purpurascens

ASCLEPIAS

FIGURE 89

    G. quinquefolia, agueweed (1 ft.), has ovate leaves. The flowers are in dense cymes on stalks nearly ½ inch long. The corolla is pale violet-blue or white; the five lobes are tipped with very slender bristles. There are no plaits between the lobes. § Late summer: woodlands and prairies, Me. to Minn., s. to Fla., Tenn., and Mo. *Fig. 88.*

    G. porphyrio (2 ft.) is a handsome species of the coastal plain pine barrens from N. J. to S. C. The flowers appear singly at the ends of main stem and branches. The corolla is bronze-green with bright blue lobes. The leaves are very narrow. § Late summer and autumn.

DOGBANE FAMILY (*Apocynaceae*)

    Most species of this family have a milky juice. Some are poisonous. The flower parts are in fives. There are two ovaries which share a single style and stigma; they form two pods. Besides the native species described below, the common cultivated periwinkle or myrtle, *Vinca minor,* is often found growing wild. It is a creeping plant with opposite leaves and erect blue or white flowers. In the western and southern states, species of *Amsonia* are found, with star-shaped flowers in terminal clusters and narrow, erect leaves.

THE DOGBANES (*Apocynum*)   PINK OR WHITE
    The dogbanes have paired leaves, with no teeth, on short stalks or without stalks, the blunt tip generally equipped with a short sharp point. The small bell-shaped flowers are in numerous clusters. Some of the species have apparently interbred, making identification sometimes difficult.

    A. androsaemifolium (to 20 in.) forks repeatedly, without any erect main stem. The uppermost flower clusters overtop the leaves; the flowers mostly hang down. The corolla, ¼ inch across, is pink, with stripes of deeper pink; it is fragrant. § Summer: dry thickets and fields, nearly throughout. *Fig. 89.*

    A. cannabinum, Indian hemp (3 ft.), has generally one erect main stem with side branches. The leaves generally have short stalks. The flowers are greenish or white, many with the corolla opening upward. § Summer: open places, throughout. *Fig. 89.*

    A. sibiricum (to 18 in.) has the general aspect of *A. cannabinum,* but the leaves are rounded or heart-shaped at the base and stalkless or nearly so. The flowers are white. § Summer: sandy or rocky places, throughout.

MILKWEED FAMILY (*Asclepiadaceae*)

    The Milkweed Family includes herbs, shrubs, and vines, mostl with paired leaves and milky juice. The flower parts are in five The stamens adhere to each other and to the stigma, forming

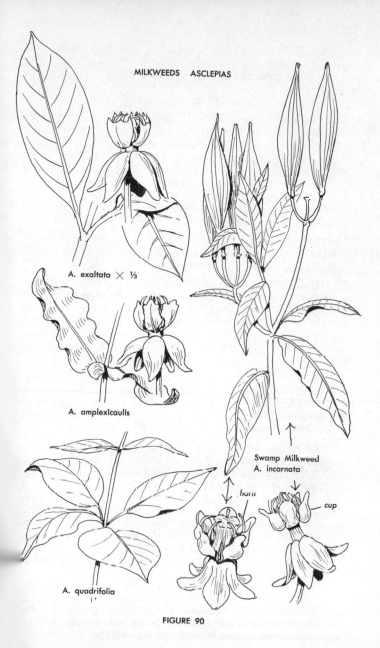

A. exaltata × ⅓

A. amplexicaulis

A. quadrifolia

Swamp Milkweed
A. incarnata

horn

cup

FIGURE 90

complex central body. There are two ovaries below the single stigma; they form two pods. The seeds are generally provided with a tuft of hair. The flowers are in umbel-like cymes (false umbels).

Genera of *Asclepiadaceae*

I. Erect herbs (compare II).

Asclepias has a flower with five horns arising from five cups (*Figs. 89, 90*); petals and sepals are bent sharply backward along the flower stalk, the sepals hidden.

Asclepiodora has cups on the petals but no horns (there is a small plate inside the cup, dividing it). The petals are green and spread apart, not bent backward.

Acerates has small greenish flowers with bent-back petals bearing cups but no horns (*Fig. 91*).

II. Vines, twining.

Gonolobus has heart-shaped leaves and brownish-purple or yellowish-white flowers (*Fig. 91*).

THE MILKWEEDS (*Asclepias*) ORANGE, RED, PURPLE, LAVENDER, OR WHITE / The milkweeds are familiar wild plants, often tall and coarse. The sharply back-bent petals support five cups from which spring the five incurved horns. The complex union of stamens and stigma results in an interesting method of pollination by insects. The flowers of some species are very fragrant. All flower in summer.

I. Species with no milky juice and orange flowers.

A. *tuberosa,* butterfly-weed or pleurisy-root (to 2 ft.), is a spreading, bushy, hairy plant. Most of the leaves grow singly on the stem. § Dry, open places, especially on sandy soil, Me. to Minn. and Colo., s. to Fla. and Ariz. PLATE 10.

II. Species with milky juice and leaves paired or in circles.

A. Species with paired leaves. These six may best be distinguished by the shape of the cups with their horns, shown in the illustrations. (Compare B.)

A. *syriaca,* common milkweed (to 6 ft.), has large, thick leaves, softly downy underneath, with short stalks. The petals are usually a dull lavender. The pods are covered with soft projections. § Fields, prairies, roadsides, N. B. to Sask., s. to Ga., Mo., and Nebr. *Fig. 89* and PLATE 10.

A. *purpurascens* (3 ft.) resembles A. *syriaca* but the petals are usually purple. The pods are downy but bear no projections. § Dry places, Mass. and N. H. to Minn. and S. D., s. to N. C., Miss., and Okla. *Fig. 89.*

A. *sullivantii* (5 ft.) also resembles A. *syriaca,* but is smooth not downy anywhere. The petals are pale purple. § Mois open places, Ont. to Minn., s. to O. and Kan. *Fig. 89.*

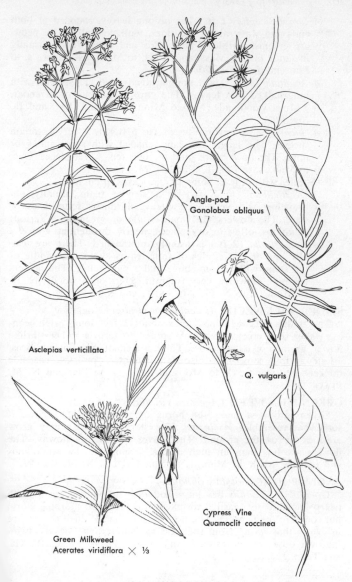

Angle-pod
Gonolobus obliquus

Asclepias verticillata

Q. vulgaris

Green Milkweed
Acerates viridiflora × ⅓

Cypress Vine
Quamoclit coccinea

FIGURE 91

A. *amplexicaulis* (2 ft.) has oblong leaves, rounded at both ends and wavy along the sides, with no stalks. The petals are greenish-purple. § Dry fields and open woods, usually in sandy places, Mass. and N. H. to Minn. and Nebr., s. to Fla. and Tex. *Fig. 90.*

A. *exaltata* (4 ft.) is a comparatively delicate species, with long-stalked thin leaves. The corolla is white or lavender. § Moist woodlands, Me. to Minn., s. to Ga., Ky., and Ia. *Fig. 90.*

A. *incarnata*, swamp milkweed (to 5 ft.), is a very common species. The leaves are lance-shaped with short stalks or none. The flowers are pink or light red. § Wet places, Que. to Man., s. to Fla., La., and N. M. *Fig. 90.*

B. Species with at least some of the leaves in circles.

A. *verticillata* (to 2 ft.) is a slender plant, usually unbranched, with very narrow leaves in threes, fours, fives, or sixes. The flowers are small, white or greenish. § Various situations, often in dry places, nearly throughout. *Fig. 91.*

A. *quadrifolia* (2 ft.) is usually unbranched. There are usually one or two circles of four leaves about the middle of the stem, with a pair above and a pair below. The flowers are pink or white, very fragrant. § Dry open woods, N. H. to Minn., s. to N. C., Ala., Ark., and Kan. *Fig. 90.*

SPIDER MILKWEED (*Asclepiodora viridis*)   GREEN

The spider milkweed has stems about 2 feet long, often leaning rather than erect. The petals spread to form a rather starlike flower, an inch or more across. There are small cups but no horns. § Late spring, sometimes also late summer: prairies, roadside thickets, dry woods, O. to Mo. and Nebr., s. to Fla. and N. M. PLATE 11.

GREEN MILKWEED (*Acerates viridiflora*)   GREEN

Green milkweed lacks the horns of the flower. Otherwise it somewhat resembles *Asclepias*. The stem (to 2 ft.) may grow erect or lie on the ground. The leaves are slightly downy. The flowers are less than an inch across. § Summer: dry woodlands and prairies, Mich. to Man., s. to Va., La., and N. M. *Fig. 91.*

ANGLE-POD (*Gonolobus obliquus*)   BROWN-PURPLE

Gonolobus obliquus has large roundish or pointed leaves with heart-shaped base (easily mistaken for those of morning-glory; but compare the figures). The flowers, less than ½ inch across, are in cymes that spring from the axils. § Summer: in thickets, twining over other plants, often in dry places, Pa. to Mo., s. to Ga. and Tenn. *Fig. 91.*

MORNING-GLORY FAMILY (*Convolvulaceae*)

Most of the species of the *Convolvulaceae* that are common i

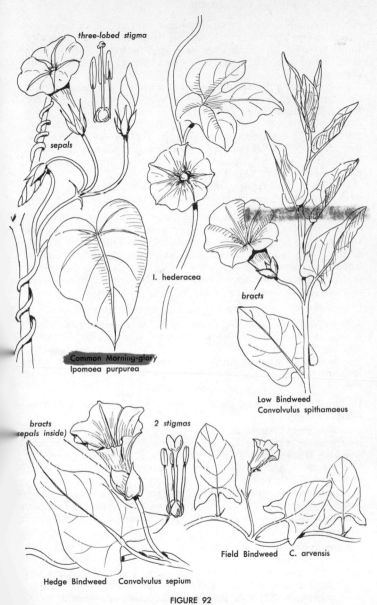

three-lobed stigma

sepals

I. hederacea

bracts

Common Morning-glory
Ipomoea purpurea

Low Bindweed
Convolvulus spithamaeus

bracts
(sepals inside)

2 stigmas

Hedge Bindweed   Convolvulus sepium

Field Bindweed   C. arvensis

FIGURE 92

our range are climbing or trailing vines with undivided leaves attached singly. The flower parts are in fives. The corolla generally forms a flaring tube with only very shallow lobes. Stigmas vary from one to four. There are only two ovules in each chamber of the ovary.

Ipomoea has a flaring, only slightly lobed corolla, blue, purple, or white. There is one style and stigma; the stigma may have from one to three lobes (*Fig. 92*).

Convolvulus has (except in one species) a pair of bracts outside the calyx and almost concealing it. The corolla is much like that of *Ipomoea,* white or pink. There are two stigmas (*Fig. 92*).

Quamoclit has a scarlet corolla which flares into a nearly flat, five-lobed disk (*Fig. 91*). There are two stigmas.

Cuscuta is a genus of parasitic vines, with yellowish or orange stems, minute flowers in dense clusters, and no leaves (*Fig. 93*).

MORNING-GLORIES (*Ipomoea*)   WHITE, BLUE, OR PURPLE

The morning-glories are familiar twining plants with long-stalked leaves and funnel-shaped corollas which are blue, purple, or white with purplish markings. Most of our species came from tropical South America and have become weeds here. The sweet potato, *I. batatas,* is also a native of South America. With us the morning-glories flower in summer and early autumn.

I. Species with three-lobed stigma and three-chambered ovary.

I. purpurea is especially abundant in moist cornfields, where it may be troublesome. The leaves are heart-shaped. § Throughout. *Fig. 92.*

I. hederacea has most of its leaves three-lobed. The sepals have long, narrow, hairy tips. § N. E. to N. D., s. to Fla. and Ariz. *Fig. 92.*

II. Species with unlobed or two-lobed stigma and two-chambered ovary.

I. pandurata, man-of-the-earth, has an edible root-tuber which may grow to an enormous size (sometimes several feet long and weighing 20 pounds). The leaves resemble those of *I. purpurea.* The corolla is white with a purplish center. § Dry soil, open or in thickets, Conn. to Mich., Ill., and Kan., s. to Fla. and Tex.

I. lacunosa has a small corolla (less than an inch long), usually white. The leaves are much like those of *I. purpurea.* § Thickets, meadows, roadsides, etc., N. J. to Kan., s. to Fla. and Tex.

THE BINDWEEDS (*Convolvulus*)   WHITE OR PINK

Convolvulus differs from *Ipomoea* in having large bracts around the calyx (except in *C. arvensis*) and two rather narrow stigmas. The leaves have more pointed basal lobes. The flowers are white or pink. Our species flower through the summer.

C. sepium, hedge bindweed, has a spear-shaped leaf with short,

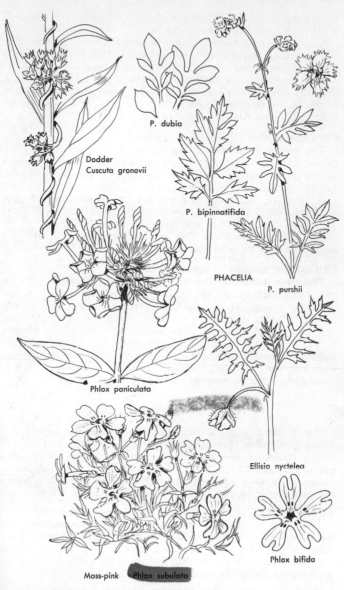

Dodder
Cuscuta gronovii

P. dubia

P. bipinnatifida

PHACELIA

P. purshii

Phlox paniculata

Ellisia nyctelea

Moss-pink   Phlox subulata

Phlox bifida

FIGURE 93

266 / Phlox Family

blunt basal lobes. The corolla is about 2 inches long. § Thickets, waste places, etc., throughout. *Fig. 92.*

C. arvensis, field bindweed, has flowers less than an inch long. The leaves are spear-shaped or triangular. This European immigrant is often a very troublesome weed. § Throughout. *Fig. 92.*

C. spithamaeus, low bindweed, is more or less erect (to 20 in.), generally downy. The corolla is about 2 inches long. § Dry open places, Me. to Ont. and Minn., s. to Va. and Ia., and in the mountains to Ga. and Ala. *Fig. 92.*

CYPRESS-VINES (*Quamoclit*)   SCARLET

Two species of *Quamoclit* are natives of tropical America, cultivated and here and there escaped into the wild. The corolla flares into a five-toothed or five-lobed flat disk at the end of a narrow tube an inch or more long.

Q. coccinea, red morning-glory, has broad leaves which may be deeply lobed or unlobed, with heart-shaped base. § N.Y. to Mich. and Kan., s. to Fla. and Ariz. *Fig. 91.*

Q. vulgaris, cypress-vine, has leaves pinnately divided into very narrow lobes. § Va. and Mo. *Fig. 91.*

DODDER (*Cuscuta*)   TAWNY OR ORANGE

The name dodder applies to a large number of species of *Cuscuta* which lack leaves and green color; they are usually straw-colored or orange. They twine about other plants and send suckers into them, living on them as parasites. The flowers are very small and often very numerous. The species are difficult to identify without recourse to technical characteristics. Two of the commonest species almost throughout our range are *C. polygonorum,* with flower parts in fours, and *C. gronovii,* with flower parts in fives. They flower in summer and autumn. *Fig. 93.*

PHLOX FAMILY (Polemoniaceae)

The Phlox Family is recognized by five joined sepals, five joined petals, five stamens attached to the corolla, and a pistil with a three-branched style and a three-chambered ovary. Two genera are common in our range: *Phlox,* with undivided leaves; *Polemonium,* with pinnately divided leaves. Several other genera and many more species occur in the western United States.

THE PHLOXES (*Phlox*)   BLUE, VIOLET, PINK, OR WHITE

The leaves of *Phlox* are mostly paired, except sometimes near the inflorescence. The flowers are in clusters at the summit of the stem and of its branches. The corolla forms a narrow tube which flares almost at right angles into five spreading lobes. The stamens are attached within the tube at different levels.

I. Species with erect stems (compare II).

A. Erect species whose stamens are completely enclosed in the corolla (compare B).

P. *divaricata,* wild sweet-William (a misleading name; sweet-William is in the Pink Family) (to 3 ft.), has ovate leaves on a more or less hairy stem. The flowers are generally a soft blue. After flowering, the plant forms stolons which, the next spring, give rise to new erect stems. § Spring: woodlands and open places, Que. to Mich. and Nebr., s. to S. C., Ala., and Tex. PLATE 11.

P. *pilosa,* also called wild sweet-William (to 2 ft.), has narrow, more or less hairy leaves. The stem may be downy. The flowers are generally purplish-pink. § Spring: mostly in woods, Conn. to Ont. and Sask., s. to Fla. and Tex.

B. Erect species whose stamens and stigma reach the opening of the corolla tube or project beyond it.

P. *maculata* (to 3 ft.) has a stem often spotted ("maculate") with purple. The pinkish-purple flowers are in a long, nearly cylindric panicle. § Summer: moist places, Que. to Minn., s. to N. C., Tenn., and Mo.

P. *glaberrima* (to 4 ft.) is slender and very smooth. The leaves are narrow and sharp-pointed. The generally pale pink flowers are in a loose dome-shaped cluster. § Summer: moist open woodlands and prairies, O. to Wis. and Mo., s. to Fla. and Tex.

P. *paniculata* (to 6 ft.) is the stoutest of these species. The leaves are lance-shaped and veiny. The magenta-pink or white flowers are on very short stalks in a broad, dense cluster. § Summer and autumn: woodlands or moist soil, N. Y. to Ia. and Kan., s. to Ga., Miss., and Ark.; elsewhere escaped from cultivation. *Fig. 93.*

II. Species that form mats of low growth.

P. *subulata,* moss-pink (neither a moss nor a pink), is cultivated in many color forms. The stems creep or trail, the leaves are almost needlelike. The flowers, rose-magenta on the wild plants, are in flat cymes. § Spring: rocky ledges and sandy soil, N. Y. to Mich., s. to N. C. and Tenn.; escaped elsewhere. *Fig. 93.*

P. *bifida* (6–8 in.) is a shrubby species, much branched. The narrow leaves are stiff. The pale purple lobes of the corolla are cleft halfway to the tube. § Spring: dry soil and rocky ledges, Ind. and Mich. to Ia., s. to Tenn. and Okla. *Fig. 93.*

JACOB'S-LADDER or GREEK-VALERIAN (*Polemonium*)   BLUE
Polemonium is recognized by its pinnately divided leaves. The stems, which frequently arch, bear small terminal clusters of handsome sky-blue flowers. The petals are joined for only a short distance, with no sharp distinction between the tube and the lobes.

P. *reptans* (about 1 ft.) has stamens the same length as the corolla tube or shorter. § Late spring and early summer: rich woods and bottomlands, N. Y. to Minn., s. to Ga., Ala., and Okla.; common and often cultivated. PLATE 11.

P. *van-bruntiae* (3 ft.) has the stamens projecting beyond the corolla tube. § Summer: swamps and bogs in woods, generally in mountains, Vt. and N. Y., s. to Md. and W. Va.

WATERLEAF FAMILY (Hydrophyllaceae)

The *Hydrophyllaceae* have flower parts in fives, but the pistil has generally but one chamber; the style has two branches in the species described below (there are many other species in the western United States). The sepals are almost separate; the petals are joined to form a bell or lobed disk. In general aspect some plants of this family resemble the *Boraginaceae;* others suggest the *Polemoniaceae.* Our species grow mostly in woodlands.

Ellisia is a small weed with pinnately cleft leaves and inconspicuous white flowers borne singly.

Phacelia has mostly pinnately cleft or divided leaves and blue or white flowers in a coiled false raceme.

Hydrophyllum contains some rather tall plants with sharply lobed or divided leaves attached singly, and white or pale violet flowers in clusters, mostly drooping. The stamens generally project from the corolla. The fruit is a round pod with a few seeds.

ELLISIA (*Ellisia nyctelea*)   WHITE

This little weed grows in woods, along streams, even in shaded lawns, most commonly in the Midwest. The leaves are deeply pinnately cleft, the lobes having a few blunt teeth. The small flowers, with petals no longer than the sepals, hang singly from the axils of the leaves. The plants disappear in the heat of summer. § Late spring and early summer: N. Y. and N. J. to N. C.; Mich. to Alta., s. to Ind., Okla., and Colo.; occasional in N. E. *Fig. 93.*

SCORPION-WEEDS (*Phacelia*)   BLUE OR LILAC

Most species of *Phacelia* are western; others, including those mentioned here, grow in the Southeast, where some in early spring carpet upland woods with their delicate bloom. They are small plants with pinnately cleft or divided leaves attached singly. The flowers are borne in false racemes, which are coiled at the tip and uncoil as the flowers pass into fruit. The fruit is a small, many-seeded pod.

P. *purshii* (20 in.) has fringed blue petals. The upper leaves, which are pinnately cleft, are stalkless. The plant is rather sparsely hairy. § Spring and early summer: woods and banks, Pa. to Minn. s. to Ala., Tenn., and Okla. *Fig. 93.*

P. *dubia* (16 in.) has lilac-blue petals with plain edges. Th

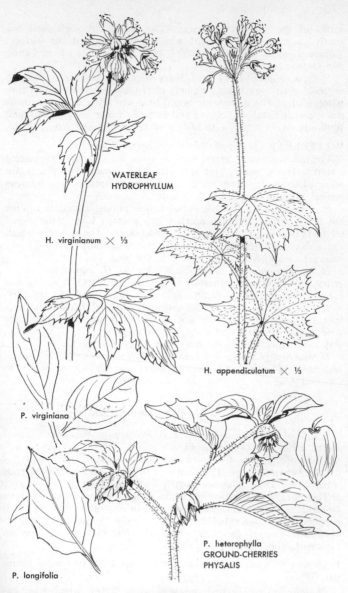

WATERLEAF
HYDROPHYLLUM

H. virginianum × ⅓

H. appendiculatum × ⅓

P. virginiana

P. longifolia

P. heterophylla
GROUND-CHERRIES
PHYSALIS

FIGURE 94

stalks of the stamens are hairy. The leaves are cleft, and are partly covered with stiff hairs which lie flat against the surface. § Spring: woods and rocky ledges, N. Y. to O., s. to Fla., Tenn., and Okla. *Fig. 93.*

P. bipinnatifida (2 ft.) has a hairy stem and long-stalked leaves, some of which are twice pinnately cleft (the lobes themselves pinnately cleft). The flowers are bright blue and fringed. The stamens have bearded stalks. § Spring and early summer: rich woods and bottomlands, O. and Va. to Mo., s. to Ga., Ala., and Ark. *Fig. 93.*

WATERLEAF (*Hydrophyllum*)   WHITE OR VIOLET

The peculiar light green markings on their leaves, suggesting watermarks on paper, give this genus its names. The plants are addicted to shady, damp woods and banks of streams. The stamens project noticeably beyond the petals.

H. canadense (2 ft.) has broad leaves almost round in outline but cut by rather shallow notches into pointed lobes with jagged teeth. It is smooth or downy with short hairs. The flowers, which are whitish, are generally lower than the uppermost leaves. § Early summer: Vt. to Mich. and Mo., s. to Ga. and Ala.

H. appendiculatum (2 ft.) is similar to *H. canadense* but is hairy and the flowers generally rise above the leaves. § Spring and early summer: Ont. to Minn., s. to Pa., Tenn., and Mo. *Fig. 94.*

H. virginianum (3 ft.) has pinnately divided leaves, the segments sharply toothed. It is smooth or nearly so. The flowers are pale violet. § Spring and early summer: Que. to Man., s. to Va., Ark., and Kan., and in the mountains to N. C. *Fig. 94.*

H. macrophyllum (2 ft.) is similar to *H. virginianum* but rough and hairy. § Spring and early summer: Va. and O. to Ill., s. to Ga. and Ala.

POTATO FAMILY (*Solanaceae*)

Plants of the Potato Family have five sepals, five petals joined at the base and flaring or united into a bell-shaped or funnel-shaped corolla, and five generally equal stamens. The pistil has usually two chambers. The fruit is a berry or pod with numerous small seeds. The leaves are usually singly attached.

The potato (*Solanum tuberosum*), the tomato (*Lycopersicon esculentum*), egg-plant (*Solanum melongena*), and red and green peppers (*Capsicum*) belong to this family. Some other genera yield well-known products: tobacco (*Nicotiana*), stramonium (*Datura*), and atropine or belladonna (*Atropa*).

I. Genera with petals joined to form a cup, tube, or funnel (compare II).

  Physalis has cup-shaped yellow or white flowers which hang below the leaves (*Fig. 94*).

Nicandra has pale blue bell-shaped flowers and almost separate sepals.

Datura has large white trumpet-shaped flowers and spiny pods (*Fig. 96*).

II. Genus with petals joined only at the base, flaring into a more or less star-shaped figure: *Solanum*.

GROUND-CHERRIES (*Physalis*)   WHITE OR YELLOW

The ground-cherries are mostly weedy plants with flowers hanging singly or in clusters, usually from forks of the stem. The most striking characteristic is the growth of the sepals to form a papery bladder which encloses the berry. The berries have often been used in making preserves. The Chinese-lantern-plant is a cultivated species of *Physalis*. The wild species are difficult to identify. The following are common or noteworthy. All flower in summer.

P. heterophylla has leaf blades round at the base. The young stems are covered with spreading hairs which are usually sticky. The corolla is yellow with a dark center. The calyx is slightly indented at fruiting. § Dry soil, Que. to Sask., s. to Ga., Ky., and Tex. *Fig. 94.*

P. virginiana (2 ft.) has leaf blades which taper gradually to their stalks; they are sparsely downy with minute curved hairs. The corolla is yellow. The calyx around the berry appears as if pushed in where the stem is attached. § Dry soil, Conn. to Ont. and Man., s. to Fla. and Tex. *Fig. 94.*

P. longifolia has leaves which are smooth or minutely downy along the veins. The corolla is yellow. The calyx is scarcely indented at fruiting. § Fields, woods, prairies, Vt. to Mont., s. to Va., Tex., and Ariz. *Fig. 94.*

P. grandiflora has white flowers 1½ inches across, with a yellow eye. It is somewhat sticky. § Que. to Sask., s. to Vt. and Minn.

P. pruinosa, strawberry tomato, is densely woolly, appearing grayish. The leaf blades are round or heart-shaped at the base. § Moist soil, Mass. to Ia. and Kan., s. to Fla. and Tenn.

APPLE-OF-PERU (*Nicandra physalodes*)   BLUE

The plant (to 5 ft.) has the general aspect of a *Physalis*, but the flowers are blue. It comes from Peru, and is most often found near dwellings and in old fields. The fruits and especially the seeds are poisonous. § Summer: N. S. to Mo., s. to Fla.

JIMSON-WEED (*Datura stramonium*)   WHITE OR VIOLET

Jimson-weed is a rank weed (4 ft.) with large trumpet-shaped flowers (to 4 in. long) which arise singly in the forks of the stem. The leaves are wavy-toothed and smooth. The fruit is a spiny pod (a form is known that lacks the spines) which contains numerous small dark seeds. All parts of the plant are dangerously poisonous. The name is said to be a corruption of Jamestown-weed, but the species seems to have come originally from Asia. § Summer and autumn: fields and waste places, throughout but more abundant southward. *Fig. 96.*

NIGHTSHADES and HORSE-NETTLES (*Solanum*)   VIOLET, WHITE, OR YELLOW / *Solanum* is recognized by the five spreading, pointed lobes of the corolla, and by the manner in which the five stamens "connive" around the pistil to make a pointed yellow center in the flower; in some species, however, one stamen is longer than the others and, with the style, points downward. The flower clusters are attached *between* the points where leaves arise —an unusual arrangement.

I. Smooth or nearly smooth species with red or black berries (compare II and III).

   S. nigrum, black nightshade (2 ft.), is bushy and spreading. The leaves are long-stalked, ovate. The flowers are white or pale violet, less than ½ inch across. The black berries are believed to be poisonous. They have often been used in cookery without harm; but those of some varieties may be poisonous if eaten raw, so that it is best to avoid them all. § Summer: woods and waste places, throughout. *Fig. 95.*

   S. dulcamara, bittersweet (to 12 ft.), a more or less woody climbing plant, has pointed leaves with a distinct lobe on either side at the base; or it may be divided into three segments. The flowers are violet or purple. The berries are red. § Summer: moist thickets, scrambling over other plants, throughout. *Fig. 95.*

II. Prickly species.

   S. carolinense, horse-nettle (to 3 ft.), has prickles on stem, leaf stalks, and main veins of leaves. The petals are white or pale violet, the corolla more than ½ inch across. The berry is yellow. § Summer: waste places and fields, especially in sandy soil, Vt. to Wash., s. to Fla. and Tex. *Fig. 95.*

   S. rostratum, buffalo-bur (to 2 ft.), is a western plant that has invaded the Midwest and is spreading eastward. The prickles are more numerous than in *S. carolinense.* The sepals enclose the berry so as to give the impression of a prickly fruit. The flowers are yellow. The lowest anther is much longer than the others and curved. § Summer: dry prairies and waste places, especially in sand. *Fig. 95.*

III. Species silvery with branched white hairs.

   S. elaeagnifolium, silverleaf nightshade (to 3 ft.), is a southwestern species now adventive in the Midwest. The plant is densely covered with white hairs which, through a lens, may be seen to be branched. There are few or no prickles. The flower is pale violet, the berry yellow. § Summer: prairies and waste places, O. to Mo., s. to Fla., Tex., and Ariz.

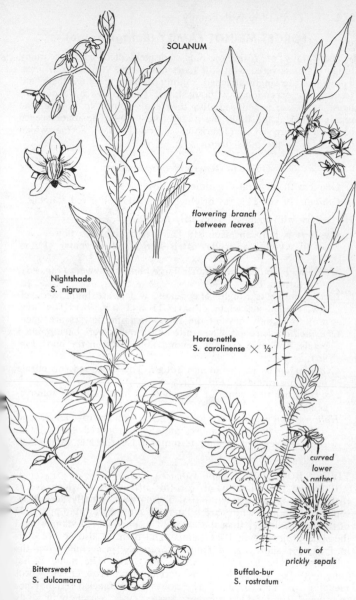

SOLANUM

Nightshade
S. nigrum

flowering branch
between leaves

Horse-nettle
S. carolinense × ⅓

Bittersweet
S. dulcamara

Buffalo-bur
S. rostratum

curved
lower
anther

bur of
prickly sepals

FIGURE 95

FORGET-ME-NOT FAMILY (*Boraginaceae*)

The family of forget-me-nots, borages, etc., contains many rough plants covered with stiff hairs, and some very smooth ones. The leaves are singly attached, mainly without marginal teeth and (with a few exceptions) without stalks. The flowers have parts in fives, mostly arranged radially, the petals joined in a tube, the sepals united at the base, the ovary four-lobed. The inflorescence of most genera is characteristic: a coiled false raceme which straightens as the buds open.

Guide to Genera of *Boraginaceae*

I. Genus with bilaterally symmetric flowers.

Echium (PLATE 11) has bright blue flowers with red stamens.

II. Genera with radially symmetric flowers.

Myosotis is not conspicuously hairy or rough; the flowers are small, sky-blue or white, often with a yellow center (PLATE 11).

Mertensia is smooth, with fairly large hanging flowers (*Fig. 96*), pink turning blue.

Lithospermum is rough. The petals, which are blunt, are yellow, orange, or white (PLATE 11 and *Fig. 97*). The style projects slightly beyond the tube when the flowers are open.

Onosmodium is rough. The white or yellow flowers have pointed petals. The style projects beyond them even in the bud (*Fig. 96*).

Cynoglossum is hairy but not rough. The blue, red, or purple petals are rounded (*Fig. 97*).

Hackelia has tiny white or blue flowers in a branched inflorescence.

Heliotropium includes a native species with narrow leaves and white flowers borne singly; and an introduced species with ovate leaves and a long terminal false raceme; both small plants (*Fig. 97*).

VIPER'S-BUGLOSS (*Echium vulgare*)   BLUE
Blueweed is another name for this bristly plant which colors roadsides in the season (to 3 ft.). The flowers, usually deep blue, sometimes pink or white, are bilaterally symmetric, the upper side of the corolla longer than the lower. The unequal red stamens and the style project beyond the petals. The plant is also conspicuous in fruit, the short, coiled fruiting branches projecting from the main stem. The leaves lack stalks and teeth. The name is not "bug-loss" but "bu-gloss"; it is derived from two Greek words meaning "ox" and "tongue." The flower has a fancied resemblance to a viper's head. § Late summer: waste places, especially in sandy soil, throughout. PLATE 11.

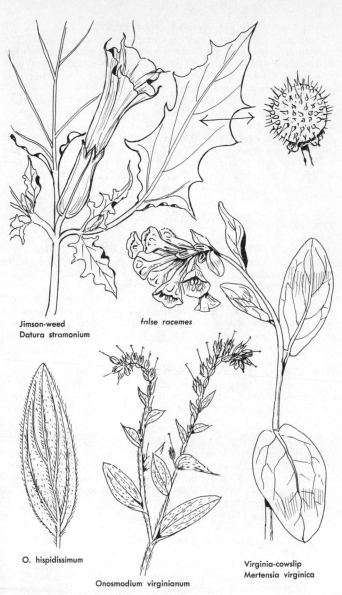

Jimson-weed
Datura stramonium

false racemes

O. hispidissimum

Onosmodium virginianum

Virginia-cowslip
Mertensia virginica

FIGURE 96

FORGET-ME-NOT (*Myosotis*)   BLUE OR WHITE
There are many species of *Myosotis,* eight in our area. The small bright blue or white flowers, some with a yellow center, are similar in all, and are all arranged in similar inflorescences. Where the tube of the corolla flares into the five round lobes, there are five small scalelike appendages.

M. scorpioides (to 2 ft.) has flowers up to ⅔ inch across, with yellow centers. § Summer: moist woods and stream banks, throughout. PLATE 11.

M. laxa has weak stems (to 2 ft. long), that tend to lie on the ground. It has hairs that lie flat against the surface of stem and leaves. The corolla is pale blue with a yellow center. § Summer: wet soil, Nfld. to Minn., s. to Ga. and Tenn.; B. C. to Calif.

M. verna (18 in.) is always erect. The sepals are hairy. The corolla is white, about ⅙ inch across. § Early summer: dry soil, Me. to Mich. and Kan., s. to Fla. and Tex.; Ida. to B. C., s. to Wyo. and Calif.

VIRGINIA-COWSLIP or VIRGINIA BLUEBELLS (*Mertensia virginica*)   BLUE / This attractive flower, which is frequently grown in gardens, is related neither to English cowslips (in the Primrose Family) nor to English bluebells (Lily Family) nor to Scottish bluebells (Bluebell Family). It is a smooth plant (to 2 ft.) with flowers which hang in a cluster from the summit of the stem. The petals are at first pink. § Spring: moist bottomlands, open or wooded, N. Y. and Ont. to Minn. and Kan., s. to S. C., Ala., and Ark. *Fig. 96.*

THE PUCCOONS and GROMWELLS (*Lithospermum*)   YELLOW OR WHITE / *Lithospermum* bears its flowers in clusters that are not obviously coiled, at the ends of the stems; they either form a flattish cluster or grow singly in the leaf axils. The roots are commonly red.

I. Species with yellow or yellowish flowers (compare II).

  L. canescens, yellow puccoon, Indian pink or paint (20 in.), is covered with soft white hairs. The bright yellow or orange flowers are about ½ inch across. § Early summer: prairies and open woodlands, n. N. Y. and Ont. to Sask., s. to Ga. and Tex. PLATE 11.

  L. carolinense, another puccoon (to 20 in.), has yellow or orange flowers to 1 inch across. It is hairy with rather loose, stiff hairs. § Early summer: mostly in sandy soil, Ont. to Mont., s. to Fla. and Tex.; the northern plants may be a distinct species, *L. croceum. Fig. 97.*

  L. incisum (to 20 in.) is recognized by the toothed edges of the petals. The flowers are about ¾ inch across. The leaves are very narrow. § Late spring: dry prairies, Ont. to B. C., s. to Ind., Ill., Mo., and Mexico. *Fig. 97.*

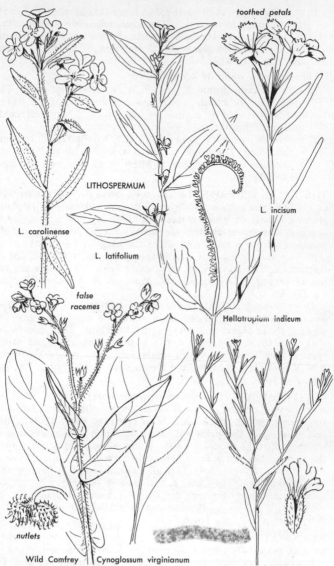

toothed petals

LITHOSPERMUM

L. carolinense

L. latifolium

L. incisum

Hellotropium indicum

false racemes

nutlets

Wild Comfrey   Cynoglossum virginianum

Heliotropium tenellum

FIGURE 97

L. latifolium, gromwell (3 ft.), has lance-shaped or almost ovate leaves, rough to the touch. The small yellowish flowers, about ¼ inch across, are in the axils. § Late spring: woodland borders and open places, N. Y. to Minn., s. to W. Va., Ark., and Kan. *Fig. 97.*

II. Species with white or whitish flowers.

L. arvense, corn gromwell (2 ft.), is an introduced weed. The small white or bluish flowers grow in the axils of the leaves, each surrounded by a circle of long bracts. § Summer: sandy roadsides, throughout.

L. officinale, common gromwell (3 ft.), has flowers only about ⅕ inch long. The leaves are narrow, each with a single vein. § Summer: roadsides, Que. to Minn., s. to N. J. and Ill.; from the Old World.

THE FALSE GROMWELLS (*Onosmodium*)   WHITISH OR YELLOW / The false gromwells are small-flowered, densely hairy plants growing mostly in waste places and blooming inconspicuously in summer. The flower clusters are sharply curved or coiled and the pale petals form a tube from which the long style projects.

O. virginianum (2–3 ft.), is covered with hairs that lie flat on the surface. The leaves have three main veins. The petals are yellow or orange. § Dry woodlands, Mass. to N. Y., s. to Fla. and La. *Fig. 96.*

O. occidentale (2 ft.) has a looser hairiness than *O. virginianum.* The leaves have one main vein. The petals are greenish-white. § Ill. to Minn. and Alta., s. to Mo., Okla., Tex., and N. M.

O. hispidissimum (about 4 ft.) is the tallest and most bristly species. The leaves have one main vein. The petals are white. § N. Y. and Ont. to Minn. and Nebr., s. to N. C., Tenn., La., and Tex. *Fig. 96.*

WILD COMFREY (*Cynoglossum virginianum*)   BLUE, LILAC, OR WHITE / Wild comfrey is a tall (over 2 ft.), softly hairy plant with large leaves which partly encircle or clasp the stem. Their texture and shape give the plant the alternate name of hound's-tongue, which is also the meaning of the Latin name. The petals spread; the stamens are not evident. The fruit consists of nutlets (one to four from a flower) covered with hooked spines. § Late spring: open woods, Conn. to Okla., s. to Fla. and Tex. *Fig. 97.*

A species from Europe, the original hound's-tongue, *C. officinale,* with red-purple flowers and an unpleasant odor, is established throughout our range.

STICKSEED or BEGGAR'S-LICE (*Hackelia virginiana*)   WHITE OR PALE BLUE / Stickseed is an erect but loosely branched plant (to 4 ft.), with very small flowers in loose, coiled inflorescences. The "seeds" that stick by their hooked bristles are really the fruits (nutlets)—four from each ovary. § Summer: woodlands and waste places, nearly throughout.

THE HELIOTROPES (*Heliotropium*)   WHITE OR BLUE

Most heliotropes are tropical plants. We have one insignificant species native in our range.

H. tenellum (1 ft.), with small white flowers in small clusters in the axils of leaves and at the summit of the stem, does not resemble the scented, purple heliotrope of gardens. Its slender stem and narrow leaves are covered with short, stiff, white hairs. § Summer: dry woodlands, Ky. to Kan., s. to Ala. and Tex. *Fig. 97.*

H. indicum (2 ft.) is coarsely hairy, with ovate leaves. The bluish flowers are in a long, dense, coiled spike. § Late spring to autumn: waste places, bottomlands, Va. to Mo., s. to Fla. and Tex.; presumably a native of Brazil. *Fig. 97.*

GROUP V OF DICOT FAMILIES. PETALS JOINED, BILATERALLY SYMMETRIC; OVARY SUPERIOR

A. Plants with a four-lobed ovary (compare B).

The **Forget-me-not Family** has mostly radially symmetric flowers, but *Echium* has bilaterally symmetric flowers, blue with red stamens.

The **Vervain Family** has four stamens. The corolla spreads into a nearly radially symmetric form, without distinct upper and lower lips (*Fig. 98*). The leaves are paired.

The **Mint Family** has two or four stamens. The corolla of most genera has distinct upper and lower lips (*Figs. 99, 100*), though in some genera the corolla has four almost equal lobes. The leaves are paired on a generally square stem.

B. Plants whose ovary is not lobed.

The **Snapdragon Family** has two, four, or five stamens (one or two of them in some genera without anthers; *Fig. 109*). The ovary has two chambers containing numerous ovules. The leaves are borne singly or in pairs.

The **Unicorn-plant Family** is identified by its curious horned fruit; the curved, sharp spine splits into two.

The **Broom-rape Family** lacks green color. The plants are small, parasitic.

The **Lopseed Family** includes in our range only one species, lopseed. The flowers are in a spike. The sharp-toothed calyx closes over the achene and bends sharply downward against the stem.

The **Bladderwort Family** includes small aquatic plants with minute bladders on the submerged leaves (*Fig. 114*) and terrestrial plants with light green, glistening leaves. There are two stamens. The lower lip of the corolla bears a spur (hollow tube).

The **Acanthus Family** has two or four stamens (flowers with four are radially symmetric; *Fig. 115*). The ovary has two chambers containing many ovules. The leaves are paired, without teeth, and practically without stalks.

VERVAIN FAMILY (*Verbenaceae*)

The Vervain Family is characterized by mostly paired leaves which in our species are toothed or cleft, and by a corolla that consists of a tube that flares into four or five flat lobes. There are generally four stamens in pairs of unequal length. The ovary is more or less four-lobed.

Verbena has a five-lobed corolla, almost but not quite radially symmetric.

Lippia lanceolata, a representative of a large genus of warmer regions, is a small trailing weed with a very small four-parted blue corolla.

THE VERVAINS (*Verbena*)   BLUE, PURPLE, PINK, OR WHITE

This is a large genus, mostly American; we have some 16 species in our range, of which the five described below are the commonest. They have flowers in spikes or flattish clusters.

V. canadensis (2 ft.) is a bushy species, the stems spreading. The leaves vary, being generally sharply toothed, cleft, and lobed. The inflorescence tends to be flat or domed. The bracts are of about the same length as the calyx. The flowers are at first blue, purple, or lilac, turning pink as they age. § Spring and summer: fields, hillsides, rocky ledges, Pa. to Ill. and Colo., s. to Fla. and Tex.; Mich.; Minn. *Fig. 98.*

V. bracteata has stems (2 ft.) that tend to recline. The leaves are hairy above and beneath, typically with one narrow lobe on each side (sometimes pinnately cleft). The flowers are purple, in spikes, only a few opening at a time. The bracts are longer than the calyx. § Summer: prairies and waste places, Ill. to Minn. and B. C., e. to Va., s. to Fla. and Mexico. *Fig. 98.*

V. hastata (5 ft.) is a handsome species with spear-shaped ("hastata") spikes, the spikes themselves clustered, a few blue or purple flowers encircling each at some one level. The leaves are generally narrow, toothed, stalked, sometimes lobed. § Summer: moist fields, throughout. PLATE 12.

V. stricta (2–4 ft.) has rather blunt spikes, a few bright blue or lavender flowers surrounding each spike at some level. The stem is not much branched. The leaves are hairy and sharply toothed, without stalks. § Summer: dry open places, N. Y. and Ont. to Mont., s. to Tenn., Okla., and N. M.; Mass. to Del. and W. Va. *Fig. 98.*

V. urticifolia (to 5 ft.) is an unattractive plant with short stalked, broad, sharply toothed leaves which recall those of nettle (*Urtica*); they are generally blotched with mildew. Th

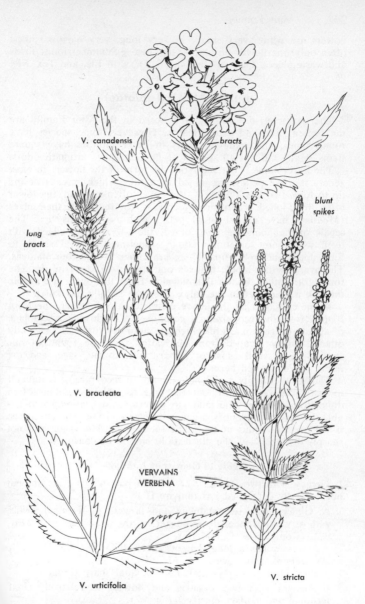

V. canadensis

bracts

long bracts

blunt spikes

V. bracteata

VERVAINS VERBENA

V. urticifolia

V. stricta

FIGURE 98

flowers are white, very small, in very long, very narrow spikes; often only one flower on a spike is open. § Summer: moist fields and waste places, Que. to Ont. and S. D., s. to Fla. and Tex. *Fig. 98.*

MINT FAMILY (*Labiatae*)

The characteristics usually first noted in the Mint Family are the square stem and paired leaves. However, some species have round stems, and some members of other families have square stems. Many but not all species of *Labiatae* have aromatic odors.

The Latin name is derived from the form of the flower: in most genera the five petals are joined in a tube which spreads at the tip to form two lips ("labia"), the upper often notched, the lower often three-lobed. There are exceptions, for the mints themselves (*Mentha*) have almost equal petals with no obvious lips. The sepals of *Labiatae* are also joined, the calyx being edged with teeth which are sometimes equal, sometimes unequal so as to form upper and lower lips. There are either two or four stamens. The ovary is four-lobed; there is one style, forked at the tip. The four little nutlike bodies that develop from the ovary are visible through a magnifier in the calyx after the corolla has fallen.

If one considers all the above characteristics together, the Mint Family is easily recognized. It comprises a worldwide assemblage of about 160 genera, 30 of which are here described. Occasionally others, mostly escaped from cultivation, may be found in our area. Several, such as savory, marjoram, thyme, sage, and the mints, are cultivated herbs.

Though the family as a whole is easy to recognize, it is difficult to distinguish genera without recourse to technical details often difficult to observe. The guide to genera, below, attempts to enable the reader to identify a genus by easily visible characteristics; if the main divisions of the guide seem somewhat vague and not sharply distinguished, the illustrations should be consulted.

Guide to Genera of *Labiatae*

I. Genera with two stamens. (A second pair may be present but not normally developed.) (Compare II.)

    A. Genera with two stamens and flowers in terminal heads, with or without other dense clusters in the upper leaf axils (*Fig. 99*). (Compare B, C, and D.)

        Monarda has a long, narrow, curved corolla, the lower lip bent sharply downward (*Fig. 99*).

        Blephilia has a calyx cleft into unequal sharp teeth.

    B. Genera with two stamens and flowers in relatively small terminal and axillary clusters (*Fig. 99*).

        Cunila has a straight, almost radially symmetric corolla with five lobes (*Fig. 99*).

Salvia (lyrata) has pinnately cleft or lobed basal leaves; the corolla is distinctly two-lipped (*Fig. 99*).

C. Genera with two stamens and flowers mostly in axillary clusters (*Fig. 100*).

Hedeoma has a two-lipped calyx, unequally cleft into three short upper teeth and two long lower teeth. The corolla is blue. The leaves are without teeth.

Lycopus has a calyx with five equal teeth. The corolla is white, with four nearly equal lobes. The leaves are toothed or pinnately cleft.

D. Genus with two stamens and flowers in a panicle rising above the leaves.

Collinsonia has yellow flowers with a fringed lower lip (*Fig. 100*). There may be four stamens.

II. Genera with four stamens, often in two pairs of unequal length. See also *Collinsonia,* above. Nine groups of genera, A to I below.

A. *Scutellaria* has a calyx which bears a hump or ridge on its upper side (*Fig. 101*). The flowers, blue in most species, are in racemes or singly in the axils.

B. *Teucrium* has a corolla split on the upper side, the stamens rising through the split (*Fig. 102*). The flowers are in a loose spike.

C. Genera with four stamens and flowers in fairly dense terminal spikes (*Fig. 102*). See also *Mentha* below (D).

Nepeta has long-stalked, downy, grayish leaves with rather blunt teeth. The flowers are white with purple markings.

Prunella has leaves with plain margins. The calyx is markedly two-lipped (*Fig. 102*).

Ajuga has a creeping stem from which erect branches rise (*Fig. 102*). The leaves are broad with plain or slightly wavy margins.

Agastache has yellowish-green flowers in a thick, very dense spike (*Fig. 103*).

D. Genera with four stamens and small flowers in dense axillary clusters which seem to encircle the stem (*Fig. 103*).

Marrubium has a calyx with teeth that are hooked at the end (*Fig. 103*). The leaves are more or less wavy-margined.

Mentha has a corolla almost radially symmetric, with four almost equal lobes (*Fig. 103*). Some species have terminal spikes as well as axillary clusters.

Leonurus has a calyx whose teeth are stiff spines (*Fig. 104*). The leaves may be sharp-toothed or jaggedly cleft.

E. Genera with four stamens and flowers in loose spikes or spikelike racemes.

Stachys has a large, three-lobed lower lip of the corolla, directed downward (*Fig. 104*).

Thymus creeps on the ground, sending up erect flowering branches. The calyx is two-lipped, three triangular teeth above, two narrow teeth below (*Fig. 104*).

Physostegia has flowers in a simple spike, one flower in the axil of each bract (PLATE 12). The leaves are narrowly lance-shaped, sharply toothed.

Perilla has flowers in a simple spikelike raceme (the flower stalks are very short). The leaves are ovate, toothed. The calyx is two-lipped (*Fig. 105*).

F. Genera with four stamens and flowers in small clusters at the summit of the stem and in the axils of the leaves (*Fig. 105*).

Hyssopus has narrow, blunt leaves with plain margins.

Lamium has round or ovate, stalked leaves with scalloped margins.

Glecoma creeps on the ground, the ends of the stems curving upward and bearing flowers (*Fig. 105*). The leaves are ovate or round, scalloped.

Galeopsis has calyx teeth ending in spines (*Fig. 106*). The flowers are pink, red, or white.

G. Genera with four stamens and flowers all in axils of leaves.

Satureia: two species are slender with narrow, mostly toothless leaves and small flowers which are not markedly two-lipped (*Fig. 106*).

Melissa has coarsely toothed, ovate, stalked leaves. The calyx is two-lipped, the upper lip scarcely divided into teeth, the lower cleft into two long, narrow teeth (*Fig. 106*).

Isanthus has narrow leaves with plain margins. The corolla is almost radially symmetric, with four lobes (*Fig. 108*).

H. Genera with four stamens and flowers in dense terminal heads, with or without dense clusters in the axils of leaves (*Figs. 106, 107*).

Satureia: one species has ovate leaves more or less toothed with blunt teeth; the stem is hairy. Only a few flowers open at once in the head (*Fig. 106*).

Pycnanthemum has flowers either in dense terminal heads with equally dense axillary clusters, or in a number of small terminal heads which together form a broad, flat inflorescence (*Fig. 107*).

Origanum has terminal heads on several branches. The leaves are stalked, and have plain margins (*Fig. 108*).

I. Genus with four long, curved stamens.

Trichostema has long-stalked, blue flowers in a loose inflorescence. The stamens rise under the upper lip and curve downward (*Fig. 108*).

THE HORSE-MINTS (*Monarda*)   LILAC, YELLOW, PINK, OR RED

The flowers of *Monarda* are long, narrow, and curved, with the lower lip directed sharply downward. They are in dense heads at

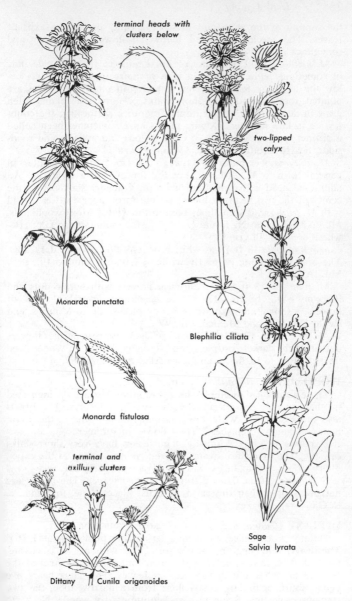

terminal heads with
clusters below

two-lipped
calyx

Monarda punctata

Monarda fistulosa

Blephilia ciliata

terminal and
axillary clusters

Dittany   Cunila origanoides

Sage
Salvia lyrata

FIGURE 99

the summit of the stem and in some species also in the axils of leaves. The species described below all flower in summer and sometimes in early autumn.

M. fistulosa, wild bergamot or horse-mint (5 ft.), has pale lilac or sometimes white flowers an inch or more long. The bracts below the head are leaflike, often tinged with pink. The leaves are pointed, toothed, and have short stalks or none. The plants often grow in dense masses, their minty fragrance permeating the countryside in late summer. Downy plants have sometimes been called a distinct species, *M. mollis.* § Open woods and prairies, and roadsides, nearly throughout. *Fig. 99* and PLATE 12.

M. didyma, bee-balm or Oswego-tea (to 5 ft.), is similar in general form to *M. fistulosa,* but the flowers are a vivid red. An additional head will sometimes arise on a slender stalk out of the center of the first head. A bright purple form, apparently a hybrid with *M. fistulosa,* is sometimes seen in the wild. § Moist woodlands, Me. to Mich., s. to N. J. and O., and in the mountains to Ga.; elsewhere escaped. PLATE 12.

M. clinopodia (3 ft.) has whitish or pink flowers with dark dots. The bracts are white or partly white. § Woods, Conn. to Ill., s. to Md., Ala., and Ky.

M. punctata (3 ft.) has yellowish flowers with purple dots and lilac or white bracts. There are generally several clusters of flowers, terminal and axillary. § Sandy places, Vt. to Minn., s. and sw. to Fla., La., and Mexico. *Fig. 99.*

M. russeliana (2 ft.) is distinguished by rose-purple flowers dotted with darker purple, and stalkless leaves. § Woods and thickets, Ind. to Ia. and Kan., s. to Ala., Ark., and Tex.

WOOD-MINTS (*Blephilia*)   LILAC
These somewhat resemble the horse-mints but are distinguished by their smaller flowers and by the two-lipped calyx. The bracts also are distinctive, with long marginal hairs; whence the Latin name, meaning "eyelashes." They flower in summer.

B. ciliata (30 in.) is downy. The leaves have very short stalks or none. The bracts are ovate, colored, veiny, as long as the calyx. § Dry woods, Vt. to Ia., s. to Ga., Miss., and Ark. *Fig. 99.*

B. hirsuta (30 in.) has distinctly stalked leaves. The bracts are narrow, shorter than the calyx. § Moist places, Que. to Minn., s. to Ga., Ark., and Tex.

DITTANY (*Cunila origanoides*)   ROSE-PURPLE OR WHITE
Dittany is a slender, branching, straggling plant (about 1 ft.). The leaves are smooth, nearly or quite without stalks, ovate, toothed. The flowers, scarcely ¼ inch long, are in clusters at the ends of branches and in the axils of leaves. The calyx bears five equal, short teeth. The petals flare from a narrow tube, the two stamens projecting. § Summer and autumn: dry woods, N. Y. to Mo., s. to Fla. and Tex. *Fig. 99.*

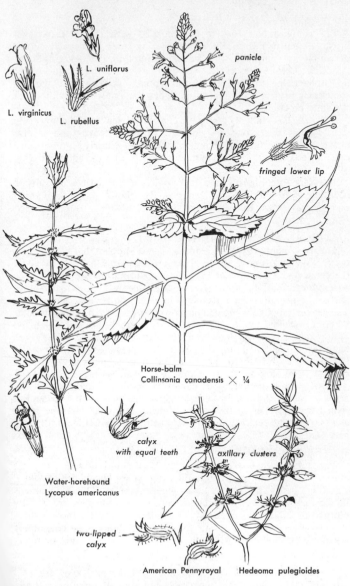

L. virginicus

L. uniflorus

L. rubellus

panicle

fringed lower lip

Horse-balm
Collinsonia canadensis × ¼

calyx
with equal teeth

axillary clusters

Water-horehound
Lycopus americanus

two-lipped
calyx

American Pennyroyal   Hedeoma pulegioides

FIGURE 100

SAGE (*Salvia lyrata*)   VIOLET

The genus *Salvia* (not to be confused with the western sagebrush, *Artemisia*) is enormous, numbering some 700 species, most of which are native in the western United States and in South America. The flowers are all conspicuously two-lipped, the upper lip often being arched, the lower spreading. The two stamens sometimes project from under the upper lip. Later they wither and the style emerges.

S. lyrata has stalked, pinnately cleft basal leaves. The flowering stem (2 ft.) bears one or two pairs of small leaves and several clusters of violet flowers about an inch long. § Early summer: dry open woods and thickets, Conn. to Mo., s. to Fla. and Tex. *Fig. 99.*

The sage used in cooking is *S. officinalis,* a native of Europe occasionally found wild in America. The herb clary, *S. sclarea,* and several other European species, may also be found escaped from gardens.

AMERICAN PENNYROYAL (*Hedeoma*)   BLUE

The true pennyroyal of Europe, a well-known herb, does not occur wild in America. Several American plants have been given the same name because of their similar aromatic odors.

H. pulegioides, common American pennyroyal (1 ft.), perfumes the air, especially when trodden, in dry woods and open fields. The leaves, about an inch long, are narrow, rather blunt, with or without marginal teeth. The flowers are scarcely ¼ inch long, the blue petals barely visible. The calyx is two-lipped, the upper three teeth triangular and joined nearly to the tip, the lower two needle-like and free nearly to the base. § Summer and early autumn: Que. to Minn. and S. D., s. to Fla., Ark., and Kan. *Fig. 100.*

H. hispida is similar, with narrower, more pointed leaves. The calyx is hairy, the upper teeth nearly as narrow as the lower but joined for more of their length. § Spring and early summer: dry soil, sandy and rocky banks, Vt. to Alta., s. to Conn., Ind., La., and Tex.

WATER-HOREHOUND (*Lycopus*)   WHITE

The genus *Lycopus* is marked by very small flowers in dense clusters which seem to encircle the stem where leaves are attached. The calyx bears four or five equal teeth or spines. The two stamens lie against the lower lip of the corolla. The leaves are mostly toothed or pinnately lobed. (Lycopus means "wolf's foot," which the leaves of some European species were thought to resemble.) All flower in summer. All grow in moist places, wooded or open.

I. Species with narrow, sharp teeth on the calyx.

L. americanus (to 3 ft.) is smooth. The lower leaves are usually pinnately lobed; the upper are toothed; all taper to a stalk. The petals are hardly longer than the sepals. § Throughout. *Fig. 100.*

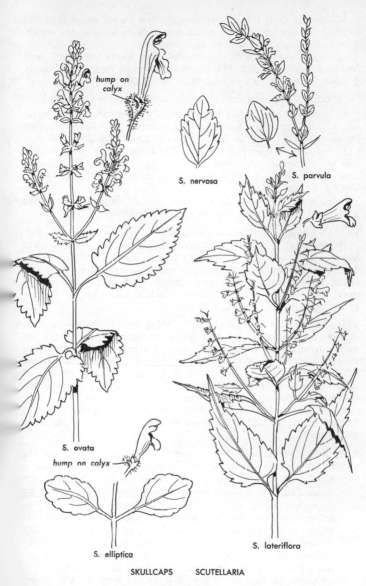

hump on calyx

S. nervosa

S. parvula

S. ovata

hump on calyx

S. elliptica

S. lateriflora

SKULLCAPS   SCUTELLARIA

FIGURE 101

L. rubellus (3 ft.) is mostly smooth. The leaves are stalked and toothed but not lobed. The petals are twice as long as the sepals. § N. E. to Mo., s. to Fla. and Tex. *Fig. 100.*

L. amplectens (to 3 ft.) is smooth. The leaves are blunt, with few teeth and no stalks. The petals are twice as long as the sepals. § Mass. to Ind., s. to Fla. and Miss. along the coastal plain.

II. Species with triangular or oblong calyx teeth, not spinelike.

L. virginicus (to 30 in.) has a minutely downy stem. The leaves are smooth, coarsely toothed, long-stalked, the blades tapering into the stalks. § Que. to Minn., s. to Ga. and Tex. *Fig. 100.*

L. uniflorus (30 in.) is smooth. The leaves are narrow, with a few inconspicuous teeth; the blades taper to each end; there is scarcely any stalk. § Across Canada, s. to N. C., Ill., Ia., Nebr., and Calif. *Fig. 100.*

Some species, notably *L. virginicus* and *L. uniflorus,* are called bugleweed, a name also applied to *Ajuga reptans.*

HORSE-BALM (*Collinsonia canadensis*)   YELLOW
Horse-balm is readily recognized by its large, ovate, stalked leaves above which rises a loose panicle of small flowers. The corolla has a four-lobed upper lip and a longer lower lip which is distinctly fringed. There are either two or four stamens. The plant has a lemon scent. § Summer: rich woods, Que. to Wis., s. to Fla. and Ark. *Fig. 100.*

THE SKULLCAPS (*Scutellaria*)   BLUE, PURPLE, BLUE- OR PUR-PLE-AND-WHITE, OR PINK / The genus gets both English and Latin names from the odd projection on the upper side of the calyx shaped like a dish ("scutella") or hat; it disappears when the petals fall. The corolla is a more or less erect tube at the end of which the upper lip is shaped like a hood. The four stamens, beneath this hood, are in two unlike pairs.

There are more than 100 American species; of the 12 or 15 known from our area, the nine described below are the most widespread.

I. Species with flowers in a cluster of racemes at and near the summit of the stem. Plants chiefly of dry woodlands, flowering in summer (sometimes in spring). (Compare II, III, and IV.)

S. ovata (2 ft.) is softly hairy. The leaves are stalked, the blade coarsely toothed, more or less heart-shaped. The flowers, up to an inch long, are blue with a whitish lower lip. § Md. to Minn., s. and sw. to S. C., Ala., Tex., and Mexico. *Fig. 101*

S. incana (3 ft.) has coarsely toothed, stalked leaves, whit underneath with a fine down. The flowers, an inch long, ar blue. § N. Y. to Ia. and Kan., s. to Fla., Ala., and Ark.

S. elliptica (2 ft.) has leaves 2½ inches long or less, blun tapering to a short stalk, scalloped on the margins. Th

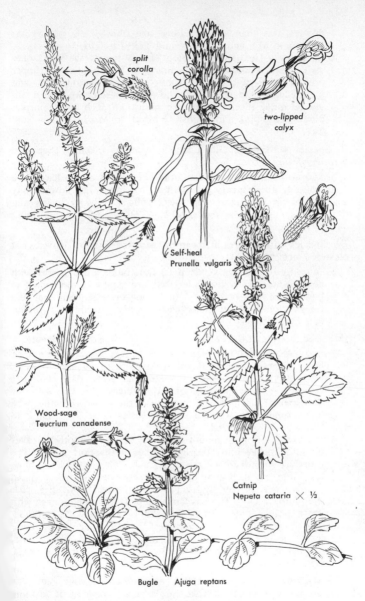

split corolla

two-lipped calyx

Self-heal
Prunella vulgaris

Wood-sage
Teucrium canadense

Catnip
Nepeta cataria × ⅓

Bugle   Ajuga reptans

FIGURE 102

flowers, less than an inch long, are blue-violet. § N. Y. to Mich. and Mo. and s. to Fla. and Tex. *Fig. 101.*

S. *integrifolia* (2 ft.) has minutely downy leaves, the lower ones stalked and scalloped at the margins, the middle and upper ones shorter (less than 2 inches long), without stalks, and plain-edged ("integri-"). The flowers are sometimes in a single terminal raceme; they are about an inch long, purple-blue or rose-pink and whitish. § Mass. to Mo., s. to Fla. and Tex.

II. Species with flowers in a single terminal raceme. (See also S. *integrifolia,* above.)

S. *serrata* (2 ft.) is nearly smooth. The blades of the leaves are ovate, toothed, tapering at the base to stalks. The flowers may exceed an inch in length; the corolla is blue. § Spring and early summer: rich woods, N. Y. to O., s. to S. C. and Tenn.; Mo.

III. Species with flowers in racemes from the axils of leaves (not clustered near the top).

S. *lateriflora,* mad-dog skullcap (2 ft.), has stalked leaves with nearly smooth, ovate blades that are coarsely toothed. The flowers are blue or pink, ⅓ inch long or less. § Summer and early autumn: moist thickets and woods, meadows, throughout. *Fig. 101.*

IV. Species with flowers singly in the axils of ordinary leaves.

S. *parvula* (8 in.) has mostly hairy leaves less than an inch long, without stalks, with one or two teeth on each margin. The flowers are blue, less than ½ inch long. The plant has creeping stems with strings of small tubers. It is very variable in degree of hairiness and toothing of the leaves. § Late spring and summer: dry woodlands and prairies, Que. to N. D., s. to Fla. and Tex. *Fig. 101.*

S. *nervosa* (1 ft.) is smooth or nearly so, with toothed leaves up to 2 inches long, the lower ones with short stalks. The veins are prominent on the under side. The flowers are blue, less than ½ inch long. § Late spring and summer: moist woods, N. J. to Ont. and Ia., s. to N. C. and Tenn. *Fig. 101.*

S. *epilobiifolia* (to 3 ft.) has lance-shaped or oblong leaves with sharp points and short stalks, the blades coarsely toothed. The flowers are blue, sometimes an inch long. Some botanists consider this identical with the European S. *galericulata.* § Summer and autumn: meadows, shores, swampy thickets etc., throughout.

GERMANDER or WOOD-SAGE (*Teucrium canadense*) PURPLE

Teucrium is easily recognized by its petals: instead of forming a two-lipped corolla, they seem to form a single five-lobed lower lip open at the top, a lobe standing erect on either side of the

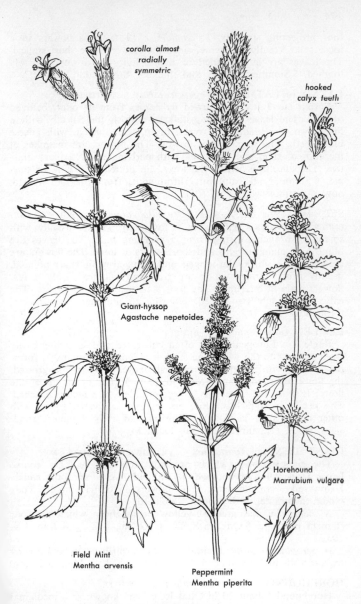

corolla almost radially symmetric

hooked calyx teeth

Giant-hyssop
Agastache nepetoides

Horehound
Marrubium vulgare

Field Mint
Mentha arvensis

Peppermint
Mentha piperita

FIGURE 103

four projecting stamens. *T. canadense* (3 ft.) has flowers in a loose spike (really a raceme, since the flowers have short stalks). The leaves are lance-shaped or ovate, hairy or downy, coarsely toothed. § Summer: shores and thickets, throughout. *Fig. 102.*

CATNIP or CATMINT (*Nepeta cataria*)   WHITISH
Catnip (to 3 ft.) has earned its names from its odor, beloved of cats. The leaves are long-stalked, whitish underneath with a fine down; the blades are ovate, often heart-shaped, with coarse blunt teeth. The stem also is downy. The flowers are in spikes at the ends of stem and branches, with perhaps a few axillary clusters. The corolla is white, the lower lip dotted with pink or purple. § Summer and autumn: throughout; from the Old World, now a common weed. *Fig. 102.*

SELF-HEAL or HEAL-ALL (*Prunella vulgaris*)   PURPLE, LAVENDER, OR WHITE / Self-heal is a low plant (2 ft.) usually with spreading branches rising from a creeping base. The leaves are blunt, with plain margins and short stalks or none. The flowers are crowded in a thick, flat-topped spike mixed with sharp-pointed, usually bristly bracts which are frequently colored; only a few flowers open at one time. The four stamens are in two pairs. The calyx is strongly two-lipped. § Spring to autumn: open places, throughout. *Fig. 102.*

BUGLE (*Ajuga reptans*)   BLUE
Bugle is a European plant often cultivated and spreading easily from gardens to the wild. The stem is creeping ("reptans"), forming a mat, with rosettes of roundish leaves next to the ground; the flowering stems stand erect (to 10 in.). The upper lip of the flower is short, the lower has a large middle lobe which is notched. The petals are typically blue, but various cultivated forms with other colors may be found. § Spring and early summer: roadsides, fields, etc., throughout but local. *Fig. 102.*

GIANT-HYSSOP (*Agastache*)   YELLOWISH OR PURPLISH
The giant-hyssops (which are not true hyssops) are coarse herbs (3–4 ft.) with toothed, ovate leaf blades on short stalks. Heavy spikes contain many small flowers mixed with bracts. They bloom in summer in dry, open woodlands.
    A. nepetoides has greenish-yellow petals, from which the four stamens protrude. § Que. to S. D., s. to Ga., Ark., and Kan. *Fig. 103.*
    A. scrophulariaefolia is similar, with purplish petals and downy leaves. § Vt. to Minn. and S. D., s. to N. C., Ky., Mo., and Kan.

HOREHOUND (*Marrubium vulgare*)   WHITE
Horehound (about 20 in.) has long been known as a medicinal herb. It was brought to this country from Europe and is often found wild along roadsides and in waste places. It has broad,

ovate, short-stalked leaves, notched along the margins and woolly with whitish hairs. The small flowers are crowded in clusters in the axils of the leaves, encircling the stem. The four stamens do not project from the corolla. The calyx bears hooked spines. The plant is aromatic and bitter. § Summer: nearly throughout. *Fig. 103.*

THE MINTS (*Mentha*)   PURPLISH, LILAC, OR WHITE

The mints have long been the despair of botanists who wished to classify and name them. The genus *Mentha* is easily recognized, being known by the four almost equal lobes of the corolla, and the four stamens. The beginner may be content with this. The species are difficult to distinguish; indeed, some of them undoubtedly hybridize, yielding intermediates which cannot be classified or named. Many of these confusing kinds have been cultivated for their essential oils. Of the ten or eleven species currently reported from northeastern North America, only one is considered native, and only two others are at all abundant. All grow most abundantly in wet places, but are also found where it is dry.

M. arvensis, field mint, has spreading, much-branched stems (to 2 ft. or more), smooth or slightly downy. The leaves are stalkless, oblong or ovate, toothed. The tiny lilac flowers, ¼ inch long, are crowded in the axils of leaves but not at the end of the stem. § Late summer: nearly throughout; a worldwide species. *Fig. 103.*

M. piperita, peppermint (to 3 ft.), has smooth leaves, lance-shaped, toothed, on stalks which may be ½ inch long. The flowers are purplish, crowded in the axils of small leaves (bracts) and at the end of the stem, forming a spike. § Summer and autumn: throughout; supposed to have come from a hybrid of two other species in Europe. *Fig. 103.*

M. spicata, spearmint (to 20 in.), is smooth, with toothed leaves almost or quite without stalks. The flowers are in long, narrow spikes and in the axils of the small leaves beneath the spikes. § Summer and autumn: throughout; from Europe.

MOTHERWORT (*Leonurus cardiaca*)   PINK

The plant may grow to 5 feet tall. Each leaf is divided into three or more sharp lobes pointing toward the tip. The lower leaves have long stalks and a more palmate form. The name *Leonurus,* which means "lion's tail," may have been inspired by these leaves, or by the generally shaggy appearance of the whole plant. The small flowers are crowded in dense clusters in the axils of the leaves, where they seem to encircle the stem. The upper lip of the corolla is hairy; the lower, which extends downward, is smooth. The calyx has five sharp teeth. § Summer: waste places, N. S. to Mont., s. to N. C. and Tex.; from Asia by way of Europe, having been formerly cultivated for supposed medicinal properties. *Fig. 104.*

THE HEDGE-NETTLES (*Stachys*)   ROSE-PURPLE

The hedge-nettles are not nettles, and, indeed, only slightly resemble those plants. Our native species have rose-purple flowers usually mottled with other purplish shades; the upper lip is hooded; the three-lobed lower lip flaring. The flowers are in the axils of the upper leaves and bracts, forming a loose spike. The leaves are pointed and in most species sharply toothed on the edges, lance-shaped or ovate. The plants are mostly downy or hairy. The common species flower in summer and grow in moist places.

S. palustris (to 3 ft.) is downy throughout with long hairs on the stem and on the calyx. It has a rank smell. The leaves are mostly lance-shaped, with short stalks or none. § Nearly throughout; a very variable species. *Fig. 104*.

S. tenuifolia (3 ft.) is usually smooth or nearly so (the stem may be rough with *short* hairs on the angles). The leaves are lance-shaped, the lower ones with stalks. § Que. to Minn., s. to N. C., Tenn., and Tex.

S. aspera (2 ft.) has a rough stem, bearing smooth leaves all without stalks and tapering to both ends. § Pa. to Ia., s. to Ga. and Mo.

S. hyssopifolia (18 in.) has very narrow leaves almost without teeth. § Mass. to S. C. along the coast, chiefly in sandy places; Ind. to Mich. *Fig. 104*.

S. hispida (to 3 ft.) is conspicuously bristly ("hispidus") on the angles of the stem. The narrow, toothed leaves are also hairy, and the calyx. § Vt. to Man., s. to S. C., Ky., and Ark.

THYME (*Thymus serpyllum*)   PURPLE

Several species and many varieties of thyme have long been cultivated for seasoning and for ornament. The common thyme found growing wild in waste places is a creeping plant with small round or oblong leaves rarely as much as ½ inch long. The flowers are on erect branches, in short spikes. The two-lipped calyx is characteristic. The corolla is about ¼ inch long. § Late summer: from Que. and Ont. s. to N. C. and Ind.; European. *Fig. 104*.

FALSE DRAGONHEAD or OBEDIENCE (*Physostegia*)   PINK-LAVENDER / These are handsome plants (to 4 ft.) with narrow, sharply toothed leaves and a terminal simple spike of pinkish-lavender flowers (one flower to an axil). The branches also may end in spikes. The flower may exceed an inch in length; the upper lip is hooded, the lower flaring and three-lobed. There are two pairs of stamens, the lower pair the longer. The first English name comes from the resemblance of *Physostegia* to *Dracocephalum,* a largely Asiatic genus called dragonhead; the second from a peculiarity of the flowers—if bent out of position they will stay where they are put.

Various forms of *Physostegia* are common in gardens, and som

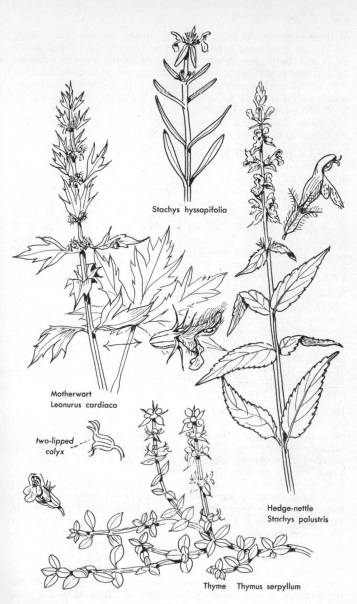

Stachys hyssopifolia

Motherwort
Leonurus cardiaca

two-lipped
calyx

Hedge-nettle
Stachys palustris

Thyme Thymus serpyllum

FIGURE 104

of these may become wild, especially in the Atlantic states. Both the species mentioned below have been commonly lumped as *P. virginiana*. Both grow in wet thickets, on shores, even in swamps. Several others are native in the southern and western states.

P. virginiana has very small upper leaves; the spike of flowers stands well above the foliage leaves. § Vt. to Ill. and Okla., s. to S. C. and sw. to Tex. PLATE 12.

P. formosior has leaves only slightly reduced in size just below the flower spike. § Me. to Alta., s. to N. Y., Mo., and Nebr.

PERILLA FRUTESCENS   WHITE

This is an Asiatic species that has spread into waste places and dry woodlands (to 3 ft.). The leaves are broad, ovate, toothed, on slender stalks; they often become tinged with red or bronze (variety *crispa* of gardens is known as beefsteak-plant). The terminal spikelike raceme is generally unbranched; others may grow from the axils of leaves. The corolla has five nearly equal lobes; it is scarcely two-lipped. The calyx is two-lipped. When brushed against after the petals have fallen, the dry sepals and leaves emit a curious metallic sound almost like the tinkling of tiny bells. § Late summer: N. E. to Ia., s. to Fla. and Tex. *Fig. 105.*

HYSSOP (*Hyssopus officinalis*)   BLUE

The supposedly medicinal herb hyssop, long cultivated in the Old World and occasionally found as a weed in America, has upright, stiff, slender stems (to 2 ft.) beset with narrow, sharp-pointed, stalkless leaves. The flowers are in close clusters in the axils of bracts and at the summit—sometimes forming a spike. The four stamens all project from the corolla, the lower lip of which is broader and longer than the upper. § Summer and autumn: Que. to Mont., s. to N. C. *Fig. 105.*

DEAD-NETTLES and HENBIT (*Lamium*)   PURPLE, RED-PURPLE, OR WHITE / *Lamium* has scalloped or bluntly toothed leaves, often on long stalks. The corolla consists of a long tube which expands abruptly into a hooded upper lip and a flaring lower lip attached to a cuplike part. The species described below are all weeds introduced from the Old World.

L. purpureum (1 ft.) is familiar to English children as (red) dead-nettle because it somewhat resembles the nettles but does not sting; it grows in roadside ditches and hedgerows where stinging nettles are common. The leaves are long-stalked except those near the flowers; the scalloped blades are often purple-tinged. The red-purple flowers, ½ inch long, are in clusters in the upper axils and at the tip of the stem. The calyx teeth end in long sharp spines The lower pair of stamens is the longer, and generally stands above the upper pair by a curving of the stalks. § Spring to au tumn: fields, gardens, waste places, Nfld. to Mich., s. to S. C., O. and Mo. *Fig. 105.*

L. album, white dead-nettle or snowflake (to 2 ft.), has coarsel

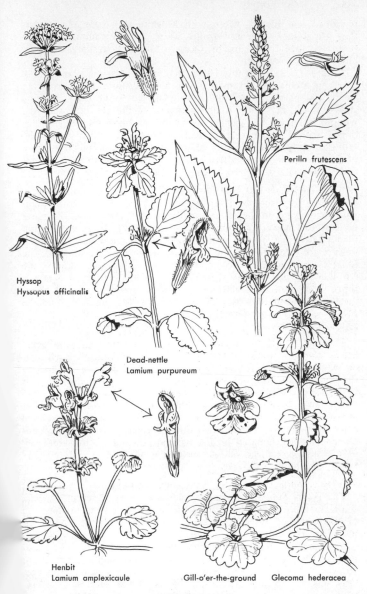

Hyssop
Hyssopus officinalis

Perilla frutescens

Dead-nettle
Lamium purpureum

Henbit
Lamium amplexicaule

Gill-o'er-the-ground   Glecoma hederacea

FIGURE 105

scalloped leaf blades, often with a white spot near the center; they are stalked. The flowers are white. § Early summer and autumn: escaped from gardens, Que. to Minn., s. to Va.; less common than *L. purpureum.*

L. amplexicaule, henbit (to 1 ft.), is a sprawling plant whose flowering stems rise from their creeping position. The leaves are small, the blades round and scalloped, the lower ones on long stalks. Early in spring many plants bear flowers that set seed without opening. The petals are visible as small magenta knobs, tipped with hairs, barely projecting from the calyx. Later the same plants produce flowers of the usual type, purple like those of *L. purpureum* but smaller. § Early spring to late autumn: lawns and waste places, Lab. to Mich., s. and sw. *Fig. 105*

GROUND-IVY or GILL-O'ER-THE-GROUND (*Glecoma hederacea*)   BLUE / Ground-ivy, as its name suggests, is a creeping plant with stems lying on the ground and rooting at the joints. The more or less erect flowering branches (to 8 in.) bear leaves with round blades scalloped at the margin and nearly smooth. The small flowers are in clusters in the axils and perhaps at the summit. The four stamens scarcely project from under the upper lip of the corolla. This is a bad weed in Europe. In this country it is sometimes planted in rock gardens, but often becomes a weed about dwellings and in woods. § Spring and early summer: Nfld. to Minn., s. to Ga.; occasional elsewhere. *Fig. 105.*

HEMP-NETTLE (*Galeopsis tetrahit*)   WHITE
This is a bristly plant (to 2 ft.) with stalked leaves, the ovate leaves coarsely toothed. The stem is swollen beneath each pair of leaves. The flowers are crowded in the upper axils and at the summit; they are generally white but may be tinted or spotted with rose or purple. There are four stamens. The calyx bears five long, sharp, slightly spreading spines. This Old-World plant has the distinction of being practically identical with a plant obtained experimentally by crossing two other species; it is therefore concluded that it originated by the natural crossing of the same parents. § Summer: waste places, across Canada and s. to N. C., O., Mich., and S. D. *Fig. 106.*

SAVORY (*Satureia*)   PINK, LAVENDER, OR PURPLISH
The genus *Satureia* embraces plants of very different aspects; some resemble *Hedeoma,* with small purplish flowers in the axils of leaves. Others have flowers in a dense head at the summit of the stem. The calyx ends in five spinelike teeth.

S. glabella (1 ft.) is a scrawny, narrow-leaved plant. The small purplish flowers, ½ inch long or less, grow singly or in small clusters in the axils of the leaves. § Summer: dry woods and barrens, Ky. to Mo. and Ark. *Fig. 106.* A similar species, *S. arkansana,* grows from Ont. to Minn. and s. to N. Y. and Tex. It may be only a variety of *S. glabella.*

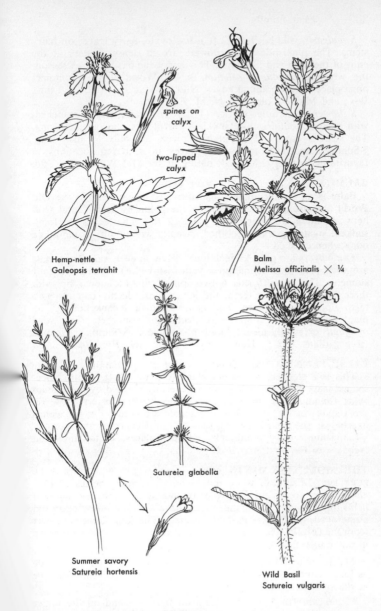

Hemp-nettle
Galeopsis tetrahit

spines on
calyx

two-lipped
calyx

Balm
Melissa officinalis × ¼

Satureia glabella

Summer savory
Satureia hortensis

Wild Basil
Satureia vulgaris

FIGURE 106

S. vulgaris, wild basil (to 2 ft.), has ovate, hairy leaves on hairy stems. The pinkish-lavender flowers are in dense clusters at the ends of the stem and branches. This is not the basil used as seasoning, which is *Ocimum basilicum,* an Old-World plant. § Summer: open places and woodland edges, Nfld. to Man., s. to N. C., Tenn., Wis., and Minn.; Colo. and N. M. *Fig. 106.*

S. hortensis, summer savory (1 ft.), is slender, much branched, with narrow, toothless and stalkless leaves less than an inch long. The stem is downy. The pinkish flowers are only ¼ inch long. § Summer and autumn: waste places in scattered locations; a favorite herb, long cultivated; native of the Old World. *Fig. 106.*

BALM (*Melissa officinalis*)   PALE BLUE

Balm is an Asiatic plant long cultivated as an herb in the Old World and brought to America by the colonists. It is found wild here and there, a rather bushy plant (2 ft.). The leaves are long-stalked, ovate, coarsely toothed, usually giving off a lemonlike odor when crushed.

The flowers are only ½ inch long, a few in each axil. The petals are very pale blue (sometimes yellowish-white). There are four stamens. The calyx forms a two-lipped cup, the upper lip with three short, triangular teeth, the lower more deeply cut into two teeth tipped with spines. The name Melissa means honey: the plant was valued as a source of nectar for honeybees. The word *officinalis* originally meant "used in medicine." § Summer: escaped from gardens, Me. to Kan., s. to Fla. and Ark. .*Fig. 106.*

FALSE PENNYROYAL (*Isanthus brachiatus*)   BLUE

This is a slender, somewhat clammy plant (1 ft.) with lance-shaped leaves; the lower leaves are generally marked by three main veins running from base to apex. The flower clusters grow on short stalks in the axils. The five sepals are equal, the five petals nearly so; the four stamens scarcely project from the corolla. § Late summer: dry woodlands and open places, Vt. to Minn. and Nebr., s. to Fla. and Ariz. *Fig. 108.*

THE MOUNTAIN-MINTS (*Pycnanthemum*)   WHITE OR PALE PURPLISH / In spite of the common name, various species of *Pycnanthemum* are found far from mountains, in both dry and wet fields, prairies, and woodlands. They have a strong minty odor and numerous small flowers in dense clusters. The four stamens project from the corolla. The species described below, the most widespread in our range, flower in summer.

I. Species with rather narrow leaves, less than one-third as wide as long, without stalks; the flower clusters in a broad inflorescence at the summit. (Compare II.)

P. *pilosum* (to 5 ft.) has hairs on the stem and on the under side of the leaves. § Dry woodlands, N. Y. and Ont. to Ia. s. to Tenn. and Okla.; occasional in N. E. *Fig. 107.*

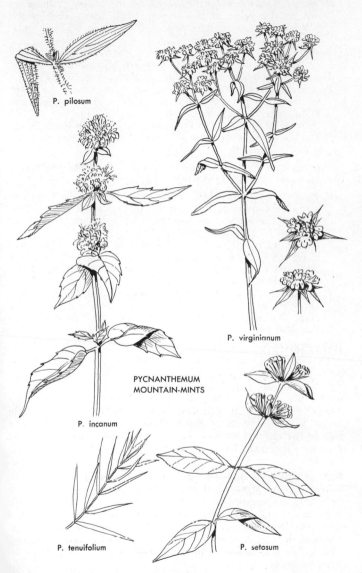

P. pilosum

P. virginianum

PYCNANTHEMUM
MOUNTAIN-MINTS

P. incanum

P. tenuifolium

P. setosum

FIGURE 107

  P. *virginianum* has some fine down on the angles of the stem
  and on the veins of the leaves, which have rough edges.
  § Woodlands and prairies, Me. to N. D., s. to Ga. and Okla.
  Fig. 107.

  P. *verticillatum* has downy stems; the leaves are downy along
  the veins on the under side; they are often toothed on the
  margins. § Upland woods, Que. to Mich., s. to N. C. and O.

  P. *tenuifolium* is smooth. The leaves are numerous and very
  narrow. § Upland woods and dry prairies, N. E. to Ont. and
  Minn., s. to Ga. and Tex. *Fig. 107.*

  P. *torrei* is finely downy in the upper parts, smooth lower down.
  The leaves are lance-shaped. § Dry woodlands, Conn. to Kan.,
  s. to Ga. and Ark.

II. Species with much wider leaves on very short stalks; the flower
clusters more scattered in the axils of leaves.

  P. *incanum* is distinguished by the white down on the leaves, at
  least on the under side. The leaf stalks are about ¼ inch long
  or less. The blades are toothed. § Upland woods, N. H. to
  Ill., s. to N. C. and Tenn. *Fig. 107.*

  P. *muticum* has leaf stalks ⅛ inch long or less. The uppermost
  leaves are velvety on the upper side, smooth on the under
  side. The blades are toothed. § Moist woods and meadows,
  Me. to Mich., s. to Fla. and Tex.

  P. *setosum* is practically smooth throughout. The leaf stalks are
  ⅛ inch long or less. The blades have plain margins. § Dry
  fields and upland woods, N. J. and s. in the coastal plain to
  Fla. *Fig. 107.*

WILD MARJORAM (*Origanum vulgare*)   PURPLISH-RED
This Old-World species, a relative of several cultivated herbs,
has become a common weed in some places. I have seen it paint-
ing the roadsides purplish-red in New York State. It is a rather
bushy, hairy plant (2–3 ft.). The stalked leaves have ovate blades
without marginal teeth. The flowers, about ¼ inch long or a little
longer, occur in heads at the ends of the branches. The lower
pair of the stamens projects beyond the petals. The calyx bears
five equal triangular teeth. § Summer: Que. and Ont., s. to N. C.
Fig. 108.

BLUE-CURLS (*Trichostema dichotomum*)   BLUE OR VIOLET
This delicate plant (to 2 ft.) is easily recognized by the four
very long, downward-curving, blue or violet stamens which give
it its name. The petals also are blue or violet. The three upper
sepals are long, the two lower ones very short. The flowers grow
singly at the tips of branches that arise from the axils of leaves
The leaves are narrow, pointed at each end, without stalks o'
marginal teeth.
  A curious feature is that when fruit is set and the petals hav

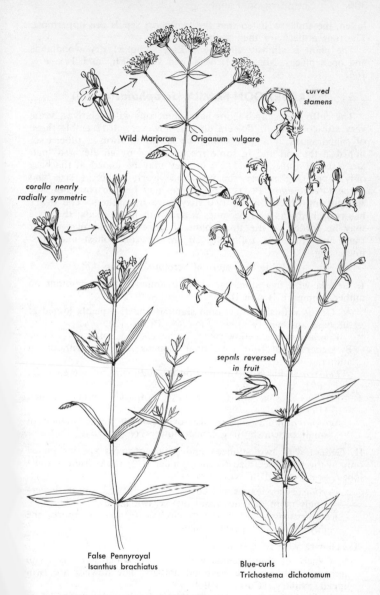

curved stamens

Wild Marjoram   Origanum vulgare

corolla nearly
radially symmetric

sepals reversed
in fruit

False Pennyroyal
Isanthus brachiatus

Blue-curls
Trichostema dichotomum

FIGURE 108

fallen, the stalk twists so that the two short sepals are uppermost. The four nutlets are then plainly visible.

The plant is slightly clammy. § Late summer: dry woodlands and open places, Me. to Mich., s. and sw. to Fla. and Tex. *Fig. 108.*

SNAPDRAGON FAMILY (*Scrophulariaceae*)

The cultivated snapdragons have numerous wild relatives, some very attractive. Their flowers do not, however, all resemble those of snapdragons. The petals may be joined to form a tube, two-lipped at the end and in some species closed by an elevated "palate" (see *Mimulus, Fig. 112*); or they may be joined at the base only, appearing nearly separate and nearly alike in size and shape (*Verbascum,* PLATE 12). There may be two, four, or five stamens, of which one or two may have no anthers. The ovary has two chambers and becomes a pod with many seeds; the style may be forked at the tip. About 40 genera are known in our range, of which the following 20 are the commonest and most interesting.

Guide to Genera of *Scrophulariaceae*

I. Genera with five stamens, all with anthers or one without an anther (compare II and III).

   A. Genus with five functional stamens and five petals joined at the base and nearly alike (*Fig. 109;* PLATE 12).

   Verbascum has yellow or white flowers in a spike.

   B. Genera with four functional stamens and one without an anther.

   Penstemon has a tuft of hair on the rudimentary stamen (*Fig. 109*).

   Chelone has a short, smooth, green rudimentary stamen (PLATE 13).

   Scrophularia has a brownish or yellowish sterile stamen in small brownish or greenish flowers (*Fig. 110*).

II. Genera with two stamens and petals of most species joined only at the base (see also *Gratiola* under III); the corolla is four-lobed, nearly radial in symmetry (*Fig. 111*).

   Veronica has leaves paired or single; it has small flowers singly or in racemes from the axils of leaves.

   Veronicastrum has leaves in circles of three or more; the flowers are in tapering spikes.

III. Genera with four stamens.

   A. Genera of small plants with two functional stamens (with anthers) and two that have no anthers. The flowers are two-lipped, axillary. (Compare B.)

   Lindernia has a tubular, five-toothed calyx; the upper lip of the corolla is much narrower than the lower (*Fig. 111*).

Gratiola has sepals separate nearly to the base (*Fig. 111*); the lips of the corolla are similar in size. The nonfunctional pair of stamens is sometimes minute or even lacking.

B. Genera with four functional stamens.

1. Genera with four functional stamens and flowers in the axils (perhaps closer together toward the summit of the stem so as to form a cluster). (Compare 2.)

a. Genera with four functional stamens, axillary flowers, and an almost radial, five-lobed corolla (compare b).

Aureolaria has yellow flowers. The tips of the stamens are hairy (PLATE 13 and *Fig. 112*).

Dasistoma has yellow flowers. The tips of the stamens are smooth.

Agalinis has pink or purple flowers (*Fig. 112*).

b. Genera with four functional stamens, axillary flowers, and a distinctly bilateral corolla.

Mimulus has a corolla partly closed by a ridge ("palate") on the lower lip (*Fig. 112*). The calyx is sharply angled.

Collinsia has the middle lobe of the lower lip folded vertically, with stamens in the fold (*Fig. 113*). The corolla is blue- or violet-and-white.

Melampyrum has a narrow yellow and white corolla. The leaves are very narrow, the upper ones without teeth (*Fig. 113*).

Euphrasia has a corolla only ⅓ inch long or less. All leaves are sharply toothed (*Fig. 113*).

Kickxia has small purple-and-yellow flowers; the corolla bears a spur (hollow extension) on the lower side (*Fig. 113*).

2. Genera with four functional stamens and flowers in dense spikes or clusters at the summit of the stem (see also *Euphrasia* in 1b).

Linaria has a spur (hollow extension) on the lower side of the corolla (PLATE 13).

Pedicularis has flowers of yellow and red or of both colors in a thick spike or head. The leaves are pinnately cleft (PLATE 13).

Castilleia has small greenish or yellowish flowers surrounded by brightly colored bracts (which may be mistaken for petals; PLATE 14).

Rhinanthus has a conspicuous calyx flattened in a vertical plane (later inflated). The corolla is yellow or bronze (*Fig. 114*).

THE MULLEINS (*Verbascum*)   YELLOW OR WHITE

The mulleins are distinguished by a corolla with five almost equal lobes; there is scarcely a trace of upper and lower lips. The five stamens all bear pollen. These are biennial plants, forming in the first year a rosette of leaves, from which in the second season a flowering stem arises. They flower through the summer and into autumn, in fields, roadsides, and waste places, mostly dry, throughout our range. All are immigrants from the Old World.

V. thapsus (to 6 ft. and even more) is the common mullein of fields, pastures, and stony hillsides, known by its rosette of large velvety leaves. The hairs on these leaves are worth examining with a magnifier: each hair is branched, like a miniature tree. The yellow flowers are borne in a tall spike. Each is individually attractive, but since only a few are open at any time, the plant has a rather ragged appearance. *Fig. 109* and PLATE 12.

V. blattaria, moth mullein (3 ft.), is nearly smooth. The stamens have violet hairs; the style is bent down; the effect is a striking imitation of the antennae and tongue of a moth. The corolla bears glandular hairs on the outside. There are two forms: in one the petals are yellow; in the other, white with purplish base. PLATE 12.

THE BEARDTONGUES (*Penstemon*)   PURPLE, VIOLET, OR WHITE / The genus *Penstemon* is a very large and difficult one; but since most of its species are western, the problem is somewhat simplified for our range. Sixteen or 17 species have been recognized in this area, of which the following are the most widespread or conspicuous. All flower in late spring and summer.

The characteristic feature of the genus is the presence of five stamens, of which one lacks an anther but (in our species) bears a tuft of hairs (whence the English name). The tube of petals flares into five lobes which make two not very distinct lips. The flowering stem rises from a rosette of stalked leaves; the leaves on the stem are paired, without stalks. The flowers are in cymes which rise from the axils of usually smaller leaves.

I. Species with a corolla an inch or more long (compare II).

   P. grandiflorus (4 ft.) has short, broad, rather thick leaves, very smooth and grayish-green. The corolla is up to 1½ inches long, the tube expanded about the middle; it is purple. A strikingly beautiful species. § Prairies, Ill. to N. D. and Wyo., s. to Mo. and Tex. *Fig. 109.*

   P. digitalis (to 5 ft.) is smooth and shining, the stem sometimes purplish. The corolla is about an inch long, sharply expanded about the middle of the tube, white sometimes faintly tinged with purple, often with purple lines inside. The anthers are usually hairy. § Woodlands, fields, roadsides, Me. to Minn. and S. D., s. to Va., Ala., and Tex. *Fig. 109* and PLATE 13.

II. Species with a corolla an inch long or less (see *P. digitalis* above).

   P. hirsutus (3 ft.) is usually hairy ("hirsute"), with glands in the inflorescence. The corolla is narrow, pale violet, with a

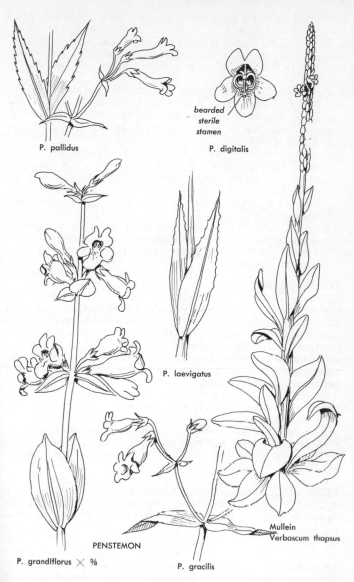

bearded
sterile
stamen

P. pallidus

P. digitalis

P. laevigatus

PENSTEMON

P. grandiflorus ✕ ⅜

P. gracilis

Mullein
Verbascum thapsus

FIGURE 109

lower lip that is arched so as to partly close the mouth. § Dry
woods and fields, Que. to Wis., s. to Va. and Ky. PLATE 13.

P. *tubaeflorus* (3 ft.) is smooth. The corolla is white; it flares
gradually to five almost equal lobes. § Prairies and woods,
Ind. to Wis. and Nebr., s. to Tenn., Miss., and Tex.; Me. to
Ont. and Pa.

P. *pallidus* (3 ft.) is downy. The corolla is white ("pallid")
with pink lines inside; it flares gradually to five almost equal
lobes. The leaves may or may not have teeth. § Dry woods
and fields, Me. to Mich. and Ia., s. to Ga., Ky., Ark., and
Kan. *Fig. 109.*

P. *laevigatus* (to 4 ft.) is smooth ("laevigatus") or hairy in
strips along the stem with very short hairs. The corolla is
violet; it is rather sharply expanded about the middle of the
tube. The anthers lack hairs. The lower leaves have teeth.
§ Fields and open woods, N. J. to Pa., s. to Fla., Ala., and
Miss. *Fig. 109.*

P. *gracilis* (20 in.) is finely downy. The corolla is violet; it
flares gradually. The leaves are narrow, the lower ones usually
toothed. § Prairies and open woods, Ont. and Wis. to Alta.,
s. to Ia. and N. M.

TURTLEHEADS (*Chelone*)   WHITE, PINK, OR PURPLE

Chelone is unusual for its family. The five sepals are scarcely
joined. The corolla forms a broad, slightly curved, two-lipped
tube, with the lips scarcely separated; the resemblance to a just-
open mouth gives the plant its names (the botanical name is from
the Greek for turtle). There are five stamens, one of which is
short and lacks pollen. The flowers are mostly in spikes at the
summit of the stem and branches. The leaves (about 4 inches long)
are narrow, toothed, paired.

C. *glabra* (to 6 ft.) generally has whitish flowers, often pink-
tipped, but it is very variable in flower color, shape of leaves, and
hairiness. § Late summer: along streams and in swamps, ditches,
and wet woods, Nfld. to Man., s. to Ga., Ala., and Mo. PLATE 13.

C. *obliqua* (2 ft.) has reddish-purple flowers. § Summer and
autumn: wet woods, Md. and Tenn., s. to Fla. and Miss.; Ind. to
Minn., Mo., and Ark.

FIGWORTS (*Scrophularia*)   REDDISH-BROWN OR GREENISH

These are rather unattractive, woody plants with small, two-
lipped flowers in a loose panicle. The middle lobe of the lower
lip extends downward at almost a right angle to the tube. There
are four functional stamens and one rudimentary one, a stalk
which forms no pollen; this will be found close under the upper
lip of the corolla. The plants grow in open woodlands.

S. *lanceolata* (to 6 ft.) has greenish-brown flowers about ½
inch long, the lower lobe yellowish-green; the rudimentary stamen is broad, rounded at the tip, yellowish-green. The leaf blades

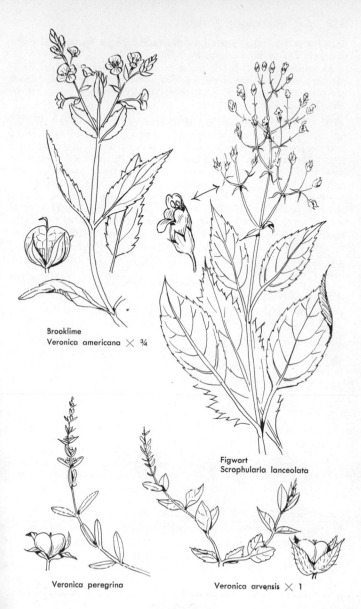

Brooklime
Veronica americana × ¾

Figwort
Scrophularia lanceolata

Veronica peregrina

Veronica arvensis × 1

FIGURE 110

about 3 inches long, taper into the stalk. § Late spring and early summer, nearly throughout. *Fig. 110.*

S. marilandica (to 9 ft.) has a reddish-brown corolla; the rudimentary stamen is club-shaped, purplish-brown. The leaf blades are rounded at the base. § Summer, Me. to Minn., s. to Ga., Ala., and Okla.

THE SPEEDWELLS and BROOKLIME (*Veronica*)   BLUE, WHITE, OR VIOLET / The speedwells get their name in England from being everywhere in fields and along grassy verges, small bright blue flowers in the grass, wishing good speed to the traveler. Several of these Old-World species are now common in America; we also have native species. The calyx makes a four-toothed cup; the four petals are joined only at the base, appearing as if separate, one a little larger than the others. There are two stamens. The flowers of most species grow singly or in small racemes in the axils of the upper leaves. The lower leaves are paired. The speedwells are recognizable even after flowering by the small heart-shaped seedpods; the differences between these (see *Figs. 110, 111*) will help in identifying the species.

All the species described below have trailing or creeping stems, the ends curving upward.

I. Species whose flowers are borne singly in the axils of leaves which are mostly attached singly (compare II).

V. agrestis has blue or white flowers, about ¼ inch across, on stalks up to ⅖ inch long. The leaves next to flowers are scalloped or toothed. § Late spring and early summer: fields, lawns, etc., Nfld. to Mich., s. to Fla. and Tex.; Old-World species.

V. arvensis has blue flowers, less than ⅛ inch across, on very short stalks (1/16 in.). The leaves next to the flowers are narrow and without teeth. The lower leaves are toothed. § Spring and early summer: fields and lawns, Nfld. to Minn., s. to Fla. and Tex.; Pacific U. S.; from the Old World. *Fig. 110.*

V. peregrina has white flowers on very short stalks (less than 1/16 in.); the petals scarcely project from the calyx. The leaves are narrow and mostly without teeth. § Spring and early summer: often a troublesome weed in lawns, across Canada, s. to Fla., Tex., and Ore.; a native species. *Fig. 110.*

II. Species with flowers in small racemes which grow from the axils of leaves.

V. chamaedrys has triangular or ovate leaves, toothed on the margins, with very short stalks. The flowers are blue with dark blue lines and a white center, less than ½ inch across. § Late spring: moist soil of gardens and fields, Nfld. to Mich., s. to Md. and Ill.; European. *Fig. 111.*

V. officinalis has toothed, somewhat hairy leaves on short stalks. The corolla, about ¼ inch across, is pale violet with dark

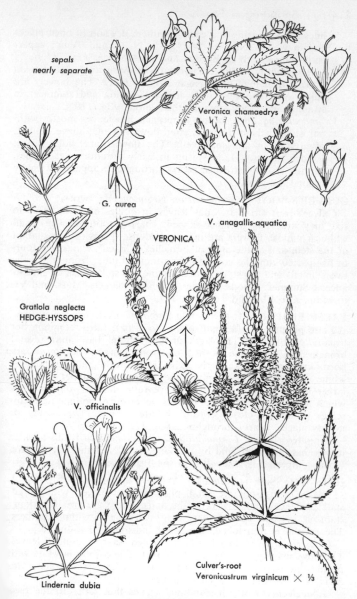

sepals
nearly separate

Veronica chamaedrys

G. aurea

V. anagallis-aquatica

VERONICA

Gratiola neglecta
HEDGE-HYSSOPS

V. officinalis

Lindernia dubia

Culver's-root
Veronicastrum virginicum × ⅓

FIGURE 111

lines. § Late spring and early summer: dry soil in open places and in woods, Nfld. to Wis., s. to N. C. and Tenn.; apparently native both in Europe and in America. *Fig. 111.*

V. *americana,* brooklime, has narrowly ovate toothed leaves on stalks which may be ½ inch long or more. The flowers are pale violet, about ¼ inch across. § Spring and summer: in swamps and along streams, throughout. *Fig. 110.*

V. *anagallis-aquatica,* brook-pimpernel, has leaves mostly without stalks (those formed after flowering may have stalks), often without marginal teeth. The flowers are violet, about ⅕ inch across. § Late spring to early autumn: wet ditches, springs, shallow streams, nearly throughout; apparently native around the world. *Fig. 111.*

CULVER'S-ROOT (*Veronicastrum virginicum*)   WHITE
Culver's-root (to 6 ft.) has leaves in circles of from three to six; they are stalked, lance-shaped, sharply toothed. The small white or pinkish flowers are in several dense spikes on the summit of the stem and at the ends of branches. The calyx makes a four- or five-parted cup, the corolla a four-toothed tube, from which the two stamens and the style project, giving the spike a fuzzy appearance. § Summer: woods, prairies, roadside thickets, Mass. and Vt. to Man., s. to Fla. and Tex. *Fig. 111.*

FALSE PIMPERNEL (*Lindernia dubia*)   LAVENDER OR WHITE
False pimpernel is a small plant (to 1 ft.), fairly common but usually overlooked. The stem divides at the base into several branches, on which the toothed leaves are paired. The flowers are borne on slender stalks in the axils. The corolla, pale lavender or white, is two-lipped, two small lobes forming the upper lip, three larger lobes the lower lip. There are four stamens, only two of which form pollen. The later flowers never open, pollinating themselves inside the closed corolla. § Late summer: wet sandy or muddy places, nearly throughout. *Fig. 111.*

A related species, *L. anagallidea,* is distinguished by its smaller leaves that lack teeth and by the longer stalks of the tiny flowers. (True pimpernel is *Anagallis,* in the Primrose Family.)

HEDGE-HYSSOP (*Gratiola*)   YELLOW OR WHITE
The hedge-hyssops are small plants of wet places, with paired, stalkless leaves and flowers in the axils. There are two functional stamens; in some species there may also be two without anthers. The corolla is four-lobed, somewhat indistinctly two-lipped.

G. *virginiana* (16 in.) has lance-shaped, sharply toothed leaves. The flower stalks are very short (⅕ in.). The corolla is white with purple lines, about ½ inch long or less. § Late spring and summer: N. J. to Kan., s. to Fla. and Tex.

G. *neglecta* (1 ft.) has toothed leaves that taper to the base and are broadest toward the tip. The flowers are on stalks up to an inch long. The corolla, less than ½ inch long, has white lobe

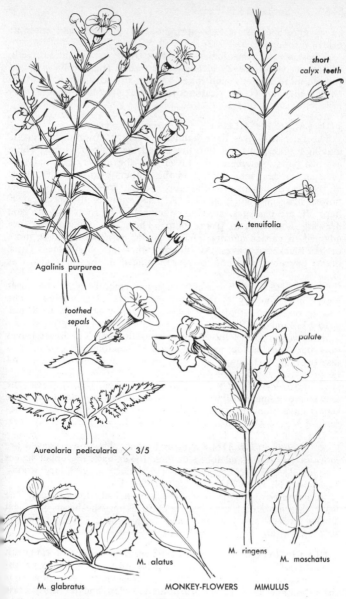

short
calyx teeth

A. tenuifolia

Agalinis purpurea

toothed
sepals

palate

Aureolaria pedicularia × 3/5

M. ringens   M. moschatus

M. glabratus   M. alatus   MONKEY-FLOWERS   MIMULUS

FIGURE 112

on a yellowish tube. § Late spring, early summer, and autumn: nearly throughout. *Fig. 111.*

G. aurea (1 ft.) has lance-shaped or ovate leaves without teeth. The flower stalks are ½ inch long or more. The corolla is bright yellow, more than ½ inch long. § Summer and autumn: Nfld. to N. Y., Ill., and N. D., scattered; s. along the coast to Fla. *Fig. 111.*

THE FALSE FOXGLOVES (*Aureolaria*)   YELLOW

The false foxgloves have handsome yellow flowers, the corolla making a tube that flares into five broad, nearly equal lobes. There are two pairs of stamens, the lower pair the longer. The stalks of the stamens bear long hairs, and the anthers also are hairy. Most of the leaves are paired; the upper ones, from whose axils the flowers arise, are much smaller. At least some of the species, perhaps all, are parasites, attaching themselves to roots of oaks and drawing nourishment from them. They are consequently not adapted to garden culture. Dried specimens generally have more or less blackened leaves. All bloom rather late in summer. These plants have by some botanists been placed in the same genus as *Agalinis.*

A. flava (to 6 ft.) has a grayish-green, smooth stem. The lower leaves are pinnately cleft. The sepals have plain margins. The corolla reaches a length of 2 inches. § Dry woods, Me. to Minn., s. to Fla. and La. PLATE 13.

A. laevigata (3 ft.) has a green, smooth stem. The lower leaves may be lobed or toothed, but often are neither. The corolla is just over an inch long. § Woods, mostly in mountains, Pa. and O., s. to Ga. and Tenn.

A. pedicularia (3 ft.) has a much-branched, downy stem. The leaves are pinnately cleft. The flower stalks are glandular. The sepals have blunt marginal teeth. The corolla is about 1½ inches long. § Me. to Ont. and Minn., s. to N. J., w. Va., and Ky. *Fig. 112.*

A. virginica (3 ft.) has a downy stem. The lower leaves are more or less ovate and lobed in their lower half, the upper leaves less lobed. The corolla is about 1½ inches long. § Dry woods, Mass. and N. H. to Mich., s. to Fla. and La.

A. grandiflora (3 ft.) has a much-branched, downy stem. The leaves are more or less pinnately cleft, as are the bracts just next to the flowers. The corolla is 1½ inches long. § Woods, Ind. to Wis. and Minn., s. to Mo. and Tex.

MULLEIN-FOXGLOVE (*Dasistoma macrophyllum*)   YELLOW

Mullein-foxglove (to 6 ft.) may be mistaken for one of the false foxgloves (*Aureolaria*). It has paired leaves, with flowers in the axils. The lower leaves are pinnately cleft and the lobes again cleft; the upper leaves are not lobed or cleft, but toothed. The foliage blackens quickly as it dries. The petals make a sort of trumpet, woolly inside (Dasistoma means "woolly mouth"), flaring into five almost equal lobes. The stalks of the stamens are hairy but the anthers are smooth. § Summer: rich woods, O. to Nebr. and Kan., s. to Ga. and Tex.

GERARDIA (*Agalinis*) PINK OR PURPLE

The species of *Agalinis* have been placed by some botanists in the same genus with *Aureolaria,* under the illegitimate name *Gerardia.* They are slender, branching plants with narrow, paired leaves and flowers on slender stalks from the axils or in loose inflorescences. The calyx is a cup bearing on its rim five equally spaced sharp teeth. The corolla is indistinctly two-lipped, the five more or less rounded, spreading lobes being much alike; the tube bulges slightly on the lower side. There are four stamens. The flowers appear in late summer and last only a day.

Some fifteen species have been recognized in our range, but several are rare or limited in distribution. The following are the most widespread.

A. maritima (6–12 in.) has a corolla ½ inch long or longer. § Salt marshes along the coast, N. S. to Fla., Tex., and Mexico.

A. purpurea (about 3 ft.) has flowers that vary greatly in size, averaging about an inch long. The largest leaves may be ⅙ inch wide. § Bogs and wet sandy shores, N. S. to Minn. and S. D., s. to Fla., Tex., and Mexico. *Fig. 112.*

A. tenuifolia (about 2 ft.) has flowers on slender stalks up to an inch long. The corolla is about ½ inch long. The calyx teeth are minute. The stem branches widely; the leaves may be hairlike; some varieties have tufts of leaves in the axils (these are more common in the Midwest). § Moist places in woods and prairies, sometimes also in dry woods, Me. to Man. and Nebr., s. to Fla. and Tex. *Fig. 112.*

A. gattingeri (to 2 ft.) is comparatively few-flowered, the flowers, ¾ inch long, being solitary at the tips of the many branches. The flower stalks may reach an inch in length. § Woods and hillsides, moist or dry, N. Y. and Ont. to Minn. and Nebr., s. to Ala. and Tex.

A. skinneriana (to 2 ft.) has a corolla up to ½ inch long. The stem is rather rough, with four sharp angles. § Dry woods and barrens, N. Y. and Ont. to Wis., s. to O. and Okla.

MONKEY-FLOWERS (*Mimulus*) BLUE OR YELLOW

In *Mimulus* the handsome flowers have a clearly two-lipped corolla; the two upper lobes stand erect, the three lower spread. The opening may be partly closed by a pair of ridges ("palate") on the lower lip (the corolla was thought to *mimic* a face). There are four stamens. The sepals form a five-angled tube. The leaves are paired, the flowers on slender stalks rising from their axils. These are plants of wet places, flowering in summer.

Species with blue (or occasionally pinkish or white) petals.

M. *ringens* (to 3 ft.) has leaves without stalks and flowers on stalks nearly as long as the leaves. § Que. to Sask., s. to Ga. and Tex. *Fig. 112.*

M. *alatus* (to 3 ft.) has stalked leaves, the blades tapering downward, and flower stalks about as long as the leaf stalks. § Conn. to Mich. and Nebr., s. to Fla. and Tex. *Fig. 112.*

II. Species with yellow flowers.

M. *moschatus* has a hairy and somewhat clammy stem which at first lies flat, the tip then rising to a height of a foot or more. The leaves are stalked, the blades round or heart-shaped at the base. The corolla is open. § Nfld. to Ont. and Mich., s. to W. Va.; also in western Canada and U. S. *Fig. 112.*

M. *glabratus* (to 2 ft.) has weak stems, nearly or quite smooth. The leaves have nearly round blades, the veins running from near the base, on short stalks. § Ont. to Man., s. to Ill. and Mo., sw. to Mexico. *Fig. 112.*

BLUE-EYED-MARY (*Collinsia verna*)   BLUE-AND-WHITE

The stems are weak, branched from the base (2 ft.). The pretty flowers give the species its name; the lower lip is bright blue, the upper white. The middle lobe of the lower lip is folded lengthwise into a small vertical envelope which encloses the four stamens; it is below the other two lobes and concealed by them. (There is a fifth stamen, but it is rudimentary.) § Spring: wooded slopes, N. Y. to Mich. and Ia., s. to w. Va., Ark., and Kan. *Fig. 113.*

COW-WHEAT (*Melampyrum lineare*)   WHITE, YELLOW, OR PURPLE / Cow-wheat is a delicate, smooth plant (to 18 in.), a parasite on the roots of other plants. The narrow leaves are in pairs, mostly without teeth; but the upper leaves may have some long teeth near the base. The narrow flowers, less than ½ inch long, grow in the axils. The corolla varies from white to pale yellow or purplish with yellow tips. There are two unequal pairs of stamens. § Summer: dry woods, pinelands, bogs, etc., across Canada, s. to Ga., Ind., Tenn., and Mont. *Fig. 113.*

EYEBRIGHT (*Euphrasia*)   WHITE OR PURPLISH

The name eyebright applies to several species of small northern plants. They have small stalkless leaves in pairs, the blades often roundish, toothed. The flowers are two-lipped, the lower lip three-lobed. There are four stamens. They bloom in late summer.

E. *americana* (16 in.) may serve as a sample of these insignificant little plants. The leaves are less than an inch long; the corolla less than ½ inch. § Late summer: fields and waste places, Nfld and Que., N. E. and N. Y. (including E. *canadensis* and E. *condensata*, only slightly different). *Fig. 113.*

CANKER-ROOTS (*Kickxia*)   PURPLE-AND-YELLOW

These are small plants whose stems lie on the ground; the leaves are singly attached. From the axils rise slender stalks about a

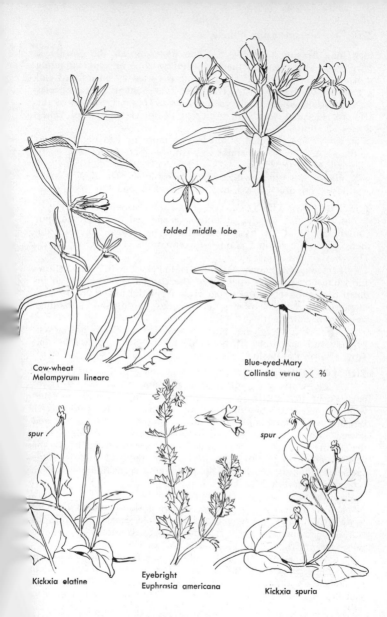

Cow-wheat
Melampyrum lineare

folded middle lobe

Blue-eyed-Mary
Collinsia verna × ⅔

spur

Kickxia elatine

Eyebright
Euphrasia americana

spur

Kickxia spuria

FIGURE 113

inch long bearing tiny flowers. The upper lip of the corolla is purple, the lower yellow; there is a hollow tube or spur extending down from the lower lip. The opening is closed by an inflated pad ("palate") on the lower lip. There are four stamens. These species were by some botanists placed in *Linaria*. They are natives of the Old World, now weeds in America in moist sandy soil. They flower all summer.

K. spuria has rounded, blunt leaves, more or less heart-shaped at the base. The flower stalks are woolly. § N. E. to Mo., s. to Fla. and Ala. *Fig. 113.*

K. elatine has leaves with pointed basal lobes. The flower stalks are mostly smooth. § Mass. to Kan., s. to Fla. and La. *Fig. 113.*

THE TOADFLAXES (*Linaria*)   YELLOW-AND-WHITE OR BLUE

The two-lipped corolla of *Linaria* is marked by a curved spur (hollow tube) at the base of the lower lip. There are four stamens. These are smooth plants with numerous very narrow leaves. They flower in summer.

L. vulgaris, also known as butter-and-eggs (2–3 ft.), has yellow-and-white flowers. The opening of the corolla is closed by an inflated projection ("palate") that rises from the lower lip (as in a snapdragon). § Waste places and gardens, throughout; a familiar weed from Europe. PLATE 13.

L. canadensis (2 ft.) has blue flowers. The corolla is not closed. § Sandy and acid soils, Mass. to Minn. and S. D., s. to Fla. and Tex.; also on the Pacific coast, and in Mexico. *Fig. 114.*

THE LOUSEWORTS (*Pedicularis*)   RED AND YELLOW

The louseworts get their unpleasant name from an old European belief that cattle that grazed these plants became infected with lice. (Perhaps they did, but not for that reason.) Our species are low but stout plants with mostly pinnately cleft leaves and flowers in a thick spike or head. The flowers are quite large, two-lipped, the upper lip narrow and curved, generally flattish in the vertical plane and with a small beak at the end and in some species teeth also, the lower lip with three spreading lobes. The four stamens are hidden beneath the upper lip.

P. canadensis, also called wood betony (to 16 in.), is a hairy plant. The flowers are yellow or red or various combinations of those shades; they are in a broad head. The leaves also may be colored. § Spring and early summer: woods, clearings, wet meadows, Que. to Man., s. to Fla. and n. Mexico. PLATE 13.

P. lanceolata (to 3 ft.) is smooth or nearly so. The flowers are pale yellow, in a thick spike. The calyx bears a toothed leaflike appendage on either side. § Late summer: wet meadows, swamps and shores, Mass. to Man., s. to N. C., Tenn., Mo., and Nebr. *Fig 114.*

PAINTED-CUP (*Castilleia coccinea*)   RED

The painted-cups have leaves attached singly and flowers in

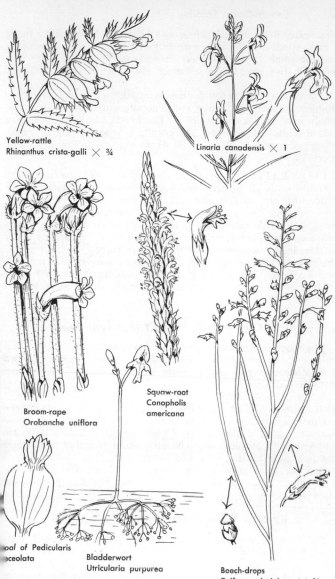

Yellow-rattle
Rhinanthus crista-galli × ¾

Linaria canadensis × 1

Broom-rape
Orobanche uniflora

Squaw-root
Conopholis
americana

...al of Pedicularis
...ceolata

Bladderwort
Utricularia purpurea

Beech-drops
Epifagus virginiana × ⅔

FIGURE 114

thick spike. Beneath each flower is a bract of characteristic form, in most species larger and more brightly colored (red or yellow) than the small greenish flowers themselves. The flowers are narrow, with two lips, the lower much the shorter. There are four stamens.

C. coccinea, also called Indian paintbrush (2 ft.), is our only common species. The leaves are generally cut more or less palmately into several narrow lobes. The bracts are red (sometimes pink or white), three-lobed. The corolla is greenish-yellow. § Late spring and summer: Mass. and N. H. to Man., s. to Fla. and Okla. PLATE 14.

YELLOW-RATTLE (*Rhinanthus crista-galli*)   YELLOW OR BRONZE

Yellow-rattle (2 ft. or more) has curious sepals, which form a bladderlike cup, at first vertically flat, later, when the fruit matures, inflated. The petals are yellow or bronze-colored, forming two lips in shape much like those of *Pedicularis* but less than an inch long. The four stamens are concealed under the arched upper lip. The leaves are paired, toothed, rather narrow, without stalks. The flowers grow in the axils of the upper leaves; they have almost no stalks. § Late spring to early autumn: fields and roadsides, even in high mountains, across Canada and s. to N. E. and N. Y. *Fig. 114.*

UNICORN-PLANT FAMILY (*Martyniaceae*)

This tropical American group is characterized by a hard pod which ends in a long spine. The flowers are two-lipped, with two or four stamens plus one or more sterile rudiments, and a one-chambered ovary.

UNICORN-PLANT (*Proboscidea louisianica*)   YELLOW-AND-PURPLE

This is a bushy plant (about 3 ft.), sticky all over, with broad leaves variously disposed. The flowers, about 2 inches long, are yellowish with purple spots. The pod, about 6 inches long, splits into two, each bearing a hooked, sharp horn. It is sometimes cultivated for these pods. § Late summer: occasional in fields and waste places, etc., in various parts of our range, especially the Midwest.

BROOM-RAPE FAMILY (*Orobanchaceae*)

The broom-rapes and their relatives are plants without fully developed leaves and without green color; they are unable to make organic food and live parasitically on the roots of other plants. The flowers, which are various in form, have four stamens and a one-chambered ovary.

BROOM-RAPE or CANCER-ROOT (*Orobanche uniflora*)   PALE LAVENDER / The white stem (2–3 in.) grows from a short, upright underground stem enveloped in scales. Each bears a single whitish or lavender flower. § Late spring and summer: shaded banks in woods, throughout.. *Fig. 114.*

SQUAW-ROOT (*Conopholis americana*)   YELLOWISH-BROWN
Squaw-root appears as a fleshy stem (6 in.), the lower part covered with yellowish-brown scales, the upper part a dense spike of flowers of the same color. The corolla is markedly two-lipped. This is parasitic on tree roots. § Late spring and early summer: rich woods, N. S. to Wis., s. to Fla. and Ala. *Fig. 114.*

BEECH-DROPS (*Epifagus virginiana*)   MADDER-BROWN OR PINK-ISH / The pale brown stem (1 ft.) is branched; it bears a few scales and many small flowers. This species is parasitic on beech roots. § Late summer and autumn: N. S. to Ont. and Wis., s. to Fla. and La. *Fig. 114.*

BLADDERWORT FAMILY (*Lentibulariaceae*)

The small flowers of bladderworts and butterworts recall those of *Linaria:* two-lipped (the opening closed in many species) and with a hollow spur. There are, however, but two stamens, and the ovary has a single chamber. These are small plants of wet places.

THE BLADDERWORTS (*Utricularia*)   YELLOW, PURPLE, OR LAVENDER / The bladderworts are named for the small bladders or sacs on leaves or branches that are submerged in water or mud; there are few or no aerial leaves. These bladders act as traps in which small aquatic animals are caught and digested; the mechanism is intricate. The submerged parts are divided into hairlike segments. The flowers bloom in summer. The species are too numerous to be here described. The following may be briefly noticed.
U. cornuta has yellow flowers, grows on wet soil, has no bladders. § Nfld. to Minn., s. to Fla. and Tex.
U. purpurea has lavender flowers, has bladders at the ends of hairlike divisions of the leaves. § Que. to Minn., s. to Fla. and La. *Fig. 114.*
U. intermedia has yellow flowers, has bladders on special branches. § Throughout except se.
U. vulgaris has yellow flowers, numerous scattered bladders. § Nearly throughout.
U. gibba has yellow flowers, very short spurs, few bladders. § Throughout.

BUTTERWORT (*Pinguicula vulgaris*)   VIOLET
Butterwort is named for its sticky, shining leaves, with inrolled edges, which catch small insects; they radiate from the base of the stem (6 in.). The flowers grow a few together on a leafless talk. § Early summer: wet soil and bogs, across Canada and s. o N. Y., Mich., Minn., and Wash.

ACANTHUS FAMILY (*Acanthaceae*)

The *Acanthaceae* are mainly tropical plants, resembling the Snapdragon Family in many ways. The chief technical difference is the hooked projection on which each seed is borne.

RUELLIA   BLUE OR VIOLET
The leaves of *Ruellia* are generally paired, without teeth, on short stalks or without stalks. The flowers, about 2 inches long, grow singly or in clusters on stalks in the axils. The corolla is almost radially symmetric, with five nearly equal lobes, 2 inches long or more.

R. strepens (to 3 ft.) is almost smooth. Short axillary branches bear two bracts and from one to three flowers. § Late spring and summer: woods and thickets, N. J. to Kan., s. to S. C. and Tex. *Fig. 115.*

R. humilis (30 in.) is hairy. The lobes of the calyx are very narrow. The flowers are borne much as in *R. strepens.* It is a variable species. § Summer: dry woods and prairies, Pa. to Nebr., s. to Fla. and Tex. *Fig. 115.*

R. pedunculata (2 ft.) is finely downy. From one to three flowers are borne on a long branch, with a pair of leaflike bracts just below. § Summer: dry woods, Ill. and Mo., s. to La. and Tex.

R. caroliniensis (to 3 ft.) has a hairy stem, bearing rather crowded leaves which may be hairy or smooth. The flowers are almost without stalks, several in an axil. § Summer: dry woods and clearings, N. J. to Ind., s. to Fla. and Tex.

WATER-WILLOW (*Justicia americana*)   PALE VIOLET
Water-willow (not to be confused with *Jussiaea,* called water-primrose and primrose-willow) grows in mud or shallow water (2–3 feet above the surface). The paired leaves are very narrow. The flowers are in tight clusters on long stalks from the axils; the corolla is two-lipped. § Summer: Que. to Wis., s. and sw. to Ga., Kan., and Tex. *Fig. 115.*

LOPSEED FAMILY (*Phrymaceae*)

This family contains only one genus, of which we have but one species.

LOPSEED (*Phryma leptostachya*)   WHITE OR LAVENDER
The upper pairs of leaves on the stem (2–3 ft.) are stalkless; the lower leaves have stalks and broad, toothed blades. The white or lavender flowers, each about ¼ inch long, are in a spike atop the stem; the corolla is very narrow, two-lipped. After the corolla falls, the calyx, containing the seedlike fruit, bends down ("lops") against the stem. § Summer: moist woods, Que. to Man., s. to Fla. and Tex.

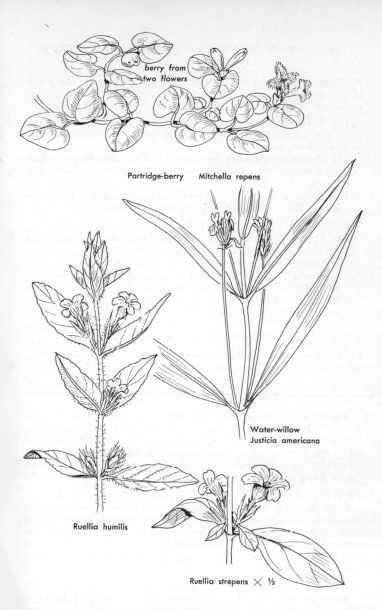

berry from two flowers

Partridge-berry   Mitchella repens

Water-willow
Justicia americana

Ruellia humilis

Ruellia strepens × ⅓

FIGURE 115

GROUP VI OF DICOT FAMILIES. PETALS JOINED; OVARY INFERIOR

A. Plants with leaves mostly borne in pairs or circles. The plants of this group treated in this book have a corolla that is radially symmetric or nearly so. (Compare B and C.)

The **Bedstraw Family** has a corolla with four lobes or teeth; there are four stamens. The petals are blue, white, greenish, or yellow.

The **Honeysuckle Family** has four or five stamens. In the genera here treated the corolla is pink, white, greenish, or dull red, five-lobed.

The **Valerian Family** has minute sepals. There are three stamens. The corolla is white or pink, five-lobed.

B. Plants with leaves mostly borne singly.

The **Cucumber Family** has a radially symmetric corolla. The stamens and pistil are in separate flowers. The three stamens are joined. These are vines.

The **Bluebell Family** has a radially symmetric corolla, white or blue. There are five stamens, separate.

The **Lobelia Family** has a two-lipped, bilaterally symmetric corolla split on the upper side; the lower lip is divided into three teeth or lobes. The stamens are joined to form a tube which projects through the split in the corolla.

C. The **Sunflower Family** has small flowers in a head that is often taken for a single flower; see the description of the family.

BEDSTRAW FAMILY (*Rubiaceae*)

This is an enormous family, mostly tropical. It includes the coffee and quinine trees. The flowers are mostly radially symmetric, with an inferior ovary. The leaves are paired, undivided, and without teeth. In our species the flower parts are generally in fours (threes in some species); the ovary has two chambers; it bears one or two styles, with two or four stigmas.

PARTRIDGE-BERRY (*Mitchella repens*)   WHITE OR PINK
Partridge-berry has a creeping stem with pairs of nearly round evergreen leaves about ⅜ inch across. The fringed flowers are in pairs at the ends of the branches. There are four stigmas on the one style. The flowers are succeeded by red berries, each pair of which coalesces into a single fruit. § Late spring and summer: woods, Nfld. to Minn., s. to Fla. and Tex. *Fig. 115.*

BLUETS (*Houstonia*)   BLUE, PURPLE, OR WHITE
Bluets are small plants with flowers at the summit of the stem. There are four narrow lobes to the calyx, four erect or spreading lobes to the corolla, and four stamens. The ovary is two-chambered, and the style bears two narrow stigmas.

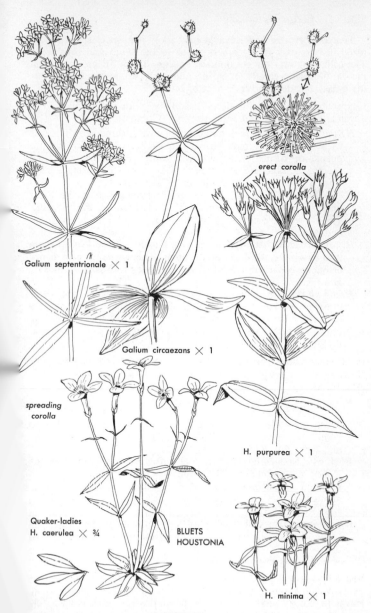

Galium septentrionale × 1

Galium circaezans × 1

erect corolla

H. purpurea × 1

spreading corolla

Quaker-ladies
H. caerulea × ¾

BLUETS
HOUSTONIA

H. minima × 1

FIGURE 116

This is a North American genus; about ten species are recognized in our area; many others occur to the south and southwest. The following are our commonest species. These all grow in open places, flowering chiefly in spring and early summer, often covering grassy meadows with a sheet of blue.

I. Species whose corolla flares gradually, with erect lobes. The flowers are clustered and short-stalked. (Compare II.)

H. purpurea (to 20 in.) has broadly ovate, three-veined leaves without stalks. It may be smooth or hairy. The flowers are purple or white. A variety (by some considered a distinct species, *H. lanceolata*) has narrower leaves with a single main vein. § N. J. to Ia., s. to Ga. and Okla. *Fig. 116.*

H. canadensis (to 8 in.) has generally oblong leaves, the basal ones slightly broader, usually all with hairs at the margins. The flowers are purple. § Me. and Ont. to Minn., s. to Tenn. and Ark.

H. longifolia (to 10 in.) has narrow, mostly smooth leaves, some in a rosette at the base of the stem. The flowers are lavender or more often white. § In dry soil, Me. to Sask., s. to Ga. and Okla.

H. tenuifolia (to 1 ft.) has very narrow leaves on the stem, those in the basal rosette being slightly broader. The clusters of purple flowers are borne at the ends of wide-spreading branches. § Dry soil, Pa. to Mo., s. and sw. to Ga., Tex., and n. Mexico.

II. Species whose corolla forms a narrow tube crowned by four abruptly spreading lobes. The flowers are single, on more or less long stalks.

H. caerulea, Quaker-ladies, innocence (to 8 in.), has a rosette of leaves at the base and a few pairs on the stems; they are oblong, or broadest near the tip. The flowers are blue or white with a yellow "eye." § N. S. to Wis., s. to Ga., Ala., and Ark. *Fig. 116.*

H. pusilla, star-violet (2–6 in.), is a tiny plant with most of the leaves at the base. The blue or purple flowers are on stalks about an inch long. The sepals are about $\frac{1}{16}$ inch long, about half as long as the tube of the corolla. § Va. to Nebr., s. to Fla. and Tex.

H. minima, also called star-violet, is similar to the foregoing, being distinguished mainly by its longer sepals ($\frac{1}{10}$ inch long, nearly as long as the tube of the corolla). § Ill. to Kan., s. to Ark. and Tex. *Fig. 116.*

BEDSTRAW and CLEAVERS (*Galium*)   WHITE, PURPLISH, OP
YELLOW / The many species of *Galium* have slender, square stems
leaves in circles, and minute, clustered flowers on branches tha
arise from the axils or at the tip of the stem. The genus is foun
all over the world, with 28 species in our range; of these, severa

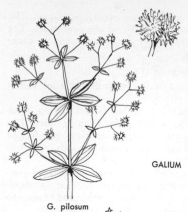

G. pilosum

GALIUM

G. verum × 1

G. asprellum × ¾

Twin-flower
Linnaea borealis × ⅔

FIGURE 117

have come in from Europe. A number are bristly or rough. The petals and stamens may be three or four. There are two styles. The fruit consists of two small spheres side by side, one seed in each; in some species they are bristly.

I. Species with bristly fruit (compare II).

A. Species with bristly fruit and leaves in circles of four (compare B).

G. *circaezans,* wild licorice (2 ft.), has broad leaves, each with three main veins. The stem may be slightly hairy. The flowers are greenish-purple, growing stalkless on forked branches from the leaf axils. § Summer: woods, Que. to Minn. and Nebr., s. to Fla. and Tex. *Fig. 116.*

G. *lanceolatum* (2 ft.) has yellowish flowers which turn purple in age. The leaves are lance-shaped, sharp-pointed, three-veined. § Summer: dry woods, Me. and Que. to Minn., s. to N. C. and Tenn.

G. *pilosum* (3 ft.) has oblong, narrow leaves with one main vein. The flowers vary from greenish-white to purplish. § Summer: dry woods, N. H. to Mich., s. to N. C. and Tex. *Fig. 117.*

G. *septentrionale,* bedstraw (3 ft.), has very narrow, sharp-pointed leaves on a smooth stem. Numerous fragrant white flowers are borne in panicles at the summit and from the axils. § Summer: various situations, across Canada, s. to Del. and N. M.; also in the Pacific states. *Fig. 116.*

B. Species with bristly fruit and more than four leaves in each circle.

G. *aparine,* cleavers (4 ft.), bears sharp hairs that point downward, so that it is rough to the touch and clings ("cleaves") to one's clothes. The stems are weak, leaning against bushes, fences, etc., often in tangled masses. The narrow leaves are in circles of eight on the main stems. The white flowers are on branches from the axils, few in a cluster. § Late spring and early summer: mostly in damp shady places, nearly throughout; also in Europe and Asia

G. *triflorum* (4 ft.) resembles the foregoing species in being a weak, straggling plant. The leaves are oblong, rough on the edges, in circles of six. The flowers are greenish-white § Summer: woods, throughout.

II. Species with smooth fruits.

G. *septentrionale,* bedstraw, has a variety with smooth fruit See under I A above.

G. *verum,* ladies' (or Our Lady's) bedstraw (3 ft.), has ve narrow leaves in circles of about eight. The flowers are ye low, fragrant, numerous in dense clusters at the summ and on branches from the upper axils. According to a cient belief, this was the "straw" in the manger at Be

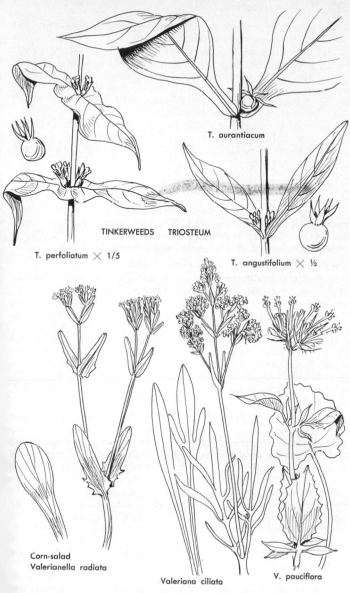

T. aurantiacum

TINKERWEEDS   TRIOSTEUM

T. perfoliatum × 1/5

T. angustifolium × ⅓

Corn-salad
Valerianella radiata

Valeriana ciliata

V. pauciflora

FIGURE 118

lehem. § Late spring and summer: fields, Nfld. to Ont. and
N. D., s. to Va. and Kan. *Fig. 117.*

G. asprellum (6 ft.) resembles *G. aparine* in having down-
pointing hairs which enable it to sprawl over other plants.
The leaves are in circles of six or fewer. The flowers are
white, in open clusters at the ends of branches. § Late
spring and summer: moist woods, Nfld. to Ont. and Nebr.,
s. to N. Y., Ind., and Mo. *Fig. 117.*

G. mollugo (3 ft.) is a smooth plant with leaves in sixes and
eights. The flowers are white, numerous in loose panicles.
§ Summer: roadsides and fields, Nfld. to Ont., s. to Va. and
Ind.

HONEYSUCKLE FAMILY (Caprifoliaceae)

Most genera of this family comprise shrubs and woody vines
and are not treated in this book. The two genera described below
have paired leaves, a five-lobed corolla which is radially symmetric or nearly so, five stamens, and an inferior ovary.

TWIN-FLOWER (*Linnaea borealis*)   PINK
Twin-flower has a creeping stem from which rise erect branches
(6 in.) bearing more or less paired leaves. The leaves are roundish, more or less toothed toward the tip. The flowers hang from
the tips of slender stalks that grow from the leafy branch. The
corolla is almost bell-shaped, ending in five small flaring lobes.

The genus was named for Carl Linnaeus, father of botanical
names, who liked to pose for his portrait with a sprig of twin-
flower in his hand. The species grows around the world in northern
latitudes; our American plants differ slightly from the European.
§ Summer: damp peaty and boggy places, across Canada and s.
to Md., W. Va., Ind., S. D., Utah, and Calif. *Fig. 117.*

THE TINKERWEEDS (*Triosteum*)   PURPLISH-RED OR YELLOW-
ISH / The tinkerweeds, also called horse-gentians, feverworts, and
wild coffee, are coarse plants with long paired leaves and small
stalkless flowers in their axils. The corolla flares into five nearly
equal pointed lobes. The fruit is an orange or red berry with a
few seeds. They all flower in late spring and early summer.

T. perfoliatum (4 ft.) has leaves that are narrowed toward the
base then expanded again to meet the corresponding part of the
opposite leaf around the stem. The stem thus seems to grow
through a single leaf. The stem and sometimes the leaves are
downy and glandular. There are from one to four purplish flower
in each axil. The berry is orange. § Woods and old fields, Mass
to Minn. and Nebr., s. to Ga. and Kan. *Fig. 118.*

T. aurantiacum (4 ft.) has leaves that taper at the base and d
not meet around the stem. The stem is hairy. The flowers ar
purplish-red. The berry is orange. § Moist woods, Que. to Ia. ar
Kan., s. to Ga., Ky., and Mo. *Fig. 118.*

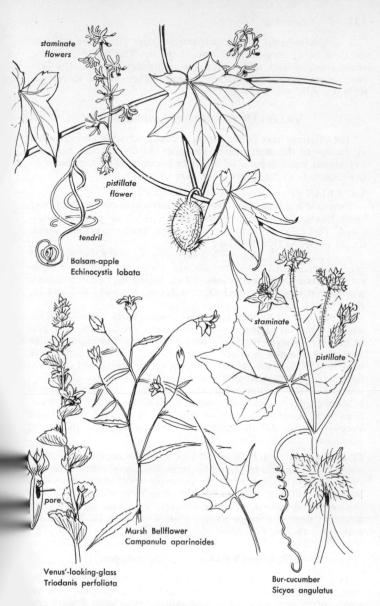

staminate flowers

pistillate flower

tendril

Balsam-apple
Echinocystis lobata

staminate

pistillate

Marsh Bellflower
Campanula aparinoides

pore

Venus'-looking-glass
Triodanis perfoliata

Bur-cucumber
Sicyos angulatus

FIGURE 119

T. angustifolium (30 in.) is sparsely hairy. The leaves taper to the base, being often broader toward the tip. The flowers are generally single in each axil, with a greenish-yellow corolla. The berries are orange-red. § Moist woods and thickets, Conn. to Mo., s. to N. C., Ala., and La. *Fig. 118.*

VALERIAN FAMILY (*Valerianaceae*)

The valerians have paired leaves and many small flowers crowded at the tips of the stem and its branches. In our species there are five almost equal corolla lobes, three stamens, and from three to five chambers in the ovary—but only one seed.

VALERIAN (*Valeriana*)   WHITE OR PINK
Valeriana has pinnately divided or cleft leaves on the stem, and basal leaves which may be pinnately divided or cleft or undivided. The calyx is composed of several feathery bristles which unroll when the fruit develops.

V. ciliata (to 4 ft.) has thick leaves with parallel veins, the basal generally undivided. The stamens and pistils are usually in separate flowers on different plants. § Late spring and early summer: wet open places, N. Y. and Ont. to Minn., s. to O., Ill., and Ia. *Fig. 118.*

V. pauciflora (30 in.) has heart-shaped basal leaves with or without a pair of segments. The stem leaves are divided, with two or more small segments at the base and a large end segment. The tube of the corolla is much longer than in other species (more than ½ inch as against about ⅛ inch). § Late spring and summer: moist soil, Pa. to Ill., s. to Va. and Tenn. *Fig. 118.*

V. officinalis, garden-heliotrope (to 5 ft.), is a rather coarse cultivated plant sometimes seen in roadside fields. The wide-branching, rounded clusters of small white or pink flowers are sweetly scented. All the leaves are pinnately divided and hairy. § Summer: Que. to Minn., s. to N. J., Pa., and O.

CORN-SALAD or LAMB'S-LETTUCE (*Valerianella radiata*)
WHITE / *Valerianella* has smooth, undivided leaves, blunt at the end, many of them of approximately the same width throughout their length. Those of *V. radiata* (2 ft.) often have a few teeth near the base. The flowers, in dense clusters, are about 1/10 inch long. § Spring: mostly in damp places, wooded or open, N. Y. to Kan. s. to Fla. and Tex. *Fig. 118.*

CUCUMBER FAMILY (*Cucurbitaceae*)

This large family is mostly tropical. The stems creep on the ground or climb by tendrils. The leaves are undivided, attached singly, often palmately lobed. The radially symmetric flowers contain only stamens or pistils, not both. Our species have three stamens, joined by their anthers. The ovary is inferior.

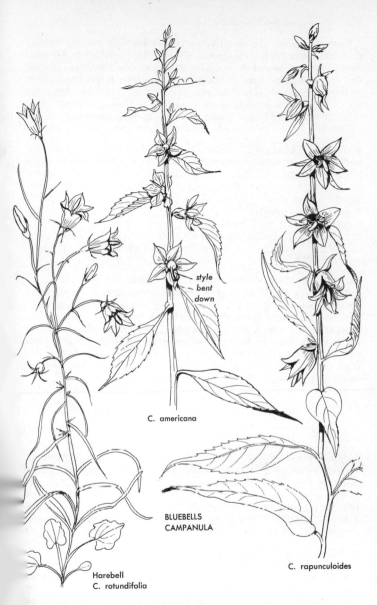

style
bent
down

C. americana

BLUEBELLS
CAMPANULA

Harebell
C. rotundifolia

C. rapunculoides

FIGURE 120

Several species are familiar in cultivation and on our tables: *Cucumis sativus* is the cucumber, *C. melo* the cantaloupe, *Citrullus vulgaris* the watermelon, and *Cucurbita* includes squashes, gourds, and the pumpkin. Any of these may occasionally be found wild in waste places. Besides the two common wild species described below, *Cucurbita foetidissima,* a western species, is found along railroad tracks and riverbanks in Missouri and westward. It has yellow flowers up to 2 inches long and leaves to 8 inches long.

BALSAM-APPLE, WILD CUCUMBER (*Echinocystis lobata*)
WHITE / The leaves of balsam-apple have from three to seven sharp lobes. It climbs by branched, coiled tendrils. The flowers have a small six-lobed calyx and a six-parted corolla. The staminate flowers are in erect racemes; the stamens are joined. The pistillate flowers hang, generally singly, from the base of the staminate raceme; but they may be missing on some vines. The fruit is oval, prickly, soft; it discharges its two pairs of seeds from two pores at the tip. § Summer: waste places and thickets, nearly throughout. *Fig. 119.*

BUR-CUCUMBER (*Sicyos angulatus*)   WHITE
The leaves of bur-cucumber somewhat resemble those of *Echinocystis,* but the lobes are usually less prominent, and their margins are generally toothed. It climbs by branched tendrils. The flowers have a five-parted corolla and calyx. The staminate flowers are in short racemes; the stamens are united. The pistillate flowers, and later the oval prickly fruits, are in tight heads on long stalks (2–3 in.). § Summer: damp soil and hedges, Me. and Que. to Minn., s. and sw. to Fla. and Ariz. *Fig. 119.*

BLUEBELL FAMILY (*Campanulaceae*)

Several very different kinds of plants are called bluebells. The name is often applied to *Mertensia* in the Forget-me-not Family. English bluebells are in the Lily Family. Bluebells-of-Scotland (which grow all over the Northern Hemisphere) belong in the Bluebell Family. The *Campanulaceae* have undivided leaves, attached singly. The blue, violet, or white flowers of our species are radially symmetric, with five corolla lobes and five stamens. The ovary is inferior. The fruit is a three- to five-chambered pod, discharging its seeds through pores in the sides.

BLUEBELLS, HAREBELLS (*Campanula*)   BLUE OR WHITE
The bluebells, as the name suggests, have mostly bell-shape flowers, with all parts in fives except the chambers of the ovar (and fruit), which in our species are three.
C. rotundifolia, harebell or bluebell-of-Scotland (2 ft.), ha apparently only very narrow, almost hairlike leaves on a wea much-branched stem. Its name is justified by a few leaves at t

base that are roundish ("rotund"). The flower is a delicate, hanging, five-toothed bell. It grows on rock ledges and in other dry places, as well as in meadows and woods, its height, the width of the leaves, and other characteristics varying greatly with the environment. § Summer: across Canada, s. to N. J., Ind., Nebr., Tex., and Calif. *Fig. 120.*

C. aparinoides, marsh bellflower (2 ft.), has a weak, branched stem, rather rough on its edges, with very narrow leaves; it grows usually among other low plants which help to support it. The flowers are scattered, on long stalks, white or pale blue. The bell is rather deeply parted, but only ½ inch long at most. § Summer: wet meadows and stream banks, N. B. to Sask., s. to Ga., O., Ill., Ia., Nebr., and Colo. *Fig. 119.*

C. rapunculoides (to 4 ft.) has leaves with lance-shaped or ovate blades, toothed, the lower ones heart-shaped and on stalks, the upper with very short stalks or none. The flowers are in a long terminal raceme; they are distinctly bell-shaped, usually deep blue. § Summer: roadsides, waste ground, thickets, naturalized from the Old World, Nfld. to N. D., s. to Md., O., and Mo. *Fig. 120.*

C. americana, tall bellflower (4 ft. or more), has ovate or lance-shaped leaves, toothed, the lower ones on a short stalk, all tapering to the base. The flowers are in a long terminal spike. They differ from those of the other species in not being bell-shaped; the five pointed lobes spread widely; they are light blue with a white line. The style is curved downward, then up at the tip. § Late summer, early autumn: woods, along streams, on roadsides, N. Y. to Minn. and S. D.. s. to Fla., Ala., and Okla. *Fig. 120.*

VENUS'-LOOKING-GLASS (*Triodanis perfoliata*)   BLUE

Venus'-looking-glass has a usually unbranched stem (3 ft.) bearing small round or ovate leaves without stalks; the basal lobes of the leaves clasp the stem. The flowers are in the axils, singly or a few together, also without stalks. The earlier ones (those lower down on the stem) have almost no corolla and never open, but form fruit by pollinating themselves. The later flowers (higher on the stem) have a corolla that flares into five pointed lobes. The pods open by "valves" that curl upward. § Late spring and early summer: open places, throughout. *Fig. 119.*

LOBELIA FAMILY (*Lobeliaceae*)

The *Lobeliaceae* are more properly united with the *Campanulaceae* (as a subfamily), when species from the whole world are compared. Our species, however, are so distinct that it is convenient to consider them separately here. We have only the genus *Lobelia*.

LOBELIA   BLUE, PURPLISH, WHITE, OR SCARLET

Lobelia is easily recognized by its bilaterally symmetric corolla, the tube of which is open along the upper side. The two upper lobes stand more or less erect on either side of this opening. The three lower lobes are pointed. The stamens are joined in a tube. Our species have flowers in spikelike racemes. They flower in summer and continue into autumn.

L. cardinalis, cardinal-flower (to 5 ft.), is named for its scarlet flowers (pink and white forms are also known). The corolla is more than an inch long. The tube of stamens (also red) stands up through the cleft. The toothed leaves are lance-shaped, tapering to short stalks. § Stream banks and other wet places, N. B. to Minn., s. to Fla. and Tex. *Fig. 121.*

L. siphilitica, great blue lobelia (to 5 ft.), is named for a reputed medicinal property. The flowers are bright blue or purplish, with white marks on the lower lobes (white-flowered forms are known); the corolla is about an inch long, the three lower lobes being broad and conspicuous. The leaves are more or less lance-shaped, tapering to both ends, without stalks. § Swamps, ditches, and other wet places, Me. to Man. and Colo., s. to Va., La., and Tex. PLATE 14.

L. inflata, Indian-tobacco (to 3 ft.), is recognized by the oval ("inflated") base of the flower, which becomes a conspicuous seedpod. The corolla is less than ½ inch long, pale blue or violet, or pinkish or whitish. The leaves are blunt, toothed, short-stalked, usually downy. § Open woodlands and fields, Que. to Sask., s. to Ga., Miss., Ark., and Kan. *Fig. 121.*

L. spicata (30 in.) has blue or white flowers ½ inch long or less. The leaves are small, lance-shaped, stalkless. § Roadsides, waste places, fields, Que. to Alta., s. to Ga., La., and Kan. *Fig. 121.*

SUNFLOWER FAMILY (*Compositae*)

The *Compositae* are the largest of all plant families. In our area alone there are over 100 genera and some 700 species that grow wild. Many are bad weeds: ragweed, wild lettuce, thistles, yarrow, cocklebur, and burdock. Besides the native and introduced wild-growing species, many are cultivated for ornament or food: chrysanthemums, dahlias, marigolds, zinnias, sunflowers, lettuce, artichoke, salsify. Some furnish aromatic herbs: artemisia, tansy. *Pyrethrum* provides an insecticide. In the tropics many *Compositae* are shrubs and trees.

Identification of genera and species of such a vast family is difficult, particularly since the flower parts are small. The botanist relies largely on certain characteristics of the stamens and styles. Such minute details can be avoided in this less technical treatment, but a few new terms must be learned before the species can be accurately described. (Even so, the reader must take warning that for

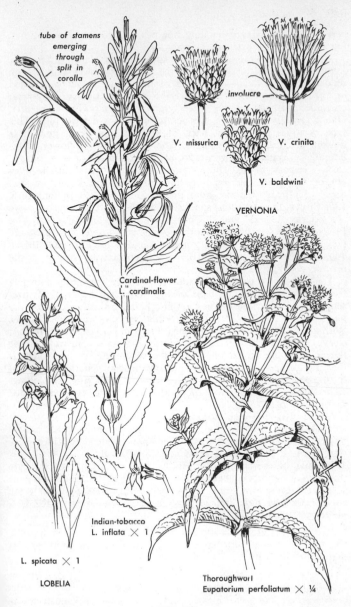

tube of stamens emerging through split in corolla

involucre

V. missurica

V. crinita

V. baldwini

VERNONIA

Cardinal-flower
L. cardinalis

Indian-tobacco
L. inflata $\times$ 1

L. spicata $\times$ 1

LOBELIA

Thoroughwort
Eupatorium perfoliatum $\times$ ¼

FIGURE 121

certain difficult genera he may not be satisfied by what follows, but must attack the technical manuals.)

While the general aspect of a sunflower or daisy is familiar, many persons do not know that the apparent flower is really an inflorescence—a head—composed of many tiny flowers all seated on the expanded end of the flowering stem. In a daisy, sunflower, or goldenrod head there are two types of flowers (*Figs. 125, 130*). One is radially symmetric, the petals forming a narrow tube. This type occupies the central part, or *disk*, of the head, and these flowers are called *disk flowers*. The other type of flower is bilaterally symmetric, the corolla being expanded on one side to form a narrow blade. These flowers form the "rays" at the margin of the head, surrounding the disk, and are known as *ray flowers*. A head that has both these types is called *radiate* (*Fig. 130;* PLATE 15). In some species, as thistles and ironweeds, there are no ray flowers, and the heads are called *discoid* (*Fig. 135;* PLATE 14). Still a third group has heads composed entirely of ray flowers; this is seen in the common dandelion (*Fig. 138;* PLATE 16). The head is surrounded by bracts collectively known as the *involucre* (*Figs. 123, 125,* etc.).

The corolla of a single disk flower is a tube, generally with five teeth at the rim. At the base of this tube are the sepals, represented only by scales, bristles, or fine hairs, collectively called the *pappus* (*Figs. 125, 131, 138*). Some species have no pappus. Within the corolla are five stamens, their anthers joined to form a sleeve, through which the two-branched stigma emerges. All these flower parts are seated on a stalklike receptacle, within which is the inferior ovary. This ripens into an achene generally crowned by the pappus—the corolla and its contents withering and falling. (The "seed" of a sunflower or dandelion is really this one-seeded fruit; *Figs. 131, 138.*)

Mixed with the disk flowers of many species are scales, collectively called *chaff*. This may be seen by pulling off a few flowers. The presence or absence of chaff is an aid in identification. Some species have bristles instead of chaff.

Because of the size of the family, it is convenient to separate the genera into ten tribes. (Some of these have been treated as separate families by some botanists.) Below is a guide to these tribes.* On the page indicated after the name of the tribe is a guide to the genera of that tribe.

I. Tribes with discoid heads (except *Inula*); a pappus of hairlike bristles (or at least with hairlike tips); no chaff; not many species with yellow flowers. (Compare II and III.)

    1. The Ironweed Tribe (p. 341). Leaves attached singly; flowers purplish (rarely white).

---

*It must again be emphasized that the "guides" in this book are good only for the species treated in it.

2. The Thoroughwort Tribe (p. 342). Leaves variously disposed; flowers blue, purple, pink, or white.

4. The Pussy-toes Tribe (p. 362). Leaves attached singly; flowers pink or whitish (*Inula* has yellow rays); bracts of the involucre mostly white or with white or translucent tips.

9. The Thistle Tribe (p. 382). Leaves singly attached; bristles mixed with flowers; flowers blue, purple, yellow, or white; involucre generally prickly (the whole plant prickly in some species).

II. Tribes with generally radiate heads (the rays lacking in some species).

3. The Aster Tribe (p. 346). Leaves singly attached; pappus of hairlike bristles or scales; no chaff; disk flat or nearly so.

5. The Sunflower Tribe (p. 364). Leaves variously disposed; pappus of scales or teeth, or a cuplike ridge, not of bristles; chaff present; disk flat, dome-shaped, or cylindric; rays of most species yellow.

6. The Sneezeweed Tribe (p. 375). Leaves singly attached; pappus of scales; no chaff; disk conical or dome-shaped; rays directed downward, yellow.

7. The Chrysanthemum Tribe (p. 375). Leaves singly attached, mostly very finely divided, generally with a marked odor which may be unpleasant; no pappus; chaff in some genera, none in others; at least some bracts of the involucre with white or translucent (not green) tips or margins.

8. The Ragwort Tribe (p. 377). Leaves single, paired, or basal; pappus of hairlike bristles; no chaff; disk mostly flat.

III. Tribe with ray flowers only, no disk flowers.

10. The Chicory Tribe (p. 385).

1. IRONWEED TRIBE (*Vernonieae*)

THE IRONWEEDS (*Vernonia*)   PURPLE

The ironweeds are generally tall plants with many leaves and numerous heads. The pappus may be purple like the corolla, or bronze, tawny, etc. They commonly inhabit fields and open woodlands, often mixed with goldenrods. All flower in late summer and autumn.

I. Species with long, hairlike tips (not bent sharply down) on the bracts of the involucre (compare II).

V. noveboracensis (6 ft.) has narrow, lance-shaped leaves, usually toothed (the teeth often very small). The bracts are broad at the base, abruptly narrowing to the long, hairlike tips. § Fields and open woodlands, Mass. to Ga., w. to Miss., inland to Ohio. PLATE 14.

V. crinita (to 9 ft. but usually much lower) has narrow leaves

with very small teeth or none. The bracts are narrow at the
base and gradually taper to the long hairlike tips. § Along
streams in woods, often in rocky places, Mo. and Kan., s.
to Ark. and Okla.; reported in O. *Fig. 121.*

II. Species with bracts of the involucre blunt or sharp-pointed,
bent down in some.

V. fasciculata (6 ft.) has a very densely flowered mass of heads
in a flattish cluster. The bracts are flat. The leaves are smooth
on both sides. On the lower side are minute pits visible
through a magnifier. § Low ground and prairies, O. to Minn.
and Sask., s. to Mo. and Tex.

V. altissima (to 10 ft.) has leaves downy on the under side, with
no pits. The bracts are flat. § Damp soil, N. Y. to Mich. and
Nebr., s. to Ga. and La.

V. baldwini (4–5 ft.) is known by the hairs on the margins of
the bracts; they interlace, forming a sort of web over the
involucre. The bracts have sharp points which curve outward and downward. § Prairies and fields, Ill. to Minn. and
Nebr., s. to Ark. and Tex. *Fig. 121.*

V. missurica (4–5 ft.) has a webbed involucre like that of *V.
baldwini;* but the bracts are purplish, and broad with nearly
flat tips. § Prairies and fields, Ont. to Nebr., s. to Ala. and
N. M. *Fig. 121.*

2. THOROUGHWORT TRIBE (*Eupatorieae*)

THOROUGHWORTS, JOE-PYE-WEEDS, ETC. (*Eupatorium*)
PURPLE, PINK, BLUE, OR WHITE / These are common plants of fields,
roadsides, and woods. The heads are usually numerous, in flat or
rounded clusters. The leaves are generally paired or in circles.
More than 20 species are known from our range, of which the
following ten are the commonest; all flower in late summer and
autumn.

I. Species with white flowers (compare II and III).

E. perfoliatum, thoroughwort or boneset (5 ft.), has paired
leaves meeting around the stem, so that the stem seems to
grow through (or "thorough") them. It is a coarse hairy
plant with wrinkled leaves, once much used medicinally.
§ Moist ground, throughout, Que. to Man., s. to Fla. and
Tex. *Fig. 121.*

E. rugosum, white snakeroot (4 ft.), has rather broad, sharply
toothed leaves on long stalks. The plants are poisonous to
cattle, whose milk may transmit the poison to man. § Woods,
Que. to Sask., s. to Fla. and Tex.; plants of sandy woods
along the coast and in the mountains may be the very similar *E. aromaticum. Fig. 122.*

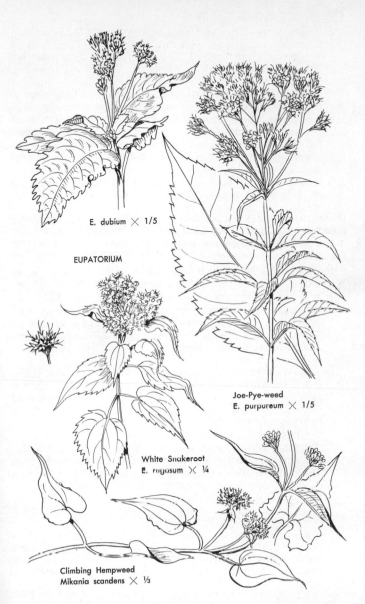

E. dubium × 1/5

EUPATORIUM

Joe-Pye-weed
E. purpureum × 1/5

White Snakeroot
E. rugosum × ¼

Climbing Hempweed
Mikania scandens × ⅓

FIGURE 122

E. *serotinum* (4–5 ft.) has comparatively narrow leaves on long stalks, the larger ones with three main veins. The bracts of the involucre are unequal. There are usually more than ten flowers in a head. § Moist woods, N. Y. to Kan., s. to Fla. and ne. Mexico.

E. *altissimum* (to 6 ft.) has very narrow leaves which taper to the base without a distinct stalk; there are generally three main veins. There are only five flowers in a head. The plant is generally covered with a white down. § Various situations, Pa. to Minn. and Nebr., s. to N. C., Ala., and Tex.

E. *sessilifolium* (4 ft.) has narrow, stalkless leaves rounded at the base; there is one main vein. There are five or six flowers to a head. The plant is smooth. § Woodlands, Mass. and N. H. to Minn., s. to Ga., Ala., and Ark.

II. Species with pink or purplish flowers. These are all commonly called Joe-Pye-weed. They have leaves in circles and may reach 9 feet in height. There are intermediate forms, perhaps due to hybridization.

E. *dubium* has broad, stalked leaves in threes and fours, often with three main veins, coarsely toothed. § Moist sandy places, N. S. and N. H. to S. C. on the coastal plain. *Fig. 122.*

E. *maculatum* has narrower leaves almost without stalks, four or five in a circle; there is one main vein. There may be 20 flowers in a head; the heads form a rather flat cluster. § Common in moist places, across Canada, s. to N. C., Ind., Nebr., N. M., and Wash.

E. *purpureum* has mostly narrow, short-stalked leaves in threes and fours. There is one main vein. There are only from five to seven flowers in a head. The heads form a round-topped cluster. When they are dried or bruised the plants emit the fragrance of vanilla. § Open, often dry woods, N. H. to Minn. and Nebr., s. to Fla. and Okla. PLATE 14 and *Fig. 122.*

E. *fistulosum* has as many as seven leaves in a circle, stalked, and scalloped rather than toothed. There is one main vein. The stem is hollow, purple. The heads form rather rounded clusters. § Moist meadows, thickets, etc., Que. to Ia., s. to Fla. and Tex.

III. Species with blue or violet flowers.

E. *coelestinum,* mist-flower (to 3 ft.), has many flowers in a dense, flattish cluster of heads. The paired leaves are fairly broad, with three main veins and short stalks. § Woods and fields and along streams, N. J. to Kan., s. to Fla. and Tex.

CLIMBING HEMPWEED (*Mikania scandens*)   WHITE OR PINK
This is a vine clambering over bushes, the stems reaching lengths of 15 or 20 feet. The leaf blades are heart-shaped at the base,

pointed, sometimes toothed, on long stalks. The clusters of flower heads grow from the axils. § Summer and autumn: thickets and swamps, Me. and Ont. to Fla. and Tex. *Fig. 122.*

THE BLAZING-STARS (*Liatris*)   ROSE OR PURPLE
   The heads of *Liatris* are arranged in long and often dense spikes or racemes. The stems are generally unbranched; they bear numerous, mostly narrow, singly attached leaves. Most species grow from an underground corm or tuber. The species (15 or more in our area) hybridize readily, yielding plants that are difficult to classify. Some kinds are cultivated for ornament. Except as mentioned, the species described below are plants of dry, open places. All flower in late summer and early autumn.

I. Species with plumose pappus: i.e., each bristle bears side bristles, and so appears feathery. The leaves are very narrow and stiff. (Compare II.)

   L. squarrosa (3 ft.) has usually from 20 to 45 flowers in a head. The involucral bracts have pointed tips that spread loosely or are even bent downward (in which case they are "squarrose"). § Del. to O. and S. D., s. to Fla. and Tex.
   L. cylindracea (2 ft.) has from 30 to 60 flowers in a head. The involucral bracts are ovate with abrupt sharp points, pressed tightly together. § Ont. to Minn., s. to N. Y., O., and Ark.
   L. punctata (3 ft.) has not more than eight flowers in a head. The involucral bracts are often hairy at the margins; they lie flat. § Mich. to Minn. and Alta., s. to Ark., Nebr., and Tex.

II. Species with plain pappus (a magnifier may reveal minute side branches).

   L. borealis, the New England blazing-star (3 ft.), has crowded leaves, the lower with a narrow blade tapering down to a stalk. The involucral bracts are reddish, broad, rounded, with a narrow almost petal-like margin. There are from 35 to 60 flowers per head. § Me. to Mich., s. to N. J., W. Va., and Ark. *Fig. 123.*
   L. aspera (4 ft.) has lance-shaped leaves which are rough ("asper"). The bracts of the involucre are roundish, the upper ones with broad translucent margins. There are from 25 to 40 flowers per head. § Ont. to N. D., s. to N. C., La., and Tex.
   L. spicata (6 ft.) has numerous narrow leaves. The involucral bracts are rounded or blunt, rather sticky, sometimes tinged with purple. There are only about ten flowers to a head. § Wet places, N. Y. to Wis., s. to Fla. and La.; elsewhere escaped from cultivation. *Fig. 123.*
   L. pycnostachya (4–5 ft.) has numerous narrow, hairy leaves. The involucral bracts have sharp tips which curve outward. There are from six to eight flowers in a head. § Damp prairies, Wis. to Minn. and S. D., s. to Ky. and Tex.

3. ASTER TRIBE (*Astereae*)

Genera of *Astereae*

I. Genera with yellow rays (compare II).

Grindelia has a single large head, often sticky, at the tip of each flowering branch. There are not more than eight bristles in the pappus of one flower.

Chrysopsis has a double pappus: an inner circle of fine hairs, an outer circle of short bristles or scales.

Solidago (the goldenrods) has small heads mostly clustered in large inflorescences. The pappus is a single circle of fine hairs (*Fig. 125*).

II. Genera with blue, lavender, pink, or white rays. (One species of *Solidago* has white rays; see above.)

Aster has a pappus of many fine hairs. The involucre is composed of overlapping bracts in several circles, the outer ones shorter than the inner (*Fig. 126*). The asters bloom in late summer and autumn.

Erigeron has a pappus of many fine hairs. The involucre is composed of bracts all about the same length, in one circle (*Fig. 128*). The species of *Erigeron* bloom mostly in spring and summer.

Sericocarpus has a pappus of many fine hairs and cream-white flowers. The leaves are broad, toothed toward the tip. The achenes are silky.

Boltonia has a pappus of a few short bristles. The rays are white, pink, or purplish. The leaves are narrow.

TAR-WEEDS and ROSIN-WEEDS (*Grindelia*)   YELLOW

Grindelia is a large genus in the West; two species are found in the western part of our range. The leaves are narrow, toothed, without stalks. The large heads are borne singly at the tips of mainly leafy branches. Both rays and disk flowers are yellow.

G. *squarrosa* (3 ft.) has narrow, sticky involucral bracts which curve out and down. § Summer and early autumn: open places, Minn. to B. C., s. to Mo., Tex., and Nev.; naturalized in the East.

G. *lanceolata* (5 ft.) has narrow but scarcely sticky involucral bracts; they are loose but not curved outward. § Late summer and autumn: rocky, dry places, Tenn. to Kan., s. to La. and Tex.

GOLDEN-ASTERS (*Chrysopsis*)   YELLOW

These plants are found mostly in dry sandy places. They are more or less hairy, with narrow, pointed leaves, mostly not toothed. The pappus is double, the outer circle being of small scales or bristles. Both disk and ray flowers are yellow. They flower in late summer.

C. *mariana* (2 ft.) has heads about an inch across, crowded at the tips of the branches. The leaves are woolly when young, be-

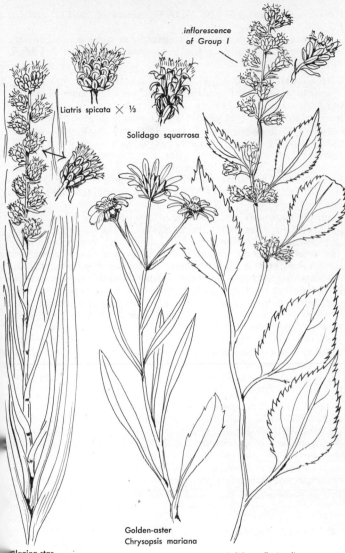

inflorescence
of Group I

Liatris spicata × ⅓

Solidago squarrosa

Blazing-star
Liatris borealis

Golden-aster
Chrysopsis mariana

Solidago flexicaulis

FIGURE 123

coming smooth in age. § N. Y. to O., s. and sw. to Fla. and La. *Fig. 123.*

C. falcata (1 ft.) has a stem covered with white wool. The very narrow leaves are more or less sickle-shaped ("falcate"). § Mass. to N. J. near the coast.

THE GOLDENRODS (*Solidago*)   YELLOW (OR WHITE)

Everyone knows the goldenrods—but very few know them. To state this paradox differently, the genus *Solidago* is easy to recognize, but many of its species are extremely difficult (even for a botanist) to distinguish. (1) They are very numerous; one authority lists 75 species in northeastern North America. (2) The flower heads are small and offer few characteristic differences visible without considerable magnification. (3) Many species are very variable, including varieties and forms that come close to those of other species. (4) Many species hybridize, giving rise to intermediate forms.

In this book it is not practical to describe all or even the majority of the species that grow in this area. The 23 species named and characterized below are a selection of the commoner ones. The brief descriptive remarks that accompany each name will serve to distinguish these species as well as is possible for the beginner. But even this is not altogether feasible without recourse to technical characteristics; and when it is remembered that there are many other species, not mentioned here, that resemble those that are included, it is evident that such a book as this cannot provide sure identifications of goldenrods—only probabilities. However, several common species will be recognizable from what follows; and this account will set the ambitious amateur on the way to the more technical treatments of the manuals.

All the goldenrods flower in late summer and autumn. The species here described fall into three groups.

I. Species that have some flower heads on short stalks in the axils of foliage leaves (these leaves being like the other leaves of the plant but perhaps smaller); the rest of the heads are crowded on the upper part of the stem (*Fig. 123*). The inflorescence is long and narrow; if there are branches, the heads are attached on all sides of the branches, in a more or less cylindrical manner; the branches tend upward. These are mostly plants of woodlands.

S. flexicaulis (4 ft.) has a zigzag stem ("caulis") and broad, sharply toothed, long-pointed, long-stalked leaves. The small clusters of heads are mostly in the axils. § Woodlands. Que. to N. D., s. to Ga., Ark., and Kan. *Fig. 123.*

S. macrophylla (3 ft.) has large, long-stalked lower leaves, very coarsely toothed, hairy on the under side. The heads are tightly clustered in the axils and at the summit. § Cool moist places, Lab. and Nfld. to Ont., s. to Mass. and N. Y. *Fig. 124.*

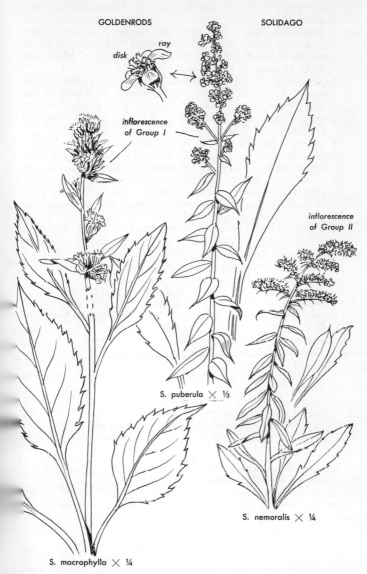

GOLDENRODS   SOLIDAGO

ray
disk

inflorescence
of Group I

inflorescence
of Group II

S. puberula × ⅓

S. nemoralis × ¼

S. macrophylla × ¼

FIGURE 124

S. speciosa (5 ft.), the most beautiful ("speciosus") of this group, has a long, dense, cylindric inflorescence of large heads (the rays are up to ⅕ inch long). The leaves taper to a long stalk; they may be toothed, scalloped, or plain on the edges. § Thickets and open rock ledges, Mass. and N. H. to Sask., s. to Ga. and Tex.

S. squarrosa (5 ft.) has long-stalked, sharply toothed lower leaves. The heads are densely clustered in axils and on the upper stem. The bracts of the involucre curve out and down (they are "squarrose"). § Rocky woods, Que. to Ont., s. to N. C. and Ky. *Fig. 123.*

S. caesia, blue-stemmed or wreath goldenrod (3 ft.), has a very smooth stem covered with a whitish bloom. The leaves taper to each end without distinct stalks, and are sharply but sparsely toothed. The stem often bends to an almost horizontal position, forming, with its axillary clusters of flowers, the "wreath." § Woods and thickets, Me. to Wis., s. to Fla. and Tex. PLATE 14.

S. hispida (3 ft.) is more or less hairy. It has a persistent tuft of large, long-stalked basal leaves, very variable in shape and toothing; the upper leaves are smaller, have short stalks or none. § Dry woods and rocky places, Nfld. to Man., s. to Ga. and Ark.

S. bicolor, silver-rod (4 ft.), is similar in general stature and foliage to *S. hispida;* but it is easily distinguished from all other goldenrods by the white rays. § Dry woods, N. S. and Que. to Wis., s. to N. C. and Mo.

S. randii (3 ft.) may be smooth or slightly downy and sticky. The basal leaves are narrow, widest near the tip, tapering downward to a long stalk, often but not always toothed; the upper leaves are similar but have short stalks or none. § Rocky places, N. S. to Que. and N. Y.; Mich. to Minn.

S. puberula (3 ft.) is downy and slightly sticky. The leaves are narrow, some of them broadest toward the tip; only the lower leaves have stalks and teeth. § Open places, generally sandy or rocky, Que. to N. Y., s. to Fla. and Miss. *Fig. 124.*

II. Species whose flower heads are situated usually along the upper side of spreading, often curved branches (*Fig. 125*). In a few of these the heads are at the ends of short branches rather than on one side of long branches, forming a dense cluster. These species grow mostly in fields and roadsides, but many are found also in woodlands.

A. Species of Group II whose larger leaves have three main veins running from near the base of the blade toward the tip (*Fig. 125*). The leaves are rather narrow, are toothed, tape both ways, have practically no stalks. These are some of the common tall goldenrods of fields. (Compare B.)

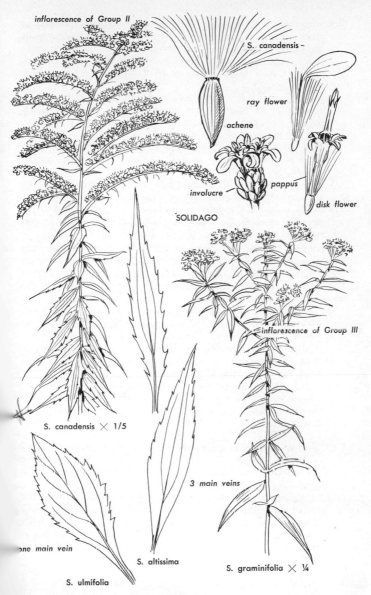

inflorescence of Group II

S. canadensis –

ray flower

achene

involucre

pappus

disk flower

SOLIDAGO

inflorescence of Group III

S. canadensis × 1/5

3 main veins

one main vein

S. altissima

S. graminifolia × ¼

S. ulmifolia

FIGURE 125

S. altissima (6 ft.) is one of the commonest goldenrods. The stem is covered with a gray down; the leaves are rough on the upper side, more or less downy on the under side, narrow, generally with a few blunt teeth. The involucre is about ⅕ inch high. § Que. to N. D., s. to Fla., Tex., and Ariz. *Fig. 125.*

S. canadensis (5 ft.), also very common, has a stem that is smooth in its lower parts, more or less downy or hairy toward the top. The leaves are typically very narrow, sharply toothed, smooth or nearly so. The involucre is not more than about ¹⁄₁₀ inch high (noticeably smaller than in other species). § Nfld. to Sask., s. to N. C., Tenn., S. D., and N. M. *Fig. 125.*

S. gigantea (8 ft.) is the largest goldenrod. The stem is smooth or somewhat whitened with a bloom. The leaves are generally hairy on the under side, narrow, sharply toothed especially toward the tip. The involucre is about ⅙ inch high. § Que. to B. C., s. to Fla., La., and N. M.

B. Species of group II whose leaves have a single main vein (some may have a weaker vein extending up the blade on either side). Except in *S. odora* and *S. rugosa,* and sometimes in *S. ulmifolia,* the basal leaves are much larger than those on the flowering stem.

S. nemoralis (3 ft.) has its larger leaves generally broadest near their tip, the lower ones toothed toward the tip and tapering downward to a long stalk, and grayish with a fine down. The inflorescence is rather narrow for this group. § Woods ("nemora") and open places, N. S. to Alta., s. to Fla., Tex., and Ariz. *Fig. 124.*

S. patula (6 ft.) has a smooth stem, generally square in cross section with sharp angles. The leaves are thick, rough on the upper side. The inflorescence is beset with white hairs. § Wet meadows and woods, Vt. to Minn., s. to N. C. and La.

S. arguta (4 ft.) is quite smooth (except the inflorescence) with thin, sharply toothed leaves; the lower leaves have broad blades tapering to long stalks. § Meadows and woodland clearings, Me. to Ont., s. and sw. to N. C. and Ky.

S. ulmifolia (5 ft.) has a nearly smooth stem, with rather rough and hairy leaves which are very coarsely toothed ("elm-leafed"). The leaves near the inflorescence are without stalks and teeth and much smaller. § Dry, rocky places in open woodlands, N. S. to Minn. and Kan., s. to Ga. and Tex. *Fig. 125.*

S. uliginosa (5 ft.) has a smooth stem and rather thick smooth leaves. The lower leaves taper to a long stalk which sheathes the stem. The inflorescence is narrow for this group, the side branches short; but this varies consider

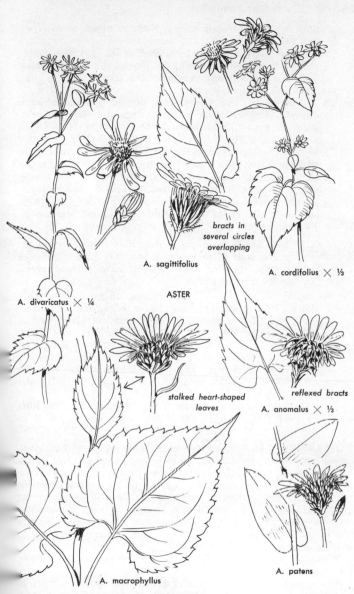

bracts in
several circles
overlapping

A. sagittifolius

A. cordifolius × ⅓

A. divaricatus × ¼

ASTER

stalked heart-shaped
leaves

reflexed bracts

A. anomalus × ⅓

A. macrophyllus

A. patens

FIGURE 126

ably. § Bogs and peaty places, Nfld. to Minn., s. to N. C. and Ind.

S. sempervirens, the seaside goldenrod (8 ft.), has thick, smooth leaves without teeth, the upper ones lacking stalks. § Salt or brackish marshes near the coast, Nfld. to Fla., Tex., and Mexico.

S. odora (5 ft.) has leaves with the odor of anise when crushed. The leaves are narrow, without stalks, and with plain margins. § Dry woodlands, Mass. and N. H. to Okla., s. to Fla. and Tex.

S. rugosa (5–6 ft.) is "hopelessly variable," with leaves more or less hairy, sometimes rough, more or less sharply toothed, usually tapering about equally to both ends, mostly without stalks. "Rugosus" means "wrinkled" and refers to the prominent veins. The involucre is about ⅕ inch high or less. § All sorts of places, Nfld. to Ont. and Mich., s. to Fla. and sw. to Tex.

III. Species with flower heads in a flattish or round-topped inflorescence, at the ends of many branches, not along their sides (*Fig. 125*). Except the first, these species have narrow leaves. They grow mostly in open places.

S. rigida (5 ft.) is variable, smooth or more commonly downy, the leaves elliptic and rather blunt, the lower ones on long stalks, the numerous upper ones much smaller and with no stalks. § Mass. to Alta., s. to Ga., Tex., and N. M.

S. graminifolia (4 ft.) has either smooth or hairy leaves, on a smooth, roughish, or finely hairy stem. The leaves are narrow, sharp-pointed. The upper leaves mingle with the flower heads. § Nfld. to B. C., s. to Va., Ky., S. D., and N. M. *Fig. 125.*

S. tenuifolia (3 ft.) is smooth. It is distinguished by the tufts of small leaves in the axils of the larger leaves. § N. S. to Mich., s. to Fla. and Ind.

THE ASTERS (*Aster*) (RAYS) BLUE, LAVENDER, PURPLE, PINK, OR WHITE / The genus *Aster* is known in our gardens as the "hardy asters"—not to be confused with China-aster (*Callistephus*). Like *Solidago,* it is a large and difficult genus: 68 species are listed for our range in one current treatment. It is distinguished from the goldenrods by the color of the rays, which are never yellow. The disk flowers are in general yellow; those of some species are reddish or purplish, especially as they age. The pappus is composed of hairlike bristles.

These are plants of open fields, of cliffs, of woods, flowering in late summer and autumn.

The remarks made above on identification of species of goldenrods apply here also. The species here described fall into three groups.

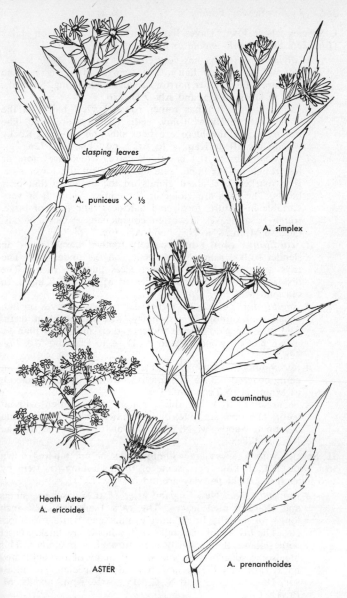

clasping leaves

A. puniceus × 1/3

A. simplex

Heath Aster
A. ericoides

A. acuminatus

ASTER

A. prenanthoides

FIGURE 127

I. Species whose lower leaves have heart-shaped blades on stalks (*Fig. 126*. See also *A. undulatus* in Group II.)

    A. divaricatus (3 ft.) has very coarsely toothed lower leaves, smooth or sparsely hairy. The stem is often zigzag. The rays are white, rather narrow, about ½ inch long. § Woods, Me. to O., s. to Ga. and Ala. *Fig. 126.*

    A. anomalus (3 ft.) has rather rough leaves, hairy on the under side, rarely with any teeth. The rays are blue. The bracts of the involucre are bent out and down. § Rocky woodlands, Ill. to Kan., s. to Ark. and Okla. *Fig. 126.*

    A. macrophyllus (5 ft.) has thick leaves which are more or less rough on the upper side and hairy on the lower side. It is marked by stalked glands on the branches that bear heads. The rays are violet or sometimes white. It is very variable in stature, form, and hairiness. The tufts of large, rough basal leaves are often conspicuous. § Open woods, Que. to Minn., s. to N. C. and Ala. *Fig. 126.*

    A. cordifolius (4 ft.) has coarsely toothed basal leaves on slender stalks, rather rough, hairy on the under side. The rays are purplish, rather short (less than ½ inch). The disk is often red. § Woods, Que. to Minn. and Kan., s. to Ga. and Mo. *Fig. 126.*

    A. sagittifolius (4 ft.) has rather narrow basal leaves on flat, broad stalks, more or less hairy, with rather blunt teeth. The rays are pale blue or violet, rather short (less than ½ inch). § Open woods, Vt. to N. D., s. to Fla. and Mo. *Fig. 126.*

    A. drummondii (4 ft.) resembles *A. sagittifolius* except in being covered with a fine grayish down. § Open woods, O. to Minn., s. to Tenn. and Tex.

    A. azureus (5 ft.) has thick, rough leaves, often without teeth. The rays are blue, or sometimes pink. § Prairies and dry open woods, w. N. Y. and Ont. to Minn., s. to Ga., Ala., and Tex.

II. Species whose leaves are without stalks or are tapered down to a wide, flat, stalklike part, some of them clasping the stem by two lobes that extend partway around it (*Fig. 127*).

    A. novae-angliae, New England aster (8 ft.), has hairy stems and sharp-pointed leaves. The rays (sometimes ¾ inch long) are usually bright purple; pink and white forms occur. The involucre and stalks of the heads are thickly beset with stalked glands, easily seen through a magnifier. This handsome species is an ancestor of many of the cultivated hardy asters. § Fields and roadsides, especially in moist soil, Que. to Alta., s. to N. C., Ky., Ark., Kan., and N. M. PLATE 14.

    A. patens (4 ft.) has more or less rough leaves (or they may be hairy) with blunt ends, little more than an inch long

The rays are blue, about ½ inch long. The bracts of the involucre bear minute glands or hairs. § Dry places, wooded or open, Me. to Minn. and Kan., s. to Fla. and Tex. *Fig. 126.*

A. puniceus (8 ft.) is a very variable aster. The stem is commonly bristly. The leaves are rough, more or less lance-shaped, with rather few teeth, or none; they clasp the stem only slightly. The rays vary from light violet to pink and white; they are ½ inch long or longer. § Moist meadows and thickets, swamps, etc., Nfld. to Sask., s. to Ga., Ala., and Ia. *Fig. 127.*

A. oblongifolius (3 ft.) is a spreading, bushy plant with a stem covered with a harsh grayish down and many small, narrow, rough leaves which sometimes scarcely clasp the stem. The rays are bright blue or violet, ½ inch long. The involucral bracts tend to curve outward. § Dry places, often sprawling over rock ledges, Pa. to Minn. and Wyo., s. to N. C., Ala., Okla., and N. M.

A. novi-belgii, New York aster (4 ft.), has leaves much like those of *A. novae-angliae* but smooth except for some hairs on the margins, and sometimes with a few teeth. The rays are violet, pink, or white. The involucral bracts have tips that spread or curve outward. § Moist places, even by salt marshes, Nfld. and Que. to Ga.

A. prenanthoides (3 ft.) has lines of fine hairs on its stem, which is often zigzag. The leaves are rough and hairy or smooth; the lower ones taper suddenly to a broad stalklike part, which expands into the two lobes that clasp the stem. The rays are pale blue or violet, about ½ inch long. § Moist places, along streams and in woods, Mass. to Minn., s. to Del., Tenn., and Ia. *Fig. 127.*

A. laevis (3 ft.) is very smooth, even sometimes with a grayish bloom. The leaves are thick, mostly without teeth, the upper ones stalkless and clasping, the lower sometimes on flat stalks. The rays are purplish, ½ inch long. § Open places, roadsides, etc., Me. to B. C., s. to Ga., Kan., and N. M.

A. undulatus (4 ft.) might be looked for in Group I, since the lower leaves may be heart-shaped and on long stalks. But the stalks are broad at the base and clasp the stem, as do the stalkless leaves farther up the stem. The leaves are generally rough on the upper side, hairy on the under side, with wavy margins. The stem has a fine whitish down. § Dry woodlands, N. S. to Minn., s. to Fla., La., and Ark.

II. Species that have no heart-shaped basal leaves on stalks and no stalkless leaves that clasp the stem.

A. Species of Group III with numerous heads and small white rays (mostly ¼ inch long or less). The heads are on spreading branches mixed with short, narrow leaves. (Compare B and C.)

A. ericoides (3 ft. or more) is covered with fine gray hairs. It is bushy with numerous stiff and narrow ("heath-like") leaves. The sharp green tips of the bracts of the involucre curve outward. § A common weed of abandoned fields and other dry open places, Me. to B. C., s. to Ga., Ala., Tex., and Ariz. *Fig. 127.*

A. pilosus (5 ft.) may bear white hairs (being then "pilose"), or it may be smooth. The heads tend to grow on the upper side of spreading branches. The bracts of the involucre are straight, sharp. § Open places, mostly dry, Me. to Minn. and Kan., s. to Ga., Ala., and Ark.

A. lateriflorus (4 ft.) is smooth or hairy, with roughish lance-shaped leaves (the lower round ones soon fall), with or without teeth. The heads are borne in a wide branching inflorescence. The involucral bracts have a green midrib. § Open woodlands and fields, Que. to Minn., s. to Fla.; Tenn., and Tex.

A. vimineus (5 ft.) is similar to *A. lateriflorus.* The stem is smooth and tinged with purple. § Moist places, Me. and sw. Que. to Mich., s. to Fla., La., and Tex.

B. Species of Group III with longer white rays (to ½ in.) and less numerous heads.

A. simplex (5 ft.) is smooth. The leaves are lance-shaped, with a short stalk or none, and usually a few very short teeth. It has from 20 to 40 rays to a head. § Moist open places, Nfld. to Sask., s. to N. C., Ky., and Kan. *Fig. 127.*

A. umbellatus (6 ft.) is smooth, with lance-shaped leaves which lack teeth. The heads are often numerous in a wide, flat inflorescence. There are from two to 15 rays about ⅓ inch long in a head. § Moist places, Nfld. to Minn. and Nebr., s. to Ga., Ky., and Ia.

A. acuminatus (3 ft.) has a downy or hairy stem and sharply toothed, mostly small leaves which taper to both ends. There are from 10 to 18 rather long rays (⅜ inch long) in a head. § Woods, Nfld. and Que. to Ont., s. to Ga. and Tenn. *Fig. 127.*

A. tradescanti (2 ft.) resembles *A. umbellatus.* It has not more than 25 rays, ⅓ inch long. § Along streams and on rocky beaches, Nfld. to Mich., s. to Mass. and n. N. Y.

C. Species of Group III with blue or violet rays.

A. spectabilis (3 ft.) is hairy or more usually beset with glands. The leaves are rough, with a few teeth or none, the basal ones stalked. The rays are bright violet, sometime nearly an inch long. § Sandy soil, often among pines, Mas to S. C.

A. linariifolius (2 ft.) has wiry, downy stems bearing ver

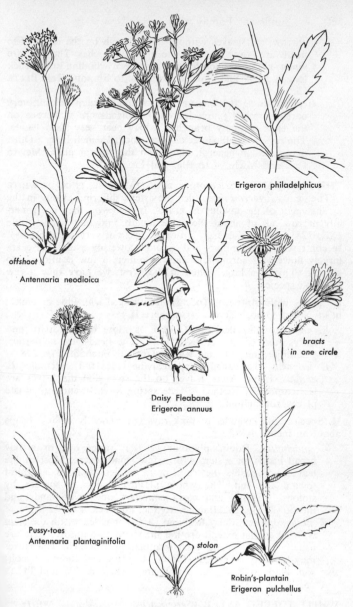

Erigeron philadelphicus

offshoot

Antennaria neodioica

bracts
in one circle

Daisy Fleabane
Erigeron annuus

Pussy-toes
Antennaria plantaginifolia

stolon

Robin's-plantain
Erigeron pulchellus

FIGURE 128

narrow, stiff leaves without teeth, rough on the edges. The heads are borne singly at the tips of branches. The rays are violet, about ½ inch long. § Dry open woodlands and rock ledges, N. B. and Que. to Minn., s. to Fla. and Tex. PLATE 15.

A. *dumosus* (3 ft.) has an almost smooth stem bearing very narrow, rather rough leaves. The heads are numerous on the ends of many branches, which bear very short leaves. The rays are pale violet or blue, about ⅓ inch long. § Open dry places in general, chiefly on the coastal plain, Me. to Ont. and Mich., s. to Fla. and La.

THE FLEABANES (*Erigeron*)   BLUE, LAVENDER, PINK, OR WHITE
    The genus *Erigeron* resembles the asters, differing chiefly in the arrangement of the involucral bracts. In *Erigeron* they are generally narrow, all of about the same length, and in a single circle (*Fig. 128;* some species have an outer circle of very small bracts). In contrast to the summer- and autumn-flowering asters, these are largely flowers of spring and early summer; a few continue into autumn. This is a large genus in the West; we have only a few common species.

I. Species with white rays (occasionally tinged with blue or pink); heads about ½ inch across. (Compare II.)

E. *annuus,* daisy fleabane (5 ft.), is more or less hairy and leafy, most of the leaves toothed. The heads· are numerous. § Summer and autumn: waste places, throughout. *Fig. 128.*

E. *strigosus,* also called daisy fleabane (to 3 ft.), resembles *E. annuus.* It has fewer leaves on the stem and the leaves are less commonly toothed. § Late spring to early autumn: waste places, throughout.

II. Species with lavender or pink rays (occasionally white); heads about an inch across.

E. *pulchellus,* Robin's-plantain (2 ft.), raises one or a few broad heads on a stem with a few small leaves. Most of the leaves are basal; they are more or less toothed, broadest toward the end. The whole plant is hairy. It spreads by stolons. § Spring and early summer: open woodlands and meadows, Me. to Minn., s. to Fla. and Tex. *Fig. 128.*

E. *philadelphicus,* daisy fleabane (3 ft.), has leaves on the stem with lobes that extend around the stem, clasping it. There are usually several heads, each terminating a branch. The leaves may be hairy or almost smooth. § Spring and summer: moist soil, Nfld. to B. C., s. to Fla. and Tex. *Fig. 128* and PLATE 15.

WHITE-TOPPED ASTER (*Sericocarpus asteroides*)   WHITE
    This is much like an aster, and has been placed in the genus *Aster* by some botanists. The involucral bracts are whitish with

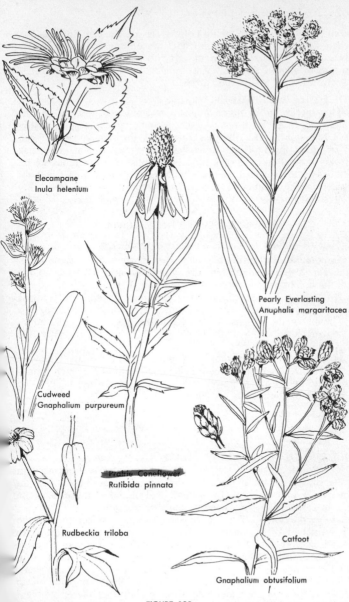

Elecampane
Inula helenium

Cudweed
Gnaphalium purpureum

Prairie Coneflower
Ratibida pinnata

Rudbeckia triloba

Pearly Everlasting
Anaphalis margaritacea

Catfoot

Gnaphalium obtusifolium

FIGURE 129

green tips. The rays are cream-colored, as are the disk flowers. The achenes are densely silky. The leaves are oblong, or often broader toward their tip, stalkless or tapering to stalks, with a few teeth, on a stem about 2 feet tall. § Summer: dry woods and clearings, Me. to Mich., s. to Fla. and Miss.

BOLTONIA ASTEROIDES LILAC
This species, as its name implies, resembles an aster. It is distinguished from the asters by the pappus, which consists chiefly of a few spines. Also the disk on which the flowers stand (seen by scraping them off) is cone-shaped instead of flat. The disk flowers are yellow, the rays lilac or purplish or sometimes white. The leaves are thickish, smooth, without teeth and almost without stalks, on a stem about 2 feet tall. § Autumn: sandy and muddy shores and thickets, N. Y. to N. D., s. to Fla. and Tex.

4. PUSSY-TOES TRIBE (*Inuleae*)

I. Genera without rays (the heads are discoid).

Gnaphalium has pistillate and perfect flowers in the same head. The leaves on the stem are about as large as those at the base. The plants are woolly and whitish or yellowish.

Antennaria has staminate and pistillate flowers on separate plants. The basal leaves are larger than those higher up. The hairs of the pappus are joined at the base so that the entire pappus falls as a unit. The plants are generally woolly and whitish.

Anaphalis has an involucre of pearly white bracts. The very narrow, numerous leaves are covered with white wool. Staminate and pistillate flowers are mostly on separate plants. The hairs of the pappus are all separate.

II. Genus with rays (yellow).

Inula has many slender rays. The leaves are woolly on the under side.

CUDWEEDS (*Gnaphalium*) WHITE OR YELLOWISH
Cudweeds are woolly plants, often somewhat yellowish, with quite similar leaves at the base and on the stem. The flowers in the center of each head have pistil and stamens, those near the margins, which are very narrow, have pistils only.

G. purpureum (1 ft.) has leaves generally widest toward the tip (which is often round), downy especially on the under side; they lack teeth. The heads are in the axils; their bracts are brownish or purplish. § Spring to autumn: open places, especially in sand, throughout. *Fig. 129.*

G. obtusifolium, catfoot (to 3 ft.), has long, narrow, sharp leaves, downy on the under side, lacking teeth, but the edges often crinkled or wavy. The numerous heads are in a wide, branched inflorescence. The bracts of the involucre are yellowish. § Summer and autumn: roadsides, clearings, etc., N. S. to Man., s. to Fla. and Tex. *Fig. 129.*

G. uliginosum (less than 1 ft.) has narrow, blunt leaves. The flower heads are clustered in the axils, their bracts brown or green. § Summer and autumn: along streams and in other moist open places, across Canada, s. to Va., Ind., Wis., Kan., Utah, and Ore.

PUSSY-TOES (*Antennaria*)   WHITE

Antennaria resembles *Gnaphalium* in general aspect, but the leaves are chiefly at the base, those on the stem being smaller and fewer. The pistils and stamens are in separate flowers and these are on separate plants. (The staminate flowers have a functionless style that lacks the two branches of the pistillate flowers. In many species staminate flowers are rare or even have never been found.) The heads are in a cluster at the top of the stem. The plants grow in open or lightly shaded ground, flowering in spring and summer. The species are difficult to distinguish, so much so that certain botanists deny that many species exist. In fact, the professional botanist may have more difficulty here than the amateur, for some characteristics are more apparent in living plants than in the herbarium.

A. plantaginifolia, ladies'-tobacco (1 ft.), is the commonest species in much of our area. It has broad basal leaves with three or five veins running from stalk to tip. The stem leaves are small and narrow. Runners are formed at the base, bearing smaller leaves. § Que. to Minn., s. to Ga. and Mo. *Fig. 128.*

A. neglecta (10 in.) has narrow basal leaves, usually with one main vein. It forms very slender stolons with few leaves. § N. S. to Minn., s. to Va. and Kan.

A. neodioica (10 in.) has basal leaves somewhat wider toward the tip, with one main vein. It forms offshoots on short, curving basal branches, thus forming dense mats. Staminate plants are rare. The species is highly variable. § Nfld. to Minn., s. to Va., Ind., and Wis. *Fig. 128.*

PEARLY EVERLASTING (*Anaphalis margaritacea*)   WHITE

Pearly everlasting (to 3 ft.) is named for its dry, white involucral bracts. The leaves are long, narrow, of about the same length from the base to the cluster of heads at the top, all covered with white wool. As in *Antennaria,* pistillate and staminate flowers are on separate plants (the pistillate heads may have a few staminate flowers in the center). § Summer: open, dry places, across Canada, s. to N. Y., W. Va., O., Wis., S. D., N. M., and Calif. *Fig. 129.*

ELECAMPANE (*Inula helenium*)   YELLOW

This is a plant brought from Europe and escaped from cultivation. Its coarse, hairy stem (to 6 ft.) bears coarsely toothed leaves, some of them clasping the stem, woolly on the under side. The involucral bracts are large and broad. The slender rays are about ½ inch long, and numerous. § Summer: fields and waste places, Que. to Ont. and s. *Fig. 129.*

5. SUNFLOWER TRIBE (*Heliantheae*)

This is our largest tribe of *Compositae* (having the most genera). It includes not only sunflowers, zinnias, coneflowers, and the like, but also ragweeds and cockleburs, which have no ray flowers or pappus; they are not treated here.

Guide to Genera of *Heliantheae*

I. Genera with disk flowers forming a cone-shaped or columnlike mass (*Fig. 129;* PLATE 15). (Compare II.)

Rudbeckia has yellow rays; the disk flowers are in a dome-shaped or globular mass. The leaves are singly attached.

Ratibida has yellow rays, extending downward. The dark disk flowers form a cylindric column. Leaves are singly attached, pinnately cleft or divided.

Echinacea has pink or purplish rays, directed downward.

Heliopsis has yellow rays and a yellow disk which is cone-shaped. The leaves are paired, unlobed and undivided.

II. Genera with flat (or nearly flat) disk.

A. Genera of Group II whose disk flowers form achenes (compare B).

1. Genera of Group II A whose involucral bracts are alike in form and color (*Fig. 130*). (Compare 2.)

Helianthus has mostly rough or hairy, undivided leaves. The rays are yellow (*Fig. 130*).

Verbesina forms flat achenes with or without thin marginal "wings" (*Fig. 131*); the stem of some species has "wings." The rays are yellow.

Actinomeris has disk flowers pointing in all directions, the yellow rays extending downward; the stem has "wings"; the achenes are flat, generally with marginal "wings" (*Fig. 131;* PLATE 16).

Galinsoga is a small weedy plant with tiny white rays.

2. Genera of Group II A with two kinds of involucral bracts: the outer green and more leaflike than the inner (*Fig. 131*).

Bidens has achenes crowned by from two to four backwardly barbed spines. Rays are lacking in some species (*Fig. 131*).

Coreopsis has achenes with upwardly barbed or barbless spines, or with no spines (*Fig. 132*).

B. Genera of group II whose ray flowers only form achenes (PLATE 16).

Polymnia has thick achenes. Pappus is lacking. The plants are sticky. The rays are pale yellow or whitish and short (*Fig. 132*).

Silphium has flat achenes with thin, "winged" margins. Pappus is mostly lacking. Rays are yellow. The plants are mostly large and coarse (*Fig. 133*).

Parthenium has very short white rays. The leaves are thick and rough (*Fig. 133*).

CONEFLOWERS (*Rudbeckia*)   YELLOW

The disk of *Rudbeckia* is conical or dome-shaped. Each disk flower is enveloped in a scalelike bract (all forming the chaff). In our common species these flowers are dark brownish-purple. The rays are yellow or orange. If pappus is present it is minute.

R. serotina, black-eyed Susan (to 3 ft.), is coarsely hairy and rough. The leaves are undivided, with or without teeth, with several main veins running from base to tip. The yellow rays are commonly bent down in the middle. § Summer and autumn: fields, roadsides, and other open places, a common weed, N. S. to Man. and Colo., s. to Fla. and Tex. PLATE 15.

R. triloba (4–5 ft.) has some deeply three-lobed leaves, mixed with undivided leaves. The rays are rarely more than an inch long, somewhat darker yellow than those of *R. serotina,* or orange. § Summer and autumn: woods and shady places, N. Y. to Minn. and Kan., s. to Fla. and Okla. *Fig. 129.*

R. laciniata (to 9 ft.) has large, nearly smooth leaves cleft into a number of lobes and these again cut and toothed. The cone of disk flowers is yellow. The rays extend downward. § Summer: moist open places, Que. to Ida., s. to Fla., La., and Ariz. PLATE 15.

PRAIRIE CONEFLOWERS (*Ratibida*)   YELLOW

These are distinguished from *Rudbeckia* chiefly by the height and shape of the mass of disk flowers. There may also be a pappus of one or two very small teeth. The rays extend downward.

R. pinnata (4 ft.) is hairy. The leaves are pinnately divided into from three to seven segments which are often toothed. The column is an inch high or less, shorter than the rays, oval in outline. § Summer: prairies and dry woods, n. N. Y. and Ont. to Minn. and Nebr., s. to Ga. and Okla. *Fig. 129.*

R. columnifera (4 ft.) is coarsely hairy. The leaves are very deeply pinnately cleft *almost* to the midrib into from five to nine narrow, toothless lobes. The cylindric column of disk flowers may reach a length of more than an inch, longer than the rays. § Summer: prairies, Minn. to Alta., s. to Ill. and Mexico. PLATE 15.

PURPLE CONEFLOWERS (*Echinacea*)   PALE REDDISH-PURPLE

These coneflowers have long purple or pinkish rays hanging straight down. The disk flowers form a conical mass. There is a pappus of minute teeth. Both species mentioned below are prairie plants, blooming in summer.

E. purpurea (to 5 ft.) has broad, ovate, rough, usually toothed leaf blades on long stalks. The rays tend to a reddish shade. § O. to Ia. and s. to Va., Ga., Ala., and Okla. *Fig. 130.*

E. pallida (to 3 ft.) has narrow, hairy leaf blades, lacking teeth, with several veins running their length. The rays tend to be a pale purple. § Mich. to Mont., s. to Ga., Ala., La., and Tex. *Fig. 130.*

OX-EYE (*Heliopsis helianthoides*)   YELLOW

Ox-eye resembles a sunflower (*Helianthus*) but is distinguished by the conical disk, as well as by the formation of achenes in the ray flowers. No pappus is easily seen. The stem (5 ft.) bears paired, stalked leaves with broad, toothed blades, smooth or (in a variety) rough. § Summer and autumn: dry woods, prairies, etc., Que. to B. C., s. to Ga. and N. M.

THE SUNFLOWERS (*Helianthus*)   YELLOW

Sunflowers are mostly tall and coarse; many are rough. The leaves are undivided and generally paired. Most species are perennial, growing from a rhizome, tuber, or thickened roots. The pappus is composed of two or four thin scales. Some 20 species grow in our range. The ten commonest and most widespread are here described.

I. Annual species, without a rhizome or tuber; the leaves are generally singly attached.

   H. annuus (to 12 ft.) is the common garden sunflower, a native of the western states and escaped from cultivation farther east. It is rough throughout. The leaves have broad, more or less heart-shaped blades on long stalks. The heads, in cultivation, may be enormous—9 inches broad, or even more—and hang from their stalk. § Summer: prairies and dry open places generally, throughout. *Fig. 130.*

II. Perennial species; the leaves are generally paired.

   A. Perennial species with smooth stems (except in the inflorescence). (Compare B.)

   H. divaricatus (5 ft.) has rough-hairy leaves which taper from near the base to a long, narrow tip; they have no stalks or almost none, and short teeth or none. § Summer: dry woodlands, shady roadsides, Me. to Sask., s. to Fla., La., and Nebr. *Fig. 130* and PLATE 15.

   H. strumosus (6 ft.) has lance-shaped, rough-hairy leaves which usually taper to a short stalk, with small teeth or none. § Summer: woodlands, Que. to N. D., s. to Fla. and Tex. *Fig. 130.*

   H. decapetalus (5 ft.) has slightly rough, lance-shaped leaves which taper to a short stalk and are coarsely toothed

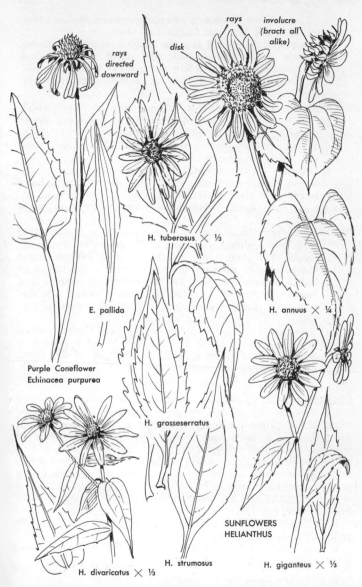

rays directed downward

disk

rays

involucre (bracts all alike)

H. tuberosus × ⅓

E. pallida

H. annuus × ¼

Purple Coneflower
Echinacea purpurea

H. grosseserratus

H. divaricatus × ⅓

H. strumosus

H. giganteus × ⅓

SUNFLOWERS
HELIANTHUS

FIGURE 130

§ Late summer: in woods and along streams, Me. and Que. to Minn. and Nebr., s. to Ga. and Mo.

H. grosseserratus (to 14 ft.) has rough, lance-shaped leaves, sharply or coarsely toothed, with stalks that may reach 1½ inches in length. § Summer and autumn: moist soil, including prairies, N. Y. to Sask., s. to O., Ark., and Tex. *Fig. 130.*

B. Perennial species with hairy stems (some are rough also).

H. mollis (3 ft.) has ovate leaves with no stalks and almost no teeth. The whole plant is white with soft hairs or down. § Summer: Mich. to Ia., s. to Ga. and Tex.; escaped from cultivation farther east.

H. hirsutus (5 ft.) resembles *H. divaricatus* except in the coarse hairiness of the stem. The narrow, rough-hairy leaves have short stalks, sharp teeth. § Summer and autumn: dry places, wooded and open, Pa. to Minn., s. to Fla. and Tex.

H. tuberosus, Jerusalem artichoke (to 10 ft.), has large ovate leaves almost like those of *H. annuus* but not heart-shaped. The English name refers to the edible tuber, and has nothing to do with Jerusalem, being a corruption of Italian *girasole,* "turning to the sun." § Late summer and autumn: waste places, fields, etc., Ont. to Sask., s. to Ga. and Ark.; often escaped from cultivation elsewhere. *Fig. 130.*

H. giganteus (10 ft.) has rough, lance-shaped blades, toothed or plain, on short stalks. It is a widely branched plant with flower heads that seem small for the size of the plant. § Late summer and autumn: Que. to Alta., s. to Fla. *Fig. 130.*

CROWNBEARDS (*Verbesina*)   YELLOW OR WHITE

The crownbeards are tall, coarse weeds with lance-shaped or ovate leaves, paired or singly attached, on angular stems from which thin flanges or "wings" project. The rays spread upward or outward. The disk is yellow. The pappus consists of from one to three small bristles. The achenes are flat, often with a thin flange or "wing" extending around the margin. The crownbeards flower in late summer and autumn in woodlands and prairies.

V. virginica (6 ft.) has small, white rays. § Va. to Kan., s. to Fla. and Tex. *Fig. 131.*

V. helianthoides (3 ft.) has singly attached leaves. The rays are yellow. § O. to Kan., s. to Ga. and Tex.

V. occidentalis (6 ft.) has paired leaves. The rays are yellow. § Md. and Va. to Mo., s. to Fla. and Tex.

WINGSTEM (*Actinomeris alternifolia*)   YELLOW

Wingstem resembles the crownbeards in general appearance and size, but has fewer bracts in the involucre (about 20), the rays

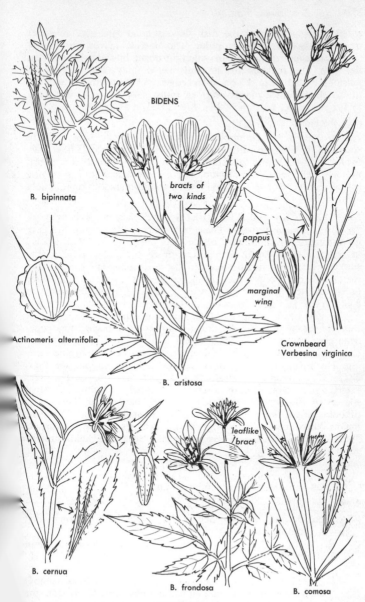

BIDENS

B. bipinnata

*bracts of
two kinds*

pappus

*marginal
wing*

Actinomeris alternifolia

Crownbeard
Verbesina virginica

B. aristosa

B. cernua

*leaflike
bract*

B. frondosa

B. comosa

FIGURE 131

extend downward, and the disk flowers (and later the achenes) point in all directions, moplike. The narrow leaves are mostly singly attached, their margins running down into the "wings" on the stem. The achenes are flat and may or may not have the extensions called "wings" on their edges. § Late summer and autumn: shady waste places or open moist soil, n. N. Y. and Ont. to Ia., s. to Fla., La., and Okla. *Fig. 131* and PLATE 16.

GALINSOGA WHITE

Two species of *Galinsoga,* natives of tropical America, are small (2 ft.) but troublesome weeds in our range. They have ovate, toothed leaves on stalks, small heads with a few short, toothed white rays, and a pappus of narrow scales almost as long as the corolla. *G. ciliata* is hairy, *G. parviflora* smooth or minutely downy.

BEGGAR-TICKS and TICKSEEDS (*Bidens* and *Coreopsis*)

YELLOW, PINK, OR WHITE / These two genera, as a group, are easy to distinguish from other *Compositae;* but it is not always easy to separate them from each other, or to recognize some of the species. Some are handsome wild flowers, some are unattractive weeds. All have two circles of bracts in the involucre, the outer green and leaflike, the inner usually differing from the outer in color, form, and size (*Figs. 131, 132*). The achene is flat or four-angled and bears a pappus of two or more spines. The spines of *Bidens* have minute, usually down-pointing teeth, barbs; they penetrate clothing and cause the achenes to stick there. The spines of *Coreopsis* are upwardly barbed or smooth; or spines may be lacking. The form of the achene is an aid in identification; see *Figs. 131, 132. Coreopsis* generally has yellow rays, in some species tinged with red or pink, in others white; some are cultivated. Most species of *Bidens* have yellow rays; some have none. The leaves of both genera are paired, those of some species divided. *Bidens* means "two teeth"—referring to the achenes. *Coreopsis* means "buglike"; the achenes of several species resemble small beetles.

Species of *Bidens*

All flower in late summer and autumn.

I. Species with rays (compare II).

    A. Species with rays an inch or less in length, and undivided leaves (compare B).

        B. laevis (3 ft.) has smooth, lance-shaped leaves without stalks, toothed at the edges. § Wet places, Mass. and N. H., s. to Fla., Mexico, and Calif.

        B. cernua (3 ft.) has smooth, lance-shaped leaves without stalks and those of a pair sometimes meeting around the stem, usually coarsely toothed. It is distinguished by the

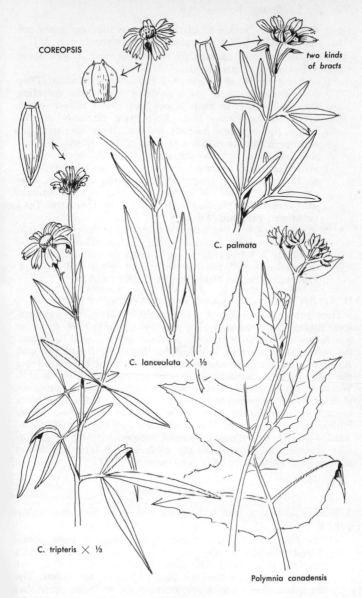

COREOPSIS

two kinds
of bracts

C. palmata

C. lanceolata × ⅓

C. tripteris × ⅓

Polymnia canadensis

FIGURE 132

drooping or "nodding" of the heads as they age (they are "cernuous"). § Wet places, nearly throughout. *Fig. 131.*

B. Species with rays an inch or more long, and at least some leaves divided or deeply lobed.

B. *aristosa* and B. *polylepis* (4–5 ft.) are very similar. They are handsome weeds of wet fields, sometimes carpeting them with gold. In such places they are a valued source of nectar for honey bees. Both have pinnately divided leaves, the segments coarsely toothed. Both have oval flat achenes with thin edges and usually two spines. B. *aristosa* has from eight to ten outer bracts in the involucre, no longer than the inner bracts. B. *polylepis* has from 12 to 25 outer bracts, longer than the inner ones. § B. *aristosa:* Me. to Minn., s. to Va., La., and Tex.; commoner westward. B. *polylepis:* O. to Colo., s. to Tenn. and Tex.; occasional eastward. *Fig. 131.*

B. *coronata* (4 ft.) has leaves very deeply pinnately cleft into very narrow lobes, some of these again similarly cleft. The involucre has from six to eight outer bracts. The achenes are wedge-shaped, bearing two strong spines. § Wet places, Ont. and Mass. to Nebr., s. to Fla., Ky., and Ia.

II. Species with no rays (rarely one or two may be present).

Here belong a number of weeds unlikely to attract the amateur. Among them the following may be mentioned: B. *frondosa* has leaves divided into stalked, toothed, lance-shaped segments; the outer bracts are long and leaflike. *Fig. 131.* B. *connata* and B. *comosa* are so similar and so variable that some botanists avoid the difficulty of distinguishing them by assigning both to the Old-World B. *tripartita;* they have coarsely toothed leaves, sometimes cleft or divided, tapering to flat stalks; they have a few long outer bracts; the achenes of B. *connata* generally have four spines barbed upward; those of B. *comosa,* three spines barbed downward. *Fig. 131.* B. *bipinnata,* Spanish needles, has very long, narrow achenes, often found in the clothes of hikers; and leaves divided and redivided or cleft pinnately. *Fig. 131.*

Species of *Coreopsis*

I. Species with undivided leaves and yellow or pink rays (compare II).

C. *lanceolata* (2 ft.) has narrow leaves, without teeth, lance-shaped with the broader end upward, mostly clustered near the base of the stem. The inner bracts of the involucre are longer and broader than the outer. The rays are yellow. The flat achene has a broad thin membrance or "wing" on either side. § Spring and summer: dry, sandy soil, Ont. and n. N. Y

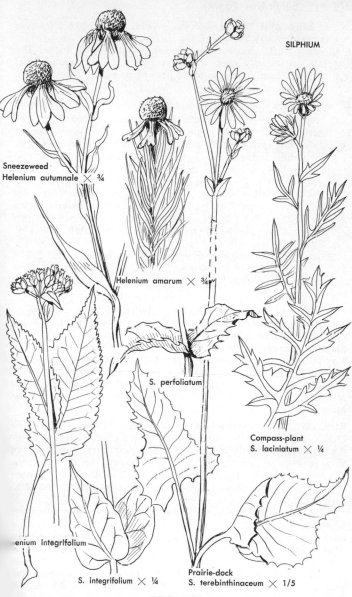

Sneezeweed
Helenium autumnale × ¾

Helenium amarum × ¾

S. perfoliatum

Compass-plant
S. laciniatum × ¼

enium integrifolium

S. integrifolium × ¼

Prairie-dock
S. terebinthinaceum × 1/5

FIGURE 133

to Mich. and Wis., s. and sw. to Fla. and N. M.; elsewhere escaped from cultivation. *Fig. 132.*

C. rosea (2 ft.) has very narrow, almost threadlike leaves. The rays are usually pink, sometimes white. § Late summer and early autumn: moist sand or peat or in water, N. S. to Ga. along the coast.

II. Species with divided leaves and yellow rays about an inch long.

C. tripteris (to 9 ft.) has the lower leaves divided into from three to five narrow segments, without teeth, on a slender stalk. The outer bracts are only ⅛ inch long or even less. § Summer and early autumn: various situations, Mass. and Ont. to Wis., s. and sw. to Fla. and Tex. *Fig. 132.*

C. palmata (3 ft.) has leaves cleft into three almost equal, narrow lobes, often without a common stalk so that they seem like three leaves; they lack teeth. The outer involucral bracts are of about the same length as the inner. § Summer: prairies and open woodlands, Mich. to Man., s. to Ind., Ark., and Tex. *Fig. 132.*

C. tinctoria, with leaves divided into narrow segments and a red-brown zone at the base of the ray, is found here and there in our range, mostly as an escape from cultivation; it is a western native.

LEAF-CUP (*Polymnia canadensis*)   WHITE OR PALE YELLOW
Leaf-cup is a coarse plant (5 ft.), fairly smooth or often hairy and sticky in the upper part. The leaves are broad and thin, stalked, pinnately lobed and coarsely toothed and generally paired; the upper ones may be unlobed but angular, and singly attached. The stalks are usually broadest at the base. The rays are not over ½ inch long, sometimes lacking. Only the marginal flowers form achenes. § Summer and autumn: moist woods, Vt. and Ont. to Minn., s. to Ga. and Okla. *Fig. 132.*

ROSINWEEDS, INDIAN-CUP, COMPASS-PLANT, PRAIRIE-DOCK (*Silphium*)   YELLOW / *Silphium* is a genus of coarse, striking plants with mostly rough leaves and rays from 1 to 2 inches long. It produces achenes from ray flowers only. There is no pappus, or only two teeth which prolong the marginal flanges ("wings") of the achene. All species flower in late summer and early autumn.

S. perfoliatum, Indian-cup (to 8 ft.), gets its name from the paired leaves which meet around the stem to form a cup. The blades are coarsely toothed. § Prairies, fencerows, ditches, woods, waste places, Ont. and n. N. Y. to S. D., s. to Ga. and La. *Fig. 133* and PLATE 16.

S. integrifolium (5 ft.) has paired leaves without stalks and without teeth. § Prairies, roadsides, woodlands, O. to Minn. and Nebr., s. to Ky., Miss., and Okla. *Fig. 133.*

S. trifoliatum (6 ft.) has most leaves in threes and fours, or short stalks, coarsely toothed. § Prairies and woodlands, Pa. to Ind. and s. to Ga. and Ala.

S. laciniatum, compass-plant (to 9 ft.), has large, pinnately cleft leaves, attached singly, with blades vertical and commonly directed north and south. § Prairies, O. to Minn. and S. D., s. to Ala. and Tex. *Fig. 133.*

S. terebinthinaceum, prairie-dock (10 ft.), has leaves only at the base except for a few bracts on the tall flowering stem. The basal leaves reach a length of 2 feet; they are long-stalked, heart-shaped, coarsely toothed. § Prairies, Ont. and O. to Minn., s. to Ga., Ala., and La. *Fig. 133.*

WILD QUININE (*Parthenium integrifolium*) WHITE

The basal leaves are thick and rough, on long stalks, with blunt rounded teeth. The leaves on the stem (3 ft.) may lack stalks. The heads are numerous, clustered. The ray flowers are only about $\frac{1}{12}$ inch long, white; they alone form achenes. § Summer and early autumn: open woodlands, prairies, rocky bluffs, N. Y. to Mich. and Minn., s. to Ga. and Tex. *Fig. 133.*

The Mexican and Central American guayule, which yields rubber, is a species of this genus. True quinine is in a different family.

6. SNEEZEWEED TRIBE (*Helenieae*)

SNEEZEWEEDS (*Helenium*) YELLOW

The sneezeweeds have narrow, undivided leaves attached singly. The disk flowers stand on a hemispherical surface, the broad, three-lobed rays hanging down at the rim. The pappus is of small scales. There is no chaff. The achenes are angular, ribbed. Several species are troublesome weeds. All flower in summer and autumn.

H. amarum (2 ft.) is easily known by its very numerous, very narrow leaves. The disk flowers are yellow. It is a weed from the Southwest, rapidly spreading eastward. § Dry soil, Va. to Kan., s. to Fla. and Tex.; spreading n. *Fig. 133.*

H. autumnale (to 4 ft.) has lance-shaped or even ovate leaves, some of them toothed at the edges; the edges are continued down onto the stem as narrow wings. The disk flowers are yellow. § Moist soil, nearly throughout. *Fig. 133.*

H. nudiflorum (3 ft.) resembles *H. autumnale* but has brown disk flowers. The leaves are narrower. § Moist soil, Mass. to Mich., s. and sw. to Fla. and Tex.; spreading n.

7. CHRYSANTHEMUM TRIBE (*Anthemideae*)

. Genera with very short rays or none, and without chaff.

Artemisia has numerous greenish flower heads in a tall, much-branched inflorescence.

Tanacetum has yellow heads in a flattish inflorescence (*Fig. 134*).

II. Genera with easily seen rays and chaff.

Achillea has many flat heads crowded in a flattish inflorescence. The rays are white or pink (*Fig. 134*).

Anthemis has single, dome-shaped heads at the ends of branches. The rays are white or yellow (*Fig. 135*).

III. Genera with easily seen rays and no chaff.

Matricaria has leaves very finely cleft and cleft again; the disk flowers are on a dome-shaped or conical surface.

Chrysanthemum has leaves pinnately toothed or lobed. The disk is flat or somewhat convex (*Fig. 134*).

WORMWOOD, SAGE (*Artemisia*)

The genus contains many species, chiefly shrubby plants of dry regions, among them the sage-brush of the arid west. (This sage must not be confused with *Salvia* in the *Labiatae,* which furnishes the culinary herb.) Some of the western species have spread eastward as weeds of railroads, roadsides, and wasteland. Some Old-World species also have become established here as weeds, notably *A. vulgaris,* mugwort. Well-known species cultivated as herbs are southernwood (*A. abrotanum*) and wormwood (*A. absinthium*). Dusty-miller (*A. stelleriana*) is grown for its white foliage.

TANSY (*Tanacetum vulgare*) YELLOW

Tansy (3 ft.) is an Old-World plant often grown in our gardens, and established as a weed throughout our range. It has many small, golden-yellow flower heads in a flat cluster. There may be some ray flowers, but usually there are none. There is no chaff. Pappus is practically lacking. The foliage is finely divided and segments deeply cut; it is strong-scented. It blooms in late summer and autumn. *Fig. 134.*

YARROW (*Achillea lanulosa*) WHITE OR PINK

Yarrow (2 ft.) is a common weed from coast to coast. It is recognized by its narrow, curved, woolly, aromatic leaves which are finely divided into innumerable narrow segments. The flower heads form a flat inflorescence. The disk flowers are mixed with chaff. The rays are white or sometimes pink or purplish. There is no pappus. *Fig. 134.*

There is another species, *A. millefolium,* from the Old World, introduced in places. It is practically indistinguishable from the native species except by microscopic details.

CHAMOMILE, DOG-FENNEL (*Anthemis cotula*) WHITE

This species was known to me in my youth as "scentless May flower," because, my father said, it does not flower in May and has a strong odor. (I think he was confusing it with *Matricaria.* It has become a common and unsightly weed throughout America known by the threadlike segments into which its leaves are divided, and by the white rays which tend to droop. The central dome bears the yellow disk flowers and some chaff. There is no pappus. It flowers from spring to autumn. *Fig. 135.*

CHAMOMILE (*Matricaria maritima*)   WHITE
This species closely resembles *Anthemis cotula* in foliage and flowers, but is not ill-scented, and the rays do not droop so markedly. The technical distinction is the lack of chaff in this genus. The divisions of the leaves are even more hairlike. § Spring and summer: waste places, e. U. S., and Pacific coast.

Two other species, *M. chamomilla* and *M. matricarioides,* have become established in this country; these when crushed have the odor of pineapple. The last-named has no ray flowers.

OX-EYE DAISY (*Chrysanthemum leucanthemum*)   WHITE
It is hard to realize that this familiar daisy is not a native of America but was introduced from Europe. It has become a weed in open places throughout the United States. The leaves are irregularly and bluntly toothed or lobed along the sides, tapering to a stalklike portion which however bears some small lobes. The upper leaves are very narrow, with more or less parallel sides, slightly lobed. There is no pappus or chaff. § Spring to autumn. *Fig. 134.*

8. RAGWORT* TRIBE (*Senecioneae*)

I. Genera with yellow flowers (compare II).
Senecio has leaves attached singly on the flowering stem, besides stalked basal leaves (*Fig. 134* and PLATE 16).
Arnica has either paired leaves on the flowering stem, or basal leaves without stalks.
Tussilago has only scales on the flowering stem; the basal leaves are long-stalked (*Fig. 134*).

II. Genera with flowers of colors other than yellow.
Petasites has flowers ranging from cream-colored to purple. They are hairy plants with broad-bladed, long-stalked basal leaves.
Cacalia has (in native species) white disk flowers, no rays. The corollas are five-toothed (*Fig. 135*).
Erechtites has white disk flowers, no rays. The corollas are deeply four-lobed.

THE RAGWORTS or GROUNDSELS (*Senecio*)   YELLOW
Senecio is an enormous genus, mostly tropical. We have some 20 species. Most have yellow rays and disks; some lack rays. There is no chaff. The pappus is of numerous soft white hairs (giving the name to the genus, from senex, "old man"). Most of our

*Ragworts should not be confused with ragweeds (*Ambrosia*), which are not included in this book. "Wort" is an old word meaning "plant," used mostly for medicinal plants.

species are covered with matted hairs, but these may disappear at maturity.

I. Species without rays.

   S. *vulgaris* (18 in.) has pinnately lobed, sharply toothed leaves, only the lower ones having stalks. § Spring to autumn: waste places, throughout; native of Europe.

II. Species normally with rays about ½ inch long.

   S. *obovatus* (2 ft.) has short-stalked basal leaves which are sometimes pinnately cleft; they are broader toward the end. The leaves on the stem are much smaller, more or less pinnately cleft. § Spring and early summer: woods, among rocks, N. H. to Mich., s. and sw. to Fla. and Tex.; commoner s. *Fig. 134.*

   S. *aureus,* golden ragwort (to 3 ft.), has basal leaves with heart-shaped blades, scalloped or toothed, on long stalks. The other leaves are pinnately toothed or cleft. A variable species. § Spring and summer: wet soil, Lab. to N. D., s. to Fla., Ala., and Ark. *Fig. 134* and PLATE 16.

   S. *plattensis* resembles S. *aureus* in stature and sometimes in its basal leaves. It retains its woolly hairs. § Spring and summer: dry places, Vt. and Ont. to Sask. and Wyo., s. to w. Va., Ind., La., and Tex.

   S. *pauperculus* (18 in.) is extremely variable. The basal leaves taper to their stalks, which are about as long as the blades. The plant is soon smooth except for tufts of wool in the axils of leaves. § Spring and summer: meadows and rocky places, Lab. to Alaska, s. to Ga., Ala., Ill., Nebr., N. M., and Ore.

ARNICA (*Arnica*)   YELLOW

Our species of *Arnica* all have yellow disk and ray flowers and paired leaves. They are chiefly northern plants, or mountain-dwellers, with large, handsome flower heads.

   A. *mollis* (2 ft.) is hairy, with toothed leaves, the basal ones on long stalks, all lance-shaped with the broad end out, or ovate. The pappus is yellowish or brownish; the hairs are branched. There is no chaff. § Late summer: Que. to Me., N. H. and N. Y., chiefly in mountains; also in the Rocky Mountains and Calif.

   A. *acaulis,* leopard's-bane (3 ft.), is hairy. The basal leaves have no stalks; there are five or seven prominent veins. The leaves on the flowering stem are few and small. § Spring and summer: open woodlands, especially in sand, Del. to Pa. and s. on the coastal plain to Fla.

COLTSFOOT (*Tussilago farfara*)   YELLOW

Coltsfoot is a small weed of damp soils, coming from Europe It has several marginal circles of rays, which are not much longer than the disk flowers. The pappus is of bristles. There is no chaff

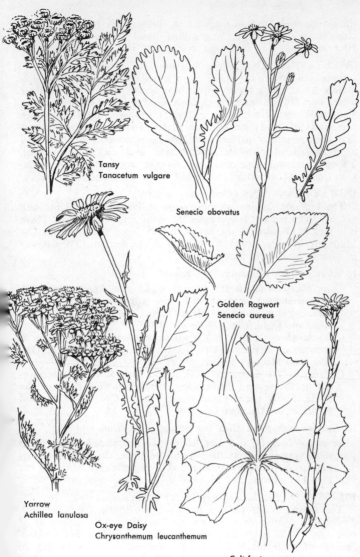

Tansy
Tanacetum vulgare

Senecio obovatus

Golden Ragwort
Senecio aureus

Yarrow
Achillea lanulosa

Ox-eye Daisy
Chrysanthemum leucanthemum

Coltsfoot
Tussilago farfara

FIGURE 134

Flowering stems (18 in.) appear in spring; they have no leaves, only scales. The large, long-stalked basal leaves appear later. Nfld. to Minn., s. to N. J. and O. *Fig. 134.*

SWEET-COLTSFOOT (*Petasites palmatus*)   WHITE

Sweet-coltsfoot (18 in.) has long-stalked, broad-bladed, palmately lobed basal leaves which bear loose white wool on their under side. On the flowering stem are smaller leaves without stalks. The small heads are in a dense spike. There is no chaff. There are two kinds of heads, on separate plants. One kind bears flowers that are apparently perfect but form no achenes; the other kind is composed of pistillate flowers (ray and disk) which fruit. § Spring and summer: meadows and wet woods, across Canada, s. to Conn., Mich., Minn., and Calif.

INDIAN-PLANTAINS (*Cacalia*)   WHITE

The Indian-plantains are mostly coarse, large-leaved plants with no rays. The pappus is composed of many fine white hairs. There is no chaff. Bracts of the involucre are long and narrow. The heads are in wide, rather flat clusters at the summit. They flower in summer and early autumn.

I. Species with five flowers in a head.

C. atriplicifolia (to 10 ft.) is smooth and pale. The lower leaves have triangular or roundish blades, with large teeth, on long stalks. § Dry woods, N. J. to Minn. and Nebr., s. to Fla., Ala., and Okla. *Fig. 135.*

C. muhlenbergii (to 10 ft.) is similar but not pale. The stem is grooved or angular. § Dry woods, N. J. to Minn., s. to Ga., Ala., and Mo.

C. tuberosa (to 6 ft.) has oval, long-stalked lower leaves without teeth; several main veins run lengthwise through the blade. § Wet prairies and marshy fields, Ont. to Minn. and Nebr., s. to Ala. and Tex. *Fig. 135.*

II. Species with more than five flowers in a head.

C. suaveolens (4 ft.) has leaves like spearheads with sharp lobes spreading from the base of the blade; the teeth are comparatively small. § Moist ground, along streams, Mass. to Ia., s. to Fla., Tenn., and Mo. *Fig. 135.*

FIREWEED (*Erechtites hieracifolia*)   PALE YELLOW

The flower heads of this fireweed, not to be confused with *Epilobium,* contain disk flowers only, no rays. The pappus is of many fine white hairs. The bracts are narrow and do not overlap. Several of these heads decorate the summit of the stem (to 10 ft.), which bears narrow leaves with jagged edges, attached singly. The plant gets its name from being especially abundant after fires. § Autumn: clearings, burned areas, marshes, Nfld. to Minn. and Nebr., s. to Fla. and Tex.

Canada Thistle
Cirsium arvense × ⅔

Bull Thistle
Cirsium vulgare × ⅔

C. tuberosa

C. suaveolens

Dog-fennel
Anthemis cotula

Cacalia atriplicifolia

FIGURE 135

9. THISTLE TRIBE (*Cynareae*)

Cirsium has a feathery pappus: each hair bears branch hairs on its sides. The plants are prickly (*Fig. 135*).

Centaurea has a pappus of plain hairs, or in some species of scales, or none. The plants are not prickly, except for the involucre of a few species (*Fig. 136*).

Arctium has a pappus of short bristles. The involucre is composed of numerous bracts with spiny, hooked tips, forming a bur. The leaves are not prickly (*Fig. 136*).

THISTLES (*Cirsium*)   PURPLE, PINK, YELLOW, OR WHITE

Thistles are well known as troublesome weeds especially in grainfields; some are also remarkably beautiful wild flowers. The prickly leaves and spine-tipped bracts of most species are familiar. The actual flowers are very slender, the corolla deeply notched to make five long lobes (instead of merely five teeth), surrounded by the feathery pappus. There are no rays. The pappus forms the "thistledown" atop the "seed"—which is the achene. Most species are biennial, the flowering stem rising from a rosette of leaves formed the year before; at the end of the second summer the whole plant dies. Some species are annual, some perennial. Many species are hairy, some with cobwebby hairs; but these hairs are often lost as the plant matures.

Of the 16 or 17 species reported from our area, the following eight are widely distributed and fairly easy to recognize. All flower in summer and most continue into autumn.

I. Species with prickly wings running down the stem from the edges of the leaves (compare II).

> *C. vulgare,* bull thistle (6 ft.), has a spiny involucre. The heads are single, on long stems. The leaves are broad, pinnately lobed. § Roadsides and fields, throughout; from Europe. *Fig. 135* and PLATE 16.

> *C. palustre* (6 ft.) has no spines on the involucre. The heads are clustered. The leaves are narrow and very prickly. § Moist ground, Nfld. to Mich., s. to N. Y.

II. Species without prickly wings on the stem.

> **A.** Species of Group II with spiny involucre (compare B).

>> 1. Species with leaflike outer bracts (compare 2).

>> *C. horridulum* (3 ft.) has leaves cut into short lobes with many yellowish prickles. The flowers are usually pale yellow, sometimes pale purple. § Spring and summer: sandy and peaty places, Me. to Fla. and Tex., on and near the coastal plain.

>> *C. altissimum* (to 10 ft.) has the principal leaves on the stem undivided and unlobed, tapering to each end; they are white underneath with a thick wool. The flowers are pink or purplish. § Woods and banks, Mass. to Minn. and N. D., s. to Fla. and Tex. See also *C. discolor.*

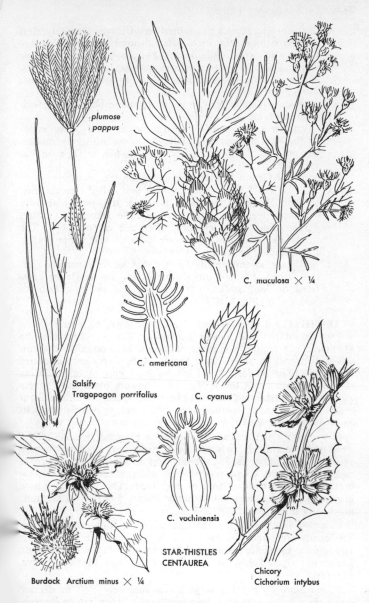

*plumose
pappus*

C. maculosa × ¼

C. americana

Salsify
Tragopogon porrifolius

C. cyanus

C. vochinensis

STAR-THISTLES
CENTAUREA

Burdock Arctium minus × ¼

Chicory
Cichorium intybus

FIGURE 136

C. discolor (to 10 ft.) has rather broad leaves pinnately cleft into large lobes, the lobes often themselves cleft. They are white with wool underneath. The flowers are purple or white. There are intermediates between this and *C. altissimum.* § Various situations, Que. to Man., s. to Ga., Tenn., and Kan.

2. Species of Group II with spiny involucre but without leaf-like outer bracts.

C. pumilum (3 ft.) has very large flower heads. The leaves on the stem are narrow, shallowly lobed, with very numerous prickles. § Dry fields, open woods, Me. to O., s. to Va. and N. C.

B. Species of Group II that lack spines on the involucre.

C. arvense (to 5 ft.) is the common pest called Canada thistle (though naturalized from Europe). It is perennial from rhizomes deep under the surface. The leaves are mostly narrow, finely prickle-edged, often not cut or lobed. The heads are small and numerous. § Fields and waste places, throughout. *Fig. 135.*

C. muticum, swamp thistle (6 ft.), has leaves pinnately cleft into broad, toothed lobes. The heads are single or clustered on long stalks. § Wet woods and swamps, Lab. to Sask., s. to Fla. and Tex.

STAR-THISTLES (*Centaurea*)   PURPLE, BLUE, OR WHITE

The star-thistles are mostly natives of Europe, especially the Mediterranean region; a number of species have established themselves as weeds in the United States. A few species are native Americans. The flowers of all species have corolla tubes flaring at the end into large lobes; the outer flowers often have larger lobes and simulate ray flowers. In most species the involucral bracts have fringed or toothed flaps at the end, by which they can be identified (see the drawings). The leaves are attached singly.

C. cyanus (4 ft.), called cornflower in England because it is a weed of the cornfields (wheatfields in American) and known here as bachelor's-button, is an annual. The leaves are very narrow, and at least when young coated with white wool. The involucral bracts are tipped with a fringe of dark teeth. This is widely grown in gardens and has escaped in many places. § Spring to autumn: practically throughout. *Fig. 136.*

C. americana (3 ft.), is smooth or nearly so, with oblong leaves. The heads are large, the involucral bracts end in a conspicuous (through a magnifier) tongue cut pinnately into narrow lobes. § Summer: open fields, Mo. to La., Ariz., and Mexico; native. *Fig. 136.*

C. maculosa (5 ft.) has large leaves pinnately cleft or divided into very narrow segments; they are woolly when young, becoming smooth. Most of the involucral bracts end in a dark triangular flap from which many narrow lobes extend. § Summer and autumn: waste places, throughout; from Europe. *Fig. 136.*

C. vochinensis (3 ft.) has undivided leaves, the lower with stalks, the broadest part toward the tip, sometimes toothed. The plant is roughish, more or less woolly when young. The marginal flowers are large. The involucral bracts end in a tongue much like that of *C. americana.* § Spring and summer: waste places, fields, Me. to Ont., s. to Va. and Mo.; from Europe. *Fig. 136* and PLATE 16.

C. nigra, another European, lacks the larger marginal flowers; the tips of the involucral bracts are black.

BURDOCK (*Arctium*)   PURPLE, PINK, OR WHITE

The species of *Arctium* are easily identified by the numerous narrow bracts that surround the flowers, each ending in a sharp hook, and together forming the spiny bur. The flowers are narrow. These are natives of the Old World. They flower in summer and autumn, in waste places.

A. minus, common burdock (5 ft.), has short-stalked flower heads arranged raceme fashion along the upper part of each stem. The leaf stalks are hollow. § Throughout. *Fig. 136.*

A. lappa, great burdock (to 10 ft.), has flower heads on long stalks forming a rather flat inflorescence. The leaf stalks are solid. § Que. to Mich., s. to Pa. and Ill.

10. CHICORY TRIBE (*Cichorieae*)

I. Genera with plumose pappus: i.e., the hairs bear branch hairs along their sides, appearing featherlike (*Fig. 136*). (Compare II.)

Leontodon has yellow flowers, no leaves except small scales on the flowering stem. The basal leaves are toothed or cleft along the sides.

Tragopogon has yellow or purple flowers, and narrow leaves on the flowering stem. The leaves have no teeth.

II. Genera with pappus of plain (unbranched) hairs, or of scales; or with no pappus.

A. Genera of Group II with white, cream, pink, blue, or purplish flowers (not yellow, orange, or red). (Compare B.)

Cichorium has rather large blue or white flowers; the pappus is of very small scales (*Fig. 136*).

Lactuca has some species with blue or cream-colored flowers in generally erect heads. These have a pappus of fine bristles borne on a short beak or small crown at the end of the achene (*Fig. 137*), which is flat at least on one side (see also B below).

Prenanthes has white, pink, purplish, or cream-colored flowers in more or less drooping heads. The pappus is of fine bristles which are not seated on a beak or crown. The achenes are not flat (*Fig. 137*).

B. Genera of Group II with yellow, orange, or red flowers.

1. Genera of Group II with yellow, orange, or red flowers and with leaves on the same stem as the flowers, these leaves as large as any basal leaves or nearly so (compare 2).

Lactuca has some species with yellow flowers and some with prickly leaves. The achenes are flat at least on one side, and bear their pappus on a long or short beak (*Fig. 137*).

Sonchus has prickly leaves. The flowers are yellow. The achenes are flat; they have no beak.

Pyrrhopappus has a very soft pappus of reddish or tan hairs. The flowers are yellow (*Fig. 138*).

Crepis has a distinct circle of smaller outer bracts around the involucre (*Fig. 137*). The pappus is of white hairs. The flowers are yellow.

Hieracium has some leaves on the flowering stem, but the basal leaves are more conspicuous; see under 2.

2. Genera of Group II with yellow, orange, or red flowers and no leaves on the flowering stem, or if some are present they are noticeably smaller than the basal leaves. (See also *Pyrrhopappus*, above.)

Krigia has a pappus of relatively few hairs surrounded by small scales (*Fig. 138*). The flowers are yellow or orange.

Taraxacum has one head on the stem. The achenes taper to a long narrow beak which bears the pappus of fine white hairs (*Fig. 138*). The flowers are yellow.

Hieracium has generally several heads on a stem (if only one, it is a very hairy plant). The achenes have no beak. The pappus is of fine bristles which are generally whitish or brownish (*Fig. 138;* PLATE 16). The flowers are yellow, orange, or almost red.

HAWKBIT, FALL-DANDELION (*Leontodon autumnalis*)   YELLOW / Hawkbit (not to be confused with hawkweed or hawk's-beard) bears pinnately toothed or lobed leaves at the base; the flowers are on a leafless stem (to 2 ft.). The pappus is tawny and plumose (each hair bears branch hairs along its length). The rays appear as if cut off sharply at the end. § Summer and autumn: fields, roadsides, Nfld. to Mich., s. to N. J. and Pa.; from Europe.

GOAT'S-BEARD and SALSIFY (*Tragopogon*)   YELLOW OR PURPLE / The genus is at once recognized by the conspicuously plumose pappus borne at the end of the long slender beak of the achene. The involucral bracts are few and in a single circle. The leaves are narrow, somewhat grasslike. The plants are very smooth. Our species came from Europe.

T. pratensis, goat's-beard (30 in.), has yellow flowers. § Summer: roadsides, fields, etc., throughout.

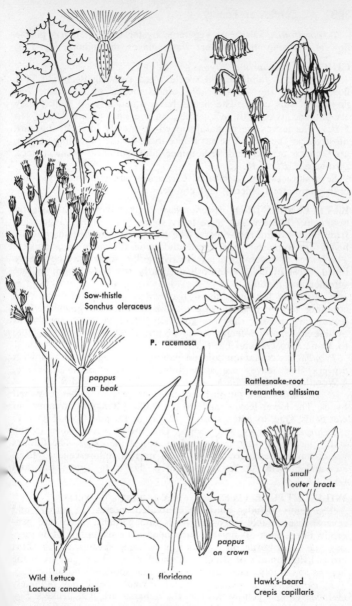

Sow-thistle
Sonchus oleraceus

*pappus
on beak*

P. racemosa

Rattlesnake-root
Prenanthes altissima

Wild Lettuce
Lactuca canadensis

L. floridana

*pappus
on crown*

*small
outer bracts*

Hawk's-beard
Crepis capillaris

FIGURE 137

T. porrifolius, salsify or vegetable oyster (to 3 ft.), has purple flowers. § Spring and summer: waste places, throughout. *Fig. 136.*

CHICORY (*Cichorium intybus*)   BLUE
Chicory is a familiar Old-World weed showing its bright blue flowers along the wayside. No other species of this tribe has flowers of this color. The heads have practically no stalks; they are situated, two or three together, on the sides of a tall stem (to 5 ft.). The leaves are pinnately lobed or merely toothed; they are mostly near the base. The rays, like those of the preceding genera, are square at the end. § Summer and autumn: waste places, throughout. *Fig. 136.*
Several races and species of *Cichorium* are cultivated, yielding both commercial chicory and endive.

RATTLESNAKE-ROOT (*Prenanthes*)   GREENISH, YELLOWISH, OR PURPLISH / These weeds have leafy stems (to 5 or 6 ft.) growing from bitter-tasting root-tubers. The leaves are attached singly. The heads are numerous and small and generally hang in a cluster. The leaves of several species are triangular, some may be deeply lobed. Most plants are smooth or nearly so. They bloom in late summer and autumn.
P. altissima has only about five bracts to a flower head (not counting the very small ones). The flowers are greenish. The leaves vary greatly; they are generally more or less triangular in outline and may be deeply lobed or not at all. § Woodlands, Que. to Man., s. to Ga. and La. *Fig. 137.*
P. alba has cinnamon-colored pappus and greenish or yellowish flowers. The leaves are something like those of *P. altissima.* § Woodlands, Me. to Sask., s. to Ga., Tenn., Mo., and S. D.
P. racemosa has purplish or pink flowers in rather crowded heads. The lower leaves taper to the stalk. § Banks of streams and wet fields, Que. to Alta., s. to N. J., Ill., S. D., and Colo. *Fig. 137.*
P. aspera is hairy and rough. The lower leaves taper to the stalk; the blades may be toothed or not at the edges. The flowers are cream-colored, crowded in a tall narrow inflorescence. § Prairies and barrens, O. to Minn. and S. D., s. to Tenn., La., and Okla.

WILD LETTUCE (*Lactuca*)   BLUE, WHITE, OR YELLOW
The genus includes both the cultivated species (*L. sativa*) and several disagreeable weeds of fields and gardens. There are generally fewer than 50 flowers in a head. The pappus is of numerous fine hairs borne on a beak (or in some species a very short crown) the summit of which is expanded. The hairs fall from the achene separately. They all flower in late summer and autumn.
L. canadensis, a widespread and variable weed, has pinnately cleft leaves and yellow flowers; the achenes are flat, beaked. *Fig 137. L. serriola* has prickly leaves; it is otherwise much like *L canadensis. L. pulchella* has leaves mostly without teeth, blu

Sunflower Family / 389

flowers, and short-beaked achenes. *L. floridana* has pinnately cleft leaves, blue or white flowers, and achenes with a crown instead of a beak. *Fig. 137.*

SOW-THISTLES (*Sonchus*)   YELLOW
The sow-thistles are coarse, unlovely weeds, whose leaves are mostly edged with prickles. The flowers are yellow. The pappus is of numerous fine hairs which tend to fall from the achene all or mostly together, as if joined at the base. These, like other objectionable weeds, came from the Old World, flowering in waste places, in summer and autumn, throughout our range. One common species is *S. oleraceus,* with sharp-pointed basal lobes of the leaves, embracing the stem. Another is *S. asper,* with rounded basal lobes. *Fig. 137.*

FALSE DANDELION (*Pyrrhopappus carolinianus*)   YELLOW
This is a slender, smooth plant (to 3 ft.); there may be basal leaves up to 10 inches long, pinnately lobed or cleft; there are usually also a few narrow leaves on the stem. The rays are about an inch long, in narrow heads. The pappus is very soft and tawny or reddish; it falls from the achene all together, with the tip of the long beak. § Spring and early summer: open, often dry places, Del. to Kan., s. to Fla. and Tex. *Fig. 138.*

HAWK'S-BEARD (*Crepis capillaris*)   YELLOW
The bracts of *Crepis* are generally of two sizes, the outer circle much shorter. The leaves on the stem are usually narrow, sometimes almost scalelike. The pappus is soft, white, on an achene with a short beak or none.
C. capillaris (1 ft.) usually bears some scattered hairs. The heads are only about ¼ inch high. § Summer and autumn: lawns, fields, etc., widespread but not common. *Fig. 137.*

THE DWARF-DANDELIONS (*Krigia*)   YELLOW OR ORANGE
These are small plants rather like dandelions, with flowers on more or less leafless stems, generally one head to a stem.
K. biflora (to 2 ft.) has a usually branched stem which bears a few leaves; these extend partly around the stem at their base, clasping it. The basal leaves may be toothed or pinnately lobed, or plain and round at the end. The pappus is composed of numerous hairs surrounded by a few minute scales. The flowers are light orange. § Spring to autumn: woodlands and fields, Mass. to Man., s. to Ga. and Ariz. *Fig. 138.*
K. virginica (1 ft.) has leaves toward the base of the stem. The basal leaves are mostly pinnately cleft and hairy. The pappus is of only a few (five to ten) hairs and as many small scales. The flowers are golden-yellow. § Spring and summer: dry open places, Me. to Mich. and Ia., s. to Fla. and Tex. *Fig. 138.*

DANDELION (*Taraxacum*)   YELLOW
Every gardener would say that he knows "the dandelion." But

botanists have found a number of species in the genus, some difficult to distinguish. (More than 1,000 have been named, mostly by European botanists; but not all agree that they are all species.) Two, however, may be found in our lawns and in waste places, blooming practically through the growing season.

T. officinale is the commoner. The flower heads are up to 2 inches across. The long bracts are surrounded by an outer circle of small bracts which curl outward and backward. After flowering, the long bracts become erect, enclosing the developing achenes ("seeds"); later they spread apart and finally point downward, exposing the mature achenes. These are rough toward the top and bear the copious fine pappus on a beak twice as long as the body. *Fig. 138.*

T. erythrospermum has smaller heads (less than 2 inches across). The leaves are more deeply cut into backward-pointing jagged lobes; the achenes are red.

HAWKWEEDS (*Hieracium*)   YELLOW OR ORANGE-RED

The hawkweeds, like the dandelions, offer great difficulties to European botanists, who have named over 10,000 species! Fortunately for us, the American species are less numerous (fewer than 20 in the northeastern United States) and more clearly defined, though several have immigrated from Europe. They are mostly hairy plants with a tuft of basal leaves and usually smaller leaves on the stem, all generally without lobes or teeth. The rays are cut off square at the end; the heads are scarcely an inch across. The pappus is of hairs which may be white but are more commonly tan or brownish. The achenes have no visible beak. The hairs on the leaves of some species are very long; in some they bear glands at the tips; in some they are branched to form stars.

I. Native species with leaves on the stems (the basal leaves are sometimes gone by flowering time). The pappus is tawny. All but one are hairy. (Compare II.)

    A. Native species with small heads in a tall narrow inflorescence; a circle of small bracts outside the longer ones. (Compare B and C.)

        H. gronovii (5 ft.) has hairs less than ½ inch long. § Summer and autumn: dry woodlands, Mass. to Mich. and Ia., s. to Fla. and Tex. *Fig. 138.*

        H. longipilum (5 ft.) has hairs from ½ to nearly 1 inch long. § Summer: dry woodlands, Ont. to Minn. and Nebr., s. to Ind., La., and Tex.

    B. Native species with small heads on long, weak stems in a loose, open inflorescence; a circle of small bracts around the longer ones.

        H. paniculatum (4 ft.) is nearly smooth. § Summer and autumn: open woods, N. S. and Que. to Mich., s. to Ga. and Ala.

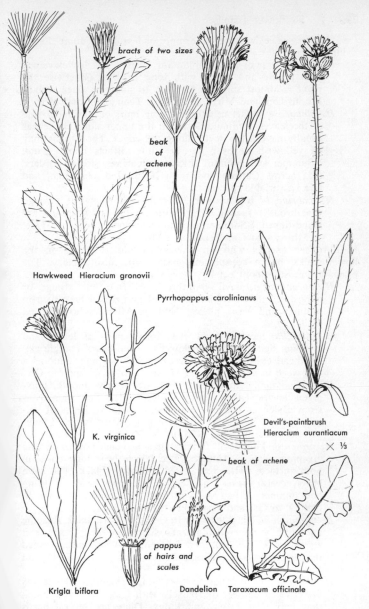

bracts of two sizes

beak of achene

Hawkweed Hieracium gronovii

Pyrrhopappus carolinianus

K. virginica

Devil's-paintbrush
Hieracium aurantiacum

× ⅓

beak of achene

pappus of hairs and scales

Krigia biflora

Dandelion Taraxacum officinale

FIGURE 138

C. Native species with heads in more or less flat or dome-shaped inflorescences.

H. venosum, poor-Robin's-plantain (2 ft.), has leaves veined with purple and edged with long bristles. Otherwise the plant is almost smooth. § Spring to autumn: open woods, Me. to Ont. and Mich., s. to Fla., Tenn., La., and Mo.

H. canadense (4 ft.) usually has long hairs on the under side of the leaves, a minute down on the upper side. The leaves usually have a few teeth along the edges. The pappus may be yellowish or even nearly white. Bracts about equal. § Summer and autumn: thickets, clearings, stream borders, etc., across Canada and s. to N. J., Ind., Ia., Ida., and Ore.; a variable species.

H. scabrum (4 ft.) has very short hairs that give it a rough ("scabrous") feeling. The hairs on the inflorescence are gland-tipped. § Summer and autumn: open woodlands, Que. to Minn., s. to Ga., Tenn., and Mo.

II. European species with no leaves, or almost none, on the flower stalks, but a conspicuous basal tuft, mostly hairy. The bracts are mostly about equal.

H. aurantiacum, devil's-paintbrush (2 ft.), has orange or almost red flowers. § Summer and autumn: a bad weed in pastures and waste places, Nfld. to Minn., s. to Va. and Ia. *Fig. 138.*

H. pilosella, mouse-ear (1 ft.), forms mats of leaves and creeping stems. The erect flowering stem bears a single yellow head (rarely two or three). § Summer and autumn: a bad weed in fields, Nfld. to Minn., s. to N. C. and O.; Ore.

H. floribundum, king-devil (3 ft.), has nearly smooth, gray-green leaves (often hairy underneath). The stem rises from a slender rhizome and bears up to 50 heads of yellow flowers. There are also creeping, leafy stems. § Summer: a weed in fields, Nfld. to N. Y. and O.

H. pratense, king-devil (3 ft.), has a slender rhizome and creeping stems or runners. The leaves bear long hairs on both surfaces. The stem hairs are often black. The stem bears several leaves and several or many heads. § Spring and summer: a bad weed in fields and roadsides, Que. to Ont., s. to Ga. and Tenn. PLATE 16.

H. florentinum, king-devil (3 ft.), has a short, thick rhizome and usually no creeping leafy stems. In other respects it resembles *H. floribundum.* § Spring and summer: a weed in fields and waste places, Nfld. to Mich., s. to Va., O. and Ia.

H. vulgatum (3 ft.) has a short, thick rhizome. The leaves are covered densely or sparsely with long, bristlelike hairs; they may have bronze markings. There are several heads of yellow flowers on the erect stem. § Spring and summer: Nfld. to Mich., s. to N. J. and Pa.

Index

INDEX